W9-API-583

949.7024 Silbe.L

Silber, Laura.

Yugoslavia : death of a
nation /
      c1996. FEB   - 1996

FEB 0 5 1996

YUGOSLAVIA

DEATH

OF A

NATION

YUGOSLAVIA

DEATH

OF A

NATION

LAURA SILBER & ALLAN LITTLE

TV BOOKS

Keeping books in the picture.

Distributed by Penguin USA

EVANSTON PUBLIC LIBRARY
1703 ORRINGTON AVENUE
EVANSTON, ILLINOIS 60201

Laura Silber is the Balkans Correspondent for the *Financial Times*. She was the series consultant for "The Death of Yugoslavia" and has been based in the region for eight years, originally as a Fulbright Scholar. Widely acknowledged among journalists, diplomats and scholars as one of the English-speaking world's leading interpreters of the causes and progress of the Yugoslav wars, she has a knowledge of the politics of the former Yugoslavia that is unequalled among foreign journalists.

Allan Little has been a correspondent with BBC radio and television news since 1988 and has covered the wars in the former Yugoslavia since the fighting erupted in the summer of 1991. He has reported from most of the theaters of conflict in Croatia and Bosnia-Herzegovina and has won widespread praise for his compassionate accounts of the war, and those caught up in it. His consistently perceptive reporting has laid bare the dynamics both of the war itself and of the failure of international efforts to end it.

Copyright © Laura Silber and Allan Little 1995 and 1996.
All rights reserved.
Maps by Aleksandar Ćirić.
Design and production by Joe Gannon.
Printed and bound in the United States.

Publisher's Cataloging in Publication Data:

Silber, Laura
   Yugoslavia : death of a nation / Laura Silber & Allan Little
   p. cm.
   Includes index.
   ISBN: 1-57500-005-9

   1. Yugoslavia—History. 2. Yugoslav War, 1991- I. Little, Allan. II. Title.

DR 1313.s55 1996   949.7'024
                                          QBI95-20785

1   2   3   4   5   6   7   8   9   10

TV Books publishes books developed from quality television.
The company is founded on the principle that books naturally extend the excitement,
enjoyment and entertainment benefits inherent in television.

TV BOOKS, INC.
DISTRIBUTED BY PENGUIN USA

This book is published to accompany the television series broadcast on the Discovery Channel. The series was produced by Brian Lapping Associates Ltd.
Associate Producer Michael Simkin
Series Producer Norma Percy
Producer/Director Angus Macqueen and Paul Mitchell

Contents

Yugoslavia 1945-1991

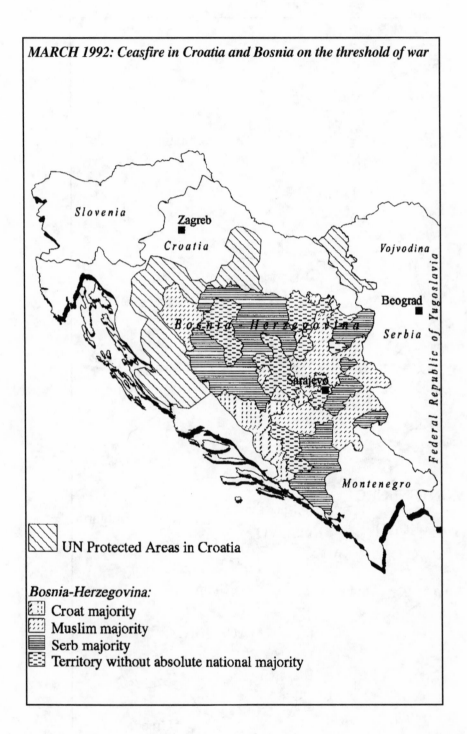

MARCH 1992: Ceasfire in Croatia and Bosnia on the threshold of war

Slovenia

Zagreb

Croatia

Vojvodina

Beograd

Bosnia-Herzegovina

Serbia

Sarajevo

Federal Republic of Yugoslavia

Montenegro

UN Protected Areas in Croatia

Bosnia-Herzegovina:
Croat majority
Muslim majority
Serb majority
Territory without absolute national majority

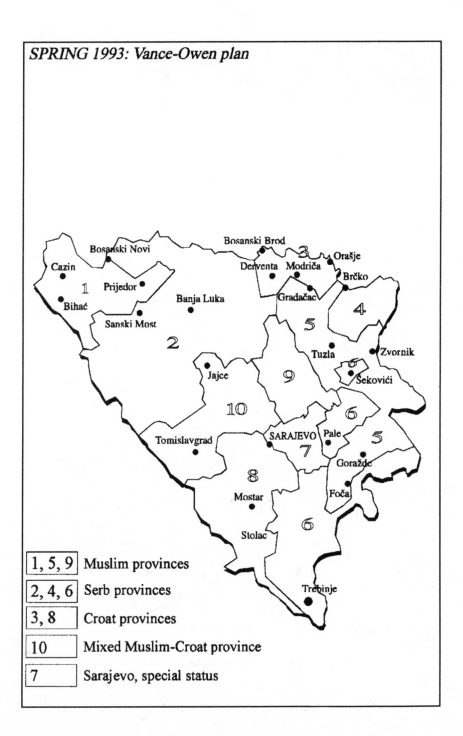

SPRING 1993: Vance-Owen plan

Bosanski Brod
Bosanski Novi
Cazin
1
Prijedor
Bihać
Sanski Most
Banja Luka
Derventa Modriča
3
Orašje
Brčko
Gradačac
4
2
5
Jajce
Tuzla
Zvornik
6
Sekovići
9
10
6
Tomislavgrad
SARAJEVO Pale
5
7
Goražde
8
Foča
Mostar
6
Stolac

Trebinje

1, 5, 9	Muslim provinces
2, 4, 6	Serb provinces
3, 8	Croat provinces
10	Mixed Muslim-Croat province
7	Sarajevo, special status

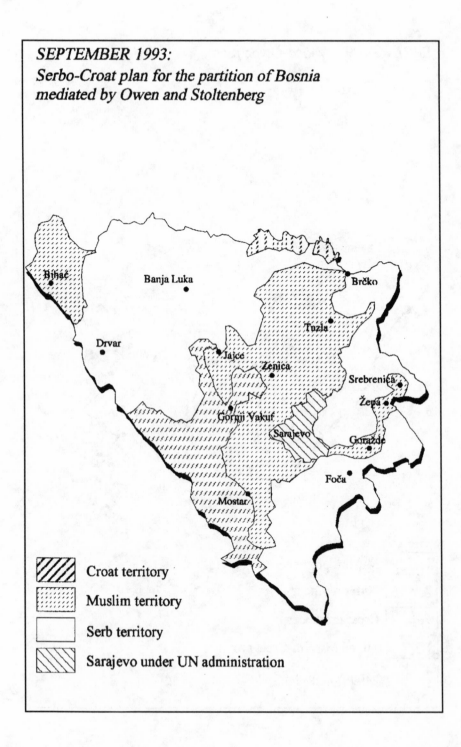

SEPTEMBER 1993:
Serbo-Croat plan for the partition of Bosnia
mediated by Owen and Stoltenberg

Bihać

Banja Luka

Brčko

Drvar

Tuzla

Jajce

Zenica

Srebrenica

Žepa

Gornji Vakuf

Sarajevo

Goražde

Foča

Mostar

	Croat territory
	Muslim territory
	Serb territory
	Sarajevo under UN administration

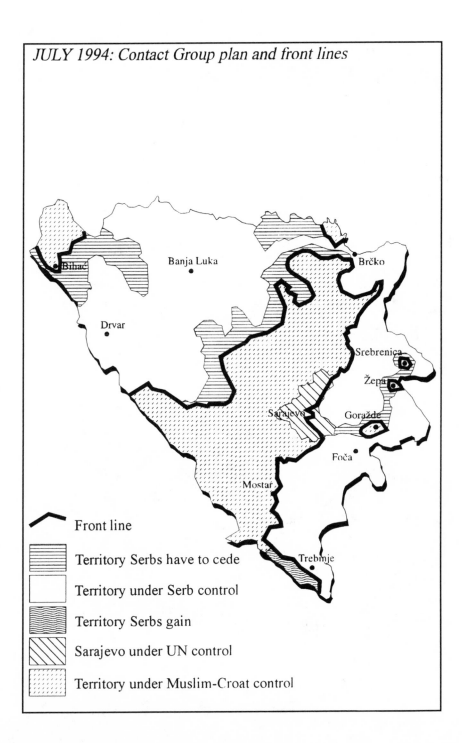

JULY 1994: Contact Group plan and front lines

Bihać

Banja Luka

Brčko

Drvar

Srebrenica

Žepa

Sarajevo

Goražde

Foča

Mostar

Trebinje

Front line

Territory Serbs have to cede

Territory under Serb control

Territory Serbs gain

Sarajevo under UN control

Territory under Muslim-Croat control

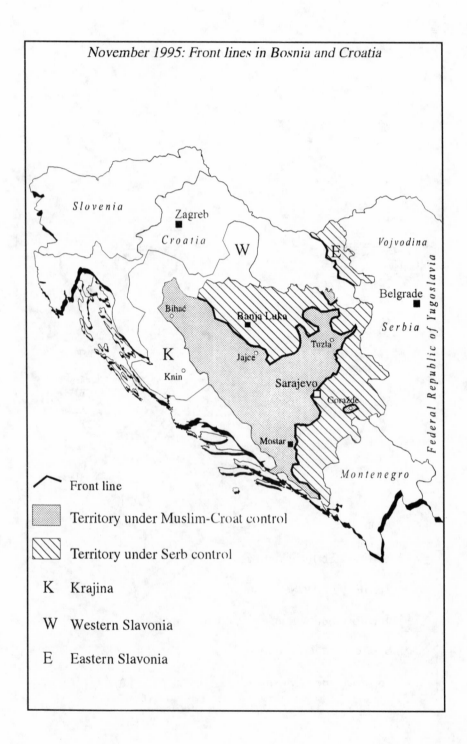

November 1995: Front lines in Bosnia and Croatia

Slovenia

Zagreb

Croatia

W

E

Vojvodina

Belgrade

Bihać

Banja Luka

Serbia

Tuzla

Jajce

Knin

Sarajevo

Goražde

Federal Republic of Yugoslavia

Mostar

Montenegro

⌐‾ Front line

Territory under Muslim-Croat control

Territory under Serb control

K Krajina

W Western Slavonia

E Eastern Slavonia

Cast of Characters

Abdić, Fikret – Muslim leader of the breakaway "Autonomous Province of Western Bosnia" in northwestern Bihać. Allied with Serbs before his mini-state collapsed in a joint Croat-Muslim offensive in August 1995.

Adžić, Blagoje – General. JNA Chief of Staff (1991) and Federal Defense Minister (1992).

Akashi, Yasushi – Senior UN envoy to former Yugoslavia (December 1993-October 1995)

Aksentijević, Milan – JNA General in Slovenia – imprisoned in Croatia – transferred to Sarajevo when war began. Unceremoniously pensioned by Milošević.

Andjelković, Radmila – Milošević aide during his rise to power.

Azemi, Husamedin – Ethnic Albanian. One of Milošević's placemen in the Communist Party of Kosovo.

Babić, Milan – A central figure in the self-styled Republika Srpska Krajina in Croatia (1990 - 1995). Held a number of positions, foreign minister at the time of Croatian offensive in August 1995.

Badinter, Robert – French Constitutional Court Judge, Chairman of the EC Arbitration Committee on Yugoslavia (1991).

Bajramović, Sejdo – Appointed Kosovo's representative on the Yugoslav Federal Presidency in 1991 – unswervingly loyal to Milošević.

Baker, James – US Secretary of State (1991).

Bavčar, Igor – Slovenia's Deputy Defense Minister, and first Police Minister after independence.

Bilandžić, Dušan – Tudjman's advisor (1991). Since 1994 Deputy Head of the Croatian office in Belgrade.

Bildt, Carl – European Union peace envoy, replaced Lord David Owen (spring 1995). Former Swedish Prime Minister.

Boban, Mate – Bosnian Croat leader. Declared separate Croat state in Bosnia. Ousted under US pressure when the Muslim-Croat federation was created.

Bogdanović, Radmilo – Interior Minister of Serbia. Ousted after demonstrations on March 9, 1991. Remained one of Milošević's closest confidants.

Bogićević, Bogić – Bosnia-Herzegovina's representative on the Federal Presidency. Serb who remained loyal to Bosnia's government during the war.

Bokan, Dragoslav – Ultranationalist politician. Serb paramilitary leader.

15

Boljkovac, Josip – First Interior Minister of independent Croatia, responsible for recruitment of thousands of new Croat police in 1990–91.

Boras, Franjo – Croat representative on Bosnian Presidency. Never returned to Sarajevo after May 1992.

Borštner, Ivan – Slovene non-commissioned officer – leaked (planted) documents to *Mladina* (1988).

Boutros-Ghali, Boutros – UN Secretary General.

Brezak, Ivan – Croatian Deputy Interior Minister (1991).

Brovet, Stane – Slovene, JNA Admiral who was Deputy Defense Minister. Pensioned in the first big purge in 1992.

Broz, Josip – TITO – Founder of Communist Yugoslavia. Ruled from 1945 until his death in 1980.

Bućin, Nenad – Montenegro's representative on the Federal Presidency who resigned along with Jović in March 1991. Unlike his Serbian colleagues he never returned.

Budimirović, Boško – Kosovo Serb activist.

Bulatović, Kosta – Kosovo Serb activist.

Bulatović, Momir – Came to power on Slobodan Milošević's coat-tails. Youngest Montenegro Party Chief and later elected President of Montenegro.

Carrington, Lord Peter – First EC peace envoy (1991-92).

Christopher, Warren – US Secretary of State (from 1992).

Churkin, Vitaly – Russia's special envoy to former Yugoslavia (1993-94).

Čkrebić, Dušan – Serb Communist functionary. Staged mock resignation ordered by Milošević in 1988.

Ćosić, Dobrica – Influential Serbian nationalist writer seen as spiritual father of Serbs. President of FRY (from 1992-93).

Cvetković, Jovan – Mayor of Svetozarevo, confronted Milošević at Mayors' meeting in March 1991.

De Michelis, Gianni – Italian Foreign Minister (1991).

Dedaković, Mile-Jastreb – Croatian commander of Vukovar. Arrested after accusing Tudjman of not helping defend the town.

Degoricija, Slavko – Prominent HDZ official. Held several key positions in Croatia.

Delimustafić, Alija – Muslim Bosnian Interior Minister (1991-92). Ally of Fikret Abdić.

Divjak, Jovan – General. Serb. Deputy Commander of the Bosnian government army.

Dizdarević, Raif – Bosnia's representative to the Federal Presidency, replaced by Bogić Bogićević in 1989.

Djukić, Slobodan – Mayor of Valjevo. Attended March 16 Mayors' meeting when Milošević warned: "At least we know how to fight."

Djurdjevac, Vojislav – General. JNA Commander in Sarajevo.

Doko, Jerko – Croat. Bosnian Defense Minister (1991).

Drašković, Vuk – Charismatic Serbian nationalist opposition leader. Jailed briefly by Milošević in 1991 and 1993 later tactical ally.

Drnovšek, Janez – Slovenia's representative on the Yugoslav Federal Presidency and later Prime Minister of independent Slovenia.

Duraković, Nijaz – Bosnian Communist Party leader, remained in opposition to Izetbegović.

Eagleburger, Lawrence – Former US Ambassador to Yugoslavia. Acting Secretary of State (1992).

Frasure, Robert – US envoy to Contact Group. Tragically killed in a road accident on Mount Igman, while travelling to Sarajevo in August 1995. Architect of the US initiative.

Galbraith, Peter – First US Ambassador to Croatia (from June 1993).

Ganić, Ejup – "Yugoslav" representative to the Bosnian Presidency, but SDA leader. Emerged in 1992 as Bosnia's *de facto* Vice President.

Genscher, Hans Dietrich – German Foreign Minister. Railroaded EC into Croatian recognition in 1991.

Gligorov, Kiro – Veteran of five decades of Yugoslav politics. President of Macedonia from 1991 who guided the republic to independence. Seriously injured in assassination attempt in October 1995.

Gračanin, Petar – JNA General. Serbian President (1988-89). Interior Minister in Ante Marković's Government.

Granić, Mate – Croatian Foreign Minister (from 1993).

Gregurić, Franjo – HDZ official. Held several functions, including Prime Minister of Croatia (1991).

Gvero, Milan – JNA spokesman and later Deputy Commander of the Bosnian Serb army. Purged in October 1995.

Hadžić, Goran – Secretary of the Vukovar branch of the SDS (1991). Briefly held title "President" of Krajina.

Hadžifejzović, Senad – Sarajevo televison news anchorman.

Hafner, Vinko – Old Slovene Communist. Member of the Central Committee of Yugoslavia. Warned Milošević that he was leading the country towards disaster.

Halilović, Sefer – First Commander of Bosnian Army.

Holbrooke, Richard – Assistant US Secretary of State. Led the US peace initiative from summer 1995.

Hurd, Douglas – British Foreign Secretary (until July 1995).

Izetbegović, Alija – Founding leader of the Muslim Party of Democratic Action (SDA). Elected President of the Presidency of Bosnia-Herzegovina after multiparty elections in 1990. Presided over Bosnia's declaration of independence and war.

Jackovich, Victor – First US Ambassador to Bosnia-Herzegovina (until spring 1995).

Jagar, Vladimir – JNA colonel, Croat, at Virovitica, who betrayed General Špegelj, Croatia's Defense Minister, over clandestine gun-running operations.

Janša, Janez – Slovene journalist and opposition activist, who became Defense Minister in independent Slovenia.

Janvier, Bernard – Lieutenant General of France. Commander of UN forces in former Yugoslavia (from February 1995). His reluctance to authorize NATO air power was a major factor in UN-US rift.

Jashari, Kaçusha – Ethnic Albanian Party Chief of Kosovo, ousted with Vllasi.

Jokanović, Žarko – A leader of student demonstrations in March 1991. Later MP.

Jovanović, Vladislav – Serbian Foreign Minister (until summer 1995).

Jović, Borisav – Serbia's representative on the Federal Presidency. Held a host of party and political posts. A close associate of Slobodan Milošević.

Juppé, Alain – French Foreign Minister (until he was appointed Premier in 1995).

Jurić, Perica – Croatia's Deputy Police Minister (1990).

Kacin, Jelko – Slovene Information Minister – credited with media blitz during Slovene war.

Kadijević, Veljko – JNA General. Federal Defense Minister (1988-1992).

Cast of Characters

Karadžić, Radovan – Bosnian Serb leader (from 1990). Psychiatrist. Indicted by International Tribunal in The Hague for war crimes 1995.

Kavaja, Burhan – Ethnic Albanian Head of Trepča mine. Imprisoned after miners' strike in 1989.

Kertes, Mihalj – One of the leaders of the "Yogurt" revolution. Milošević's reliable ally in secret police. Instrumental in arming Serbs in Croatia.

Kljuić, Stjepan – Croat member of Bosnian Presidency. Advocated unified Bosnia. Removed by Boban in 1992, reinstated in 1994.

Koljević, Nikola – Bosnian Serb "Vice President." Member of Bosnian Presidency before the war.

Kolšek, Konrad – General. Commander of the JNA's Fifth Army District.

Komšić Ivo – Croat member of Bosnian Presidency (1993). Backed Muslim-Croat federation.

Kordić, Dario – Bosnian Croat journalist turned key HVO commander in Muslim-Croat war (1993-94). A leader of Croat mini-state in Bosnia. Indicted by International Tribunal in The Hague for war crimes (1995).

Koschnick, Hans – German EC Mayor of Mostar (from 1994).

Kostić, Branko – Acting President of rump Yugoslavia after Croatian Mesić withdrew from the Federal Presidency.

Kostić, Jugoslav – Vojvodina's representative on the Federal Presidency (1991).

Kozyrev, Andrei – Russian Foreign Minister.

Krajišnik, Momčilo – Serb. Speaker of pre-war Bosnian Parliament. Speaker of Bosnian Serb assembly. Nicknamed "Mr. No" for his tough stance.

Krunić, Boško – Vojvodina Party official, ousted in the Anti-Bureaucratic Revolution in 1988.

Kučan, Milan – Slovene Communist Party leader who became the first president of independent Slovenia.

Kukanjac, Milutin – General. JNA Commander of Sarajevo.

Lagumdžija, Zlatko – Bosnian (reformed) Communist leader. Remained in opposition to Izetbegović.

Lilić, Zoran – President of FRY (from 1993). Took instructions from Milošević.

Lokar, Sonja – Slovene (reformed) Communist official.

MacKenzie, Lewis – General. Canadian UN Commander in Sarajevo (1992).

Mahmutčehajić, Rusmir – SDA leader – advocate of forming the Patriotic League in Bosnia.

Mamula, Branko – JNA Admiral. Yugoslav Defense Minister until 1988.

Manolić, Josip – HDZ leader and, until a rift in 1994, one of Tudjman's most trusted advisors.

Marković, Ante – Last Federal Prime Minister (1989-91). Introduced market and, to a lesser extent, political reforms.

Marković, Mirjana – Slobodan Milošević's wife. Powerful and influential figure. Belgrade university professor.

Martić, Milan – President of breakaway Serb state in Croatia. Rose to Knin police chief with his own paramilitary group in 1991. Fled Croatian offensive in August 1995. Indicted for war crimes by the International Tribunal in The Hague.

Mendiluce, José Maria – Top UNHCR official in former Yugoslavia (1991).

Mesić, Stipe – Croatia's representative on the Federal Presidency, HDZ leader and, until a rift in 1994, one of Tudjman's most trusted advisors.

Milošević, Slobodan – President of Serbia. Singled out by the international community as most responsible for Yugoslavia's violent disintegration. Later praised for efforts towards peace.

Mitević, Dušan – Confidant of Milošević and Chief of TV Belgrade.

Mitsotakis, Konstantin – Greek Prime Minister (1993).

Mladić, Ratko – General. Commander of Bosnian Serb Army from 1992. Previously Commander of Knin Corps. Indicted for war crimes by the International Tribunal in The Hague.

Morillon, Phillipe – Commander of UN Forces in Bosnia (1990-93).

Morina, Rahman – Milošević's token Albanian. Head of the Communist Party of Kosovo and previously police chief. Died 1990.

Nambiar, Satish – General. First UN Commander in former Yugoslavia.

Okun, Herbert – Cyrus Vance's right-hand man. Former US Ambassador.

Opačić, Jovan – Serb rabblerouser from Croatia who helped found SDS.

Orić, Naser – Leader of Srebrenica defenders (from 1992). Former bodyguard of Milošević.

Cast of Characters

Owen, Lord David – EC mediator, co-chairman of the Peace Conference on former Yugoslavia (1992-95).

Panić, Života – General. Commander of the First Army District during Vukovar operations. Later VJ Commander-in-Chief. Purged in 1993.

Panić, Milan – Belgrade-born, California millionaire. FRY Prime Minister (1992).

Pankov, Radovan – One of the leaders in the Anti-Bureaucratic revolution in Vojvodina. Minister in Serbian Government.

Paraga, Dobrosav – Founded Croatian Party of Right. Long-time nationalist Croatian dissident.

Paspalj, Mile – Speaker of Krajina Assembly.

Pavelić, Ante – Leader of the pro-Nazi Ustaše Independent State of Croatia, 1941-45.

Pavlović, Dragiša – Belgrade Party Chief (up to 1987) and Stambolić's protégé.

Peterle, Lojze – Slovene Prime Minister (1990).

Plavšić, Biljana – "Vice-President" of self-proclaimed Bosnian Serb state. Was a member of pre-war Bosnian Presidency.

Pohara, Armin – Journalist turned Bosanski Brod defender.

Poos, Jacques – Luxembourg's Foreign Minister (1991).

Praljak, Slobodan – Theater director. Commander of Bosnian Croat Militia (1993), instrumental in the destruction of the bridge in Mostar.

Pučnik, Jože – Former Slovene dissident. Leader of DEMOS opposition coalition in 1990 elections.

Račan, Ivica – Croatian Communist leader. Abandoned the last Party Congress after the Slovenes. Lost 1990 elections.

Rašeta, Andrija – JNA General. Deputy Commander of the Fifth Army District.

Rašković Jovan – Founder of the Serbian Democratic Party in Croatia. Moderate. Eclipsed by Milan Babić.

Ražnatović, Željko-Arkan – Commander of fierce paramilitary unit and briefly MP. Worked for Serbia's secret police. Accused of war crimes in Bosnia and Croatia.

Redman, Charles – US special envoy to peace talks (1993-94).

Reihl-Kir, Josip – Osijek regional Police Chief who tried to keep war from erupting. Murdered by HDZ extremists.

Ribičić, Ciril – Slovene Communist leader.

Rose, Sir Michael – British Lieutenant General. Commander of UN troops in Bosnia. (January1994-January 1995).

Rugova, Ibrahim – Leader of Kosovo ethnic Albanians (from 1989).

Rupel, Dimitrij – Slovene Foreign Minister (1991).

Sacirbey, Muhamed – Bosnian foreign minister (June 1995). Formerly Bosnian ambassador to the United Nations.

Sapunxhiu, Riza – Kosovo's representative on the Yugoslav Presidency, fired in 1991.

Scowcroft, Brent – Leading US foreign policy-maker. US National Security Council (until 1992).

Šešelj, Vojislav – Ultranationalist MP who commanded paramilitary unit during war. Milošević named him his favorite politician and helped him create his party. Later jailed him.

Silajdzić, Haris – Prime Minister of Bosnia-Herzegovina. Formerly Foreign Minister.

Šipovac, Nedeljko – One of the leaders of the Anti-Bureaucratic revolution in Vojvodina.

Školjč, Jože – Head of the Slovene Youth Opposition (1989).

Smith, Rupert – Lieutenant General, Commander of UN forces in Bosnia. (January-November 1995)

Šogorov, Milovan – Vojvodina Communist chief, ousted in 1988.

Šolević, Miroslav – Kosovo Serb activist.

Špegelj, Martin – Croatia's first Defense Minister. Former Commander of the Fifth Army District in the Yugoslav Army.

Stambolić, Ivan – Communist politician. Helped Milošević rise to power only to face betrayal. He was ousted by his best friend in 1987.

Stanovnik, Janez – President of Slovenia (1988).

Stoltenberg, Thorvald – UN envoy to International Conference, replaced Cyrus Vance (1993-95).

Šuklje, Borut – Slovene Communist. Yugoslav Central Committee member.

Šušak, Gojko – Croatian Defence Minister. Prominent in the extreme nationalist diaspora who returned to Croatia in 1990 - and became one of Tudjman's closest allies, leader of the HDZ right wing.

Šuvar, Stipe – Croatian Communist leader. Head of Yugoslav Party (1988-89). Croatia's representative on Federal Presidency 1989-90.

Tasić, David – *Mladina* journalist. Arrested in 1988 for passing on a secret military document.

Tharoor, Shashi – Special assistant to the UN head of peacekeeping.

Thornberry, Cedric – UNPROFOR civilian official.

Todorović, Zoran – Serbian party activist. Protégé of Mira Marković.

Trgovčević, Ljubinka – Member of Serbia's Presidency. Sided with Stambolić.

Tudjman, Franjo – Founding leader of the Croatian Democratic Union (HDZ) and first president of independent Croatia.

Tupurkovski, Vasil – Macedonian politician. Member of Yugoslavia's Presidency (1991).

Tus, Antun – Croatian, JNA General. Took charge of Croatia's Armed Forces in 1991.

Unković, Slobodan – President of the Serbian Parliament (1991).

van den Broek, Hans – Dutch Foreign Minister (1991).

Vance, Cyrus – UN envoy and co-chairman of the Peace Conference on former Yugoslavia (until 1993).

Vasiljević, Aleksandar – Head of JNA counter-intelligence (KOS) (1991). Fired in May 1992 in purge of Generals.

Vico, Ratomir – Close associate of Milošević. Head of Belgrade Serbian television. Information Minister.

Vllasi, Azem – Ethnic Albanian Kosovo Party leader. Chief of Kosovo Communist party. Jailed in 1989 after Milošević pledged to arrest him at mass rally. Convicted of counterrevolution, released in April 1990.

Wijnaendts, Henri – Dutch Ambassador to France, Carrington's deputy.

Zavrl, Franci – Editor in Chief of *Mladina*. Arrested as part of Ljubljana Four in 1988.

Zimmermann, Warren – Last US Ambassador to Yugoslavia (1989-92).

Zubak, Krešimir – Bosnian Croat, President of Muslim-Croat Federation in Bosnia (from 1994).

Zulfikarpašić, Adil – Bosnian Muslim businessman in Switzerland. Financed SDA and signed "Belgrade initiative" with Milošević in 1991.

ABBREVIATIONS

DEMOS	Democratic Opposition Coalition of Slovenia
EC	European Community
EU	European Union
FRY	Federal Republic of Yugoslavia
HDZ	Croatian Democratic Union
HVO	Croat Council of Defense
IMF	International Monetary Fund
JNA	Yugoslav Peoples' Army
KOS	JNA counterintelligence
MASPOK	Mass movement in Croatia 1971
NDH	Independent State of Croatia (1941)
SAO	Serbian Autonomous Region
SDA	Party for Democratic Action
SDB	secret police
SDS	Serbian Democratic Party
SFRJ	Socialist Federative Republic of Yugoslavia
SPS	Socialist Party of Serbia
SKJ	League of Communists of Yugoslavia
TO	Territorial Defense Force
UN	United Nations
UNHCR	United Nations High Commissioner for Refugees
UNPROFOR	United Nations Protection Force

NOTE ON PRONUNCIATION

c is "ts" as in bats
č is "ch" as in archer
ć is "tj" as in tune
dj is "dg" as in bridge
dž is "g" as in gentle
j is "y" as in you
lj is "lli" as in million
nj is "n" as in new
š is "sh" as in sharp
ž is "zh" as in treasure

INTRODUCTION

On that day we'll say to Hell: "Have you had enough?"
And Hell will answer: "Is there more?"
Toga dana mi ćemo reći paklu: "Jesi li se napunio?"
A pakao će odgovoriti: "Ima li još?"
Meša Selimović, *Derviš i Smrt*

Muslim refugees run into the woods, crowd into trucks, some are shot dead while trying to escape a Serb onslaught. Serb refugees form endless convoys of tractors, fleeing a Croatian advance. Blackened skeletons of buildings shape Sarajevo's skyline. Mediators and politicians wring their hands, wondering how to stop the wars in former Yugoslavia, whose waves of wrenching violence have provoked such public outrage.

Over the past five years, the images have become familiar. They have faithfully conveyed the anguish of the time.

We wrote this book to shed light on the decisions which led to the horror and destruction. It is an attempt to identify, clinically and dispassionately, the crucial events, the secret meetings, in both the lead-up to war and in its progress once the fighting had started, and to reconstruct those events through the accounts of those people who took part in them – the milestones, if you like, on the road to catastrophe. It does not condemn, or condone, or justify any of the players in the unfolding tragedy. It tries simply to relate what happened, and why, and at whose behest.

The war in Yugoslavia was not the international community's fault. The war was planned and waged by Yugoslavs. It was not historically inevitable. To attribute the calamity that engulfed the peoples of Yugoslavia to unstoppable forces is to avoid addressing oneself to the central dynamic of the war. It is also to let the guilty off the hook. And, it also provides a justification for the failure of the West, for so long, to intervene with sufficient will and vigor to end the war. This book examines why Western governments failed to intervene decisively, and analyzes the means by which they intervened in the end.

This book shows that Yugoslavia did not die a natural death. Rather, it was deliberately and systematically killed off by men who had nothing to gain and everything to lose from a peaceful transition from state socialism and one-party rule to free-market democracy. We trace the origins of the war to the rise of Serb nationalism among Belgrade intellectuals in the mid-1980s, and the subsequent harnessing of nationalist rhetoric by Slobodan Milošević. The book traces Milošević's conscious use of nationalism as a vehicle to achieve power and then to strengthen his control first over Serbia, and then over Yugoslavia. His original dream was to step into the shoes of Josip Broz

25

Tito as leader of the whole of Yugoslavia. But by 1991, when he found this unattainable, he chose an alternate project, the creation of a new enlarged Serbian state, encompassing as much territory of Yugoslavia as possible. His centralizing, authoritarian leadership and calculated, clever manipulation of the politics of ethnic intolerance provoked the other nations of Yugoslavia, convincing them that it was impossible to stay in the Yugoslav federation and propelling them down the road to independence.

One of the central themes of our book is that under Milošević's steward-ship, the Serbs were, from the beginning of Yugoslavia's disintegration, the key secessionists. This is not to say that Milošević was uniquely malign or solely guilty. The foot soldiers of Yugoslavia's march to war were legion and were drawn from all the nationalities in the country.

This book is also a lament for the failed promise of Yugoslavia. As Communism declined in the late 1980s, Yugoslavia was, in many ways, better placed than any other Communist state to make the transition to multi-party democracy, either as a single state, or as a group of successor states. There was a real chance for Yugoslavia to take its place in a new and, at that time, hopeful community of European nations. That this chance was deliberately snuffed out, in the ways this book describes, turned out to be Europe's loss and that of all democracies, as well as Yugoslavia's, and a mortal blow to many of the key moral certainties of our age.

Yet in retrospect the appearance of a stable and prosperous Yugoslavia may have been deceptive. Ethnic grievances had been suppressed, not dispelled, by the centralized Communist system. Peaceful change to a liberal political system would have required very careful management, from inside and outside.

It is now clearer than ever that exactly the opposite happened. As the presidents of Yugoslavia's six republics – Bosnia-Herzegovina, Croatia, Macedonia, Montenegro, Serbia, and Slovenia – quarreled in public about the country's future structure in the run-up to war, some of them were cyni-cally plotting the path to disintegration.

We chose to start the book with Milošević's rise to power, and then plot how he sustained himself in power by provoking successive crises in Serbia; and how he extended his power base beyond the borders of his own republic. Finally, by hijacking the Yugoslav People's Army (JNA) – the single most important, and eventually the only truly functioning, pan-Yugoslav federal institution – and harnessing it to the cause of the Serbs outside Serbia, he was able to present the other nations in Yugoslavia with a simple sinister choice: either stay in Yugoslavia on my terms, or fight a war against one of the largest armies in Europe. President Milan Kučan of Slovenia and President Franjo Tudjman of Croatia jumped to take the challenge. Slovenia won a lightning-quick war, while Croatia initially lost nearly a third of its territory to the JNA, but won international support. Under the cloak of the UN and backed by the US and Germany, Croatia spent the next four years arming and preparing to redeem lost territory that would send the biggest single exodus of refugees since World War Two fleeing east, towards Serbia, seeking refuge with the man who had led them into their calamity in the first place. Bosnia's President Alija Izetbegović took the challenge too, with disastrous consequences. The ill-fated leader of Bosnia's Muslims differed from his Slovene, Croatian and Serbian counterparts in one striking respect: while their actions drove events, he seemed perpetually to be swept along by circumstances and activity well beyond his control. All the leading politicians knew war was coming as the country disintegrated. At least two of them, Milošević and Tudjman, made determined preparations.

In the slide to war, the presidents of Serbia and Croatia jostled for position in their coming battle for the spoils of Yugoslavia. They began with a tacit agreement about the partition of Bosnia between Serbia and Croatia, without regard to the interests of that republic's two million Muslims, and at their expense. The Muslims, unprepared for conflict, were to become the biggest victims – driven from their homes, the traces of their cultural heritage, mosques and graves obliterated. Minarets and Orthodox and Catholic churches jumbled together in an architectural expression of multiethnic coexistence which, though it had frequently been interrupted by periods of conflict, had characterized this region for centuries.

When the international mediators entered the fray, they behaved as though war were self-evidently futile and irrational; as though all that they needed to do was to persuade the warring parties of this truism and, once the scales had fallen from their eyes, the guns would fall silent. What the diplomats often failed to realize is that despite the appearance of chaos, the wars have been prosecuted with terrifying rationality by protagonists playing long-term power games.

It is also important to state what this book is not. It is not a *crie de coeur* of the "Save Bosnia Now" type (though we both believe that Bosnia could, and should, have been saved). It is not a polemic against the failure of the West to protect the weak against the strong, or even to honor its own promises. And it is not a book about journalism or journalists; it is not a "we were there and it was horrible" account of life on the front line.

We have charted what we believe to be the principal stages in the country's violent disintegration. In this context, and in a futile attempt to keep the book down to a manageable length, many important events have been omitted. The fate of Macedonia has been overlooked. Its somewhat specific and wider set of circumstances makes it possible to separate it from its northern neighbors. We have also left the continuing, and as yet unresolved, conflict between Belgrade and the Kosovo Albanians largely untold even though it was the first point of conflict and the first disaffected community against whom the army was deployed. Kosovo enters our narrative only to the extent that it was the centerpiece of modern Serb mythology, and the grievance of Kosovo's small Serb minority against the ethnic Albanian majority was the first card to be played by Milosevic. Nor have we chronicled the fortunes of opposition movements in the various republics. War had the effect of hardening public opinion and of shoring up the power bases of the republics' leaders; *they* have been the principal actors in this disaster.

Working with documentary film producers Brian Lapping Associates, we have conducted hundreds of interviews with all the leading players. As a rule, quoted personal recollections are taken from those interviews, or from our own direct experiences and observation at the time, unless otherwise stated.

The first Yugoslav state was created after World War One on the smoldering ruins of the Ottoman and Hapsburg empires. It was called at its foundation the Kingdom of Serbs, Croats and Slovenes and was only later rechristened Yugoslavia. It was ruled by the Serbian dynasty Karadjordjević, and embodied the nineteenth-century dream of unity for the south Slav peoples (južni slaveni) which has been nurtured by intellectuals of all the south Slav nationalities, who yearned for liberation from foreign – that is to say Austrian and Ottoman – domination. The young Yugoslav monarchy quickly became a dictatorship. Croatian intellectuals, in particular, initially enthusiastic about the Yugoslav ideal, grew disillusioned and embittered.

Josip Broz, a locksmith who was half Slovene and half Croat, was known to his army of Partisan guerrillas as Tito. In 1941, the Axis powers invaded and partitioned Yugoslavia. Tito counted among his enemies Germans, Italians, Croatian fascists (Ustaše) and Serb monarchists (Chetniks). Communist Yugoslavia was founded by a declaration at Jajce, in central Bosnia, on November 29, 1943.

In 1945, the Soviet Army liberated most of Eastern Europe from German occupation and Moscow installed Communist governments in Warsaw, Berlin, Prague and Budapest. They were led mostly by men who had sat out the war years safely in Moscow. The Yugoslavs had, in contrast, substantially liberated themselves. Though Tito remained, initially, loyal to the Soviet way, he was the only post-war Communist leader in Europe to have built his position from the bottom up, and not to have been installed by a Soviet occupation force. From Moscow's point of view, he was dangerously independent, and too ambitious. Yugoslavia was expelled from the common institutions of the eastern bloc in 1948.

After his split with Moscow, Tito steered Yugoslavia between east and west. He was feted in Cold War western Europe as an anti-Moscow Communist leader. He used the country's unique position to secure financial backing. Yugoslavia grew accustomed to a prosperity that was beyond its means.

Throughout his stewardship of Yugoslavia, Tito worked to prevent his state from suffering the same fate as its predecessor – from falling under the hegemony of the biggest nation, the Serbs, who were twice as numerous as the second biggest, the Croats. Successive post-war constitutions were designed to balance institutional power between the republics, as a way of spreading power among the nations.

In his eternal battle to keep the nations on an equal footing, Tito ruthlessly suppressed any expression of resurgent nationalism. Enforcing his doctrine of "Brotherhood and Unity," he carried out purges of Serbs, Croats and Muslims, Slovenes, Macedonians and Albanians, balancing his repression of any one nation against that of the others. Nationalists were forced into exile, where they nurtured their resentment in expatriate communities that proved fertile breeding grounds for extreme nationalism. Or they were jailed.

By the time of the promulgation of the 1974 constitution (Tito's last), the country was decentralized to an unprecedented extent. Yet while Tito was alive, that decentralization was notional, rather than real: there were no doubts about who held the reins of power. Tito was himself a one-man single-party state. There was a pay-off for the lack of democratic accountability this implied: Yugoslavs were allowed to travel, to work abroad, and they did not suffer the same suffocating restrictions that prevailed throughout the Soviet bloc.

Tito was frequently likened to a great oak tree, in the shade of whose immense branches nothing else could grow. In his last years, no heir apparent emerged. Wary of appointing a successor, Tito created a hopelessly inefficient inheritor of his mantle: the collective head of state which was to replace him was an eight-member presidency, comprising one representative from each of the six republics, and one from each of Serbia's two autonomous provinces, Vojvodina and Kosovo. The presidency of this body would rotate annually between its members. As head of state, the eight-member presidency was also commander-in-chief of the army.

Yugoslavia had a federal parliament, six republican parliaments and two provincial parliaments. There were ten Communist Parties– one for each of the six republics, one for each of the two provinces, one for federal Yugoslavia, and one for the Army.

When Tito's health began to deteriorate, federal institutions deteriorated with him. Yugoslavia became a country composed of little more than eight regionally–based and separate Communist Parties, the secret police and the Army. When he died at the age of eighty eight, in May 1980, there was a genuine outpouring of patriotic grief among all of Yugoslavia's nations. The ethnic Albanian Communist, Mahmut Bakalli, later remembered: "We all cried, but we did not know we were also burying Yugoslavia."

Yugoslavia would die more than a decade later. After the collapse of the Warsaw Pact, Yugoslavia lost its strategic importance to Washington. Preoccupied with the Gulf War, and the future of the disintegrating Soviet Union, the US left the handling of the conflict's early stages to the European Community, which proved lamentably incompetent. James Baker, Secretary of State under President George Bush, bluntly explained the US's lack of interest by saying, "We don't have a dog in that fight."

Four years later, the United States was driving international diplomacy in the region. After months of maneuvering behind the scenes, during which time the US had shifted the balance of power on the battlefield decisively in favor of the Croats and Muslims, Washington emerged center stage, universally acknowledged as the only power capable of producing a settlement. To the power brokers of the region, it seemed that geopolitical calculation, rather than morality, was the factor that brought the US back into the region. Washington's belief that southeastern Europe was again growing in strategic importance prompted it to return with a mixture of force and diplomacy which its allies could not match.

The fall of the self-styled Serb state of Krajina in Croatia in August 1995, and the subsequent Serb losses in Bosnia, combined with a massive NATO bombing campaign, heralded a new age in Western engagement. Shuttling between the Balkan capitals, and backwards and forwards from Washington, Richard Holbrooke, the US envoy, gave the impression that the region was too important, too sensitive to be allowed to fester. By the end of 1995, for the first time in years, there was a realistic prospect of a political settlement on which a lasting peace would be built. Domestic considerations influenced US motivation in pushing the peace process with such focused determination: Bill Clinton needed a foreign policy triumph as he entered the last year of his first term as president; better still a triumph in the very region that had repeatedly confounded all previous attempts at peace-making. But the peace being built was – and this was acknowledged by all – a peace that became possible only as the result of decisive military victories on the ground, and the forced exodus of millions of people to areas where their ethnic group predominated.

At the time of writing, it seems likely given the extent of Washington's leverage over the protagonists that they will reach an agreement. The next drama surrounds the dispatch of up to 20,000 US troops pledged to form part of a peace implementation force. What remains completely uncertain is whether the parties are ready to agree to a lasting peace or whether they will simply calculate, as they have in the past, that a ceasefire will give them a chance to re-group and re-arm in order to improve their positions for the next battle.

Washington aimed to cut the Balkan warlords down to size; history suggests that may prove impossible. All too often, the region's leaders have proven themselves able to drag more powerful states deeper into conflict than they ever planned to go. Yet former Yugoslavia is the clearest illustration to date of a central strategic reality of the post-Cold-War world: if the United States does not take a lead, then no one does. By the end of 1995, it had become apparent that the only chance for peace was if Washington, with its unique military and political authority, was prepared to see it through.

PART ONE: LAYING THE CHARGE

1

"THIS IS OUR LAND"
The Stirring of Serb Nationalism

It was the dream of all nationalists in Yugoslavia to put their vision down on paper and then make it a reality. They knew their plans could not be executed immediately, but they were content to wait. The Memorandum of the Serbian Academy of Sciences and Arts remains shrouded in mystery nearly a decade after its existence was revealed. Was the Memorandum an attempt to settle political scores in Serbia? How did Slobodan Milošević, the ambitious Party chief, avoid taking a public stand? Was this revival of Serbian nationalism the first step towards dismembering Yugoslavia?

In this rough document, a cabal of Serbian academics[1] had catalogued their nationalist grievances. They had not yet intended to publish it, but somehow this unfinished draft appeared in the press. Set against the savagery of the next decade, the Memorandum now seems pale and hackneyed, but, when excerpts were published on September 24, 1986, in *Večernje Novosti*, the mass-circulation daily, it was a political bombshell. The country was convulsed.

Serbs were in such an unjust position in post-Second World War Yugoslavia, argued the document, that their very existence was threatened. They were the victims of economic and political discrimination by their Croat and Slovene countrymen. Serbs had made the greatest military contribution (and suffered the most casualties) over the last century and, far from being rewarded, were being punished in peacetime. The Serb nationalist conviction that it had always been the Serbs' fate to "win the war and lose the peace," was gaining popular currency. For the Serbs in Kosovo and Croatia, the Memorandum alleged, the situation was even worse. In Kosovo and Metohija, the traditional Serbian name for the republic's southern province, Serbs faced total genocide. It said they were facing the greatest defeat in their liberation struggle waged since 1804, the Serb revolt against the Turks. The status of Serbs in Kosovo had long been a subject of resentment in Serbia, but the draft Memorandum went a step further, sounding the alarm about the position of Serbs in the other republics:

Except during the period of the NDH (the Independent State of Croatia, proclaimed in 1941 by the pro-Nazi Ustaše), Serbs in Croatia have never been as endangered as they are today. The resolution of their national status must be a top priority political question. If a solution is not found, the conse-

31

quences will be damaging on many levels, not only for relations within
Croatia but also for all of Yugoslavia.[2]

Yugoslavia, in its present form, was no longer an adequate solution to the Serbian question. The Memorandum argued that the country was disintegrating, and that forty percent of Serbs had been left languishing beyond the frontiers of the motherland. The blame, it said, rested with the Comintern legacy, the national politics of the Yugoslav League of Communists, and their faithful and ignorant Serbian followers. The seventy-four-page tract accused Slovenia and Croatia of conspiring against Serbia. The campaign had been allegedly spearheaded by Tito himself and Kardelj, the Slovene architect of Self-Management: Yugoslavia's own brand of socialism, based on the concept of social rather than state ownership[3].

Serbia's Academy of Sciences and Arts wielded considerable influence. Removed from the public gaze, along with the Writers' Union, it was one of few institutions not totally controlled by the Communist Party. In Croatia and Slovenia, these two organizations had a similar status. In Serbia, part of the intelligentsia had enjoyed a century-long tradition of comfortable coexistence with the rulers of the day. Memoranda had been used as a means of political communication in Serbian history. In writing theirs, the nationalist academics were drawing on a Serbian tradition that pre-dated Yugoslavia.

Dobrica Ćosić, the writer seen as spiritual father of the Serb nation, denied that he contributed to the Memorandum. It is, however, the undoubted distillation of his ideas, and he defended it when it came under attack[4]. A member of the Academy, Ćosić went so far as to explain, rather unconvincingly, that the Memorandum was not "nationalist" but "anti-Tito and pro-Yugoslav."

An icon for Serbian dissidents, Ćosić, silver-haired and bespectacled, spoke in the accent of a Serbian peasant. His quiet manner did not mask his belief, and that of his fellow nationalists, in the authority of his message. Despite having been the powerful cultural ideologue in Tito's regime, Ćosić is credited with making sure that Socialist Realism – the mandatory form of expression elsewhere in Eastern Europe – was not enforced in Communist Yugoslavia. His almost mythical status was ensured in 1968, when he was expelled from the Central Committee for accusing ethnic Albanians of separatism and anti-Serbian sentiments. In the 1970s, disgruntled intellectuals rallied around him. Ćosić held clandestine monthly meetings on the need for democratic reform in Yugoslavia. The police watched him constantly, but he was never arrested. He called this "pragmatic tyranny." To imprison him would have been counter-productive.

The President of Serbia, Ivan Stambolić, heard secret police reports that the Academy had undertaken a covert project, but was told that it consisted simply of a socioeconomic assessment of the current situation. However, when the Memorandum was made public in September 1986, its contents shocked even the Belgrade leadership.

Stambolić and his protégé, Dragiša Pavlović, the Belgrade Party chief whose domain traditionally included the media, roundly denounced the document. For Stambolić, a Serbian nationalist in the eyes of Croats and Slovenes, but accused of being too soft by Serbian hardliners, the Memorandum was an ominous indication of rising chauvinism. He called it a requiem for Yugoslavia. The Academy assailed the federation for dividing rather than uniting Serbs, which, according to Stambolić, turned the country's biggest nation into its most dangerous. The fact that the Memorandum lambasted the Serbian leadership for arrogance and inaction spurred Stambolić to respond. He was depicted as totally ineffectual and ripe for removal.

The draft Memorandum did not create nationalism, it simply tapped sentiments that ran deep among the Serbs, but which were suppressed and, as a result, exacerbated by Communism. The Academy's tract echoed opinions whispered throughout Serbia.

The Serbian press outdid the other republics in the severity of its attacks on the Memorandum and the Academy. Indeed, the Slovene daily, *Dnevnik*, praised the Belgrade media for its determination to get rid of nationalism. Croatian politicians bashed the document. Liberals, who disagreed with the text itself, supported the Academy's right to speak its mind. In the midst of the political furor, only a tiny handful of Academicians spoke out against the document.

Throughout Yugoslavia, Communists hurled invective against the Memorandum and the Academy. Except for Milošević. The leader of the Serbian Communist Party, who usually castigated anyone who deviated from the official line, remained silent. He let others speak in his place, making sure the document was condemned – this was, after all, his duty – but shied away from a public expression of his views.

At a session of the Belgrade Party, Dušan Mitević, a close friend of Milošević and his wife Mirjana, denounced the Memorandum as dangerous for Yugoslavia and the Serbian nation. The fact that his speech was carried as a commentary in the State-run Belgrade daily, *Politika*, meant that Milošević supported it. Milošević also made sure the speech was distributed at a Party meeting.

Stambolić and Pavlović put pressure on the portly Mitević to find out why Milošević was keeping silent. "Milošević answered that there was already too much discussion and he did not want to add to the confusion. He is like a football player who usually plays a supporting role but then scores the goals," said Mitević, then a city Party official.

Cracks were appearing in Stambolić's twenty-five-year friendship with Milošević. But Stambolić failed to appreciate the extent of the danger until their fateful showdown at the Eighth Session of the Serbian League of Communists.

Promoted by his powerful uncle Petar, Ivan Stambolić had engineered Milošević's advancement to the post of Party chief. In the style of a typical Communist ruler, he had silenced dissent within the leadership over the promotion of his friend, who was then little more than the colorless head of Tehnogas, a state fuel company. At the time, Stambolić justified the purge as an attempt to revitalize the Party with fresh blood. At the age of fifty, Stambolić was stepping down from the more powerful Party leadership to become Serbian president. He wanted to devote himself to changing the constitution.

The Yugoslav constitution, adopted in 1974, devolved substantial power to Yugoslavia's six republics, giving each a central bank and, separate police, educational and judicial systems. It gave the same to Serbia's two provinces, Kosovo and Vojvodina. The provinces elected deputies to the Serbian parliament, as well as having their own assemblies. The two provinces were made constituent members of the federation, giving their leaders seats on Yugoslavia's rotating presidency, which assumed power when Tito died. On several occasions, they sided with the other republics against Serbia. In this way, the enormous disparity between Serbia and the other republics was diminished. Serbia was no longer a republic of ten million people, more than twice that of the next biggest republic, Croatia. By virtually abolishing Belgrade's authority over Kosovo and Vojvodina, the constitution cut Serbia, now with a manageable population of six million, down to size. Serbs often complained that the expression "weak Serbia – strong Yugoslavia" embodied the attitude of their countrymen. While the constitution gave Serbs something to gripe about, it also calmed the other republics who feared domination by their big brother.[5]

With the promulgation of the 1974 constitution, Serbia's position in the federation preoccupied a succession of leaderships.[6] The question of the status of Kosovo became the most pressing concern. Although ninety percent Albanian, Kosovo was regarded by Serbs as the cradle of their civilization. It was the seat of the Serbian church, the Patriarchate at Peć. Serbian politicians and intellectuals have wrestled for more than a century with the thorny question of Kosovo.[7] The balance of power had already shifted dramatically in the southern province when Tito's hard-line interior minister, Aleksandar Ranković, was ousted in 1966.[8] Over the next twenty years, and especially after 1974, ethnic Albanians ruled the roost, holding most positions of power in the province.

In the autumn of 1981, a year after Tito's death, ethnic Albanians took to the streets, demanding independence from Serbia and that Kosovo become the seventh republic. The protests were crushed by the Yugoslav Army and federal police. While the province's powers almost matched those of the republics, they stopped short of the right to secede, which the republics arguably enjoyed. Of course, a decade later in Croatia it would become clear that the right of secession was little more than notional, impossible to exercise without bloodshed. Secretly encouraged by Ćosić, a group of Kosovo Serbs dissatisfied with their position began to organize. "They complained about their position and I advised them to write a petition and to put forward their demands," said Ćosić. But Ćosić was not their only support. They had a silent backer in the Serbian government. A trio of local Serb activists, Miroslav Šolević, Kosta Bulatović and Boško Budimirović, soon circulated their first protest petition. It attracted just seventy-six signatures. But, later, they were to garner wider public support with their frequently repeated simple message: "This is our land. If Kosovo and Metohija are not Serbian then we don't have any land of our own."

Over the next four years, a motley protest group calling itself the Committee of Serbs and Montenegrins sought to ignite Serb emotions. They told tales of woe, of being forced to move under pressure, of rapes and harass-ment.[9] In 1986, the group easily collected more than 50,000 signatures from Serbs calling for a change in Kosovo.

Even though the secret police had infiltrated Šolević's organization, the Party apparatus had not yet taken the movement under its wing. On April 2, 1986, Bulatović was arrested in Kosovo Polje – and the police questioned him regularly in the months that followed. His cronies went to Belgrade for help. Late that night, they met the dissident nationalist writer, Vuk Drašković, in the Hotel Moskva. Drašković took them to meet Ćosić in the nearby Hotel Slavija. Ćosić told them to come later to his house in the exclusive Belgrade suburb of Dedinje, where the Communist establishment rubs shoulders with foreign diplomats.

Budimirović noticed that Ćosić was shaking visibly, as he greeted the Kosovo activists by the front gate. It was midnight. Inside, he guided his guests to the cellar, where dusty books lined the walls. They sat there until two o'clock in the morning:

> *They came to me in the cellar and we agreed how they should struggle, what they should do, and which forms of resistance they should offer.*
> *I helped them in everything they did. I cooperated with them in their illegal struggle.*

Ćosić rang Dušan Čkrebić, the Serbian President. The next morning at eight o'clock, he received the delegation in Parliament. Čkrebić told them: "This is where you should be. Not where you were last night." It was a key moment. No longer would the movement be confined underground. The Communists were about to hijack the nationalists' cause. Recognizing its usefulness, official Serbia began its headlong and ultimately disastrous descent into nationalism. It tapped a rich seam of national grievance, official-ly stifled but privately nurtured for decades. Its primitive appeal, the Communist leadership believed, would revive Serbia's stagnating political and economic system. Eight months after the Memorandum sent shock-waves throughout the country, its basic message was beginning to take root.

1 The Serbian economist Kosta Mihajlović, who later became one of Milošević's closest advisors, is widely believed to be the Memorandum's main author. While he never acknowledged that he wrote the Memorandum, papers he published later contained an identical rationale.

2 Memorandum, p.64.

3 Celebrated as a monumental achievement in the Socialist world, Self-Management was actually a convoluted system based on "social ownership," meaning factories are owned by workers and their councils rather than by the state, but in fact it was very difficult to define who owned what.

4 Ćosić was active in the Committee for Freedom of Speech, which defended those throughout Yugoslavia, who were prosecuted for their political views. The accused would later become a Who's Who of the break-up of Yugoslavia. Franjo Tudjman, arrested for Croatian nationalism, in 1990 would become Croatian President; Alija Izetbegović, jailed for Muslim fundamentalism would become President of Bosnia in 1990; Vojislav Sešelj, Serbian ultra-nationalist paramilitary and MP; and Dobroslav Paraga, a Croat extremist and paramilitary leader, etc.

5 Stambolić recalled that once over a fish dinner with Kardelj, even he, the architect of the constitution, admitted it caused problems for Serbia. Seen as Tito's heir apparent until he died in 1979, Kardelj said Stambolić and his comrades should work towards changing the constitution. But by Tito's death in 1980, no progress had been made, and afterwards the question was shelved.

A Yugoslav ideologue from Slovenia, Kardelj also tried to reassure Stambolić that the country would survive without him and Tito. "Whoever attacks the equality of nations, the federated set-up, whoever attempts to take away the factories from the workers, or to raise the question of Yugoslavia's independence – we'll break his neck!"

6 Yugoslavia promulgated three constitutions in the post-Second World War period: 1946, 1963, and 1974. Until 1974, the question of regulating relations in Tito's Yugoslavia was a key topic with a multitude of constitutional amendments adopted in the meantime.

7 Dobrica Ćosić and other members of his nationalist dissident clique secretly devised a scheme to partition the province, giving Serbia its treasured Orthodox monasteries. The remainder would be handed to the Albanians, leaving them free to unite with their kinsmen across the border in Albania. Ćosić never unveiled his plan, insisting the public was not ready to give up even part of Kosovo.

8 Aleksandar Ranković was expelled from the Yugoslav League of Communists on July 1, 1966, for abuse of power in the secret police, i.e. wire-tapping Tito. In Kosovo, Ranković's name was synonymous among Albanians with a reign of terror. For Serbs, he ruled with a strong hand and kept a lid on Albanian nationalism. When he died on August 20, 1983, tens of thousands of Serbs attended the funeral in what became the first mass-protest about the status of Serbs in Kosovo and Yugoslavia in general. The turn-out signalled the rise of nationalism. Ivan Stambolić, then Belgrade City Chief, said: "All across Yugoslavia they criticized me for not controlling it – should I have put tanks round the cemetery?"

9 In fact, statistics indicate that the incidence of rape was much lower in Kosovo than elsewhere in Yugoslavia.

2

"NO ONE SHOULD DARE TO BEAT YOU"
The Rise of Slobodan Milošević
April 1987–December 1987

There was nothing about the Serbian Communist leader's visit to Kosovo Polje on April 24, 1987, to suggest it would change the course of history. But for the first time Slobodan Milošević donned the mantle of protector of all Serbs. It was a stroke of good fortune for the young Party chief. The Serbian President, Stambolić, should have gone to Kosovo himself for talks with local leaders, but casually sent Milošević in his place. It was a careless move which set in motion a train of events that would cost him his career.

On the eve of the trip, Milošević's wife, Mirjana Marković, a professor of Marxism at Belgrade University, feared for her husband's safety. "Mira was frightened for him, and with reason," their close friend Dušan Mitević claimed. "There had been reports from the police that it wasn't safe. An advert in the Albanian émigré press had been published, putting a price on his head. I offered to go down with him to comfort Mirjana, but Slobodan phoned the next morning to say there was no need."

Galvanized by the fact that Belgrade was finally paying attention to their plight, thousands of local Serbs pressed forward, trying to shake the Party leader's hand as he entered the drab House of Culture in Kosovo Polje. Frantic to gain his attention, demonstrators screamed about Albanian oppression. While Milošević met local Serb representatives, police, fearing violence, used batons to drive the crowd away. The protesters chanted: "Murderers" and "We are Tito's, Tito is ours."[1]

Suddenly, people started hurling rocks – seized from a truck which local activists had conveniently parked nearby. Inside the hall, politicians and reporters tried to find out what was going on in the street, but the doors were locked. Miroslav Šolević, one of the main organizers of the protest, told the local functionaries that the demonstrators were intent on getting into the building to meet Milošević. Azem Vllasi, the black-haired blue-eyed ethnic Albanian Kosovo Party chief, suggested they rig up a sound system in order to calm the seething mob. After all, he believed, the purpose of Milošević's trip was to stop the increasingly frequent demonstrations by Kosovo Serbs.

Apparently shaken by the screaming outside, Milošević said he wanted to see what was happening. He watched the crowd from the balcony before going downstairs to give what was to become one of the most important speeches of his career. "No one should dare to beat you," he bellowed, unwittingly coining a modern Serb rallying call. The mood suddenly changed, the crowd outside started chanting: "Slobo, Slobo." "This sentence enthroned him as a tsar," said Šolević. He joked that Milošević was, in fact, telling the police that no one had the right to attack them when he uttered the phrase that would secure his mythical status among Serbs. But, as Šolević admitted, with a deep laugh, there was not a single policeman who did not get a beating that night. By parking the truck full of stones, the Kosovo Serbs had had their weapons ready.

Milošević's speech set the tone. Speaker after speaker attacked the ethnic Albanian Party leaders, calling for a state of emergency, for the abolition of Kosovo's autonomy, and even the expulsion of Albanians. They warned they would abandon Kosovo, that their lives were in danger at the hands of their Albanian neighbors.

That day in Kosovo Polje, Vllasi advised Milošević to distance himself from the bigoted tirade. "But he never said anything." The stormy session lasted all night. If Milošević realized he could become the most powerful man in Yugoslavia by playing on the discontent of the Kosovo Serbs, he was giving little away. But the whole episode had provided him with a ready formula for rousing nationalist sentiments.

For the first time, Milošević felt the pull of the masses.

You should stay here. This is your land. These are your houses. Your meadows and gardens. Your memories. You shouldn't abandon your land just because it's difficult to live, because you are pressured by injustice and degradation. It was never part of the Serbian and Montenegrin character to give up in the face of obstacles, to demobilize when it's time to fight... You should stay here for the sake of your ancestors and descendants. Otherwise your ancestors would be defiled and descendants disappointed. But I don't suggest that you stay, endure, and tolerate a situation you're not satisfied with. On the contrary, you should change it with the rest of the progressive people here, in Serbia and in Yugoslavia.

"Milošević was transformed, set afire by Kosovo," said Ivan Stambolić, the Serbian President and then-undisputed leader of Serbia. The two men had been virtually inseparable for twenty-five years. They had met as first-year students at the Law Faculty of Belgrade University. Both were from provincial Serbia, both were ambitious, diligent and bright. Ivan had worked his way through university, and helped Slobodan get his first job in the Party. Over the next two decades, he made sure his friend followed in his footsteps. In time, they became an awesome political duo.

Stambolić had already visited Kosovo on April 6, 1986, when more than 10,000 local Serbs gathered to protest against the arrest of the activist, Bulatović. A year later, aware that the situation could boil over, Stambolić gave his protegé, Milošević, advice before he left Belgrade: "Be careful, keep a cool head!"

Dispatching Milošević to Kosovo was the first of Stambolić's many mistakes. The bedraggled and increasingly radical Kosovo Serbs never forgave him for not taking them seriously. When Milošević made his pilgrimage, his friend, Stambolić, forfeited his right to be their leader. It would soon become clear that whoever commanded them would become the leader of all Serbs. After Milošević's visit, the Kosovo Serbs found themselves the center of attention. For Dušan Mitević, Deputy Director of Television Belgrade, and a propaganda genius, it was a simple task to generate popular interest. "We showed Milošević's promise over and over again on the TV. And this is what launched him." The message found fertile ground in Serbia.

But Milošević's "conversion" to nationalism was not a chance affair. He had been to Kosovo four days earlier to meet Communist officials. The visit was conveniently forgotten, giving the impression that Friday's events were entirely spontaneous. At the first meeting, local Serb activists rallied 2,000 people and many accused Milošević of refusing to address their complaints. "Comrade president, you gave a monologue, but we invited you for a dialogue," Šolević told Milošević. "We want you to come again." Milošević agreed to return at five o'clock on Friday.

Over the next few days, Milošević's minions were busy making preparations. "Milošević sent a senior party official to Kosovo Polje on the Tuesday and Wednesday to stir things up," said Vllasi. "He came down unofficially, without contacting me, and talked to Šolević and the others. They devised a way to get the masses there." The Albanian Party chief realized the visit was of great importance to the Serbian leadership. "We knew about it from our intelligence sources and the fact that the Belgrade media and TV were all prepared to come down for this special event. Local TV usually covered these things."[2]

Before the April visit, Milošević had shown little interest in the situation in Kosovo, or, for that matter, in moves to change the 1974 constitution. He then realized that, by seizing this agenda, he could become the Serbian leader. Through pressure and lobbying over the summer, his placemen were able to stack the deck against Stambolić. "Following Milošević's speech at Kosovo Polje, the rift between us grew deeper. There were no longer two currents in one party. There were now two policies," said Stambolić.

Milošević made his next move. He arranged for a session of the Yugoslav Communist Party on the situation in Kosovo. On June 16, 1987, Milošević showed Šolević an advance copy of an introductory speech, reassuring him that it would be sufficiently tough on the Albanians. But Šolević feared that the deputies from Croatia, Slovenia or Kosovo might block it.

In order to make their point, 3,000 Kosovo Serbs gathered in Pioneer Park, across from the federal parliament, in the heart of Belgrade. Public demonstrations were a major event. The political and military establishment was on edge.

In the absence of volunteers, Ivica Račan, a Croatian member of the Yugoslav Party leadership, was sent to calm the crowds. Serbian leaders were pleased that Croatia would now see that Kosovo was not just Serbia's problem, but that it warranted attention from the top ranks of Yugoslavia's leadership.

Later that night, Račan and Šolević sat in the Belgrade city hall. One hundred meters away, the crowd hurled invective at the country's leaders, calling them thieves and monkeys. The Serbs screamed for the abolition of Kosovo's autonomy. Račan considered it one of the most humiliating episodes of his life, and one which revealed the malicious nature of Milošević's politics. After hours of heated talks, the Kosovo Serbs agreed to leave Belgrade. But the crowd had delivered an unmistakable message – the sheer power of their numbers could easily disrupt daily life.

Milošević understood what it meant. For the first time he saw that an angry crowd could unsettle the Yugoslav leadership. He turned to Stambolić and said: "The fatherland is under threat." Stambolić was astounded and asked what the matter was. He saw that Milošević was shaking. It struck Stambolić as a decisive alarming moment. "And that's how it all began. The nationalists ran into his embrace. They grabbed him. He didn't really enjoy it very much. But he knew that it was politically very profitable."

The lure of nationalism had always dangled before Serbian politicians. At times, they had flirted with it to bolster popular support. Stambolić – a product of the old Communist regime – had shunned it, believing it too dangerous to tamper with. Milošević sensed early on that the promise of change was an elixir. Serbs were tired of the seemingly endless discussion about Kosovo, which had made the Serbian leadership seem incompetent. When Milošević offered resolute action, he won immense popular support. By contrast, Stambolić had always been reluctant to make public promises of change. This discrepancy was a portent of their future and final conflict.

The entire political establishment was scheming – except Stambolić. He steadfastly refused to admit that a showdown was imminent, concentrating instead on pushing through constitutional changes, in the mistaken belief that this would save him.

In September 1987, a rapid series of events unfolded which together changed the face of Serbia's political landscape: the sensational murder of four army recruits, an unprecedented public attack on Milošević by the Belgrade Party chief, and the televised overthrow of Stambolić. In three weeks, Stambolić would be politically dead. His executioner, Slobodan Milošević, would be in charge.

In the early hours of September 3, at the Paraćin barracks in central Serbia, Aziz Kelmendi, a nineteen-year-old ethnic Albanian recruit, opened fire on four of his fellow soldiers, killing them as they slept. Several hours later Kelmendi was found dead half a mile from the barracks. The army said he had committed suicide. The dead included two Muslims, a Croat and a Serb, but the frenzied Belgrade media called it an act of Albanian separatism against Serbia. Ten thousand people attended the funeral of the Serbian recruit. Against the wishes of his parents, the ceremony became a political demonstration against the Kosovo Albanian leadership. The bereaved father turned to the demonstrators, pleading with them to stop abusing the death of his son.[3] For days on end the event obsessed the Belgrade media, which had been gradually co-opted. For Milošević, the event was timely, providing him with the ammunition he needed for the political assassination that was to follow.

A fortnight later, in an atmosphere of hysteria and anti-Albanian propaganda, Dragiša Pavlović, Belgrade Party chief, took steps to defuse the tension. He called Belgrade media bosses to a briefing to warn against a resurgence of Serbian nationalism. He arrived in a confident mood, but failed to see that Milošević was already driving the pace of events.

He told the editors:

> *The general situation in Kosovo is not improving with the necessary, desired or easily promised speed... This is creating a dangerous atmosphere in which every word spoken against Serbian nationalism is seen as giving in to Albanian nationalism. Explosive words bring nothing but fire... The range of possible solutions for Kosovo has now been narrowed down to such an extent that the smallest mistake, even made in good faith, could be tragic not only for Serbs and Montenegrins in Kosovo, for the Serbian nation, but also for the basic stability of Yugoslavia.*

Without naming him, Pavlović was sounding a battle cry against Milošević, and drawing the front line in Serbian politics. Pavlović thought his warning would be enough to sober up the media and send a message to Milošević and his allies that they were courting disaster. Unfortunately for Pavlović, courting disaster was part of Milošević's strategy.

At home, Slobodan was relaxed. Sitting in his living room, his feet on the table, he told Mitević: "We'll take care of this on Monday." He and Mirjana then set off for a weekend at their villa in the eastern Serbian town of Požarevac, where they had grown up together.

Slobodan and Mirjana watched the Pavlović press conference on television. She saw it as an attempt to denigrate her husband. She accused Pavlović of trying to destroy the "frail hope" her husband had given "these poor, oppressed people," the Serbs of Kosovo.

The Miloševićs were extraordinarily attached to each other. From their school days in Požarevac, Slobodan and Mirjana were inseparable. The fact that each had suffered considerable tragedies may have brought them together. They were both children of the Second World War. Slobodan's father studied to be an Orthodox priest at the Faculty of Theology in Belgrade. After the war, he returned to his native Montenegro as a school teacher. It was a time of uncertainty. His wife, Stanislava, stayed with her two young sons in Požarevac. A rigid Party activist, she was to instill ambition and faith in Communism in her two children, Slobodan, and his older brother, Bora. She would also try to conceal the news of their father's suicide until the boys had grown up.[4] A decade later, Stanislava would also commit suicide.

Slobodan kept to himself. A plump and awkward child, he did not like sports. By all accounts, however, he clung to his friend, Mirjana, who, as a child, adopted her mother's Partisan *nom de guerre*, Mira. Growing up in the shadow of death and betrayal, she would never know her mother and lived apart from her father. Her mother was shot as a traitor to the Party in 1942, at the height of war in Belgrade. The details remain unclear, but, under interrogation and torture, she divulged the names of her comrades.[5] Baby Mirjana's father was a Partisan chief, who became Party boss of Serbia after the war, and remarried, leaving his daughter to be raised by her grandparents. Mira spent summers with her father on the Adriatic island of Brioni, where the hand-picked Communist élite and their families took their holidays.

During the weekend, Mira and Slobodan planned a counter-attack. A cavalier Milošević knew that the key media were already under his control. Two days later, *Politika Ekspres* launched a blistering attack against Pavlović. The commentary accused him of destroying Serbian and Yugoslav unity. It was attributed to an editor but was, in fact, written by Mira Marković.[6]

The unprecedented ferocity of the newspaper's attack surprised the Serbian President, Stambolić. He wanted to defend Pavlović, but the editor of the most influential Serbian daily, *Politika*, Živorad Minović, who was usually servile towards the Communist leader, tried to avoid him. When they finally spoke, Stambolić found him cold and arrogant. It became clear whose side Minović was on when *Politika* reprinted the article damning Pavlović.

Determined to fight back, Pavlović told Stambolić he would call a meeting of the Belgrade Party leadership. It seemed a good idea to Stambolić, who now feared for his own political future. He wrote a letter supporting his friend, an act which would return to haunt him. It would, he said, "finish off my political life." Nevertheless, the letter may have helped to win over the Belgrade Party leadership. At the party session, most of the forty-five speakers sided with Pavlović. However, his victory was short-lived. Radmila Andjelković, a member of the Serbian Party presidency and one of Milošević's disciples, stood up to announce that the matter was not finished. The more powerful presidency of the Serbian Central Committee would meet the next day to "examine the case of Dragiša Pavlović." Milošević had trumped Pavlović.

Even some of Milošević's supporters were taken aback by how quickly he was closing in for the kill. "In Communist countries, when you are on the Central Committee agenda," said Dušan Mitević, "there is an eighty percent chance that you're dead."

As soon as he heard about the session, Stambolić rang Milošević. He said he felt personally threatened by the agenda. "He told me not to worry – there was no problem in it for me."

Despite the warning signs, Stambolić refused to face reality. He thought he had enough support, but Milošević and his most trusted allies had contacted every member of the Presidency to find out who was going to side with whom. They believed they could win.

On September 18, 1987, Milošević scored a key political victory, presiding over the session. Forty-nine people spoke at the two-day session – but only twenty had the right to vote. The first item set the tone for the rest of the meeting. In the naive belief that he still wielded authority, Stambolić said:

*I would propose one other thing: let's not be angry, because it is not so impor-
tant. It would be good for Sloba and Dragiša to meet for coffee every day for
a half-hour. Or let them drink lemonade. But they should meet to overcome
the difficulties; I know people, and I will not accept they cannot find human
solutions. I will not accept that.*

Milošević showed no mercy, cutting short Stambolić and his pathetic attempts at reconciliation.

*This question cannot be minimized by describing it as a personal conflict, as
two kids having a squabble... This is not personal animosity or sympathy
and these are not things that can be simplified in that manner.*

In this tense atmosphere, Milošević was called to the phone. Mira Marković listened to her husband recount the meeting, sounding uncertain and nervous. "There's no going back now," she said, "you're too exposed." With that, Milošević returned to the ring.

That night Milošević's friends, most of whom were also members of the Presidency, gathered at the Milošević's modest flat in central Belgrade. They discussed the session, planning their next move. "Milošević said it was very difficult, that he was very disappointed with some people, that he couldn't believe what some people said," later remembered Mitević. But it was Mitević who devised a plan of action. It was brilliant and brought victory within reach.

The next morning he met four other members of the Belgrade Party committee, and persuaded them to sign a letter saying that Stambolić had pressurized them into supporting Pavlović at the city council a few days earlier.

The Serbian Presidency meeting resumed. Milošević's performance shattered any illusions Stambolić may have nurtured that the two men could remain friends. "I thought the Russians had invaded, that the Third World War had begun," said Stambolić when he saw Milošević's face. His voice raised, Milošević interrupted the debate:

Comrades, I have hesitated for the last hour or two. We have received a letter. First I asked for it to be checked as authentic, that there wasn't some mistake. Then I doubted whether one could really read out this letter at the Presidency itself. Maybe I will be making a mistake...

Stambolić was now implicated in conspiring against the Party's hierarchy. Of course, Milošević, despite his convincing performance, had already known about the letter. Mitević's idea had put the noose around Stambolić's neck.

It seemed to Milošević that he was ahead, so he called a vote on expelling Pavlović from the party. Eleven voted in favor, five against and four abstained. Their winning strategy rested with the representatives from Vojvodina and Kosovo. They did not like Stambolić, who was always harping on about constitutional changes. He seemed more of a threat than the faceless, big-eared Milošević. But Azem Vllasi objected to the way the meeting was being run, and refused to vote for Pavlović's expulsion, in effect backing Stambolić against Milošević.

Milošević offered some words of comfort that made Stambolić's blood freeze. "I sincerely hope, I believe in it firmly, that Comrade Stambolić was manipulated and not guilty."

Pavlović's fate was left up to the Eighth Session of the Central Committee of the Serbian Party. Milošević's camp did not lose a minute in planning for the Eighth Session, as it has come to be known. Borisav Jović, Milošević's faithful co-conspirator, who wore glasses and was small in stature, led the charge. The group fanned out through Serbia. They invited sixteen presidents of regional or district committees, who were also members of the Central Committee, to Belgrade, in order to persuade them how to vote. In this way, they easily spun a web ensnaring the regional bosses who, in turn, also met the local members of the Central Committee. They had even planned how the Presidency members supporting Milošević would act and speak. Milošević was in charge of seeing that speakers opposing him did not speak one after the other. It was easy, since, as president, he chose who was given the floor.

By contrast, Stambolić did not plan his defense before the Eighth Session.

On the eve of the meeting, he sat among friends, wondering what they should do. His reasoning was simple: "I was keen that we should say what we think. For our grandchildren."

As the Eighth Session opened, the Communist machinery went into motion. There was another twist aimed at heightening tension in the assembly hall and throughout Serbia. The meeting was televised: for the first time the Communists let the public inside their dark and treacherous realm. It was a shock. For the next two days, people throughout Serbia were glued to their TV screens, watching the showdown. It was supposedly broadcast live, but, as the meeting went on, the speeches were delayed for the news. Then Television Belgrade began cutting the speeches, Mitević blatantly giving preferential treatment to the winning side.

Life ground to a halt on the streets of Belgrade as people discussed the debate. Stambolić seemed paralyzed, unable to mount a counter-attack. It was as if he did not believe what was happening. Ljubinka Trgovčević, a historian who was a central committee member, described seeing Stambolić transfixed by his impending execution:

> *He was completely incapable of thinking. He comes from a patriarchal environment, where you don't hit your best friend and where you never betray your Party.*

Throughout his political career, Stambolić had skirted many of the traps laid by his rivals. By his own admission, he had only himself to blame for failing to see what Milošević was up to. "When somebody looks at your back for twenty-five years, it is understandable that he gets the desire to put a knife in it at some point. Many people warned me but I didn't acknowledge it."

The man who had eliminated all previous challengers would fall at the hand of his best friend, Milošević. Three months after the Eighth Session, Stambolić confided in Trgovčević. "He told me that he loved Milošević more than his own brothers and that he had spent more time with him."

The session opened with a speech commemorating the fiftieth anniversary of Tito as head of the Party. Both sides used Tito as a foil. Milošević praised the Communist leader for fostering unity. "He implied that we were not with Tito. It was a public lynching," said Stambolić.

In the unrelenting barrage on Pavlović and, by association, Stambolić, the next speaker offered one of the few bright spots. Milošević picked the blond-haired, attractive Trgovčević, believing she was an inexperienced politician who would not dare to fight. But television pictures showed him holding his head in his hands during her speech: "I am afraid we are returning to certain methods which were abandoned long ago and I don't want to use those methods." Her words, she said, infuriated Jović. "He got angry and said I was accusing them of

Stalinism, but I told him that it could be fascism, too," said Trgovčević, who left politics soon afterwards, returning to her work as an historian.

While Milošević's side held the upper hand from the outset, it was not clear who would win. After all, Stambolić was an institution. His downfall would bring many down with him. It would be the end of an era. Trgovčević watched the delegates sweat.

> *The atmosphere was terrible. People were standing and biting their nails in the café. Everyone turned greyer and greyer. Some people carried two different speeches in their pockets, depending on how things turned out. You must realize that ninety percent of those people's careers and futures depended on the outcome of the meeting.*

During the breaks, Milošević's team lobbied any potential supporters. Jović was like a bee, buzzing round the restaurant.

Milošević tried to cajole Vllasi, who resembled the archetypal Communist functionary, becoming fatter with each step up the ladder. An eager head of Yugoslavia's Communist youth, Azem had been Tito's pet. "This is now or never. Vote for me and tell the members of your delegation to do so, too. You'll see I will pay you back later," said Milošević. Vllasi refused: "You have hardly helped me in the past and I cannot help you now." Milošević was furious. "He called me a 'cunt,'" said Vllasi, "and I told him that he was a 'liar and a cheat.'" Two years later Milošević would get his revenge on Vllasi, jailing him on charges of counter-revolution. By then, Vllasi would cut a starkly different figure, a thin and determined victim of Milošević's regime.

Leaving nothing to chance, the Communist machinery churned out "telegrams of support." These were read aloud, generating a momentum of their own. Once a provincial leader heard that a neighboring municipality had sent a telegram, he understood that it would be propitious if he also sent a message. Telegrams from Kosovo Serbs particularly helped to stir public emotions and boost support for Milošević.

As the session went on, Milošević's supporters moved to the back of the hall. By the end, Stambolić was sitting by himself. When a vote was called and Pavlović was expelled from the Presidency, it was clear that Stambolic would not last long. Dušan Čkrebić said: "Serbia is tired of leaders and does not need new ones." Milošević had won.

The television broadcast yielded handsome dividends. "Milošević looked good because he was saying 'We have had enough of all this empty talk, this blah-blah that brought us here,'" later remarked Mitević, whose ability to manipulate the sequence of events made him the Serbian Orson Welles.

Surprisingly, leaders from around Yugoslavia welcomed Milošević's triumph.

Only a handful of federal officials wanted to put it on the Government agenda. Slovenia was uninterested. Croatian functionaries went so far as to criticize their own press for objecting to Milošević and the way that he had removed Stambolić. In fact, Stipe Šuvar, Croatia's representative on the Federal Party Presidency, later explained why he had then defended his future foe:

> *Stambolić was the most feared politician on the Yugoslav scene, so the grey bureaucrat Milošević made us feel that we could control him. You must remember he was clearly not a nationalist – everything he did was in the name of Yugoslavia – and his argument that the Albanians were secessionists was basically right.*

They did not realize that the implications of Milošević's rise to power would extend far beyond Serbia. His fellow Communists failed to understand that Milošević was about to become the first strongman after Tito.

After the Eighth Session, Milošević was free to turn his attention elsewhere. "Then," believes Stambolić, "Milošević became aware that Kosovo was only the launch pad. The goal was Yugoslavia."

> *He used his populist method throughout Yugoslavia... It was the red rag to the bull of other nationalisms. When the biggest nation begins to wave flags, the smaller nations were obviously afraid.*

Before coming into direct conflict with Slovenia, Milošević argued by proxy over the issue of Kosovo. He carried out a Stalin-style purge of everything from the Belgrade media to the head waiter at the Serbian government villa. After months of lurking in the shadows, Stambolić was officially dismissed on December 14, 1987.

1 Kosta Bulatović, a Kosovo Serb activist who is actually from Montenegro, explains that few people had been invited and that many of those who actually received invitations were *"Takojevići,"* a made-up word for people who say *"tako je –* That's the way it is." In other words, those who blindly obey the political line.

2 Two of Milošević's close associates, Ratomir Vico and his deputy Dušan Mitević, were running television at the time.

3 Djukić, Slavoljub, *Izmedju slave i anateme: politička biografija Slobodana Miloševića,* Filip Višnjić, Belgrade, 1994, p. 68.

4 Djukić, *Izmedju slave i anateme,* pp. 13-17.

5 Her sister, another Partisan was rumored to be Tito's lover during the war. She died of tuberculosis and was reportedly buried in his backyard. There were even rumors that Tito was really Mirjana's father.

6 Djukić, *Izmedju slave i anateme,* p. 71.

3

"NO WAY BACK"
The Slovene Spring, 1988

As Milošević consolidated power, the authorities in Slovenia were relaxing their hold. In the early eighties, the tiny northwestern republic embarked on a period of liberalism unprecedented in the Communist world. Alternative groups were tolerated and even flourished, functioning almost as political parties. They covered a wide spectrum, from ecology to gay rights. Slovenia was the most accustomed to pluralism of all the republics when multiparty elections were called. At the same time, the movement known as *Neue Slowenische Kunst* (New Slovenian Art) appeared to challenge parochial Slovenia. The musical group, Laibach, became the standard bearer of avant-garde in Slovenia, in Yugoslavia and outside, creating a following in the West. At first, the group's Nazi uniforms and frequent use of German upset Yugoslavs.[1] After all, mocking the Second World War was heresy, akin to bludgeoning the very foundation of Yugoslavia. By the mid-1980s, Slovenia's Socialist Youth organization took a shine to the music, giving Laibach the official stamp of approval.

For the first time, Ljubljana was a cultural magnet outdoing the other Yugoslav capitals. Until then, Slovenia was considered the most developed, and Slovenes the most industrious, but also the most conservative. Indeed, throughout history, revolution was an alien concept to this devoutly Catholic, mostly peasant population. The farmers prospered, most owned their own land and were faithful servants in the Austro-Hungarian empires. The neatly-tended gardens and wooden chalets, which dot the Slovene countryside, distinguished this Alpine republic from the rest of the country.

The diminutive Milan Kučan, head of Slovenia's Communist party since 1986, turned a blind eye to the new political trends – from radical to national-ist. This accomplished politician realized early on that Slovenia's future, and his, lay in reform.

> *It was clear to me there was absolutely no chance for Slovenia without seri-ous reform. This is when the constant conflict began, between me and Milošević, in particular after he had taken over from Stambolić.[2]*

Slovene youth was already in hot water with the Yugoslav establishment. They had caused a furor over Youth Day, Tito's birthday, by proposing a Hitler youth poster to promote Yugoslavia's annual relay race which marked the celebrations. Eight years after Tito's death, the Yugoslav Communists still took the anniversary extremely seriously. The poster was a gesture of defiance against the Communist regime and the Army, which remained the protectors of Titoism and of the legacy of the Partisan battle against the Nazis. Admiral Branko Mamula, federal defense secretary, dismissed the proposal as an attack on Yugoslavia.

It was not only the youth who were in trouble. Slovenia's nationalist intellectuals were also on the Yugoslav Peoples' Army's (JNA) black list. In February 1987, they advanced Slovenia's national program in the journal, *Nova Revija*. The Communist establishment saw it as an answer to the Serbian Academy's Memorandum. The manifesto called for a closing of national ranks and a return to Slovenia's Christian tradition. Moreover, Issue 57 of *Nova Revija*, argued that the Slovenes would be better off outside Yugoslavia.

Once again, Party organizations throughout the country disparaged the upsurge of nationalism and the attacks on Yugoslavia's socialism. But while official Yugoslavia was up in arms, Slovene and Serb nationalist dissidents enjoyed regular and warm contacts, even though their visions of the future of Yugoslavia seemed to conflict. The Serbs wanted centralization and the Slovenes the opposite. Yet they had much in common: more than a decade before the outbreak of war, both had begun to question the tenets of faith that held Yugoslavia together. At that time the nationalisms were not mutually threatening because they were not from neighboring republics.[3]

Kučan played a clever game. The Slovene Communists dismissed "Contributions To The Slovene National Program," the document published in *Nova Revija*, as a rehashing of old ideas. The only stroke of originality, his Slovene Party statement said, was that it singled out the Communists as responsible for everything. The Party would ignore "the sham, high-sounding argumentation" of the authors, turn the other cheek and call for tolerant democratic debate. It accused the Slovene chauvinists of "national intolerance and falsifying history."

The Yugoslav Army, however, refused to turn the other cheek. It was furious about the *Nova Revija* document. Calling it another Memorandum, Admiral Mamula said Slovene nationalists and the bourgeois right were scheming to destroy the Yugoslav community. "They negate the national revolution, self-management and non-alignment. They hope to ally with traitors, and use the Catholic Church to seize power." He said the Program attempted to launch a new concept of defense, proposing that republican armies take precedence over the Yugoslav People's Army.[4]

Mamula asked Kučan, whose large, round, blue eyes gave him a beguilingly angelic appearance, if he understood what was happening in Slovenia. He warned there would be trouble if the Slovene government ignored what was happening. Kučan's apparent dismissal of the importance of the new political

49

groups and the increasing attacks on the Army left the Admiral disappointed. He tried to flatter Kučan, praising him for encouraging reform, while warning about "those radicals who want to secede from Yugoslavia or attack Yugoslavia as a state."

The Army was convinced it would have to draw the line. The JNA had been formed to defend Yugoslavia against Western capitalist countries and, after 1948 and the break with the Soviet Union, Eastern European Communist states. The more enemies there were abroad, the more potential there was for betrayal at home. The Army was vigilant. Steeped in Communist Titoist dogma, JNA officers were isolated from the outside world. They were not allowed to travel abroad. They were even isolated from the society that gave them their privileges. Indeed, since its foundation, the JNA had been more secretive than the Soviet Red Army. Officers often started their training as fourteen-year-old boys. These youths, typically from the countryside, would grow up in military academies away from home, later making up the vast majority of the officer corps. It was a strange upbringing in a country where traditional family bonds and limited economic prospects made it unusual for "children" to leave home, even if they were married with offspring of their own. In their intensely sheltered world, it was not uncommon for officers to be summoned to a confidential briefing, only to be informed of events that had already been made public six months earlier. After 1980, the JNA knew that, along with the League of Communists, it was the glue that was holding Tito's Yugoslavia together. Even up to the outbreak of war in 1991, most officers genuinely believed in the multinational union of six Socialist republics, and in "*bratstvo i jedinstvo*," the official slogan of Brotherhood and Unity.

For all its determination, the JNA could not halt the process of politicization in Slovenia. It saw every move as an attack on Communism and the Yugoslav Federation. *Mladina*, the weekly magazine of the Socialist Youth organization, and a remarkable mix of satire and muck-raking, launched a campaign to expose the JNA as "an undemocratic institution always ready to stage a military coup." The Slovene judiciary, prompted by Belgrade, had charged Franci Zavrl, *Mladina*'s editor-in-chief, with authorizing an article entitled "Mamula Go Home"; and Andrej Novak, of the Slovene *Teleks* magazine for his essay "Generals and Generations." A year later the federal prosecutor took up the case, saying the Slovene courts had not pursued it.

Mladina's first target was Mamula himself. It dubbed him the "Merchant of Death" for selling weapons to the government of famine-stricken Ethiopia.[5] The government would use the arms against its own starving people, wrote *Mladina*. The magazine revealed how JNA conscripts had built the admiral an enormous villa in Opatija, a famous Adriatic resort town popular with Viennese high society before the First World War. This exposé of

Mamula's opulent standard of living gave even the most loyal officers pause for thought. General Milan Aksentijević, then a colonel in the Ljubljana garrison, says he remembers the day the article was published: "I had mixed feelings, I must say. From the article I learned that Mamula was building a castle – and here I was desperately trying to scrape the money together to get an apartment."

In March, Mamula struck back.

> *I wanted to warn them that there were limits... Direct attacks on the Army were forbidden in the constitution; I was not against democratization and reconstruction according to European values – though I did believe in the one-party system – not so much personally but as a representative of the Army.*

Frustrated, the JNA was convinced the Slovene leadership was using *Mladina* for its own ends. When they complained about the magazine, the Slovene response was that the Army should not be upset by a bunch of kids. For the generals, this tolerance was tantamount to approval. "You must remember this was during Communism," said Colonel Aleksandar Vasiljević, deputy commander of military counter-intelligence (KOS). "The Slovenes could have stopped them in a moment if they wanted to."

Mamula later realized that he had unwittingly helped to bolster the opposition. "One Slovene noted that, with my threat against the Slovene opposition, I did more for Slovene independence than anyone else. But what else was I supposed to stand up for?"

General Veljko Kadijević, who had recently taken over as Defense Minister, decided to make an example of *Mladina*. Mamula believed this left only one course of action for the JNA – a court-martial. A media war began between Slovenia's independent newspaper and the glossily-packaged JNA magazine, *Narodna Armija*, which accused *Mladina* of "joining the hostile émigré press and certain foreign papers to disseminate anti-JNA rumors." On March 20, *Dnevnik*, a daily newspaper from Serbia's northern province of Vojvodina, joined the fray. It criticized *Mladina* and *Nova Revija*, warning Kučan that he had been slow to realize that the "children had moved into an open and relentless struggle for power. Yesterday they advocated the democratization of society, while today they have already negated the leading role of the League of Communists." The Vojvodina daily called for the Slovene League of Communists to take a resolute stand.

As the first step in its crackdown, the JNA called a meeting of its Military Council, a body responsible for state security, to discuss how to bring Slovenia into line. The Council ruled that *Mladina* was "counter-revolutionary," charging that there was a foreign-backed conspiracy to overthrow the regime. Next, General Svetozar Visnjić, the Ljubljana Commander, went to see Kučan to ask how Slovenia would react if charges were brought against the authors of the anti-JNA articles. He asked Kučan whether he expected significant public outcry. If so, warned Visnjić, the Army would protect military barracks and Army personnel who were put in danger. Kučan told Visnjić: "Any action which does not take into account the extremely delicate political situation in Slovenia, would have irreparable consequences." Refusing to discuss politics with the Army, Kučan turned to the Party. He requested a special meeting of the Yugoslav Central Committee to discuss the Military Council. "The anti-Slovene campaign being waged in Serbia and elsewhere must stop. An anti-Yugoslav mood is growing in Slovenia in reaction to the growth of the anti-Slovene mood in the rest of the country. It is absurd to say the editors of *Mladina* are instruments of a special war being waged in Yugoslavia by world capitalism," Kučan told the other members of the Party leadership.

At this meeting he became more convinced than ever that there was a coalition hardening against Slovenia. Kučan saw that Slovenia was in the dock, with the JNA as chief prosecutor. He was worried that the JNA would do something drastic and urged the Central Committee to weigh its next step carefully. "This problem could break apart the country." An uncompromising Milošević disagreed. "Communists should support the people in the struggle against anti-Communism. The question is whether the Military Council was right in its actions. I think it was, because it is not right that the Army should be put in the position where it has to defend itself."

An alarmed General Kadijević uttered what was to become his stock warning: "Yugoslavia is on the brink of disintegration."

> *The very existence of Yugoslavia as a socialist state is under threat by counter-revolutionaries. There are connections between these circles in Yugoslavia and émigré circles... They have great influence on the foreign banks and the IMF and they put conditions on their aid, too, for us – more freedom and human rights and democracy.*

> *Enemy forces are in acceleration. The CIA has concluded that the* Mladina *editorial board is similar to Solidarnošč in Poland. The CIA has concluded the fall of Communism in Yugoslavia has begun. We must stop the counter-revolutionary actions.*

Kadijević dismissed Kučan's suggestion that the Presidency members travel to Slovenia to see how best to defuse the problem. He lashed out again:

Our conclusions don't need further study. Kučan is attacking the Presidency of the League of Communists of Yugoslavia in order to cover up his own mistakes in letting an anti-Army atmosphere develop in Slovenia. We did not need to consult with the Slovene political leadership at all. In the future the Army will act the way it sees fit.

This exchange shows the extent to which relations were already strained within the Central Committee. As Milošević carried out his purges, the battle lines would be redrawn, but the essence of the dispute would remain the same. Even Kadijević's threats did not spur the Slovene Central Committee into devising a formula to quell the dissidents. Despite intense anti-Slovene propaganda in the rest of Yugoslavia, no one made a move. It seemed that the danger had passed. But the JNA was not put off that easily.

Less than a month later, *Mladina* had a scoop – a secret document from the Ljubljana military district 5044-3 of January 8, 1988, listing instructions on how to prepare for martial law. Franci Zavrl later revealed that the document came from Ivan Borštner, a Slovene non-commissioned officer, who was about to leave the Army and was looking for contacts in the civilian world.

The JNA was already watching Borštner. Vasiljević said the Army had learned that Borštner was an extreme Slovene nationalist. "So we removed him from his high-security position as an Army cryptographer. At the end of 1987 he left the Communist party. He later explained that the Slovenes were being degraded and impoverished within Yugoslavia."[6] But Borštner had remained in the Army and got in touch with *Mladina*.

Zavrl was unfazed, and gave the document to Janez Janša, the activist who was Mladina's JNA expert. The magazine already had copious contacts in the military and political establishment. "This was nothing special... the document itself was silly and unimportant." But another, far more incendiary document would soon emerge. Janša secured a transcript of the Central Committee's March 25 session, called to discuss the Military Council meeting on Slovenia – the one where Kučan finally realized that the JNA meant business. Janša held on to the original, not realizing that the police were watching him. That night Slovene police broke into Mikro Ada, the computer company run by Janša and his friends, and discovered copies of the classified documents. The Slovene leadership was informed the next day, but took no action.

On May 13, *Mladina* published "Night of the Long Knives," a story about Army intervention which said the Army had drawn up a list of people it was proposing to arrest *en masse*.[7] The story was based on the Yugoslav Central Committee session, but the authors, afraid the authorities would ban the issue, did not quote directly from the transcript. None the less, the article caused a sensation. In a few days the issue was pulled from newsstands. Ljubljana was awash with rumors about a planned military coup. Kučan was under pressure. Later, he would reap the benefits of occupying the middle ground between the radical opposition and the reactionary JNA, but, for the time being, he was unsure what to do. How could he explain the document, which Belgrade was convinced he was responsible for leaking? He insisted the Army was overstepping its bounds: the main point was not the lists but the JNA's interference in politics. After meeting the Slovene police, he agreed to launch an investigation to find out how the transcript became public. Kučan told Belgrade what he had done, while his police were obliged to inform the JNA about the document they found in Janša's computer company.

When Mamula took early retirement in May 1988, it was up to Kadijević to implement the Army's plan to bring Slovenia to heel. He sent his crack KOS agent, Colonel Vasiljević, to Slovenia. Vasiljević had worked his way up through the ranks of the most élite of the military and security services' counter-intelligence. He had masterminded the JNA's covert action to crush ethnic Albanian unrest in Kosovo in 1981. He now arrived in Slovenia prepared to ferret out the "mole" who had leaked the military documents to *Mladina*. Although a specialist in clandestine operations, Vasiljević informed the Slovenian secret police of his plans. "They knew everything about me: I met their head, Ivan Eržen, every evening to review events. Tomaž Ertl, his boss, also knew of my presence in Ljubljana." Kučan later denied that he knew of Vasiljević's presence. "This was a matter dealt with by the Army and especially their secret services. The Slovene State Presidency was not informed by the Army about it." He never admitted that he had cooperated with the JNA.

Vasiljević and his team were ready to move. On Sunday morning at 5:30 Janša was suddenly woken up. "They searched my home and the Mikro Ada offices, then put me in a cell without a bed or daylight," he said.

> *They may say they arrested me for that military document but they never even bothered to ask about it. They were only interested in how I got hold of the transcript of the Central Committee meeting in March. They wanted to know who my contacts were in the government and the military.*

The circumstances surrounding Janša's arrest remain mysterious. Janša, who three years later would rise to prominence during Slovenia's "ten-day war," accused Kučan of collaborating with the JNA against him. News of the arrest spread quickly. Igor Bavčar, Janša's friend and business partner, was able to get a short report in the city edition of the Ljubljana daily, *Delo*. In Belgrade the next day, Slovenia's party leaders attended a session of the

Yugoslav League of Communists. Among those attending was Borut Šuklje, a Socialist youth leader and member of the Central Committee. Kučan turned to Šuklje and said: "Your friend, Janez Janša, has been arrested." Šuklje was alarmed.

> *I got scared. I didn't know at that time if this circle of arrests would end with Janša or would continue. At the same time it became clear to me that there was no way back. I got the feeling that Kučan was really surprised, and that he hadn't known in advance what would happen. I couldn't say whether the Slovene leadership collaborated with Belgrade or not.*

General Kadijević said the Slovene leadership had been kept informed of all developments. During a break in the Party conference, Kadijević told one of his fellow Communists that several men would be arrested in Slovenia for stealing military documents.

The next day the Slovene police handed Janša over to the JNA. Sergeant Borštner, who had leaked the incriminating document (it turned out to be a "plant") was arrested, as was the *Mladina* journalist, David Tasić, who had passed on the secret military document Order 5044-3. According to Yugoslav law, Slovenia was then obliged to allow the JNA to take over the investigation, since the three were suspected of possessing secret military documents.

In military jail, Janša was interrogated by Vasiljević, who had perfected his technique over two decades.

> *He told me in jail that it wouldn't be a problem even if all Slovenes supported me, because there are only a handful of us in the country, and they could kill all of us, if they wanted to. Really. He was very tough. He said: 'We can kill you, we can sentence you for fifteen years, we can ruin your family, we can kill your children, we can do anything in the interest of the state.'*

Two weeks later the JNA arrested Franci Zavrl. There was an immediate and intense public outcry. Bavčar founded the Committee for the Defense of Human Rights, known as *Odbor* – rallying together journalists, professors and other Slovene intellectuals. The arrests were the catalyst which effectively created an organized Slovene opposition movement. "It was interesting, at the time, all old conflicts just vanished," says Bavčar. "Very quickly we found out that this case would become a politically crucial case for Slovene democracy."

A petition calling for the release of the Ljubljana Four, as they became known, quickly collected 100,000 signatures, mostly, but not exclusively, from Slovenia. Crowds gathered to sign, causing spontaneous mini-demonstrations on Ljubljana's usually placid streets. The numbers were staggering, particularly for Slovenia, which had one of the most conservative populations, and where complaints about economic exploitation were far more widespread than those about human rights. Laibach and other exponents of the *Neue Slowenische Kunst* might have contributed much to expanding the Slovene social scene, but the JNA arguably contributed more.

As the JNA bulldozed on, the face of Slovene politics changed irreversibly. The leaders shifted towards the dissidents. Janez Stanovnik, President of Slovenia, made the unprecedented move of receiving Bavčar's Committee. This was a clear statement to Belgrade: Slovenia's leadership was supporting the Ljubljana Four. Stanovnik admits the meeting was in fact not planned. Bavčar, a huge man, showed up for a private meeting with a crowd of reporters and television cameras in tow. The mustachioed Stanovnik, looking for all the world like a throw-back to the days of the Austro-Hungarian Empire, told the impromptu press conference: "Look, people, I sympathize with what you are doing, I commit myself to take all the necessary steps on the federal level."

Despite official appeals, the trial went on. Each day crowds gathered round the courthouse. For the JNA Colonel Aksentijević, the public abuse the Army suffered during the trial struck hard. He had spent nearly forty years of his military service in Slovenia and had come to regard the republic as his home. Now it seemed it was turning against Yugoslavia, the country he had spent his life upholding.

> *My barracks were the host for the court. We had massive demonstrations outside the building all the time – and I had to make sure we were properly defended in case they got out of control. It was very painful. I would have to walk through the crowds and they would boo me and shout.*

For Franci Zavrl, the trial was pure Kafka.

> *The judge was not sure what was going on. We could hear the people outside the court. Nothing we, in the opposition, had ever tried to do to rally people had worked as well as that trial. It was a symbol: the dissident, the journalist, the soldier – all young and with popular appeal. We were the perfect ingredients for the Slovene spring.*

Juxtaposed against these perfect patriots of the new Slovenia was the JNA – acting like a bull in a china shop. The Army made one mistake after another. The public was barred from attending. The defendants were not allowed their own lawyers. The trial was conducted in Serbo-Croat instead of Slovene – this in itself helped to sway the opinions of many Slovenes, for whom language is crucial to national identity.[8]

The Army refused to bend. The Slovene leadership protested, but not too loudly. Kučan was not yet ready to mount an open challenge to the JNA. The Ljubljana Four received sentences ranging from eight months to four years. Instead of relaxing its grip, the federal establishment tried to force the Slovenes to climb down. An appeal from President Stanovnik for clemency was refused.

If the trial was Kafkaesque, the imprisonment was Ionesco. "I served the sentence in an open prison with a friendly Governor," said Zavrl. "I spent my days editing the magazine in my office and my nights in prison. On one occasion, when I was late getting back, I had to break into the prison over the wire!"

The trial took Slovenia one step further from Yugoslavia. It unified the tiny republic against the JNA – the symbol of the Communist Federation. "In early 1989, I and most others would still have opted for Yugoslavia," recalls Zavrl. "But then began Milošević's attacks in Kosovo, the attacks on Slovenes in the Army, and the whole irrational pressure from Serbia and Milošević. It drove us out much faster."

1 *Laibach*, the German word for Ljubljana, was the first written reference to Ljubljana in 1144 – two years later the town was mentioned in Slovene.

2 Stambolić and Kučan have remained on good terms since his fall from power.

3 The usually docile Macedonians, who revered Tito for giving them a state within the Yugoslav federation and recognizing them as a distinct ethnic community after the Second World War, reacted sharply to the Slovene document for negating the national identity of Macedonia and other Yugoslav nations.

4 Mamula, himself, wrote a book on Yugoslav defense, *Odbrana malih zemalja*, so he may have felt especially piqued.

5 Before 1991, Yugoslavia earned US $2 billion annually on arms exports, mostly to developing nations.

6 Vasiljević's observations were common complaints, more frequent in times of economic deprivation, about how Slovenia was supporting the rest of Yugoslavia. At the same time, Serbia made the same complaints on how the rest of the country was exploiting Serbia's rich raw materials.

7 In fact the list of names was never revealed and according to Ali Žerdin, the respected Slovene journalist, it is doubtful whether it existed at all.

8 Through centuries of foreign rule, the Slovenes had vigilantly preserved their culture, pressing for the right to use their language – whose first written records date back to the twelfth century.

4

"COMRADE SLOBODAN, THINK HARD"
Milošević's Anti-Bureaucratic Revolution
July 1988–March 1989

The Slovene spring gave way to the heat of Serbian summer. Throughout Yugoslavia's biggest republic, Serbs turned out by the million for rallies. They flocked to so-called "Meetings of Truth" about Kosovo clamoring for Slobodan Milošević. They resembled religious revivals. The steely Milošević rode the wave of nationalism which whipped through Serbia. Having secured absolute control over the Serbian League of Communists, he turned first on the two provinces of Serbia, then on tiny Montenegro, and finally on Yugoslavia itself. The emergence of nationalism was vaunted as the rebirth of dignity. Serbs believed that, after fifty years under the enforced slogan of "Brotherhood and Unity," Milošević had once again given them back their national identity, the right to say they were Serbs. Their fervor was fanned by the press. The daily newspapers doubled and tripled the number of faithful who attended the rallies. Each day the headlines got bigger, the messages more explosive. They sowed fear in the rest of the country. But there seemed to be nothing anyone could do.

On October 5, a crowd armed with triangular cartons of yogurt and milk, laid siege to, and then ousted, the leadership of Serbia's northern province of Vojvodina. The leadership was living a comfortable life running the province with little mind to what Belgrade thought. The "Yogurt Revolution," as it came to be known, was the final act in a drama that had begun three months earlier. The fate of the Vojvodina leadership had been sealed when Miroslav Šolević, the man who had established his loyalty in Kosovo Polje by rallying the crowds from 1987 on, and helping to stage-manage Milošević's dramatic Kosovo Polje speech, had organized a rally in the provincial capital, Novi Sad. For Šolević, a bear of a man, the rally was an immense success, the first in a chain of protests round Serbia. However, Belgrade thought it was too early for a rally to be effective against the Novi Sad leaders. Milošević sent his envoy to dissuade the Kosovo Polje group from travelling north to Vojvodina, where, in the jumble of national groups, Serbs comprised over fifty percent of the population. But Šolević refused. Milošević's people "wanted it to appear that all they had to do was press a button and we would respond to their call," he said. Instead, bearing signs saying: "We believe in the League of Communists of Yugoslavia," "Down with the 1974 constitution," and "Peace," they set off. The slogans were brilliant in their simple appeal: "Kosovo is Serbia." "Vojvodina is Serbia." "Together we are stronger."

58

By his own admission, Šolević did everything possible to provoke a conflict with the Novi Sad leadership. He was not disappointed. The Party chiefs went to great lengths to stop the rally from being held. They even turned off the power-and-water supplies. It was an ill-considered move. The Vojvodina leadership appeared to be attacking the "downtrodden" Kosovo Serbs, who were portrayed in the Belgrade media as martyrs for Serbdom. In a show of solidarity, Serbs from Novi Sad joined their Kosovo brothers marching to the town center. Women wept. This test-case cemented Milošević's conviction that "protests" were the perfect vehicle for stirring up popular opinion and destabilizing local Party leaders. By taking to the streets in this way, he could install his people throughout Serbia and its provinces. Šolević was the front man, the one the public came to know as the organizer of Milošević's Anti-Bureaucratic Revolution. But behind the scenes, the SDB, the secret police, helped to get the crowds out from factories and other work-places.[1] Under the illusion that Milošević had delivered their national freedom, it took little effort to stir up the masses.

On July 10, Boško Krunić, one of the Vojvodina Party leaders, tried to defend his province's autonomy against Milošević's drive to bring it under his control. Speaking in a village in Srem, Krunić insisted, pathetically, because he was terrified of what would happen, that he did not oppose the constitutional changes Milošević was forcing through. He admitted that negotiating the changes had been "difficult," but called on Belgrade to halt its "unprecedented efforts" to undermine his leadership. In fact, Vojvodina was trying to block the constitutional changes sought by Serbia's leaders. But afraid of provoking the wrath of Belgrade, Krunić, even at this late hour, tried to shift the blame on to Kosovo for the protracted negotiations. Krunić reminded Milošević that, unlike the restive, mostly Albanian province, the fertile prosperous plains of Vojvodina were peaceful:

> We all know that the most serious political problem in Yugoslavia today is the emigration of Serbs and Montenegrins from Kosovo... At the same time, we are forced to react to groundless accusations. We in Vojvodina never asked to be a republic. Why, and to whom, and how long are we to go on repeating this?

An attack on Vojvodina's autonomy was also an attack on Krunić's leadership and, obviously, all the privileges that came with the job.

His plea did not halt Belgrade's smear campaign. To no avail, Vojvodina tried to gain support within the ranks of the Yugoslav Party. On October 5, 1988, Mihalj Kertes, an ethnic Hungarian who was one of Milošević's most faithful executioners, led a crowd of factory workers by foot, bus and even tractor from the town of Bačka Palanka to Novi Sad, forty kilometers away. The bombastic Kertes recruited the protesters from state factories in his native Palanka. In a performance starring Kertes, Radovan Pankov and Nedeljko Šipovac, who would become Vojvodina's next leaders, the crowd of 15,000[2] jeered at the Party leadership. Hurling stones at the assembly, people chanted: *"Dole foteljaši"* – "down with the armchair governors." They splashed the building with yogurt, christening the "Anti-Bureaucratic Revolution" that was making Milošević the most powerful man in Yugoslavia.

Inside the building, the Vojvodina leaders began to panic. Dušan Mitević, head of Belgrade television, and Milošević were watching the events unfold on a live broadcast. They had a direct telephone link with the beleaguered officials. Mitević said the trapped men were terrified, afraid for their lives. Fearing the crowd would storm the assembly, they called for Army intervention. Belgrade blocked the deployment. If the Army had been engaged, the embattled leaders might have succeeded in garnering support among the politicians in other parts of Yugoslavia, who were watching the developments with growing concern. Macedonia's Lazar Mojsov, then President, gave the go-ahead to the Army. General Nikola Ljubičić, Serbia's representative to the federal presidency, surprisingly also said yes – even though he was one of Milošević's key supporters. The dispatch was blocked by another Partisan hero of the Second World War, General Petar Gračanin, President of Serbia, who was clearly acting at the behest of Milošević. Moreover, the JNA judged the Novi Sad events in a different light from those in Slovenia the previous spring. In Milošević, the Army saw a Communist who wanted Yugoslav unity; in the Slovene leadership, it saw reactionaries intent on destroying the country. The generals were blinded by their ideological persuasion.

The crowd swelled, screaming into the autumn night. Milovan Šogorov, head of the Vojvodina Party, desperately phoned Milošević appealing for help. He replied coolly: "Okay, I'll save you, but there is one condition: you must all submit your resignations. If you resign, I'll save you." That was it. The regime crumbled. Milošević was in control. The leaders of the Yogurt Revolution would be rewarded for their faithful service.[3]

Milošević attained almost divine status among the Serbs. No one anticipated the adoration which he would command. Suddenly he was everywhere. His photograph or portrait, often both, hung in every store window, in trucks, offices and government buildings. There were even jokes about his portrait. In one, Milošević stares at one of the thousands of pictures of himself. Finally, he breaks down and asks: "What will happen to us?" The picture answers: "One day they'll take me down. But they'll hang you." It was impossible to walk through the heart of Belgrade, the Serbian and Yugoslav capital, without constantly meeting Milošević's confident gaze. Tito's image began to disappear. Carrying his photo, at the scores of rallies over the next six months, people would chant that Milošević had replaced

Tito. Serbs loved Milošević for his pledge to protect them – to reunite Serbia divided by the 1974 constitution.

Montenegro was next. It was Yugoslavia's smallest republic, with just 604,000 inhabitants. Like the other republics, under Tito, Montenegro had its own central bank, steel works, aluminum plant and Academy of Sciences and Arts, but it was bankrupt. Workers were demanding higher wages. The republic seemed ripe for social unrest. Divided into thirty-five tribes, Montenegrins still know which clan they belong to. They had traditionally cast themselves as a warrior nation, hailing from the forbidding craggy peaks of the Dinaric mountains. Of all the other communities in Yugoslavia, their history, religion, and identity was most closely intertwined with the Serbs. There are two traditions which run deep in Montenegro: one the Greens, for independence, the other, the Whites, who call themselves Serbs and want union with Serbia. Milošević knew that his Serbian revival would find fertile ground in Montenegro. After all he was a native of Montenegro.

A trio of rallies, several months apart, and an amalgam of economic and political demands broke the existing Montenegrin regime. On October 7, hot on the heels of Vojvodina's Yogurt Revolution, crowds turned out in Titograd in protest, after police used truncheons and tear-gas to prevent a demonstration by steel workers. Seven men were injured after the police captain ordered his forces to baton-charge the crowd. The event was later manipulated by the Belgrade media which accused the Montenegrin leadership of cruelly suppressing the national will. The rally shifted from economic concern to demands for change in Kosovo. The occasion marked the political birth of Branko Kostić, Vice President of the Montenegrin government. At his advanced age of fifty, Kostić told the crowd, he was not there to make a name for himself but to see how he could help. In just three years, by demonstrating his blind loyalties, the pro-Serb Kostić would be acting President of rump Yugoslavia.

The Montenegrin regime stayed in power another three months. In the meantime, a group of young Montenegrin Communists, led by Momir Bulatović, appeared launching open harsh attacks on their leadership. They knew that the criticism would go unpunished because their mentor was in Belgrade. At thirty-four, Bulatović became the Party chief of Montenegro. Milošević's control was extending beyond the borders of Serbia itself.

After Montenegro, what next? The Yugoslav political establishment was shaken by Milošević's revolution road-show. On October 17, at the Seventeenth Session of the Central Committee, the Yugoslav League of Communists tried to stop Milošević. The federal Party chief, Stipe Šuvar of Croatia, proposed a vote-of-confidence in each member of the Politburo. It was clear that Šuvar's target was Milošević.

Šuvar, who earlier had been a Milošević supporter, was now convinced that the Yugoslav Party should vote to oust him. However, Milošević protested on the grounds that he was a member of the Politburo because he was chief of the Serbian Party, so the Yugoslav body had no authority over him. He won. Using this procedural loophole, the Party bosses from the six republics and two provinces were exempt from re-confirmation. There is little doubt that if Milošević had been forced to place himself for re-election before the federal Party, he would have lost. Indeed, the only candidate to fail the ballot was Milošević's closest ally, Dušan Čkrebić, Serbia's man on the federal Party. By voting against him, the Yugoslav Communist bosses were signalling their opposition to Milošević. They had sufficient support to fire Milošević, but the rules did not permit it.[4] The Yugoslav Party was powerless to stop this former banker whose gamble had paid off.

Indeed, Milošević even manipulated the rules to score another point. By invoking the powers of the Serbian over the Yugoslav Party, Milošević rescued the elderly Čkrebić. At the insistence of the Serbian Party, Čkrebić was reinstated.

With this move, Milošević made clear his strategy towards the Yugoslav federation: when it was opportune he invoked the supremacy of the federal institutions over the republics; but when it was in his interest, he claimed that Serbia would not obey the dictates of the federation. In a strident and prescient warning, Vinko Hafner, a veteran Slovene Communist and a Partisan, took the floor, pointed his finger across the podium and, fixing his gaze on Milošević, said: "Comrade Slobodan, think hard about which road you have chosen."

Belgrade carried out a series of purges with ruthless efficiency. A policy called differentiation was in full gear; anyone, from local authorities to factory managers, who refused to kow-tow to Milošević, was fired. On November 17, 1988, the leadership of the Kosovo Party was dismissed. Already the mood in Kosovo was nervous. Ethnic Albanians, the overwhelming majority of the province's 1.9 million population, were bracing themselves for a crack-down. As the Serbian rallies became more feverish – men wearing Chetnik nationalist war mementoes demanded the arrest of Albanian functionaries – Belgrade prepared to strip Kosovo of its autonomy. The Serbian leadership tightened its grip, while among Albanians popular support swelled for the embattled leaders, Kaçusha Jashari and Azem Vllasi. While the Party Committee met to rubber-stamp the dismissals, secured by Belgrade, miners abandoned their pitheads in Trepča, marching fifty-five kilometers to Priština. For the next five days, along with Albanian students, they braved freezing temperatures as they camped out in front of the provincial Party headquarters in protest against the fall of their Party leaders. It was a scenario reminiscent of the Yogurt Revolution in Vojvodina, except that this time the popular protest was in support of the local leadership and against Belgrade.

Over whisky a few weeks later, Milošević asked Vllasi whether he had been behind the November demonstrations. "He wanted to know how so many people could turn up and take the police completely by surprise," recalled Vllasi. "He said that the police could not work out who had been organizing them."

"They turned up of their own will. I certainly did not have the money to pay for them and bus them in," said Vllasi in a retort which irked Milošević.

They were the last Albanian protests *not* to end in bloodshed. The police remained on the sidelines. In three months, the Army and the police were to assert control over the southern province. Belgrade dismissed the protest as "counter-revolution." Serbia's propaganda was at fever pitch. The press warned of Albanian separatism, dismissing the nation as primitive. Intellectuals banded together with the politicians to warn of a conspiracy against Serbia from Ljubljana to Tirana.

On November 19, after several false starts, "the Meeting of All Meetings" was held in Belgrade. Whenever Serbia argued with other Yugoslav republics, the Belgrade leadership would threaten to hold the biggest rally ever. On that grey November day, Milošević warned his countrymen: "We are not at all afraid. We enter every battle intending to win." The local press said at least one million people turned out to listen to their leader pledge victory "even though Serbia's enemies abroad are uniting with those inside the country." Looking out at the sea of people, Milošević said: "Every nation has a love which eternally warms its heart. For Serbia it is Kosovo. That is why Kosovo will remain in Serbia." Milovan Vitezović, a poet and Party hack, coined the phrase: "The people have happened." It became the catch-phrase for the national awakening which propelled Milošević to the height of power, the most powerful politician since Tito.

Milošević's people set up a company to provide the transportation and organize the meetings. Tens of thousands of workers were bussed in from provincial factories. They were given sandwiches and drinks instead of working their shifts. State enterprises forced their employees to go together to attend the "Meeting of All Meetings."

For the politicians elsewhere in the other republics, Milošević's pledge to make Serbia whole again sounded the death-knell for Yugoslavia. Kučan, Party chief of Slovenia, saw the significance: "By abolishing the autonomy of both provinces of Vojvodina and Kosovo, Serbia would directly control three-out-of-eight votes in the Federal Presidency – in comparison with the other republics that had one vote each. That meant turning Yugoslavia into Serbo-slavia." With a loyal Montenegro, Milošević was, eventually, to control half the votes on the Yugoslav Federal Presidency, effectively ensuring that the collective head of state could not take a single decision without his explicit approval.

Milošević paid no heed to the intense criticism provoked by his populist methods, bulldozing over the existing institutions. His scorn for his opposite numbers was evident at a Party session in January, when he made clear he would achieve his goals regardless of their protest. "The solution will be found through politics supported by the majority of people in this country. Either through the existing institutions or not. On the streets or inside, by populist or élite methods."[5] Milošević was stating explicitly that if he did not get his way within the existing power structures, he would rally the masses in order to achieve his goal. He had already begun.

Milošević pressed on with the constitutional changes, with the republics unable to stop him.[6] The federal parliament, on November 25, adopted amendments which cleared the way for the new Serbian constitution. There were only a few loose ends. The Kosovo assembly had to vote in favor of its own demise. In other words, Milošević needed to make sure his men controlled Kosovo's Communist Party. The official Serbian media divided Albanians into "honest" and "separatist." Milošević had already picked three "honest" Albanians, Rahman Morina, Husamedin Azemi and Ali Shukria, to carry out his bidding.

After the November demonstrations, Vllasi topped the blacklist as leader of the "secessionists." "I was aware that the ground was being prepared for revenge or even my arrest. Serbia was fairly open about it: they thought that until they got me out of the way, it would be impossible to pass the constitutional changes they wanted," he said. Once a favorite of Tito, Vllasi was now expelled from the Central Committee. Milošević lost no time in installing his trio of faithful Party apparatchiks. The constitutional changes were almost in the bag.

On February 20, the Trepča miners went into action again. They refused to leave the pits until their demands were met – the first of these was the resignation of Milošević's "placemen" from the Kosovo Party leadership. Scenes of the pale-and-determined miners crowded into dark dank pits were broadcast throughout Yugoslavia. Grim lines cut their shadowed faces. They pledged to stick to their demands until death if necessary. Outside their families waited, afraid of what would come next.[7]

Kosovo came to a halt. Protests broke out everywhere. In Belgrade, Milošević wanted the strike over. He pushed for the declaration of a state-of-emergency. To Burhan Kavaja, head of Trepča mine, the Serbian leadership did not even feign concern about the miners' lives. At an emergency meeting to try to end the strike, Kavaja warned Yugoslavia's leaders that he was worried about the potential for disaster. "I explained that there were 2,400 kilograms of explosives in the mines. There were 1,300 miners there. Someone could easily set it off by mistake. To my surprise, they did not seem to care." Only Yugoslav President Raif Dizdarević received the news with apparent distress. Petar Gračanin of Serbia dismissed his appeals and, to Kavaja's astonishment, began a monologue about his own exploits in Kosovo during the Second World War.

The diminutive General Gračanin then made the exaggerated warning that more than 50,000 armed Serbs and Montenegrins were ready to march to Kosovo. Throughout Serbia it was common to hear men pledge themselves ready to fight in Kosovo. It seemed like bluster, a confident swaggering boast that would never be tested. But as tensions rose, fears of an armed confrontation grew. The Yugoslav leadership argued violently over whether to declare a state-of-emergency in the province. There were accusations that the Slovenes and Croats were sending food and money to Kosovo to keep the strike going. Milošević wanted to deploy the JNA to end it. Kučan told him that he had no right to resort to military means, explaining that the strike was prompted by the changes to the Serbian constitution, which Milošević himself had strong-armed.

Intent on stopping the strike, Milošević phoned Vllasi in Priština. He told the ethnic Albanian leader to persuade the miners to call off their strike. In response Vllasi said: "I have been to the mines and am convinced that they won't give up, unless their demands are met." Furious, Milošević warned Vllasi that "someone will have to answer for this." Ignoring the clear threat, Vllasi agreed: "Of course, the one who is responsible. But the miners won't leave until their demands are met." Milošević tried to cajole him into coming to Belgrade for talks, but Vllasi shrugged off the suggestion. This was their last conversation.

Tensions were at fever pitch. Milošević made it plain to the Yugoslav Party Politburo that he would not abandon the constitutional changes. After all, that was the political platform which sustained his leadership. If the Party would not back the amendments, Milošević told Kučan at a meeting of the party leadership, "Serbia would do what it wanted, using any means it deemed necessary, be it in accordance with the law or not." "Then this is the end of Yugoslavia," answered Kučan.

That night, Milošević made a tactical maneuver to buy time. His three minions on the Kosovo Party leadership offered their resignations. The miners, 180 of whom were already in hospital, ill after a week underground, abandoned the strike. But it was too late. The situation had spiraled out of control.

The next day, the Slovene capital, Ljubljana, turned out for a rally in the concert hall, Cankarjev Dom, organized by Bavčar's Committee for Human Rights. The entire Slovene political leadership took part, siding with the strikers against Belgrade. In Serbia, the public was shocked. Despite their current war of words, the Serbs and Slovenes generally had enjoyed good relations. Condescendingly, Serbs often pointed out that they had sheltered Slovene children during the Second World War when they fled Nazi occupation. In total 8,600 Slovenes took shelter in Serbia after Heinrich Himmler ordered the expulsions of "disloyal Slovenes." Another component of the new-born Serb nationalism was the constant comparison of the suffering of the Serbs during the Second World War to that of the Jews.[8] It is difficult to imagine a slogan more likely to rile the Serbs than the speech made that night, at Cankarjev Dom, by Jože Školjč, then head of the Slovene Youth organization. "Albanians in Yugoslavia are in a position similar to that of the Jews in World War Two." For Serbs, this struck at the essence of their rekindled mythology: they were the martyrs.

On February 27, speaker after speaker in Ljubljana condemned the Serbs for repression in Kosovo. Belgrade had become the tormentor. "Yugoslavia is being defended in the Trepča mine. The situation in Kosovo shows that people are no longer living together but increasingly against one another. Politics cannot be pursued on the streets or when lives are put at risk," said Kučan.

> *The Trepča miners are defending the rights of citizens and Communists in Kosovo to elect their own leadership. Slovenes are not casual visitors in Yugoslavia. We helped create it and are responsible for its future. We protest against fanning the psychosis of the state-of-emergency. We are warning that a quiet coup is taking place before our eyes which is changing the face of Yugoslavia.*

Watching the Cankarjev Dom rally on Ljubljana Television, Dušan Mitević, Belgrade TV chief, made what he called an "unintentionally" dangerous decision. He decided to broadcast the rally. Within a few hours, complete with Serbo-Croat subtitles translated from the Slovene, the rally sent electric jolts through Serbia, a nation inured to its own nationalist rhetoric. The Serbs appeared not to see that, when the Slovenes protested against the Serbs in Cankarjev Dom, it was after a full year of Serbian nationalist rallies echoing through Yugoslavia. The reaction was instantaneous.

"They criticized the Serbs so much in Cankarjev Dom. They said such awful things about us which I, as a human being, could not understand," Gračanin later remembered.

He was incensed, and so was the rest of Serbia. It was inconceivable that the clever Mitević, even if only paying half a mind, did not see the shock-value of his broadcast. It is more likely that he welcomed the unexpected ammunition in the intensifying war of words between Belgrade and Ljubljana. "As soon as I got home the phone began to ring," said Mitević:

> *Friends told me people were gathering outside their blocks of flats in heated discussion. Ten minutes later someone told me students were leaving the campus. I realized something would happen that night, so I returned to the office to organize coverage of events in Belgrade... By 8.00 a.m., there were a million people in front of the Federal Assembly. They were upset for no clear political reason apart from one transmission from Slovenia where they had heard so much abuse against themselves.*

It remains in question how many people turned out spontaneously that night in Belgrade, but Serbs were truly astounded. Party functionaries visited key factories around Belgrade. The federal President Dizdarević said:

> *That evening we received information from federal state security that several Belgrade factories were being organized to call meetings for tomorrow to coordinate and to put pressure on the federal structures. The factory bosses received direct orders from Zoran Todorović, a Party official, widely known as "kundak" (rifle-butt).*

Party functionaries frantically phoned round for instructions as reports came in through the night that thousands of students were marching on the city. "I told Gračanin to stop it," said Dizdarević. Gračanin tried to ease Dizdarević's worries, promising to divert the students outside the city center. Dizdarević took his word. But he woke to the news that hundreds of thousands of demonstrators had gathered in front of the federal parliament smack in the city center.

The Miloševićes were away for the weekend in Vrnjačka Banja, a spa in central Serbia. Mira Marković said they did not watch the Slovene demonstration on television, and claimed to be shocked when told about it. Early the next day, they decided to return to Belgrade.

As usual Milošević was in no hurry to address the rally. The longer he kept it waiting the more momentum the protest gained. Workers arrived from Rakovica, the nearby industrial district in Belgrade. They were chanting: "Slobo, Slobo." They would not settle for anyone else. "Milošević was like a saint to them, not an icon, but a living saint, they believed his every word and would not go home until he spoke to them," said Borisav Jović.

The Serbian and federal politicians held crisis-sessions all day. Milošević wanted to declare a state-of-emergency in Kosovo. Kučan was dead-set against this. He knew that Serbia could use the same excuses against Slovenia in the near future. In the end Milošević got his way.

It seemed that the leadership was losing control. At one point, Jović exclaimed euphorically: "Serbia is on fire." Outside the crowd was calling for Milošević. Gračanin said: "Slobo was psychologically incapable of speaking in front of such large crowds."[9] After hours of resisting, Dizdarević, the federal President, agreed to speak, believing that, as a Bosnian, he would not provoke the wrath of the crowd. Šuvar of Croatia refused – "No, they'll attack us," he said. Dizdarević's speech was painful. Gračanin had advised him to say: "As far as the '74 constitution is concerned, we're working on it. And I promise you that we'll succeed. As far as Kosovo is concerned, Kosovo is part of Serbia. As far as Yugoslavia is concerned, we are in favor of Yugoslavia."

A young Milošević activist stood behind Dizdarević prompting him what to say: "Tell them that you'll do everything to protect Yugoslavia." His whisper was audible over the public address system. Dizdarević's humiliation showed just how weak the federal institutions were; they had no power against this maddened crowd. People hung from the trees, screaming for the heads of the Kosovo leadership, jeering at Dizdarević, calling for the arrest of Vllasi and demanding to be armed.

The crowd did not disperse. It waited into the night, and was still there the next morning. Twenty-four hours after the crowd had gathered, Milošević finally appeared. Again he appealed directly to the masses, over the heads of the Yugoslav leaders:

> *This rally shows that no one can destroy the country because the people won't let them, the people are the best guarantee, we are going to get all honest people in Yugoslavia to fight for peace and unity. Nothing can stop the Serb leadership and people from doing what they want.*
>
> *Together we will fight for unity and freedom in Kosovo. We have to change our constitution, and this will mean progress for all people in Yugoslavia. Unity for the Communist Party and the people.*

The crowd roared, screaming for the arrest of the Albanian Party leaders. Milošević answered: "I can't hear you, but we will arrest those responsible including those who have used the workers. In the name of the socialist people of Serbia I promise this."

Dušan Mitević said it was Milošević at his best.

> *It was a show of power – to keep a crowd waiting for hours. The federal President speaks, and they don't leave. Finally Slobodan comes. He speaks briefly for four minutes. The crowd shouts: 'Arrest Vllasi!', Slobodan did not hear it properly and repeated: 'We will arrest those who have to be arrested! No matter what function they hold.' 'Now go home!' and they did... It showed his power and that he was their unassailable leader.*

Vllasi was driving through Belgrade. The car radio was on. Milošević's pledge to arrest him tempted Vllasi to turn up at the rally. He was jailed one day later.

The crowd dispersed. For days afterwards, the demonstrations were likened to March 27, 1941, when the Serbian people had come out in defiance against a pact with Hitler's Germany. *"Bolje rat nego pakt"* – "better war than a pact," the war-time crowd had famously asserted. The Serbs prided themselves on being prepared to go headstrong into war rather than accept the dictates of others. General Gračanin remembered the day when the "people reacted spontaneously to the pact with the Germans... I was eighteen at that point":

Chapter 4: "Comrade Slobodan, Think Hard"

There were streams and streams of people throughout Serbia. And I said to Slobodan later: 'This is the 27th of March' and I told him: 'You weren't even born at that time.'

The new constitution was announced, ratified by the Kosovo assembly. The vote to strip itself of autonomy and submit itself to the authority of Belgrade was assured by the JNA tanks and the Serbian police surrounding the building and deployed throughout Kosovo. On March 28, 1989 the political élite of Serbia turned out to celebrate the new constitution. The entire front page of *Politika* trumpeted that Serbia was whole again. Belgrade had brought the provinces under its control. While girls in white dresses sang the Yugoslav national anthem in a chorus in a Belgrade concert hall, twenty-two ethnic Albanians and two policemen were killed during two days of protests against the new constitution. Official Belgrade said not one word of regret about the deaths of the ethnic Albanians. The changes had been brought on bayonets. The day was declared a state holiday in Serbia.

1 *Telegraf:* November 9, 1994.

2 Estimates vary wildly – by some accounts there were even 150,000 people present.

3 Kertes was to hold a host of key positions from Chief of the Federal Secret Police to Head of Customs in 1994 (in a country under embargo, where all trade was smuggling, that was a choice post). Another secret policeman, Jovica Stanišić, grew up next to Kertes. He would rise to the top, becoming one of Milošević's most trusted allies. In May 1995 Milošević appointed Stanišić his "special envoy" designated for freeing UN hostages in Bosnia.

4 Radiša Gačić, Serbia's other man in the Yugoslav Politburo, who had been on Stambolić's side in the Eighth Session passed the ballot. Milan Pančevski, a pro-Milošević Macedonian, almost did not make the cut-off with eighty-six.

Djukić, Slavoljub, *Izmedju slave i anateme: politička biografija Slobodana Miloševića,* Filip Višnjić, Belgrade 1994.

5 Slobodan Milošević, *Godine raspleta*, BIGZ, Belgrade, 1989, p. 333.

6 In fact, they were relieved to let Belgrade deal with it. Slovenia often protested against the huge contributions to the federal fund for the less-developed regions of Yugoslavia – Kosovo, Macedonia, and Montenegro.

7 Serbia traded accusations with Croatia and Slovenia as to whether the miners were actually on a hunger-strike. The charges were aimed at compromising the miners. Since 180 men were hospitalized, and they all looked wan and ill, it seems unlikely, and, in any event, irrelevant, whether they were eating or not.

8 Prominent Serbian intellectuals in 1989 founded the Serbian-Jewish Friendship Society. The group opposed non-aligned Yugoslavia's pro-Arab, anti-Israeli policy. It soon received considerable official backing with its secretary, Klara Mandić, later to be involved with several prominent Serbs from Radovan Karadžić, to Captain Dragan who had his own paramilitary unit in Knin, the Kninjas.

9 Rumors have persisted that Milošević hates to speak in public. Even though he came to power on a wave of rallies, he seldom addressed crowds.

5

TSAR LAZAR'S CHOICE
March 1989–January 1990

The ubiquitous smile of the new Yugoslav Prime Minister, Ante
Marković, became a trademark for his seemingly boundless optimism.
He strove to implement free-market reforms, meeting resistance from the
leaders of Serbia, Slovenia and Croatia, who wanted to keep control over the
economy. His program offered hope for a country caught in a dangerous spi-
ral of nationalism, generated from Serbia. In a short time, the silver-haired,
blue-eyed Marković became the most popular politician in all six republics,
even though he was vilified by their governments. Even now the mention of
his name recalls an era of prosperity and optimism.

But he is also remembered for presiding over, and lacking the power to
stop, Yugoslavia's excruciating descent into war. During his tenure, the first
multiparty elections since the Second World War were held in the six
republics. Nationalist parties captured most of the vote. Marković came into
conflict with Serbia, Slovenia and Croatia. Yet he was at their mercy. His program hinged on the compliance of each regime, but they selectively obeyed
or violated it. Indeed the republics, at odds over everything, forged an
unlikely alliance to overthrow him. The Prime Minister was hit from all
sides. Milošević tried to block reforms which would weaken his monopoly
over power. In a tactical maneuver to distance itself from the federal government, Serbia launched a separatist drive, even appointing its own Foreign
Minister, the first Yugoslav republic to do so. It became popular to say that
Serbia could survive on its own. But these were only tactics. Milošević's real
intention was to take over the Yugoslav federation.

Slovenia refused to follow the same rules as the other republics. Croatia
wanted to keep its foreign-currency earnings from tourism. Marković stubbornly tried to defend Yugoslavia, even when there was nothing left to
defend, pleading for reason over nationalism. On December 20, 1991, he
resigned, ostensibly in protest against the federal budget which he called a
war budget. Betrayed by everyone, he controlled little more than the cav-
ernous and sprawling federal government building. Finally, he lost that too.

By supporting Marković's candidacy in January 1989, Serbia had hoped to
wring concessions from Croatia and Slovenia. The pay-off for Belgrade's
approval of Marković, a Croat, was a free hand with Kosovo and constitutional changes. The choice was a compromise for Milošević, particularly since the
other main candidate was Borisav Jović, one of Milošević's most trusted collaborators. Marković, a pragmatic technocrat, picked a government mostly

70

composed of market-oriented politicians. To win support for his reforms, Marković tried to keep the republics happy. While he was in office, the dinar, the national currency, was made convertible and pegged to the German Mark. Marković liberalized imports and pushed through a package of privatization laws. He wanted to anchor the economy in sound fiscal and financial policy, rather than political whim, believing that people would prefer to have a color television set, a car and foreign travel rather than nationalist slogans, war and isolation. He was wrong.

Despite the lure of shiny foreign labels, Serbia was still blinded by the radiant glare of nationalism. On June 28, 1989, a million Serbs flocked to Kosovo to worship at Milošević's feet, during celebrations to mark the six-hundredth anniversary of Serbia's defeat by the Turks. The date resonates throughout Serbian history. On the same day, in 1914, Gavrilo Princip, a Serb nationalist revolutionary, assassinated Austrian Archduke Franz Ferdinand in Sarajevo, triggering the First World War. But far more important to the Serb national psyche is St Vitus's Day, 1389, when a Serbian army was vanquished by the Ottomans in a place in Kosovo known as the Field of Blackbirds. According to the most revered of epics, Tsar Lazar joined the ranks of Serbia's legendary heroes, in a battle that ushered in the beginning of 500 years of Turkish domination. At the start of the battle, the invading Turks offered Tsar Lazar the choice between fighting to the death and capitulation. They also offered a reward for his surrender. He refused, choosing the kingdom of heaven over worldly wealth and the betrayal of his nation to a foreign oppressor.

According to one version of the legend, Saint Elijah came with a message from the Mother of God:

> *What kingdom shall I choose?*
> *Shall I choose a heavenly kingdom?*
> *Shall I choose an earthly kingdom?*
> *If I choose an earthly kingdom,*
> *An earthly kingdom lasts only a little time,*
> *But a heavenly kingdom will last for eternity.*

Tsar Lazar chose the heavenly kingdom rather than capitulate to the foreign enemy, and the medieval Serb aristocracy died together in that battle.

> *All was holy, all was honorable,*
> *and the goodness of God was fulfilled.*

Milošević asked his followers to make the same choice. His minions

71

throughout Yugoslavia should pledge to eat roots rather than betray their nation by accepting foreign dictates. This, Lazar's choice, was inimical to the Marković reforms, which promised a kingdom on earth.

The myth of Kosovo is the centerpiece of Serbian tradition. "Beside the name of Christ, no other name is more beautiful or more sacred," said Orthodox Bishop Emilijan at a celebration marking the battle's anniversary in 1939.[1] Half a century later, pilgrims stood in line at the Orthodox monastery, Gračanica, to view Lazar's bones. The remains would be passed round monasteries in Yugoslavia, places that would be claimed as Serb lands when the war broke out in 1991. This journey, the first time that Lazar's bones had been seen in public, was celebrated as a holy national rite. Some sensed danger. Ljubinka Trgovčević, an early Milošević opponent, had already warned the Serbian leadership that the travelling exhibit – and the return of Chetnik symbols such as the double-headed white eagle of the Serbian royal house and the imagery of the Serbian Orthodox Church – could upset Yugoslavia's delicate balance. The Serbs, she said, were the biggest nation and should act responsibly towards the smaller, more vulnerable ones. But her advice was drowned by the thunderous shouts of Serbs rejoicing in the conviction that they, finally, held the country's destiny in their hands.

In an aggressive, defiant mood, Serbs flocked from around the world to take part in the ceremonial union of all Serbs under one leader. After hours spent snarled in traffic, apparently willing to endure a host of trials to see their leader, they thronged to the Field of Blackbirds. From daybreak, they waited to secure places at the front, but were separated from Milošević by a huge expanse of mud. The celebration at Gazimestan, the battlefield, differed from the anti-bureaucratic rallies, attended by tired-looking workers bussed in from factories. This was a momentous occasion. The state machinery might have delivered the crowds to Kosovo, but the people here were proud to be part of this powerful expression of Serb unity. Gazimestan was the spectacular culmination of the numbers game. No one could outdo Milošević.

In this fevered atmosphere, Milošević descended from the heavens by helicopter to deliver his grandest snub to the federation. Yugoslavia's top politicians stood on the stage, looking decidedly uncomfortable. Milošević was out in front, totally in command:

> *Serbs in their history have never conquered or exploited others. Through two world wars, they liberated themselves and, when they could, they also helped others to liberate themselves.*
> *The Kosovo heroism does not allow us to forget that at one time we were brave and dignified and one of the few who went into battle undefeated.*
> *Six centuries later, again we are in battles and quarrels. They are not armed battles, though such things should not be excluded yet.*

Almost within earshot, in Kosovo's capital, Priština, the decrepit Socialist high-rise buildings, usually teeming with children, were silent. Serb folk-music blared in the heat. The town seemed abandoned. Even though Serbs were outnumbered ten to one in Kosovo, on that day Albanians kept to themselves, fearing they could be targeted by the hordes of pilgrims, many of whom had had a generous dose of *šljivovica* (plum brandy). Milošević's deputy in Kosovo vowed to arrest Ibrahim Rugova, the ethnic Albanian opposition leader. That day, Rugova, fragile and unsure, waited for the hand of Belgrade to tighten its grip over Kosovo.

After the March 1989 constitutional amendments, Serbia was far more powerful than the other republics. By taking control over the provinces, it now had three votes in the eight-member federal Presidency. Slovenia was afraid of this unchecked influence, so the northwestern republic sought to redefine Yugoslavia: to weaken the hold of the center.

Serbia was confident that introducing "one man, one vote" would halt the centrifugal forces tearing apart the federation. Majority vote usually goes hand-in-hand with democracy, but in this climate, where perceived national interests dominated individual ones, it would have guaranteed, for example, that the numerically-superior Serbs could always outvote the Slovenes. Convinced of this, the Slovenes insisted on retaining "one federal unit, one vote" stipulated by the 1974 constitution.

In September, Slovenia tried to halt Serbia's drive for centralization. The northwestern republic proposed a package of constitutional amendments, which would spell out the right to secede, if necessary, from Yugoslavia. Independence, however, was not the goal. Most of the leadership considered the amendments, which ran the gamut from language to the military, an insurance policy that would safeguard Slovenia's special position within Yugoslavia.

By sanctioning the selective implementation of federal law, the amendments dealt a body-blow to Marković's program. They helped Ljubljana to mute the rising popular complaint, encouraged by the Slovene regime, that Yugoslavia's richest republic was being exploited and its prosperity drained by the rest of the country. After all, Slovenia accounted for eight percent of Yugoslavia's population of 23.5 million and produced nearly one-third of the country's hard currency exports. This fallacious equation did not take account of the virtually captive markets of the rest of Yugoslavia's 21.5 million people, or the cheap labor and raw materials which Slovenia had access to elsewhere – in particular, Serbia, Bosnia and Macedonia. The new constitution would empower Slovenes – and not the federation – with the right to decide how to allocate the wealth of the republic. This posed yet another obstacle for Marković, about which he could do little but hope it would not subvert his reform program.

73

A storm erupted when Belgrade got wind of the planned amendments. Serbia demanded the right to discuss the proposed changes. The Slovene leadership responded by pointing out that Serbia had amended its own constitution, regardless of what anybody else in Yugoslavia wanted, even at the cost of Albanian lives in Kosovo. Slovenia said Serbia had set the precedent: Yugoslav republics had the right to change their own constitution. Belgrade argued that the Slovenes were interfering in what was exclusively an internal affair of a federal state. For weeks, the republics waged a war of words.

The Serbian leadership was infuriated by the amendments, which, by subjugating federal to local interests, effectively made the Slovenes their own masters – an expressed goal of the regime. Slovenia would then have powers equal to, or even exceeding, those of the federation. It could decide whether the Army should take action in the republic, declare a state-of-emergency, redefine its relations with the other federal units, and choose which parts of federal law it wanted to implement. Serbian and federal military leaders debated how to stop Slovenia. Between themselves, they argued whether they should threaten to impose a state-of-emergency or actually impose one. Jović spent hours exploring the various options with Milošević and the Defense Minister, General Kadijević. "Milošević and I believed that if the Slovenes passed the amendments it would be the end of Yugoslavia." The trio decided it would be preferable to dissuade the Slovene leadership from adopting the amendments rather than deploying the Army. For the time being, Milošević decided that the threat of force was the most effective deterrent to promulgating a new constitution.[2]

Jović, as Serbia's representative on the Yugoslav Presidency, promised to persuade the federal institutions to condemn the Slovene constitutional amendments. The eight-member federal Presidency ruled against the amendments, on the grounds that they would give Slovenia a privileged status within Yugoslavia. After a meeting at the military hideaway of Dobanovci, outside Belgrade, Janez Drnovšek, a Slovene, who was then head of the rotating Presidency, explained that a harsh public statement would be counter-productive. Jović reluctantly agreed to open talks with the Slovenes in Belgrade.

It was not yet time to play hardball.

The Serbian leaders tried to cajole the Slovenes into climbing down. A senior Slovene delegation turned up in Belgrade to face the unlikely coalition of Jović, Kadijević and Marković. Drnovšek initiated the discussion by describing the political atmosphere in Slovenia. Public expectations were high, he said, the leaders could ill-afford to disappoint them. Jović, however, argued that the amendments violated the federal constitution. The Slovenes claimed the opposite. Going one step further, the Slovenes complained that Belgrade, in fact, was violating the constitution by exerting pressure on Slovenia.

The Slovenes then threw the Serbs a bone, volunteering to make some corrections to the amendments. In fact, they made a few purely cosmetic changes which did little to placate their Serbian and federal counterparts. In his legalistic and argumentative manner, Jović told the Slovenes what they already knew, that the Presidency had ruled that the amendments would directly threaten Yugoslavia's integrity. He warned that Belgrade would not tolerate the creation of an "asymmetrical federation."

A succession of meetings did nothing to improve relations. In a thinly-veiled reference to Milošević, Kučan accused "certain people" of wreaking havoc simply to further their own political ambitions. He said there were only two amendments which could possibly be interpreted as unconstitutional: that which gave the republican parliament the sole right to authorize the JNA to enter Slovenia; and another, which gave Slovenia the right to declare a state-of-emergency. By attacking the Ljubljana leadership over the past two years, said Kučan, Serbia was destabilizing Slovenia. He asked if Belgrade planned to oust the Slovene Communists, because, the Slovene Party chief said, they would be forced to step down if the amendments were blocked. Jović retorted by saying that if the changes were made, it would mean the end of Yugoslavia which Kučan apparently considered less important. The Presidency, as the Supreme Commander of the Army, would not sanction the country's demise – an argument, which, over the next three years, would be repeatedly invoked. Jović said: "I was backed by Kadijević, which meant indirectly that the Army would use every means under the law to prevent that action. Kučan was visibly upset and insisted on an explanation."

The two sides argued back-and-forth over whether the amendments violated the much-maligned 1974 constitution. Desperate to stall their adoption, Jović summoned the heads of the federal institutions to a meeting early on September 26, one day before the Slovene Parliament was due to sit. The federal constitutional Court was called in to rule on whether the amendments violated the existing constitution. Chief Justice Ivan Kristan, a Slovene, argued that his Court could not consider hypothetical legislation. The majority of the judges backed his argument. The Court's decision surprised even Kristan. The Chief Justice said: "If the Court had decided that the Slovene amendments were against the 1974 constitution, everything would have developed the way Jović wanted it." But the Serbian leadership had to find its way out of a legal entanglement which might play out in favor of the Slovenes. It was becoming clear that there was not a single body in federal Yugoslavia capable of preventing the Slovenes from adopting the amendments – except the Army.

With the two sides digging in, the Serb chiefs hoped that General Kadijević would take matters into his own hands. They agreed that he would suggest Army intervention. At the last minute, Kadijević changed his mind, proposing something completely different. His co-conspirators were dumbstruck, recalled Jović. Kadijević's sudden about-face was the beginning of a pattern, incompatible with his task at hand. With steel-blue eyes and wavy grey hair, Kadijević cut a dapper figure. He was the defense minister of a country that was being torn apart and could not make up his mind what to do. He would decide then change his mind, saying that there was no constitutional backing for armed intervention. This would shape the next and final three years of his career. He would never consider himself part of the cabal of Serbian nationalists, but lacked the courage and conviction to disavow himself of them. In the end he sided with them when they warned they, too, would go their own way and form a Serbian army. That day, Kadijević, trying to lower the temperature, suggested that if Slovenia went so far as to adopt the amendments, then the Constitutional Court should rule on them.

To the Serb leaders, "This was a major mistake and a turning point," said Jović. He later asked Kadijević why the Army changed its opinion. He said: "After analyzing the problem again, we concluded that some people might argue that any move to stop the Slovenes was illegal Army intervention." Belgrade was forced to adopt another plan.

Despite the Serbian strong-arm tactics, the Slovenes made it clear that they would go ahead with the amendments. But there was one more card to play. The day before the Slovene Parliament was due to sit, and, with no advance notice, the Slovene Communists were summoned to Belgrade for a Central Committee meeting. Kučan was nervous. "It was an attempt to put pressure on the Slovene Communists by resorting to the principles of democratic centralism – pressure on us not to adopt the amendments or to postpone the session of the Slovene parliament."

He quickly called a Slovene Party meeting, where their position on the amendments was re-affirmed. "The Slovenes are not prepared to live in Yugoslavia at all costs and will not agree to political bargaining," the Party statement said. Determined, the Slovenes called for the formation of an "asymmetrical federation," which would recognize the republic's special economic and political status. The decision to forge ahead, no matter what Belgrade did, was a move that one senior Slovene official called "crucial for the dissolution of Yugoslavia."

Full of trepidation about what Belgrade was preparing for them, the Slovenes double-checked their contingency plans. That day, the leadership, fearing an assassination attempt, took separate flights to Belgrade. Even during harmonious times, Slovenia had always had rental cars ready in case it was necessary to make an emergency departure from Belgrade. The plan now was for the entire delegation to leave by road. Their escape route would take them in the opposite direction to what was expected: not to Zagreb, towards Ljubljana; but to the Bulgarian border, for a circuitous route to Slovenia.

At the showdown in Belgrade, Kučan defended his Party's decision, warning of a direct conflict between the forces of authoritarianism and aggression, on one side, and democracy and reform on the other. He informed his fellow Communists that they were following tradition – in 1937 the Party pioneers had said: "First of all we are Slovenes and only then Communists." The Slovenes were clearly in the minority. They got a boost that night at the Central Committee of the Yugoslav Party, when, for the first time, the Croats publicly sided with them against the majority in a vote that was ninety-seven in favor of postponing the vote on the amendments and forty against.

The Croat vote was a watershed for the second biggest republic in Yugoslavia, which, until then, had disguised its support for the Slovene push towards decentralization. It further unravelled the rapidly disintegrating federal state. It was a logical move for Croatia, which saw in Slovenia the only hope of resistance to Milošević. In that heated atmosphere of intolerance and intense JNA pressure, Ivica Račan, the Croatian Communist Party chief, had little choice but to cast Croatia's fate with the Slovenes.

Slovenia lost the vote, but the Slovenes realized that Belgrade would not move against them. The JNA had miscalculated – believing that the Slovenes would back down. Croatia was now on their side; the Slovene Communists left Belgrade that day in high spirits. They did not use their special escape routes. Kučan ordered whisky and food for everyone on the plane. At the end of the sixteen-hour marathon session, the Communists arrived in Slovenia as national heroes for saying no to Belgrade.

On September 27, Slovenia declared itself a sovereign state. The Parliament erupted in thunderous applause when the deputies overwhelmingly adopted the constitutional amendments with only one dissenting vote and one abstention. In a show of unity, the entire Slovene leadership attended the Parliament session. Janez Drnovšek, then President of Yugoslavia, cut short his visit to the United Nations General Assembly in New York. His move showed that Slovenia was more important to him than his position as federal head-of-state. "The Slovene people have demonstrated in this war of nerves that they are capable of being the masters of their own fate... This is a historic moment for Slovenia," said Janez Stanovnik, at a parliamentary session. The atmosphere was exuberant. Some of the Slovene politicians began singing patriotic songs. In his typical understated fashion, Milan Kučan, the experienced Party chief who had been instrumental in winning this round, went home to sleep. He had climbed the ranks of the Communist Party, survived potentially lethal political infighting, and knew the biggest battles lay ahead.

Over the next month, the war of nerves intensified. Slovenia took a swipe at Marković, declaring the republic unable to contribute to federal funds out of its own income. While claiming to support Marković's market-oriented reforms, Slovenia criticized the fixed exchange rate, which was one of the mainstays of his program, for overvaluing the dinar and hurting Slovenia's export-based economy. The stakes were raised with an announcement that Milošević's travelling circus of nationalist rallies, dubbed again the "Meeting of Truth," was to appear in Ljubljana. Bearing the traditional bread and salt, an old Serb gesture of hospitality, the Serb nationalists said they would break down the barriers which now separated them from the Slovenes.[3] "The truth about Kosovo is not known in Ljubljana," said a Yugoslav Communist official.

Kučan's leadership pondered how to deal with this deliberate provocation by Belgrade. Slovenia banned the rally, saying that it was afraid of violence, that riots would become an excuse for military intervention. Trains from Serbia were searched before entering Slovenia. The bold move helped Kučan, who was worried about the upcoming free elections which Slovenia had called before the other republics. By standing up to the Serbs once again, he knew there would be some political cachet.

At the last minute, the Serb organizers who had warned that people could be killed at the rally claiming that the Slovenes would try to stop it by force, cancelled the meeting. But Belgrade did not allow the issue to die. Far from it. The Socialist Alliance of Serbia, an arm of the Communist Party, called on "all institutions and enterprises in Serbia to sever all relations with Slovenia on the grounds that all fundamental human rights and liberties had been suspended there." On December 1, the seventy-first anniversary of the creation of the Kingdom of Serbs, Croats and Slovenes, Belgrade struck back with a brazen diktat – the order to sever ties with the northwestern republic:

> We are saying clearly that no citizen of Serbia will beg Slovenia to remain in Yugoslavia or lower himself to offer bread and salt to those who are prepared to shoot at him.

Over the next month more than 130 major Serbian enterprises cut relations with Slovenia. The slightest resistance was punished. The Serbian newspaper, *Politika*, rounded on Yugoexport – one of the top clothing stores – for offending the sentiments of Belgrade by displaying Slovene clothes in the shop windows. The boycott was a classic manifestation of "*inat*" (spite). Belgrade wanted to hit the Slovenes where it would hurt most, regardless of how high the price for Serbia.[4] Serbian factories relied on Slovene products, too. This was just the beginning. It was a move which cut both ways.

Milošević rubbed salt in the wound. He had just been endorsed by Parliament as President of Serbia. In an address to the Assembly, the newly-elected Serbian President accused the Slovenes of depriving the rest of Yugoslavia of the chance to lead a normal life in a stable country. In a classic example of the Orwellian double-speak which so characterizes Milošević, he said:

> *This Slovene leadership is a protector of conservatism in Yugoslavia, and one of the last protectors of conservatism in the socialist countries in general. Conservatism in Slovenia, in conflict with the forces of progress in Yugoslavia, and especially with the progressive economic and political changes in Serbia, has reacted aggressively and cruelly. Such aggressiveness and cruelty as a rule distinguish all conservatism.*

The Communist chiefs began to quarrel when they heard about this inaugural speech. One of Milošević's allies screamed at Račan, Croatia's Communist leader, "I have had enough of you." Račan turned pale. His hands and voice shook: "You are doing everything to force me to take sides in a dispute I don't want to be part of."[5] A statement from the Slovene leadership blasted Milošević's speech, for its "unfounded and absurd assertions."

Minutes of Party meetings reveal the enmity fostered over two years of bitter dispute. It seemed that they could not agree on a single thing. They even quarreled about what song should open the extraordinary Fourteenth Congress of the Yugoslav Communist Party; the *Internacionale*, the national anthem, "*Hej Slaveni*" (Hey Slavs), or the popular song, "Yugoslavia." At one point Račan said: "It is not important how we begin, but it is important to finish with Yugoslavia," apparently missing the irony until the others broke out in laughter.[6]

The final showdown between Serbia and Slovenia took place at the Fourteenth Extraordinary Party Congress on January 23, 1990. Throughout the doomed session in Belgrade's Sava Center, delegates argued over the fate of the Party. Should it be divided into two groupings, Socialist and Communist, rather than according to republics? By then, the gulf between Serbia, on one side, and Slovenia and Croatia, on the other, had become seemingly unbridgeable. Indeed, the two western republics had already called free elections for the spring. Throughout eastern Europe, Communism was in its death throes. Over those three days, the country's Party leaders came no closer to agreement on the future of the organization. On the contrary, any prospects for reconciliation collapsed.

With the Communist Party falling apart, the Bosnian leadership grew nervous, caught between the two sides. Nijaz Duraković, chief of the Bosnian Party, tried to mend fences: "I have a mandate to kneel in front of President Kučan and Milošević and beg them to find some sort of compromise," he said.

The deputies roamed the halls, bars and restaurants, trying to find out what was going on in the conviction that Party decisions were never reached in public. Serbia and Slovenia continued their polemics over transforming the Party. No fewer than 458 amendments were proposed to the final Party resolution.

Delegates hurled invective at one another. Milošević warned that if the Yugoslav Party disintegrated, then the parties in each republic would become "nationalist" or "national socialist." One Slovene deputy said that it was Milošević's Party that was "national socialist," implying that the Serbian Party was fascist. Dušan Mitević rushed to Milošević's defense, praising him for his vision of Yugoslavia which was "acceptable for the working class of Serbia, the Serbian people, and the nations and nationalities of Serbia."[7] For three days and nights, Mitević made sure that the Congress filled television screens throughout Yugoslavia.

Each Slovene proposal – from human rights to Yugoslavia's role in Europe – failed to get even half the total of 1,612 votes needed to be adopted. Rounds of applause greeted each defeat. The Slovenes were humiliated. It became clear to them that the Serbian and Montenegrin delegation had been instructed to vote down any Slovene proposal. "All the Slovene amendments were rejected," said Kučan. "The substance of the Slovene proposals was completely irrelevant. Anything that we submitted would have been rejected." For most of the Slovene delegates it was not a question of if, but when, the Congress should be abandoned.

Meanwhile the Serbs goaded the Slovenes, defying them to walk out. The Slovenes had already planned a signal to leave – Ciril Ribičić would take the floor and say: "This orientation cannot be the orientation of Slovene Communists and we are leaving the Congress."

Fed up, the Slovene delegation walked out of the Congress. Sonja Lokar, a prominent Slovene party official, wept as her delegation silently filed out of the hall. Many of the remaining Serbian delegates applauded the midnight walk-out, convinced they had scored a victory against the Slovenes.

In what was one of Milošević's first political blunders, he scrambled on to center stage and called for the Congress to continue. "Let those who want to go, go, and we will make a new quorum." But his bid was ignored. The confident leader, who was used to being hailed with feverish enthusiasm, suddenly was at a loss. He had miscalculated. Ivica Račan had pledged that his delegation would follow the Slovenes if they pulled out of the Congress. Milošević had ignored this. A third of the members of the Croatian delegation were Serbs. Milošević was relying on them to keep the Croatian delegation at Congress. He was wrong. The Croat delegation abandoned the Congress in support of the Slovenes.

The Congress had dissipated into a quarrel about every aspect of political life. It ended in the disintegration of the Communist Party of Yugoslavia. The Fourteenth Congress was the last attended by all six Yugoslav republics.

The glue that was holding federal Yugoslavia together had come unstuck. Federal Prime Minister Ante Marković put a brave face on the break-up, "Yugoslavia will continue," he said grinning.

The Army High Command made their trepidation evident. Warning Momir Bulatović of Montenegro, who was chairing that session, General Kadijević said: "Defending the Party means defending the country." But there was to be no compromise. After the Croats refused to continue the Congress, the young Bulatović did not know what else to do. He called a fifteen-minute break which, as he later observed, "lasted throughout history."

1 Irena Kostić and Slobodan Vuksanović (eds), *Pesma o Kosovu: savremena srpska poezija*, Belgrade, 1991, Vidici SKZ, Jedinstvo, p. 12.

2 After the Army was called in to Kosovo in February, 1989, the leadership in Belgrade increasingly viewed it as a means of conducting, and enforcing, policy.

3 Jovića Vlahović, a man who says he lost his hand while a child courier for the Partisans, but actually injured it while dynamite-fishing in Montenegro, was one of the more colorful extremists/agents involved in the Slovenia débacle.

4 Djukić, Slavoljub, *Izmedju slave i anateme.*

5 *Vreme*, Agonija SKJ, November 5, 1990.

6 *Vreme*, Agonija SKJ, November 12, 1990.

7 *Vjesnik*, January 23, 1990.

"A CROATIAN RIFLE ON A CROATIAN SHOULDER"
The Awakening of Croatia
1989–1990

Croatia watched the rise of Milošević in silence. For twenty years, this western republic – Yugoslavia's second largest – had been known as the Silent Republic, after the crushing by Tito in 1971 of a nationalist movement called Maspok, which was led by a faction of Croatia's ruling Communists.[1] The Party leaders who had spearheaded the campaign were purged; indeed, anyone even remotely associated with it was fired or jailed. The Croatian cultural organization, *Matica Hrvatska*, was dismantled after becoming a major focus of dissent, with a nationalist platform reviving economic and historical grievances against the Serbs. Nearly two decades later, many of Maspok's ousted leaders would rise again to take part in the country's first multiparty elections since the Second World War. The winner of that poll, the Croatian Democratic Union (HDZ) rose to power with the backing of a highly-politicized community of émigré Croats living abroad, many of whom had fled Yugoslavia after the Second World War with a second wave after 1971. A hardened core of Croat émigrés had long been depicted by the Communists as the bogeymen of Yugoslavia, and had, for twenty years, stood accused of international terrorism. In the hostile climate of Milošević's reign, the HDZ was a mass movement which easily captured the vote on its pledge to realize Croatia's 1,000-year-old dream of statehood.

Croats, nursing their resentment since the crack-down on Maspok, had long awaited change. State security agents and military intelligence interrogated anyone suspected of having links with Croatian émigrés, who were supposedly committed to the revival of an independent Croatian state. For Communist Yugoslavia, Croatian independence was a taboo theme, tantamount to an attempt to rehabilitate the Ustaše Independent State of Croatia (NDH). Each arrest served as a warning – vigilant Yugoslavia would not tolerate any manifestation of Croatian nationalism. Prison sentences were meted out for singing nationalist songs or carrying the *šahovnica*, Croatia's red-and-white checkerboard emblem, which had been the coat-of-arms in the pro-Nazi NDH in 1941. It remains in doubt how many of these "hostile-activities" symbols were "planted" by police. For example, the possession of extremist propaganda could land someone in jail. If an Ustaše pamphlet was posted from Germany, it was sufficient evidence to bring charges against the unlucky recipient in Zagreb who, in fact, may have known nothing about it.

Against this selective repression, the Croat national élite cultivated a sense of separateness from the eastern parts of the country. In the Croat nationalist mind-set, Serbia was Communist, backward and poor, while Croatia – developed and modern – belonged to civilized Central Europe, its cultural heritage tied with the Austro-Hungarian for centuries. As the battle-lines were drawn, Croats would insist that they were outside the dark Byzantine world of the Balkans. They grumbled that the Serbs ran the show and were over-represented in the media and in the security forces. Interest in the Catholic Church swelled. For many Croats this was an affirmation of their identity – distinct from their Serb Orthodox countrymen – rather than an expression of faith.

By the time Communism fell in Eastern Europe in 1989, the deafening echo of Croatia's silence was reverberating throughout the western republic.[2] The rise of Milošević gave credence to those who demanded that Croatia should abandon Yugoslavia in order to get out from under the Serbian heel; and served as a warning to even the most Yugoslav-oriented Croats that it was time for urgent reforms.

Years after Serb nationalism had taken hold in Belgrade and propelled Milošević to power, the behavior of Croat nationalists was still muted, manifesting how effective the suppression of Croatian nationalism had been. The vast Serb processions and mass rallies, teeming with Serbian imagery and symbolism of domination, were often to be seen, but, as late as 1990, the Croatian counterpart was cowed and furtive. Across the political spectrum, Croatian intellectuals began whispering in cafés and strolling in city parks to elude the ear of the state. In various combinations, they debated what should be done. The most influential group included a former JNA General and historian, Franjo Tudjman. On February 28, 1989, the Croatian Democratic Union (HDZ) held its first public gathering.[3] A brief item broadcast on the late news was sufficient to attract supporters to the HDZ. The Party was not legalized until December 1989, when, following Slovenia's lead, Croatian Communists decided to call multiparty elections. The Communists had run out of steam. A feud between conservative hard-liners and reformers had paralyzed the party. Since Maspok, one of the most important criteria for entry into Croatia's ruling élite had been an absence (or denunciation) of nationalism. With Milošević at his height, a section of the Party leadership wanted to speak out – while another part counselled silence, initially even backing the Serbian leader. The reformers, such as Celestin Sardelić, saw a threat in Milošević, and at the same time were convinced that the Communist Party's role needed to change. The internal feud, however, prevented the reformers from mounting a credible electoral campaign.

In the run-up to elections, Tudjman gave the seething crowds what they wanted: a strong dose of nationalism as an antidote to the fervor coming from the east. Tudjman, unlike Milošević, was a genuine nationalist, but both leaders built their power on mobilizing the masses. Croatia's Communist chief, Ivica Račan, whose renamed Party of Democratic Change lost to the HDZ, saw Belgrade's role in enhancing Tudjman's allure.

> *Milošević's aggressive policy was the strongest propaganda for Tudjman. Milošević was sending his gangs to Croatia, where they were dancing and singing: 'This is Serbia' which provoked and liberated the national pride and the nationalist reaction of Croats which was effectively used by Tudjman.*

His pledge to deliver Croatian statehood was also Tudjman's personal obsession. Born in 1922, he was early on promoted to the rank of General. Years later he would justify his Partisan valor as his youthful struggle for a free Croatia, not Yugoslavia.

In spite of his Communist past, Tudjman's nationalist credentials were in good order. Named by Tito as Head Political Commissar, by 1967 he had been fired for nationalism. Tudjman never missed an opportunity to point out that he had been in the *avant-garde* of Maspok. He was jailed in the 1970s – at the time of the Maspok purges – and again in the 1980s. In deference to his Partisan record, Tudjman received better treatment than his fellow nationalists in prison. One inmate was dismayed when he saw the extent of the former General's prison privileges and privacy: Tudjman was accommodated in the relatively comfortable prison infirmary and had daily hot water to shave with. The irascible Tudjman was no ordinary dissident. It was rumored that the great writer, Miroslav Krleža, the *enfant terrible* of Croatian intellectuals, had intervened with Tito to suspend Tudjman's prison sentence.[4]

This preferential treatment was even more precious outside prison. It was to influence Croatia's future. Unlike many dissidents in Yugoslavia, Tudjman was allowed to have a passport. During the 1980s he travelled abroad, fostering ties with Croat émigrés, which eventually would help to secure his position as leader of the Croat nation. Of all the opposition contenders, Tudjman controlled the purse-strings of the Croatian émigrés. The election campaign in April 1990 allegedly cost four million dollars.

Once a political pariah, Tudjman had waited for years for his fortunes to reverse. He could count on one hand the faithful who had risked visiting his spacious home in the hills above Zagreb, the exclusive Tuškanac district.[5] Despite his crooked smile and strained demeanor, Tudjman carried himself as a man who believed in his august destiny. His demeanor was borne in part from his military background, but also grew from the strength of his personal conviction that he had a mission to rule.

Tudjman had fallen from grace for the sin of nationalism – among his most errant beliefs was his contention that the Communists had vastly exaggerated the number of Serb victims in the Second World War. The military establishment was outraged by his claim that the official figure of 600,000 Serbs, Jews and Gypsies killed in the Ustaše concentration camp at Jasenovac was more than a ten-fold exaggeration. Tudjman, however, insisted that, during the Second World War, the real figure of killed in all of Croatia was closer to sixty thousand. The argument about how many Serbs died at the hands of Ustaše death-squads, and in the concentration camps of Ustaše leader Ante Pavelić, has never been resolved and probably never will be.[6] With this public dispute, Tudjman gained currency with even the most radical of émigrés – it was his *mea culpa* for his Partisan past.

Nevertheless he had a soft spot for Tito. Indeed, later as a powerful president he would be ridiculed for his efforts to imitate the debonair Yugoslav dictator. In 1969, in his book *Great Ideas and Small Nations*, Tudjman wrote that Yugoslavia's peaceful and independent course could be attributed to Tito as "one of the most distinguished statesmen of new nations and of the contemporary world in general."[7]

For decades Croatian emigration had been painted in the Yugoslav media as a uniform, consummate, lurking evil, first responsible for butchering Serbs in the Second World War, then sowing the seeds of terrorism throughout the world.[8] "All Croatian emigrants were branded by the Communist authorities as fascists, Ustaše," said Tudjman, "although they lived in democratic America, Canada or Sweden." Indeed Communist Yugoslavia, obsessed with its political emigration from Croatia and elsewhere, established a special unit to liquidate them abroad. One agent, Željko Ražnatović, alias Arkan, would become notorious during the 1991 war. There were some former Ustaše who had managed to escape after the Second World War. In fact, the émigrés ran the political gamut. Tudjman had the prescience to recognize their importance early on. He knew that Croatian émigrés would be a key to an HDZ victory. Josip Boljkovac, former Interior Minister of Croatia and HDZ Vice President, arranged for the émigrés to get Yugoslav visas through government connections.

By inviting the émigrés to Zagreb for the HDZ Congress on February 24, 1990, Tudjman made what he said was his most crucial political decision, even compared to the steps he took later while he was President of a new-born country torn by war.

> *To invite the emigration back to the homeland for a great meeting was risky to the point that even those people who were later in my leadership waited till the last minute to see whether we would be arrested or not. This is why that was a turning point in my life in terms of decision making...*
>
> *Great deeds, both in individual creative terms, and especially in social*

*innovation and even militarily, are created on the razor's edge between the
possible and the impossible.*
    *Therefore, it is in such moments that judgement is important to achieve
something that seems impossible for most people.*

It was not until 2,500 delegates packed into Lisinski Concert hall in
Zagreb, that the HDZ leaders knew they would not be arrested. By then, the
HDZ was a mass phenomenon, claiming 200,000 members. Tudjman told
the highly emotional crowd that he would strive for the Croatian right to self-
determination and sovereignty.

*Our opponents see nothing in our program but the claim for the restoration
of the independent Croatian Ustaše state. These people fail to see that the
state was not the creation of fascist criminals; it also stood for the historic
aspirations of the Croatian people for an independent state. They knew that
Hitler planned to build a new European order.*

His speech was immediately seized on by the JNA and the Serbs, particularly those from rural parts of Croatia. In a Croatia which hailed the return of
alleged war-criminals and allowed Tudjman to speak, Serbs claimed their
future was not secure. The HDZ claimed Tudjman was not rehabilitating
the violence of the Ustaše but separating out the good parts, which was the
realization of Croatian statehood in the NDH. But, when Tudjman
remarked, "Thank God my wife is not a Jew or a Serb," the hysteria grew.
    Aside from predictable attacks on Serbian nationalism, Tudjman also
made clear his total disregard for Bosnia-Herzegovina, calling the central
Yugoslav republic a "national state of the Croatian nation." Croat nationalists saw Bosnian Muslims as Islamicized Croats – their Serb counterparts
alleged they were Orthodox Serbs. Later, as President, during a meeting
with the US Ambassador Warren Zimmermann, Tudjman exploded into a
tirade about Izetbegović and the Muslims of Bosnia. He denounced them
as "dangerous fundamentalists" who wanted to use Bosnia as a springboard
for spreading Islam into Europe. Unable to keep control, despite the efforts
of his aides to silence his outburst, Tudjman said Bosnia should be divided
between Serbia and Croatia.
    The Herzegovina lobby – Croat emigrants from Herzegovina as well as
their kin in the country – formed an important pillar of Tudjman's support.
In return for financial and political backing, he was beholden to this clique.
They openly advocated the annexation of Herzegovina, the southern part of
Bosnia-Herzegovina. Extremist ambitions to extend Croatian territory as far
as Zemun, a town just north of the Serbian capital Belgrade, even entered
popular humor at the time. One joke said HDZ stood for *Hrvatska do*

Zemuna, which means Croatia all the way to Zemun. The Herzegovina lobby eventually would come to blows with the continental Croats who did not share the expansionist drive of their kin.

At the two-day Congress, speaker after speaker asserted Croatia's right to secession and to freely forge alliances with other countries – shaping the HDZ's election platform. In order to foster Croatia's spiritual rebirth, the HDZ pledged that perceived historical imbalances would be redressed – such as fixing the disproportional representation of the Serbs who made up thirteen percent of Croatia's 4.7 million population in the police and media. "There won't be any improvement for Croatia until a Croatian rifle is on a Croatian shoulder, and a Croatian wallet in a Croatian pocket,"[9] proclaimed Šime Djodan, an extremist HDZ leader, who later briefly served as defense minister.

The Congress took place in an atmosphere of intense emotion and nationalism, and the audience waved banners emblazoned with the *Šahovnica*. No longer was Croatia mute from apathy or fear of being imprisoned for nationalism or anti-Communist statements. The movement had crossed the threshold, and Slobodan Praljak, a theater director who later become a commander of the Bosnian Croat militia, described how the HDZ had passed the stages of vulnerable infancy:

> *I knew at that time we would win. And so this declaration was a feeling similar to that of a director on an opening night. There is joy and also sadness that something has finished. We were no longer this exclusive group of 30 or 40. We were no longer bound to this shadow of secrecy and illegal meetings.*

The Croatian silence was shattered.

If Croatia careered towards free elections, Slovenia strolled. It was a different game altogether in this northwestern republic, where the official five-month campaign had actually begun long before. Quasi-political interest groups had existed since the early 1980s. The Slovene Communists were forward-looking enough to initiate democratic reforms on their own, rather than waiting for public pressure to build.

In September 1989, the reformist Communist Party President Milan Kučan led the drive to adopt constitutional amendments, which laid the ground for elections and Slovenia's sovereignty. In December, the Slovene League of Communists changed its name, retaining its initials as a memory of the past, while emphasizing the Party's transformation: ZSK Party of Democratic Reform. Its message, put forward in cheery child-like colorful shapes, was "Europe Now!" The reformed Communists and the opposition parties all shared what Kučan described as a "Slovene perspective" with "no fundamental differences" between them. The main point of contention among the political parties was the prospect for reform within Yugoslavia. Despite the intense political disagreement, the reformed Communists believed it was possible to transform Yugoslavia into a modern democratic state.

The electoral campaign revolved around the question of Slovenia's role in Yugoslavia. Should the most developed, modern republic remain part of the Yugoslav federation? DEMOS, an unwieldy seven-party opposition coalition, campaigned on a pledge to hold a referendum on independence.

The elections were a complicated, three-round proportional system which gave a wealth of parties representation in the Parliament. Slovenia's were the first free elections in any of the six republics. They were testament to a successful and positive democratic transformation. In the second round of polling, Kučan defeated DEMOS presidential candidate, Jože Pučnik, a former political prisoner in the 1950s who had left Slovenia as a *gastarbeiter* and gone on to become an academic in West Germany.

Rewarded for his defiant stand against Milošević, Kučan became Slovenia's first President – quickly giving up his Party membership in order to represent all Slovenes. DEMOS won fifty-five percent of the vote and the reformed Communists seventeen percent. This victory resulted in a jumble of political options because DEMOS included such divergent parties as the conservative Christian Democrats and the Greens. The Christian Democrats emerged as the strongest party, although they actually won fewer votes than the Communists or the Liberal Democrats (the former Socialist youth), whose magazine *Mladina* had led the charge against the JNA.

In the run-up to the elections, the federal Defense Minister, General Kadijević, who was half-Croat, half-Serb, made several visits to the Fifth Army region, which encompassed Slovenia and Croatia. The visits fuelled speculation that the JNA would strike if the country's first free elections went contrary to the Army's wishes. On April 7, the eve of the poll in Slovenia, Kadijević travelled to Ljubljana. He openly threatened to retaliate against any political party which called into question Yugoslavia's territorial integrity:

> *Those who today negate all values and achievements of development in the elections, who offer a fratricidal war, redrawing the borders and tearing apart the country, must realize that this will be stopped.*
>
> *A high price was paid for our freedom, which must be preserved and maintained by engaging all patriotic forces. The JNA and the armed forces as a whole will still be committed to the path of reform of society. It will make its full contribution to the development of democracy and those processes which*

*make a man's life more human and richer, but it will, according to its consti-
tutional role, decisively combat the forces which are digging up the foundation of the SFRJ, and weakening its powers of defense and security.[10]*

In Slovenia, Kučan pondered how seriously he should take the Army's
threats:

*Even so I knew how this paper tiger thought, what powerful means it holds
in his hands and how little it would take to go 'insane' in the euphoric mood
in JNA circles, which was supported by the Party and the federal bodies.*

JNA threats against what it called the dangerous HDZ only served to bolster Tudjman's popularity. Admiral Branko Mamula, a close friend of
Kadijević and former Defense Minister, urged the Croatian Communists to
use their majority in the Sabor, the Parliament, to ban the HDZ, which he
said was possible under the electoral law prohibiting extremist parties.

Mamula told Ivica Račan that, ever since the HDZ Congress, the Serbs in
Croatia had been frightened of another genocide – of a return to the Second
World War. He tried to persuade him that the Croats must speak out in
defense of the Serbs. The JNA was extremely concerned about recent developments – particularly about the return of émigrés, some of whom the Army
had been looking for and dealing with for years. He urged Račan to stop the
émigrés who were being issued passports at the airport in Zagreb.

Faced with JNA arm-twisting and threats, Račan responded that the
Yugoslav military was to blame for allowing Milošević to go so far. Račan told
Kadijević:

*We are not breaking apart Yugoslavia because we are taking the democratic
route. It is Milošević and your refusal to resist him.*
  *Should you make a tragic mistake and intervene in Croatia by armed force,
you'll first have to liquidate me and my friends, and then maybe the nationalists in Croatia.*

The JNA made clear its disdain for the weak leadership of the Croatian
Communists who did not stand a chance of mounting a challenge to the
HDZ. After one particularly heavy-handed attempt to intimidate the
Croatian leadership, Kadijević turned up accompanied by ten generals.
General Martin Špegelj, a leading Croatian in the JNA, later recalled that he
was taken aback by Kadijević's anger:

*He launched into a harsh, unpleasant lecture on how they should not have
allowed the formation of parties along national lines, how they can't allow*

separatism and how the army is strong enough to stop such tendencies. He
said that elections should only be allowed within the framework of the
Socialist Alliance. He attacked nationalists in Croatia and then as usual: the
CIA; all West European countries that want to rule Yugoslavia; and the
Vatican.

Efforts by the federal political and military establishment to frighten voters
away from the nationalist opposition failed in Croatia, just as they had in
Slovenia. In two rounds of voting, Tudjman's HDZ won 205 of the parliament's 356 seats. The reformed Communists took seventy-three seats and
the remaining places in the Sabor were distributed among the centrist
Coalition of National Understanding, the Serbian Democratic party (SDS)
and six smaller parties.

In fact, the electoral victory appeared more resounding than it was. The
HDZ got 1.2 million votes to 994,000 for the reformed Communists. But
Croatia's British-style first-past-the-post, single-member-constituency electoral system gave Tudjman's party an absolute majority of the seats in the
new Sabor, even though it had won fewer than half the votes cast in the
country. Small parties were weeded out – the system favored a mass movement, such as the HDZ, which was well-organized throughout the country.
Tudjman's message – *Odlučimo sami o našoj sudbini* (We'll decide our fate by
ourselves) – hit the target.

Everything seemed to backfire in the Communists' lackluster campaign.
One disastrous poster showed a huge picture of Ivica Račan with the unfortu-
nate message "*Ne*" splattered across his chest, which perhaps was his defiant
"No" to Belgrade, but seemed more like a warning not to vote for Račan.
The name-change and the fact that Račan had guided, albeit haltingly,
Croatia towards a multiparty system did little to convince Croats that the
reformed Communists, if elected, would fight for their national interests.

Within days of the HDZ victory, a brawl at a football match in the
Croatian capital between Belgrade's Red Star and Zagreb's Dinamo football
teams left seventy-nine police and fifty-nine spectators injured. The horrified nation watched on television as the Serbian "*Delije*" club charged the
Croatian "Bad Blue Boys." The police were quickly overpowered and crazed
fans tore off the plastic seats, hurling them in the air. In vain, the announcer
appealed for calm. The clash surpassed the usual fierce football rivalry, and
the chaos and destruction sent waves of fear throughout Yugoslavia.

On May 30, amid considerable pomp, Tudjman was formally inaugurated
as the first democratically-elected President of Croatia. He wore a red-white-
and-blue sash. The *šahovnica* was displayed in the background, the
Communist red star abandoned. The Croatian President had not yet, however, accomplished what he wanted. Just out of reach was his dream of a

Croatian state. There was one problem – the Serbs. All five SDS deputies boycotted the session.

1 Maspok is short for *masovni pokret*, mass movement.

2 Term used by Slavko Goldstein, a liberal Croatian intellectual and publisher.

3 On that same day, February 28, the Belgrade media was reporting that one million Serbs had gathered in front of the Federal Parliament in protest against the Slovene rally in Cankarjev Dom.

4 Hudelist, Darko, *Banket u Hrvatskoj: prilozi povijesti hrvatskog višestranačja* 1989-1990 (Zagreb: Bibilioteka Dnevnik, 1991), pp. 9-37.

5 Hudelist, *Banket u Hrvatskoj*, p. 396.

6 Djilas, Aleksa, *The Contested Country: Yugoslav Unity and Communist Revolution 1919-1953* (Cambridge Harvard University Press, 1991), pp. 103-127.

7 *Federal Tribune*, January 25, 1994, excerpts from Franjo Tudjman's *Great Ideas and Small Nations*, Matica Hrvatska, Zagreb, 1969.

8 *Danas*, Zagreb, April 17, 1990, pp. 27-29.

9 *Danas*, Zagreb, April 17, 1990, p. 90.

10 *Danas*, Zagreb, April 17, 1990, p. 90.

PART TWO: LIGHTING THE FUSE

7

"THE REMNANTS OF A SLAUGHTERED PEOPLE"
The Knin Rebellion,
January–August 1990

Milan Babić's political education began beneath a mulberry tree in the garden of his parents' home in the village of Vrlika. There, as a boy, he learned the twin instincts of distrust and fear, and established in his mind an unbreakable link between his own survival and that of the Serbian nation:

> *In 1990 my closest neighbors were the most active people in forming the HDZ party branch in my village. Their father in 1941 was the head of the Ustaše government of the village. In the summer of 1941 he brought a group of Ustaše killers to slaughter my family. My father was 12 years old at the time, and escaped only because his family had fled from their home.*
>
> *When this man came to kill the family and found no one at home, he took a great carving knife from our house. He used it to make a gash in the bark of the mulberry tree in our garden. The tree has since grown large, but the scar· remained. And we children who were born after the war were shown the tree – and that scar.*

Babić was born in 1956 – fifteen years after the cutting of the scar, and over a decade after Tito's Partisans had victoriously – in the official parlance of the post-war Communist regime – reunited all Yugoslavia's nations in Brotherhood and Unity. But the passing of the scar (in Babić's case literally as well as metaphorically) from generation to generation was typical of the atavism which would come to characterize the mentality of Serb nationalism, and, later, of the Yugoslav conflict itself: the deliberate evocation of atrocities that had long passed from living memory; a consciously-fostered paranoia fed at least as much by rumor and myth as by historical reality; the use of the past as a weapon of conflict, and, later, of war; and, above all, in common with Communist societies everywhere, the sublimation of individual identity to that of the collective – in this case, the Serb nation.

When Milan Babić began to talk publicly about genocide and fascism he was appealing not only to the real experience of the people but also to a folk-loric belief, in which it is the fate of the Serbs to be attacked at home, betrayed abroad and left alone, the sole guardians of their own destiny.

Not all atrocities had passed from living memory. The summer of 1941 had burned a deep impression on the consciousness of the Krajina Serbs. In April of that year, the Axis Powers had invaded and partitioned Yugoslavia. In Croatia and Bosnia, the Croatian fascists, led by Ante Pavelić, declared the Independent State of Croatia (NDH) a pro-Nazi regime founded by Pavelić's Ustaše movement, which, in the 1920s and '30s, had been an outlawed terrorist group living mostly in exile. Pavelić's declared intention was to create a pure Croatian nation-state. In Ustaše rhetoric, Serbs were either racially inferior or – in an apparent contradiction – simply lapsed Croats who had betrayed the nation to foreign interests, by converting to Orthodox Christianity. Pavelić's Ustaše forces, dressed in the distinctive black uniforms that were to re-emerge in the 1990s,[1] embarked on a killing spree, levelling Serb villages, rounding up and killing the inhabitants, sometimes in their village, sometimes after loading them into trucks and driving them into remote countryside. In the most notorious cases, entire villages were locked into the local Orthodox church, which was then set on fire. No one knows how many victims there were; the figures are disputed. But there is little doubt that hundreds of thousands of Serbs died either in concentration camps, or at the hands of the Ustaše death-squads. Often, the victims were buried in open pits, which, in the interests of preserving Brotherhood and Unity, were never spoken of in Tito's Yugoslavia – at least not publicly. With the revival of nationalism in the 1990s, mass graves were disinterred with great ceremony and political symbolism.

The method by which Pavelić sought to create his ethnically-pure territory was the annihilation of the Serbs as a people. In a phrase which, even in 1990, carried a deep and abiding sense of terror among the Serbs, he sought to "kill a third, expel a third, convert a third (to Catholicism)." It was easy for nationalist leaders to evoke the horror of 1941, and to awaken, in the Serbs, a desire to avenge the sufferings of the past. The last time there was an independent Croatia, they argued, the Serbs had only saved themselves from extinction by taking up arms. The Krajina people were the descendants of those who survived by fighting back – the remnants of a slaughtered people.[2] The historical memory of an independent Croatian state that extended as far east as the Drina River – Bosnia's border with Serbia – made the Serbs, living west of the river, consider themselves the most vulnerable of all. To them, the demand for a single state which would embrace all Serbs had particular appeal.

The word Krajina comes from the Serbo-Croatian word *kraj*, meaning end, or edge. The name of the region, *Vojna Krajina*, means Military Frontier. It is one of the great geo-strategic fault lines of European history, across which the warring empires of Austria-Hungary and the Ottoman Turks ebbed and flowed. The Austrians created the Krajina. They recruited Orthodox Christians who had fled the Ottoman subjugation of Serbia, settled them on the land, and employed them as a permanent defensive barrier against Ottoman expansion. In return, the Krajina Serbs enjoyed autonomy, being ruled neither from Zagreb nor from Budapest, but directly by the Imperial capital, Vienna. Thus Krajina embodied, from its very creation, two traits that were to burst on to the Yugoslav stage again in 1990, and with violent expression: a fierce pride in local independence; and an enthusiastic resort to arms.

But at the start of 1990, Milan Babić was a young provincial dentist in a town that most Yugoslavs knew only as a railway junction. Knin is a lonely dust-bowl of a place in the isolated barren wastelands of Croatia's Dinaric mountains. Krajina forms the hinterland of Croatia's prosperous Adriatic coast, with which it had traded and intermarried for centuries. Knin, and Krajina generally, were economically integral parts of southern Croatia. The Serbs of Knin spoke the western variant of Serbo-Croatian and wrote mostly in the Latin script.[3] Croatia, in turn, needed Knin because it was the vital rail and road junction connecting Zagreb to the southern coast. The interdependence of Krajina and the rest of Croatia had been self-evident for generations. Each, without the other, was economically untenable.

In appearance, Babić cut an unlikely figure as a warlord. His boyish round face, soft pale skin and wire-rimmed glasses gave him an almost cherubic expression. Babić was an unimportant, unremarkable figure on the fringes of Croatia's ruling Communist Party. He had broken with the Party in 1989, determined, at first, to form a new political organization. His ambitions were modest. He had in mind a local party to be called the Democratic Union of Knin. Although predominantly Serb in population, many Croats also lived in Knin. The party of Babić's early aspirations had no explicit national orientation.

But a radical new alternative presented itself and Babić first seized it, then dominated it, and, finally, reshaped it to his own design.

Even before they founded their own party the previous year the Serbs had held a rally on July 9 in the echo of Milošević's fiery words at Gazimestan. This celebration of the six-hundredth anniversary of the battle of Kosovo was organized by Croatia's Communists. Their message at this rally was completely different. It was that the future hinges on the communities remaining together in Yugoslavia. But the program was disrupted by a group of local Serbs led by Jovan Opačić, a clerk. He told the crowds that the Serbs should abandon the myth about Yugoslavia. They should channel their energy into strengthening the Serb political and spiritual identity.

Opačić was arrested and jailed for three months, at Šibenik on the Croatian coast.

His persecution struck a chord with Serb nationalists throughout Yugoslavia. Dobrica Ćosić sent a telegram of support to Opačić in prison. On his release, the two met in Belgrade, in December 1989. Opačić was still reeling from the shame of a prison term and Ćosić urged him to contact Jovan Rašković, a psychiatrist in the town where Opačić had served his time in detention, and with whom Ćosić had been in regular contact since the early seventies.

Rašković was from Knin and had spent his entire life in Croatia, attending high school in Zagreb and taking his PhD at the University there. In January 1990, he emerged – anointed by the hand of his friend, Dobrica Ćosić – as the leader of Croatia's Serbs. He was a magnetic orator, and his long grey-brown beard, bushy hair and hypnotic eyes made him instantly recognizable. Among Serbs, he was a crowd-puller and the masses loved him. Among Croats he quickly acquired a reputation as a dangerous enemy. He was not, however, to last long. He was to be eclipsed by Babić, the man anointed by the hand of Slobodan Milošević.

Early in February 1990, Rašković and Opačić agreed to turn a cultural club, *Zora*, into a political party. Rašković wanted to leave national orientation out of the name of the Party altogether – to call it simply the Democratic Party, an early indication, despite his firebrand reputation, of the moderate nationalism that was to discredit him in the eyes of an increasingly radicalized Serb community. It was Opačić who insisted that the Party must be a vehicle for the expression of the national interests of the Serbs. The Serbian Democratic Party (SDS) was born in Knin on February 17.

The formation of the SDS brought Rašković and Babić together for the first time. Their differences were immediately apparent. Rašković firmly rejected any move to take the Serbs of Croatia out of the republic. In June, he addressed a rally of 10,000 people in Petrinja, a small town south of Zagreb, whose population was half Croat, half Serb. His firebrand rhetoric disguised the fact that his demands were in fact moderate.

Belgrade radio reported:

> *Addressing the crowd, Jovan Rašković... said that the Serbs respect the Croatian people's right to their sovereign state, but they [the Serbs] demand in that state an equal position for the Serbian and other peoples. The Serbs do not want a second state in Croatia, but they demand autonomy... The Serbian people in Croatia should be allowed to speak their language, to write their script, to have their schools [cheers], to have their education programs, their publishing .iouses, and their newspapers.*

Despite Rašković's profile, the SDS was not, organizationally, ready for the 1990 election, and it polled badly, fielding only a handful of candidates and winning only five seats in the Croatian Assembly, all of these confined to a cluster of municipalities around Knin. Most Serbs in Croatia opted for a party that had no exclusive national orientation, the reformed Communists, now renamed the Party of Democratic Change (SDP). Despite the "ancient enmity" that was later reputed to characterize relations between Croats and Serbs in Croatia, most Serbs expressed faith in a party that was led by a Croat – the outgoing Communist President, Ivica Račan.

Tudjman's HDZ was a broad church, more a movement than a party, of moderate and extreme nationalists. Tudjman spanned both wings. Rašković's SDS enjoyed a surge in popularity after Tudjman's election triumph. Croatia's rural Serbs, in particular, many of whom lived in exclusively Serb villages and communities, were stunned by the scale of his victory and frightened by the tone of his subsequent pronouncements. In spite of the SDS's poor showing in the election, Tudjman none the less recognized Rašković as the legitimate leader of this belligerent and alarmed community. In response, he looked for some conciliatory gesture to offer to Rašković, but one that would not alienate his own anti-Serb constituency. In May, Tudjman and Rašković met. Tudjman courted the leader of the Serbs with offers of government jobs in the new coalition. Rašković had little or no interest in entering Tudjman's government himself. First and foremost, he wanted the Serbs to be defined as a constituent nation in the new Croatia, along with the Croats, and on an equal footing. They should not be reduced to the status of a national minority. This struck at the heart of Tudjman's very *raison d'être* in politics – to secure for the Croatian people a nation state of their own. Rašković's daughter, Sandra,[4] later said the talks with Tudjman had produced no result:

> He [Rašković] said that it was very difficult to talk with Tudjman because he has some sentences that he repeats all the time. 'Croatia is an independent country. I want Croatia to be independent. We waited nine centuries for this.' Tudjman was tortured by one delusional idea, to be the Messiah of the Croatian people and that he was going to give them a free state.
>
> My father told him that this could create a great problem, because the Serbs don't want it. He gave him the advice not to hurry with the new Constitution and to wait a bit.

Rašković's demands were vague. He wanted autonomy for the Serbs, but this had no explicit territorial dimension. There was to be no specific autonomous region; the Serbs were to enjoy national rights, as individuals and collectively as a nation, wherever they lived in Croatia. Even so, it was unacceptable to Tudjman's HDZ, which saw in Serb autonomy, however mild, the negation of their over-riding objective – the founding of a Croatian nation-state. So Tudjman did not wait, as Rašković had advised. In June, his government, two months after taking office and with the minimum of consultation outside the ruling group, produced a draft constitution. Disastrously for Rašković, it defined the state of Croatia as the sovereign state of the Croatian nation. It made no reference to the Serbs. Under Communism they had been a constituent nation of the republic of Croatia. Now they were dropped from the constitution. Ethnic exclusivity was to be written into the basic law of the state. It was a hammer-blow to Rašković. It strengthened the hand of Serb nationalists much more radical than he: those who wanted territorial autonomy, and, finally, secession from Croatia.

Tudjman blamed Belgrade for initiating and manipulating the Krajina Serbs' rebellion. He saw Rašković as the willful agent of an insurrection both inspired and sustained by Milošević, and as little more. Rašković's final humiliation came in August. Tudjman's office, in an apparent attempt to discredit Rašković among his own supporters, leaked the transcript to the Croatian weekly *Danas* of what was supposed to be a private conversation, in which Rašković had confided to Tudjman that the Serbs were a "crazy people," and that he had nothing in common with the "Communist Milošević."

The leaked conversation ruined Rašković's reputation among the Serbs. But if Tudjman thought he could destroy the Krajina rebellion by destroying Rašković, this was among the most crass of his many blunders. It had, if anything, the opposite effect. For, while Rašković and Tudjman were talking in Zagreb, Milan Babić was laying the groundwork for the real insurrection of the Serbs, and not, as Rašković had advocated an "uprising without weapons,"[5] but an uprising armed, supplied and directed by Belgrade, the purpose of which was not to secure for the Serbs autonomy inside Croatia, but to take the Serbs, and the land on which they lived, out of Croatia altogether.

Within the Serb leadership in Croatia, Babić now led an assault on Rašković. By now he was number two in the SDS hierarchy, and Mayor of Knin. He began by building an alternative power-base, taking advantage of the Rašković-Tudjman dialogue to buy time. In May, he established the Association of Serbian Municipalities. One by one, Babić toured the areas in which the Serbs constituted a majority of the population. By mid-summer a handful of local municipalities neighboring Knin had signed up to his Association: Obrovac, Dvor, Vojnić, Donji Lapac.

But by no means all the Serb-populated areas backed Babić's rebellion. Many were interested in dialogue with Zagreb, and were far from hostile to the new government. In these areas, Babić used force to impose his authority. In Korenica, for example, the SDP members formed a majority on the local assembly. They did not join Babić's Association. Instead, they invited Tudjman's local government minister, Slavko Degoricija, to visit the region. They wanted to talk about internal investment, and about plans to develop the tourism potential of the Plitvice National Park, a vast and beautiful lake-land wilderness whose spectacular waterfalls were one of the most popular and successful tourist attractions in Yugoslavia. Babić preempted the meeting by sending forty armed men from Knin the night before Degoricija was due to arrive. In the weeks that followed, the SDS staged a series of rallies in Korenica until the SDP deputies were drummed out of office. By Babić's own admission, the local leadership had to be changed three times before the SDS finally secured control of the municipality. When it did, another chunk of what Babić was to turn into the independent Republic of Serbian Krajina had fallen into place. The Serb demand for autonomy was acquiring territorial definition.[6]

In July, Babić completed the second phase of his exercise in state-building. He sought to turn the Association of Serb Municipalities into a national entity by convening a Serb assembly. "By that," he said, "we wanted the self-governing region which we founded through the association of municipalities to transform itself into an autonomous region to preserve the [Serbs'] sovereign national rights." The Assembly met on July 25, Rašković still nominally its leader, and announced the event that was to mark the start of open, armed hostility between Croatia and the Krajina Serbs: the August "referendum" on Serb sovereignty.

Tudjman's first serious indication of the extent to which he had lost control over the dispute with the Krajina Serbs came in early July. Milan Martić, a Knin police inspector and a man already trusted by Babić, wrote to the Federal Interior Ministry in Belgrade (bypassing his superiors in Zagreb) to inform it that he and his officers would refuse to wear the new uniforms of the Croatian police, in particular the hated *šahovnica* checkerboard shield, which Serbs strongly associated with the atrocities of the NDH. Babić's SDS had evoked the terror of those years repeatedly during the election campaign and after. The re-emergence of the symbolism of an independent Croatia was, in SDS rhetoric, certain evidence of the re-emergence, too, of Croatian fascism, and, along with it, a predisposition towards genocide against the Serbs. Tudjman's insistence on the *šahovnica* as the symbol of a sovereign Croatia, and his insensitivity towards legitimate Serb anxieties, were grist to the mill of Babić's party. Guided by Belgrade, the SDS consciously revived memories of the 1940s. Tudjman had handed them one of their most powerful propaganda devices.

Martić's letter provoked what seemed, at the time, a comic interlude in the mounting tension. Tudjman sent a three-man delegation to Knin on May 5 to bring the rebel Serbs to heel: the Croatian Interior Minister Josip Boljkovac, his deputy Perica Jurić, and Ante Bujas, the commander of the Šibenik police, within whose regional command the Knin municipality fell. The trio addressed a meeting of ninety members of the Knin police, in the town's police station. They were received with silent, impassive hostility. Across the republic, Serb policemen were losing their jobs: fired to be replaced by Croats in a ham-fisted effort by Tudjman's government to redress the national imbalance in a police force which he said was sixty percent Serb, but was in fact no more than twenty percent Serb.[7]

Boljkovac spoke first. He had been a Partisan during the Second World War, and felt some sympathy toward the Serbs. He was conciliatory. He told them he was prepared to forgive them for the breach of discipline that the letter represented, and to find a solution through dialogue. The Knin police had not sought forgiveness nor did they believe they had done anything to be forgiven for. They made no response. Boljkovac argued that the question of the new national symbols was a matter of trivia, of secondary importance. He reminded them that one of the first acts of the Tudjman administration had been to increase the salaries of the police. Some officers were earning ten times as much as they had under Communism.

At that, Martić took the floor. Martić was not a physically impressive man. He was short and round, and wore a clipped little moustache, which, coupled with his puffed-up arrogance and cocky swagger, would have made him, in other circumstances, an easy figure of fun, a backwoods Napoleon in a small town in the middle of nowhere. Martić said he was insulted by this latest contribution from Boljkovac, which was, he said, an attempt at bribery, an effort to persuade the Serbs to sell their national dignity for higher salaries. "Gentlemen," he told them:

> *...you have forgotten one fact. Yes, it is nice to live well, to have good pay, to have good clothes, a good car. However there is something which money cannot buy. What cannot be bought is our Serb dignity. We would rather go hungry, as long as we are together with our Serb people. We will eat potatoes and husks, but we will be on the side of our people. We will remain human.*

Jurić spoke next. He was more aggressive. He told them they had committed one of the worst criminal offenses against the constitution of the republic that was paying their salaries, that this was unforgivable and that they would face the consequences. The meeting erupted. According to Jurić, "They all jumped up like devils." Boljkovac grew nervous. A crowd, thousands-strong, had gathered outside the police station. The three visitors were trapped. The purpose of their visit was forgotten, and their priority now was to get out in one piece. Boljkovac spoke again. "Gentlemen," he said. No response. Then "Friends!." Still nothing. Finally, desperately, since the term was never used in Croatia's new nationalist political culture, he appealed to them as "Comrades!." Then, according to Jurić, Boljkovac lost his nerve. "Let's promise them anything," he said, "as long as we get out of here alive. These are Chetniks! You don't know what that means – they'll hang us!"

It was an ignominious end to a visit that had begun with the confident purpose of stamping Zagreb's authority on a group of rebels who were still not regarded with the seriousness they now, so clearly, warranted. It was a triumph for Martić, the author of the defiant letter and the outspoken hero of the hour. By the end of the meeting he had established control. These three, their security, their very lives, were in his hands. He rose to the occasion, condescendingly granting them a security escort past the waiting crowd and out of town. It was the last time an official delegation from Zagreb was to set foot in Knin. A part of Croatian territory had been taken out of Croatian jurisdiction. Much more was to follow.

Events were gathering pace: so much so that even Jovan Opačić, whose Serbian cultural society had given rise to the whole movement and who, less than a year earlier, had spent three months in jail as a dangerous radical nationalist, declared himself shocked at the direction in which Babić was moving. In May, he had sent a "very dramatic" letter to Rašković pleading with him not to approve Babić's nomination as mayor of Knin. Babić, he said, had struck him as a man who "desired power with a pathological craving."[8] But Rašković was already in political decline.

Milan Babić, increasingly dismissive of Rašković's ineffectual and vague notions of "cultural autonomy," had been making friends in Belgrade. On August 12, on Milošević's instruction, he met Borisav Jović, Serbia's man on the Yugoslav Federal Presidency, and, at that time, its President.[9] The Federal Interior Minister Petar Gračanin was also there.[10] Babić asked them for guarantees: first, that the Croatian flag would never fly above Knin: "because under this flag our fathers, our grandfathers and our nation were murdered;" second, that Croatian police should not be allowed into the area; and third that Serb policemen in Croatia should never be forced to wear black uniforms.[11]

The next day, Gračanin haughtily rebuked Tudjman's Interior Minister Boljkovac, in a telephone call. Gračanin warned him not to try to wrest control of Knin police station and impose a new force, composed of men loyal to Zagreb. Milošević's men had now explicitly taken sides in the conflict. Milan Babić returned to Knin certain that he had been given the green light to build a Serbian state in Croatia.

On August 17, two days before the scheduled "referendum" on Serb autonomy, Knin awoke to a frenzy of rumor. Croatia had declared the referendum illegal and had undertaken to prevent it,[12] and was now trying to move in on Knin once and for all. It was the first use of force by Croatia against the Krajina Serbs and it failed.

That morning, the mayor of the neighboring town of Obrovac frantically telexed Babić to warn him that a Croatian police formation was about to descend on Knin. The Croatian Interior Ministry had sent three columns of police vehicles – from Zadar, Šibenik and Karlovac – to make good Tudjman's promise to quell the Knin rebellion. The telegram warned that the police station at nearby Benkovac, which, like Knin, had a Serb majority, had been disarmed. An attempt had been made to do the same at Obrovac, but had failed. The Serb police there had distributed weapons to the people the day before. The Croatian police had deployed seven armored vehicles for the operation, from a total of ten at the Interior Ministry's disposal for the whole republic. It was the heaviest show of force the Croats could muster.

At the same time, three Interior Ministry helicopters took off from Zagreb, bound for Knin, loaded with police reservists. JNA jets, sent on a direct order from the Chief of Staff in Belgrade, intercepted the helicopters, first buzzing them from above. Perica Jurić, the Deputy Interior Minister, was on board the lead helicopter:

> *The jet stream threw us toward the ground. We barely managed to stay in the air. Then they blocked our radio connections and we couldn't even communicate with each other. After a few minutes the MiG pilot contacted us and his order was very short: either we return directly to Zagreb, or they would shoot us down. We had one minute to do so.*

The helicopter raid ended in farce, with the federal authorities able to claim, plausibly, that they had intercepted the flight for no other reason than that the helicopters had, deliberately, or so it seemed, strayed from their scheduled flight path.[13]

In Knin, Babić's defense committee was meeting. All afternoon, Serbian Radio Knin was feverishly broadcasting reports on the events at Obrovac and Benkovac. The Mayor of Obrovac had appealed to the JNA to intervene, to prevent the Croat police from moving in. Early in the evening, Radio Knin announced that Babić had declared a "full state of alert." Shops and workplaces closed. The streets filled with people. Radio Belgrade reported: "the people are demanding arms and are being given them." Martić, the hero of the show-down with Tudjman's Interior Minister, now firmly installed himself as police chief, and ordered his men into action.

> *I literally took over the police station. I issued the order to the policemen to take their rifles. We broke into the warehouse where other arms for the police were stored and gave arms to the people.*

An hour later, Knin Radio announced that Babić had declared a "state of war" in the region. There was chaos and panic. People took to the hills and woods outside the town, convinced that they were fleeing an imminent

Croatian armored assault. The bells of the Orthodox churches rang out to warn the people. Air-raid sirens were sounded. In Belgrade, the media announced that the JNA had moved on to the streets of Knin and taken control of public buildings, including the railway station and the post office. Roads were blocked and telephone lines went down.[14]

Babić was nowhere to be found, only appearing from time to time on Radio Knin by telephone, but not disclosing his whereabouts. He, too, had taken to flight. There was a frantic exchange of phone calls between Belgrade and Zagreb, between two national leaderships who plainly hated one another. Croatia's Interior Minister Josip Boljkovac telephoned his federal opposite number, Petar Gračanin. The Croats accused the federal authorities of using the JNA to thwart the legitimate law-enforcement bodies of the Croatian republic. The federal authorities and the Belgrade media accused Croatia of launching a genocidal attack on the Krajina Serbs. Both sides knew that they were edging closer to the brink of civil war. And each side behaved as though it were more intent on self-justification, more intent on proving itself the aggrieved party, than on avoiding the precipice.

With the helicopter reinforcement grounded, the Croatian police formations did not continue their advance on Knin. The Croatian Interior Ministry later claimed that they withdrew in order to avoid bloodshed. Serb leaders, both in Knin and in Belgrade (singing, increasingly, the same tune), claimed that the armored columns had been repulsed by a spontaneous uprising of Serb people who had seized weapons from the police stations in Benkovac and Knin, and mounted road-blocks by cutting down trees. Croats derided the events of August 17 as the Log Revolution.

And it was a revolution. At the very moment Babić had received his telex from the Serb Mayor of Obrovac, appealing for military help, the discredited SDS leader, Jovan Rašković, arrived at Knin municipal headquarters. He asked Babić to go with him, immediately, to Benkovac, to appeal to the people to stay calm. He was shocked at the speed with which events were moving, and opposed to the resort to arms. He suggested lying down in front of the Croatian police vehicles. Babić told him there was no time for meetings and for peaceful protest; the time had come for the Serbs to defend themselves. "Rašković remained speechless," Babić said.

> He didn't know what to do. [Then] one of my associates arrived – Dušan Orlović, who worked in my police – and told me that the [Croat] Special Forces were approaching on the Lika road. I told him 'Stop them.' He left. That is how the first barricades went up.

Babić later denied that he had declared a "state of war." The JNA denied that its troops had taken to the streets, though not that troops had been seen.

102

The Garrison Commander issued an implausible and, in the circumstances, almost laughable statement late that night:

> *I assert in the most responsible way that the army did not go out on to the streets and that the news broadcast earlier on concerning this does not correspond to the truth.*

"The confusion, amongst observers present in Knin," the statement continued:

> *...could have been caused by about two hundred soldiers who went off on leave. Owing to a train being late they had become caught up at the railway station and its immediate vicinity while waiting for the train.*

There is no doubt that the Krajina Serbs enjoyed the moral support and political guidance of the Belgrade regime. It is also clear, from the sheer quantity of arms that they possessed when hostilities broke out the following year, that a program of covert arming had taken place; and that individuals in the JNA and the Yugoslav Interior Ministry were engaged in arms-smuggling with tacit official approval. But there is no evidence that the JNA actively engaged in support of the rebels *as an army* as early as August 1990; that would come later. For now, the Army was still commanded by the old, politicized Communist officer corps. Babić had been received warmly in Belgrade, and given certain vague assurances. But neither he nor Martić yet trusted the JNA absolutely. Even Tudjman quickly expressed his satisfaction with the Army's behavior. In a televised address to the republic later that night he said: "The Army is not, and will not be, involved in the destabilization of Croatia."

None the less, a revolution of sorts had taken place. Croatia had used force, or at least a show of force, for the first time, to try to stamp its will on the rebel regions. And it had been thwarted. The Knin region was barricaded. An impermeable curtain had fallen across Croatia, separating SDS-controlled areas from the rest of the republic. The Krajina Serbs had drawn more closely under the protection of Belgrade, and under the control of Slobodan Milošević. Babić's nascent "state within a state" had acquired, for the first time, a definitive border, to be defended and, soon enough, to be pushed forward ever deeper into the territory of Croatia. The war in Croatia, one which was to spread far beyond the borders of that republic, had begun without a shot being fired.

1 In 1991, HOS, the military wing of the extreme nationalist Croatian Party of Rights (HSP), the political successor to Pavelić's Ustaše, wore all-black uniforms in a deliberate evocation of 1941.

2 The phrase is that of the Serb nationalist poet Matija Bećković. *Kniževne Novine*, Belgrade September 15, 1989, p. 3.

3 Serb nationalists argued that the Latin script had been forced on them. In Knin, however, while the official signs are now exclusively written in Cyrillic, the graffiti appeared mostly in Latin.

4 Rašković died, a broken and disillusioned man, in Belgrade in July 1992.

5 Thompson, *Forging War* (Article 19, London, 1994), p. 157.

6 Degoricija also visited areas that had already fallen to SDS control. In the summer of 1990, he visited Lapac, where the radical Serb nationalist David Rastović, one of Babić's closest lieutenants, was mayor. Degoricija addressed a public meeting. Rastović also spoke, demanding recognition of the Cyrillic alphabet, the Serbian language, and separate Serbian schools. Degoricija recalled that there were a hundred people at the meeting. "At one point I said 'Okay, if this is so important to you, we can remove all road-signs in Latin script and replace them with Cyrillic signs, but how shall we employ people, what are your ideas for the economy?' He said: 'We will feed on the leaves, graze the grass, but we will be Serbs!' I said, 'Well, David, this is a strong economic policy indeed' and everybody laughed." (Interview with Degoricija, May, 1994.)

7 Serbs were, traditionally, disproportionately represented, both in the police force and state security services, including the officer corps of the JNA in Croatia; historically, they had been the poorer, more rural, of the two national groups, and more dependent on state employment and armed service, even more so in Krajina, where Serbs had been settled for the explicit purpose of defending, and policing, the frontier of the Austro-Hungarian Empire. See Chapter Eight of this book: "You've Chosen War."

8 According to Opačić, Rašković ignored the advice.

9 The Presidency, since Tito's death, rotated on a one-year basis by republic. Serbia's representative Borisav Jović on May 15, 1990, took over from Janez Drnovšek as head of the rotating Presidency. Stipe Mesić of Croatia became vice president.

10 There has been speculation as to whether Babić met Milošević personally at this stage. There is no evidence that he did. Babić says he met the Serbian President for the first time in December, 1991. It seems likely that Milošević, who was still keeping a certain personal distance from the Serb rebels, would have delegated his contact with them to Jović, rather than commit himself to them publicly by meeting Babić. It is typical of Milošević's tactics not to commit himself to anything or anyone (at least not publicly) until he has to.

11 Croatia had never proposed the adoption of black uniforms for its police. The impositions, to which Martić and Babić objected, were more imaginary than real. In fact, they were deliberately invoked as a pretext on which to begin an armed rebellion.

12 The referendum was organized by the SDS and was not recognized as legal by the Zagreb government. It invited only Serbs to take part. There was no residency qualification – all Serbs born in, or resident in Krajina, could vote. And there was no specific question put: the paper read, simply, "Vote to decide Serb autonomy: For/Against."

13 Jurić later denied that the helicopters were planning to go to Knin. He insisted that they had been intended as no more than a provocation to the JNA, to demonstrate publicly that the JNA would take the side of the Krajina Serbs in the dispute. Others, including Manolić, say the helicopters were bound for Knin as part of a force that would try to storm the police station there.

14 *Tanjug*, August 17, 1990.

8

"YOU'VE CHOSEN WAR"
The Arming of Slovenia and Croatia, April 1990–January 1991

The Army wasted no time. It pounced the very day the new coalition government in Slovenia came to power. Its immediate target was the weapons stores of the Slovene and Croatian Territorial Defense (TO) forces. The TO embodied a central plank of Yugoslav defense theory – that foreign invasion could be deterred by the presence of a huge civil army that would rise up to fight a guerrilla war to render foreign occupation costly, and, ultimately, unsustainable. It was a citizens' army in waiting, and it rested on the principle that all citizens would act.

But the TO owed its allegiance not to the Yugoslav People's Army (JNA) but, dangerously, given the political hue of the incoming governments in Slovenia and Croatia, to the individual republics.[1] This had never presented a problem under the monopoly rule of the Yugoslav Communist Party. But during the run up to the Slovenian and Croatian multiparty elections, the JNA High Command had come to fear that the TO, now had the makings of separate republican armies, at the service, potentially, of secessionist governments.

The JNA was a Communist army, inseparable from the ideology on which it was founded. In the slogan-rich environment of Tito's Yugoslavia, the JNA had marched to the cry *"Armija je rodjena u Revoluciji"* – "The Army was born in Revolution!" And it still did. Its generals were confident that the collapse of Communism elsewhere in Eastern Europe would not spread to Yugoslavia. They argued that their Communist revolution had been indigenous and not imposed on an unwilling population. They even believed Communism would return to the former Warsaw Pact countries. If Communism were to fall in their own country, the Army's place in society, hitherto unassailable, would fall with it, as would the privileges enjoyed by Army officers. To a Communist Army, multiparty pluralism presented more than a threat to its own position. It presented a threat to the security of the state. On May 16, two days after the new government in Slovenia had taken office, the JNA began to disarm the Slovene TO.

The republic's new government was not informed. The incoming Defense Minister, Janez Janša, was, after all, the very man whom the Yugoslav authorities had jailed only two years earlier for publishing military secrets. The Slovene President, Milan Kučan, claimed that he heard of the mass confiscation of weapons only informally.

The mayor of Jesenice called and said they'd asked him to hand in the arms. So did the mayor of Slovengradec. I immediately tried to find General Hočevar, the commander of the Slovene TO. He said that they were replacing the WW2 arms with new ones. I was satisfied. I had no reason to disbelieve him. But the next morning messages came from many municipalities that this was not at all what was happening – that all the arms had to be handed in. I called General Hočevar again. He told me that he had been ordered to move the arms from the TO stores, that he had an order from Belgrade to conceal this from the Slovene leadership.

Kučan ordered the TO to surrender no more arms, and placed increased police protection on TO weapons stores. However, the republic had, according to Janša, already lost about seventy percent of its weapons stockpile. The JNA's disarmament program then came to a halt. A stand-off had begun between the JNA and the force that was, within little more than a year, to transform itself into Slovenia's national army. The dispute between Slovenia and Yugoslavia's federal institutions had acquired a military dimension.[2]

The crisis further widened a split in the Slovene government, which was, in any case, a broad and unwieldy coalition of parties united only by their desire for greater autonomy for Slovenia. Janša wanted to use the existing TO structure as the basis on which to build an armed force independent of the JNA. Kučan was more cautious. He was reluctant to commit Slovenia to a secret, and illegal, arms-procurement and smuggling program. Relations between Janša and Kučan had been cold[3] since Janša's imprisonment; Kučan had been head of the Slovene Communist Party during the attempted suppression of the "Slovene spring." Now, Janša did not trust Kučan: "The disarmament of the TO showed us that Kučan would be too soft, that he would accept everything he had to, that he would wait, and fall behind," he said. Janša's calculation was that the TO – a force of 70,000 men – now had fewer than 10,000 weapons between them. The shortfall had to be made up. As Defense Minister, Janša initiated a plan to buy weapons abroad, smuggling them into Slovenia in small quantities.

Igor Bavčar, Slovenia's Interior Minister, took part in the clandestine operations:

We had thought about it before the election. We knew when we came to the ministry that we would not know whom to trust, and that we would have to build a new kind of organization that would be fully under our command. In three months we built an army of 20,000 armed people. And the JNA didn't know.

In the beginning, the Slovenes acquired only small arms, and these in small quantities. In September, the JNA stepped up its campaign against the TOs. The Federal Defense Minister Veljko Kadijević announced that there would be no republican military operations or units outside the control of the Army. Slovenia then dismissed the commander of its own TO, who had already demonstrated his loyalty to Belgrade. On October 4, the JNA took control of the TO headquarters in Ljubljana.

The show-down with the JNA united Kučan's government, which earlier had been reluctant to commit money to the project, behind Janša's weapons-procurement program. Kučan now learned of, and approved, Janša's plans. Knowledge of the project was restricted to five or six leading members of the government. In December, the first anti-tank weapons arrived – shoulder-launched Ambrust missile systems. They were stored in barracks at Kočevska Reka and placed in the possession of the nascent Slovene Special Forces.

A referendum on sovereignty had been scheduled to take place later that month. Anti-Federation sentiment was running high. Janša, and his deputy, Jelko Kacin, decided to gamble on a show of defiance and a display of strength. The republic, they decided, would openly declare itself armed and ready to repel any attempt by the JNA to interfere with its new democracy. Kacin flew to Kočevska Reka in a police helicopter. A Slovene television cameraman was waiting for him. There, Slovene troops fired two or three Ambrust missiles at an old and obsolete tank. The film was broadcast on Slovene television two days later. The Slovenes were raising the stakes.

Not for the last time Slovenia had blazed a trail that left Croatia struggling to catch up. The disarming of the TO in Croatia was accomplished quickly and efficiently. The incoming government found itself with no armed force capable of acting independently of the JNA, except the police. According to the Croatian representative on the federal Presidency, Stipe Mesić, Croatia had no more than 15,000 rifles, all held by civilian police, only one armored personnel carrier[4] and no heavy weapons of any description.

With its TO disarmed, Croatia decided to turn its domestic police force into an army. The task was two-fold: not only had the force to be supplied with weapons; it also had to be de-Serbianized. Traditionally, Serbs had been disproportionately represented in the state security services as well as in the officer corps of the JNA. This had been a persistent source of grievance to many Croats, who saw, in the imbalance, Serbian hegemony. Across the republic thousands of Serbs now found their careers suddenly cut short. They were side-lined, demoted or fired. At the same time, as part of its drive to build a national state for, and of, the Croatian people, the republic's Interior Ministry ran a recruitment drive to bring young Croats into the force. Thousands responded, many of them zealous young nationalists responding to what they saw as the challenge of the day: Tudjman's as yet unspoken call-to-arms. They were hurriedly trained and, in many cases, promoted to positions for which neither their age nor experience qualified them. Belgrade accused Zagreb of mobilizing 50,000 police reservists, in addition to those brought in to the regular force. The recruitment drive promoted an atmosphere of national exclusivity and intolerance in the police. It went beyond the police; *en masse* Serbs were fired from their jobs throughout Croatia or forced to sign loyalty oaths. It explains, in part at least, why so many Serb policemen and civilians, who might otherwise have been persuaded to live in an independent Croatia, joined the rebels when the war began in earnest a year later.

The task of arming the new police force – or Croatian National Guard as it was to be renamed – was entrusted to Martin Špegelj, the republic's Defense Minister. Špegelj, a bear of a man from peasant stock, with the weather-beaten face of a hardened drinker, had had a distinguished military career. Now retired, he had been one of the JNA's most senior Croat officers, as Commander of the Fifth Military District, an area encompassing all of Slovenia, and most of Croatia. Furthermore, his commitment to Croatia's sovereignty was not in doubt: in April, he had publicly attacked the JNA for – illegally, in his view – disarming the TO. This combination of military expertise and sound national credentials made him, in Tudjman's judgement, the ideal candidate to nurture Croatia's fledgling defense force.

Špegelj proved himself more radical than Tudjman could have predicted. He secretly toured the country, establishing within each Army barracks a cadre of reliable Croatian JNA officers, who formed an alternative command structure in readiness for the day when the conflict with Belgrade would begin. He set up a network of village patrols, arming Croatian civilians and training them to organize a defense force for each municipality. He ran an arms-smuggling operation that dwarfed that of Slovenia. It used the network of Croatian nationalists abroad to fund and organize gun-running operations. Arms were brought in by ferry, by truck and, in countless small consignments, by private car – a method those involved referred to as "small four-wheeled ant." While Croatia was arming, the Yugoslav Army counter-intelligence service (KOS) was watching.

By December, Špegelj believed Croatia was sufficiently armed and organized to face down the might of the JNA once and for all. In an interview in Belgrade, General Kadijević, who had already accused Tudjman of rekindling the fires of 1941, of fascism and genocide against the Serbs, launched a blistering attack on Croatia, and explicitly threatened, for the first time, to use force to disarm Croatia's police.[5] The situation in Yugoslavia was "drastically deteriorating," he said. Civil war was now a possibility:

The biggest danger for the country's integrity and security comes from the intensive work towards setting up purely national armies. They are driving the country further towards the abyss of a fratricidal war. Yugoslavia cannot and will not become another Lebanon. All armed formations set up outside the army will be disarmed. Those responsible for setting them up will be held accountable before the law. Since, under the law and constitution, this comes under the competence of the armed forces, there will be no negotiations or compromises. Those who try to oppose the army by force will be thwarted by force.

In Zagreb, Kadijević's remarks were taken as the signal of an impending military coup.

In secret, General Špegelj now unveiled his plan to an incredulous and plainly nervous meeting of Croatia's small defense council. Špegelj argued that the JNA was too weak to launch the war that Kadijević was threatening. The JNA was made up, he said, of eighteen- or nineteen-year-old conscripts, the majority of whom were non-Serbs, and who would not be prepared to fight. Špegelj argued that the Croatian police should lay siege to JNA barracks in Croatia, and cut off food, water and electricity supplies and telephone lines. The garrisons, he said, were by JNA convention all physically separated from the logistics' units on which they depended. If the two were separated for long enough the garrisons would fall apart by themselves. Their members – the officers and men – could then be invited to transfer their loyalty, *en bloc* or individually, to the new armed forces of the Croatian republic.

My idea was to put the JNA up against a wall and say 'If you want to take our weapons, there'll be a war right now.' If we had disarmed the JNA then we would have gained 3,000 artillery pieces, 1,000 tanks, ammunition for two years of war, and 700,000 small arms. With this change of power, there probably would not have been a war.

Tudjman was stunned. The meeting fell into silent disbelief. No one supported Špegelj's plan. Tudjman dismissed it out of hand:

It was clear to me that it would be political suicide for democratic Croatia. We had no possibility at that time of disarming the JNA, no possibility of crushing the insurgents in Knin. Had we accepted that plan we would have been condemned by the world as outlaw secessionists who wanted to overthrow the constitutional system.

The political and diplomatic case won over the military. Špegelj believed that Tudjman was being naive.

* * *

109

Špegelj knew the JNA well enough to know that his arms-buying program would not go unnoticed. He knew that the defense establishment in which he worked was riddled with people still loyal to the idea of Yugoslav unity, and hostile to Tudjman's increasingly secessionist government. Špegelj knew he was surrounded by spies; but he did not know who they were.

In early October, 1990, Colonel Vladimir Jagar, a JNA officer at Virovitica, near the Hungarian border, contacted JNA counter-intelligence. He reported that Špegelj had tried to recruit him into a secret network of Croat agents who were distributing weapons to Croatia's growing reserve police force.

The JNA counter-intelligence officer, Colonel Aleksander Vasiljević, ran a security check on Jagar. A Croat, too, he was the son of a close, life-long friend of Špegelj. Jagar and Špegelj were from the same village. Jagar's mother had died when he was a young boy, and he was raised as part of Špegelj's own family. Špegelj loved and trusted Jagar almost as though he were his own son. Jagar's betrayal would be all the more damaging as a result. Within two days, Vasiljević had recruited Jagar as an agent.

At the same time, JNA informants in Austria reported to Vasiljević that a consignment of 20,000 Kalashnikov machine guns were to be delivered across the Hungarian border some time between October 8 and 11, at a crossing near Virovitica. Vasiljević placed the area under heavy surveillance. The operation was so sensitive that he commanded it personally. He was foiled by the weather:

> It was a foggy night, very foggy. We saw the two trucks crossing over from Hungary with the license plates that we knew they would have. At the same time they brought about 30 special police there, and they escorted the vehicle with heavy security, with a police car at the head of the column and one behind the second truck.

The area was swarming with Croatian policemen – Vasiljević estimated between two and three hundred officers. He was stunned to see, among them, four or five of the highest-ranking security officials in the republic. The two trucks were not checked by the Yugoslav customs officers on duty.[6] Instead, they were driven away, escorted by two police cars, one leading, the other following. The two trucks disappeared into the fog.

The next day, Vasiljević instructed Jagar to seek an urgent meeting with Špegelj. Jagar telephoned his old family friend, and told him he had information that he could not divulge on the telephone. Špegelj told him to come to his house in Zagreb. When Jagar arrived, Špegelj answered the door with a pistol in his hand. He signalled to Jagar that the house was bugged. Josip Boljkovac, Croatia's Interior Minister, who had responsibility for Croatia's police force, including, officially, its recruitment drive, was also there. He waved his arms frantically at Jagar to warn him not to speak. Jagar had found the two men in a state of acute paranoia, tiptoeing around the house, mouthing their conversation in silence. Eventually, the three left the house, in Boljkovac's car, where they began to talk openly. Unknown to the other two, Jagar was carrying a surveillance device. Their conversation was being recorded.

Vasiljević had ordered Jagar to encourage Špegelj to talk as much as possible about the smuggling of weapons, and to disclose details of the arms-distribution network. Vasiljević wanted to know where the paramilitaries were based, who was in charge, where the weapons were stored. He needed a detailed breakdown of the operation in order to plan a JNA campaign against it.

Jagar had a delicate and dangerous task. He had to tease the information out of Špegelj without arousing his suspicion. He did it brilliantly. Over the next six weeks Vasiljević was to gather more than a hundred hours of audio tape from Jagar, including material in which Špegelj appears to describe secret "liquidation squads" whose task would be to assassinate senior Serb officers and kidnap their families.[7] Whether such a plan ever existed remains a matter of conjecture. What mattered for now was that Vasiljević had sufficient material on tape to produce the convincing and startling case that it did.

Vasiljević and Jagar went further still. They hid a video camera in Jagar's house. Špegelj was filmed trying to persuade a colleague of Jagar's to join the secret network of officers. Špegelj knew that he was under surveillance. He knew that he was almost certainly being bugged, but not once did he suspect his trusted young friend of complicity.

Vasiljević kept the Federal Defense Minister informed throughout. Kadijević heard the first audio tapes in early October. By the beginning of December he had produced a report for the Federal Presidency, the JNA's supreme commander. One of its members was Stipe Mesić, a man whom Kadijević's report directly implicated in the arms-smuggling program.[8]

Kadijević's report was marked "Top Secret." The accusations it levelled at Croatia revealed the extent to which the JNA had infiltrated the covert weapons-distribution program. It accused Croatia of importing arms from warehouses in Hungary, under the cover of an import-export company in Zagreb, called Astra. It accused Špegelj, Boljkovac, and other members of Tudjman's government of direct involvement, laying out a case for their immediate arrest and prosecution under federal law. It described in detail the building of an illegal paramilitary force in Croatia – an armed wing of Tudjman's ruling party, the HDZ. The JNA had also uncovered Špegelj's plan to surround and disable JNA barracks in Croatia. Although, the document said, there was enough evidence to arrest and prosecute the leaders of this planned insurrection, the political consequences would be too great.

Instead, Kadijević's recommendation was that the Federal Presidency issue an order to disarm all paramilitary formations. This, he said, was the only way to avoid civil war.

The Federal Presidency session at which Mesić was to be confronted took place in mid-winter, January 9. The atmosphere was electric, with both the regular Croatian police and the JNA on full alert, in a volatile, fractious stand-off, each knowing that by now the Croatian countryside was bristling with weapons that had been secreted or stolen from JNA warehouses or smuggled across the Croatian-Hungarian border. Zagreb was seething with rumors of an impending military coup.

In an atmosphere of intense mutual distrust, Jović presented the allegations from the Kadijević document. He proposed that the JNA be given a free hand – that the paramilitaries should be disarmed, by force if necessary. To the surprise and fury of Jović, the Bosnian delegate, Bogić Bogićević, objected. The resolution failed to get the five votes it needed under the constitution. A compromise was reached. The paramilitaries should be given ten days to disarm voluntarily. It secured the majority it needed. Only Mesić and Slovenia's Drnovšek had voted against.

But Mesić had succeeded in inserting into the resolution the word "illegal." This was the loophole by which Croatia was to avoid acting on the Federal Presidency's order. Mesić returned to Zagreb, knowing that Croatia did not have the slightest intention of disarming the police, or the reservists that Špegelj had recruited and armed over the previous six months. Croatia would, instead, embark on a ten-day game of brinkmanship with the JNA, arguing that the only "illegal" paramilitaries in Croatia were the rebel Serbs in Krajina.

For seven days, no weapons were surrendered. On January 17, the US Ambassador to Yugoslavia, Warren Zimmermann, met Jović and told him the US would not accept any use of force. A democratic solution had to be found through peaceful negotiation. The Army was not to be used to round up the paramilitaries. Jović was furious. It proved, he told Zimmermann, that the US was in league with the German conspiracy to expand its influence south to gain a warm-water port, by destroying Yugoslavia. And he reiterated what were to become the mainstays of Milošević's argument: that the borders between the republics were administrative only; that if Yugoslavia were to disintegrate, the borders were no longer valid; and that only the nations, and not the republics, had the right to secede from the federation. Jović later conceded that Zimmermann's intervention had been an important factor in the JNA's reluctance to move in with force on the Croatian police.

The next day, Jović met Mesić. He told him that if force became necessary, every member of the Croatian Government would find himself on trial, accused of plotting armed insurrection against the state. Mesić agreed to go to Zagreb and try to find a compromise. Milošević, according to Jović, did not trust the Croats, and urged Jović to order the Army into action immediately, to arrest Špegelj and Boljkovac. But there were still two days to run on the ultimatum. Jović knew that Kadijević would not act without seeking further political authority from the Presidency.

On January 19, the day before the deadline for disarmament was due to pass, Kadijević showed the Špegelj film to Jović. Kadijević was convinced that the Croats were not preparing to disarm, and that the film was the evidence the JNA needed to arrest Špegelj and the others involved in the arms-distribution plan.

Jović telephoned Mesić. Mesić said he needed more time. He asked for two more days. Jović agreed.

Two days passed. Kadijević told Jović that the Croats had not handed in any weapons. Mesić telephoned Jović from Sarajevo where he had been attending a conference. He repeated Croatia's position: the only illegal paramilitaries in Croatia were the Krajina Serb rebels. Jović told Mesić: "You've chosen war."

Milošević began to press Jović for a change in the Federal Presidency's instructions to the JNA. Milošević, according to Jović, argued that if the Croats intended to secede, then Serbia should not try to prevent it.

Instead, Serbia should use its hold over federal institutions – particularly its control of half the votes on the Federal Presidency – to protect the Serbs in Croatia. Milošević's position was that the JNA should not fight the Croats, but should withdraw from places of Croat majority to areas of Croatia where Serbs predominated.

At the same time, Milošević made it clear to the Slovenes that Serbia would not try to prevent their secession from Yugoslavia. On the night of January 24 as the Federal Presidency gathered for the second time in a month to demand the disarming of the Croatian police, Milošević held a separate meeting with Slovene President Kučan. The two reached an easy agreement. According to Kučan:

> *It was obvious at that meeting that the Serbs would not insist on keeping Slovenia within Yugoslavia... We Slovenes said that we wanted the right to have our own state. Milošević said the Serbs wanted the recognition of this right for themselves, too – that is, all Serbs in Yugoslavia in one state. My reply, of course, was that the Serbs also had this right, but in the same way as the Slovenes, without hurting the rights of other nations. Milošević replied 'Yes of course, this is clear' and with that we flew home to Ljubljana.*

There were no Serbs living in Slovenia, and there was, from Belgrade's point of view, no distinction to be drawn between the Slovene nation and the Slovene republic. The same was not true for Croatia. The Serb-Slovene agreement, when it was made public, infuriated the Croats. To them, it read as though Kučan had given Milošević a free hand to partition Croatia.

Milošević, the master tactician, was, as always, keeping his options open. He had not yet abandoned the goal of preserving Yugoslavia's territorial integrity; but he had signalled that he was willing to do so should the need arise. According to Jović:

> We thought, Milošević and I, that there was no reason to keep Croatia by force in Yugoslavia and we thought the Army should have withdrawn to the Serb territories. But the Army could not understand this because they still believed they should defend Yugoslavia.

This was the primary difference, at the beginning of 1991, between Milošević and the Communist High Command of the Yugoslav Peoples Army. For Kadijević and the Generals, the unity of Yugoslavia was sacrosanct; for Milošević it was negotiable, a bargaining chip in his perpetual efforts to strengthen his hold on power. Over the months that followed, Milošević was to wrench the JNA away from its historic purpose, which was to preserve the Yugoslav state, toward a wholly different goal. He would threaten it, co-opt it, until it embraced the new goal: that of protecting the Serbs outside Serbia and of forging a new territorial entity. Gradually the Yugoslav Army would become, in its over-riding military objective, and, eventually, in its ethnic composition and ideology, the army of Greater Serbia.

On January 25 Jović wrote in his diary "Today may have changed the entire course of Yugoslavia and the crisis." He and Kadijević had prepared one last *coup de théâtre*, a final attempt to force the Croats into a corner in which they would have to disarm. This was how the stage was set.

Milošević telephoned Jović to urge him again, as Supreme Commander of the Yugoslav Army, to act to protect the Serbs of Knin. Jović told Milošević that the generals would not move without the explicit authority of the Federal Presidency. Milošević instructed Jović to convene a further meeting of the Presidency to give the Army the political authority it needed. Jović scheduled the session for two p.m.

In Zagreb, tension had reached fever pitch. Tudjman addressed a special session of Parliament. He told them he was preparing to go to Belgrade that very day. So acute was the paranoia that many delegates told him he would not come back alive. Tudjman consulted his ministers. Many of them agreed. A trip to Belgrade was too dangerous. In the event of a JNA crack-down, Tudjman would be vulnerable. Only Špegelj told him he thought the trip safe.

Croatian fears were well-founded. The Army High Command had made detailed preparations for a military takeover of the country. That night, the Army was placed on full alert. There were troop movements in Croatia, further fuelling the rumors of an impending *coup d'état*. A secret document, drawn up by the Federal Defense Ministry, was circulated to every major Army barracks in Yugoslavia, and read to JNA commanders across the land. It was called *A Report Concerning the Actual Situation in the World and Yugoslavia and the Immediate Tasks of the Yugoslav People's Army.* It welcomed recent developments in the Soviet Union, including the slowing down of the reform movement, and the growing strength of the conservative hardline faction in Soviet politics. It also welcomed the increased mobilization of the Soviet Army because, it said, "It limits the West's freedom of action and scope for influencing world events." It attacked the West for supporting "disintegrative tendencies" in the Soviet Union (and, by implication, in Yugoslavia), and accused Western governments of having plotted the overthrow of socialism in Eastern Europe in order to extend their own influence:

> *The support for democracy expressed in certain circles in the West is transparent demagogy, because for them democracy is only that which corresponds to their aims and interests.*

It attacked those whom it regarded as agents of Western imperialism – by implication, the governments of Slovenia and Croatia, who were seeking greater autonomy or independence.

> *Yugoslavia can exist only as a state. If it is not a state then it is not Yugoslavia, but something else. That which some in Yugoslavia offer as a confederation is factually not a state, nor can it be... Our basic task must be to create the conditions for the functioning of the federal state. This means, first of all, the liquidation of all breaches made in the field of unity of the armed forces: i.e. disarming and liquidating all paramilitary organizations in Yugoslavia. Implementation of this task will inflict a powerful defeat on nationalist-separatist politics...*

It was a blueprint for a military coup in every respect except one: the Army was not prepared to act alone. The generals were ready to take on the recently-acquired might of the Slovene TO and the Croatian police; it was ready to arrest the Slovene and Croatian governments and impose martial law. But it wanted to cover with a veneer of constitutional legality what amounted to a military take-over. So it sought authorization from the Federal Presidency.

Kadijević addressed the Presidency session. He repeated his determination to disarm the Croatian paramilitaries. He asked the Presidency to authorize armed intervention by the JNA in Croatia. The Slovene representative, Janez Drnovšek, fearing that the proposal would get the majority Kadijević wanted, provoked a furious row with Jović and stormed out, slamming the door behind him and announcing that he was going back to Ljubljana to hold a press conference.

When the session resumed, Kadijević's proposal was put to the vote. It was deadlocked. On the question of armed intervention, the Serbs had lost the support of Bogićević from Bosnia. It failed to get the five votes it needed to secure a majority – only Milošević's men, the representatives of Serbia, Kosovo, Vojvodina and Montenegro voted in favor. (Tupurkovski, the Macedonian representative, was not present.) Drnovšek who had been persuaded to return suggested that Tudjman be brought into the session. While the Presidency members waited for Tudjman's arrival, Kadijević sprang the surprise he had been planning for months – a final attempt to terrorize the Bosnian delegate to vote against the Croats and Slovenes. He made what seemed an innocent suggestion: that the Presidency members take a break to watch the evening television news.

The Croats sat in a separate office in the Federal Presidency building. They watched the news in stunned disbelief. Belgrade television was broadcasting Vasiljević's clandestine film of the Croat Defense Minister's arms-smuggling activities, together with a doctored audio tape of Špegelj apparently disclosing details of a plan to attack and disable the JNA in Croatia. Belgrade television devoted forty-five minutes to a grainy black-and-white film in which the Croatian Defense Minister argued that Croatia was already at war with the JNA.

Kadijević's last attempt to win over the Presidency was a spectacular piece of showmanship and manipulation, and a ringing conclusion to the whole Špegelj affair. The film had been released to Belgrade TV, which was controlled by Milošević, deliberately to coincide with the Presidency session as a way of frightening its members into compliance. But it failed. The Bosnian delegate was not impressed. He did not change his vote. The Kadijević plan was still deadlocked. There would be no Presidency endorsement of a JNA crack-down on Croatia's paramilitaries.

Kadijević lost his nerve. He would not order action that the Presidency – his supreme commander – had explicitly voted against. He and Tudjman left the room. Between them they agreed on a compromise. Kadijević would call the Army off alert in Croatia, if Tudjman agreed to the prosecution of a handful of people who had been arrested that morning in connection with the arms-smuggling operation. Kadijević also told Tudjman that he intended to have Špegelj arrested. Tudjman returned to Zagreb the next day declaring that his courageous mission to the enemy capital, undertaken at great personal risk and despite the mortal concern of his ministers, had saved Croatia from invasion.

Špegelj went into hiding. Croatian television broadcast the film of his clandestine meeting the day after Belgrade, describing it as an outrageous forgery. When he heard about it, Špegelj initially concluded that he had been betrayed by Perica Jurić, the Deputy Police Minister; Špegelj had used Jurić's car on the occasion when the film was shot. The two men met in secret. Špegelj wore two pistols in his waistband. He told Jurić there were only two people who could have colluded to produce the film: "One of them," he said, "I trust implicitly. The other is you." Only when he saw the film did he realize that he had been betrayed by Jagar. The camera had been hidden in the television set in Jagar's living room. In retrospect, Špegelj now remembered that Jagar had, on that night, insisted that he sit in a particular chair, so that the camera could film him face on. Croatian police dynamited Jagar's house in the village where the deception had taken place. Špegelj's own house, in the same village, stands less than a hundred meters from the ruins. Jagar, a Croat, was never to return to Croatia. It was not, in any case, what he considered his homeland. That was Yugoslavia, and it was disappearing beneath his feet.

Jović's prediction that January 25 would be the day that changed the course of Yugoslav history was prescient. But he, more than any other individual (with the single exception of Milošević), knew what was really taking place. Kadijević's indecision, his refusal to act without political authority, played into Milošević's hands. Jović had known of Špegelj's arms-smuggling and distribution program since mid-October. It had taken nearly four months to reach even this inconclusive compromise. Throughout that time, the federal authorities never once mounted a serious effort to prevent the arming of the Croats, either by taking control of the border crossings or instructing the federal customs. Milošević had already decided: if Yugoslavia could not be salvaged and centralized, then the Croats, like the Slovenes, would be allowed to go. But they would not be allowed to take with them those parts of their republic that Milošević's men considered Serb territory. The rebel Serbs of Krajina were being drawn ever more closely under the protection of Belgrade, and the control of Slobodan Milošević.

1 Strictly, the armed forces (*Oružane snage*) of the Federal Republic consisted of the JNA and the TO. They were designed to complement each other. They interrelated on all levels of command, up to the highest, when the TOs were relegated to the republics' defense ministries, while the JNA had its own supreme command. They then united at the level of the supreme command. They were highly integrated

– the officers were interchangeable through their careers. In the TOs only the highest officers were full-time soldiers, the rest were reservists. Most of the Army units were fully-active units. The TO kit was stored all over the place. The TO units were often based on the Partisan brigade principles, a brigade being the size of a battalion; so a big factory would have its own TO unit, or a municipality, and it would often have weapons' stores in the workplace itself. "ONO i DSZ – *Opštenarodna odbrana i društvena samozaštita*," was Tito's doctrine, which means: "general popular self-defense and society's self-protection.".. the socialization of the armed forces. Also their doctrine was: *"Moramo se spremati za rat kao da će izbiti sutra, i raditi za mir kao da će trajati stotinu hiljada godina"* – we have to be ready for war as if it will break out tomorrow and work for peace as if it will last one hundred thousand years.

2 It is not clear on whose authority the JNA was acting. The Commander in Chief of the JNA was, constitutionally, the eight-member collective Federal Presidency. The Slovene representative, Janez Drnovšek, had been President of the Presidency until May 15 – two days before the disarmament of the TOs began. He knew of no order to disarm, and later claimed that only the Serbian representative, Borisav Jović, who assumed the Presidency of the Presidency after Drnovšek, knew anything. "My term [as President of the Presidency] expired on 15 May. On May 17 this disarmament was done. They had waited for my term to expire. Only Jović was informed about it and, for the Presidency, it was a *fait accompli*. They never voted on it. I, of course, was against it, and demanded a Presidency meeting to discuss it, but the others were against me."

3 Kučan had had his doubts about the appointment of Janša and his ally, Bavčar, to positions of such sensitivity, and had expressed them to Prime Minister Peterle when he was forming the Government in 1990. Why, he asked Peterle, are you appointing a man with such a record of conflict with the JNA, as Defense Minister? And Bavčar, who had a personal history of conflict with the police, as Interior Minister? Peterle had told Kučan not to undermine his ministers by expressing these doubts in public. Kučan, despite his misgivings, accepted the appointments.

4 An unlikely claim, since Croatia was, by August, sending columns of armored vehicles, including seven APCs, to try to regain control of Knin.

5 Kadijević gave his interview the night before Serbia's first free elections. It was widely seen, at the time, as a whole-hearted endorsement of Milošević's SPS.

6 There is little doubt that the arms-smuggling operation could have been stopped. KOS's strategy was to allow the operation to continue.

7 Špegelj disputes this. He says the film and audio tapes were doctored to make him appear to be arguing for selective assassinations. He says he never advocated this, and that the audio tapes were taken from a TV interview he had once given in which he had been asked to discuss hypothetical matters.

8 Kadijević said he had evidence that Mesić had accompanied Špegelj to Budapest to buy weapons.

9

"IF WE DON'T KNOW HOW TO WORK, AT LEAST WE KNOW HOW TO FIGHT"
The Decisive Month
March 1991

March was the decisive month. Milošević set the country on the course to war.

Tanks broke the silence of Bulevar Revolucije. Scattered fires burned in front of the Federal Parliament. Gusts of wind whistled through smashed windows. There were screams as police stalked Belgrade beating up and arresting pedestrians at random.

The city stank of tear-gas. A seventeen-year old student, Branivoj Milinović, lay in a pool of blood, shot dead by a squad of fifteen policemen just a few yards from President Milošević's office. The police were intent on revenge for a colleague who had been stoned to death by angry protesters.

It had been a chaotic, frightening day during which the Serbian regime vented its anger on the hitherto quiet streets of Belgrade. It was Saturday, March 9, the day on which it became clear that President Milošević would not hesitate to use force against his own people in order to preserve power. Just four years after promising Serbs in Kosovo that "no one will ever dare to beat you," Milošević sent tanks into his own capital. The grim night-time parade stood in stark contrast to the dawn of democracy elsewhere in Eastern Europe. In fact, the display of force was planned well before the anti-government demonstration, which supposedly provoked it, got out of hand. Borisav Jović, then President of Yugoslavia's collective leadership, started ringing members of the Presidency asking for approval to deploy tanks even before the first outbreak of violence.

But the stage for bloodshed had been set earlier. The Interior Ministry, acting at the last minute, banned a city-center protest against government control of the media. Hundreds of policemen were deployed, with dogs, horses and armored vehicles. They set up roadblocks around Serbia to seal off the capital. But the ban was imposed in the certain knowledge that it would be violated. By noon on Saturday, 40,000 people, mostly supporters of the opposition leader, Vuk Drašković, and his nationalist Serbian Renewal Movement (SPO), converged on Belgrade's central square, Trg Republike. Drašković was named *Kralj Trgova* (King of the Squares) for his ability to draw a crowd – a skill at which he surpassed even Milošević. Drašković was one of the principal targets of an elaborate state-run smear campaign to discredit anyone

119

who rose to challenge Milošević. Among a plethora of wild and absurd accusations, Belgrade Television – state-run, and immensely powerful in shaping public opinion – repeatedly accused the charismatic Drašković of secretly plotting to destabilize Serbia, in an unholy alliance with the revived "Ustaše regime" of President Franjo Tudjman of Croatia.[1]

Belgrade Television was firmly in Milošević's grip. It was the ideal tool for stirring up hatred against "the enemies of the Serbian people" – first Kosovo's Albanians, then the Slovenes, the Croats, and finally, the opposition in Serbia itself. After his overwhelming victory in Serbia's first free elections in December, Milošević continued to use the media as his personal propaganda machine, refusing to give the opposition any airtime. To the anti-Communist protesters, Belgrade Television symbolized Milošević's total control over Serbia.

From the balcony of the National Theater, opposition leaders called for freedom of the press as the police moved in. Drašković cut a striking figure with his great mane of black hair and flowing beard. He called for the Bolsheviks to step aside in favor of radical change. He demanded press and broadcasting freedom, and an independent judiciary. The police tried to disperse the crowd with water cannon and salvoes of tear-gas canisters. Drašković urged his followers to resist and bellowed "Charge! Charge!" Seconds after rows of police, clad in full riot gear, surged forward. The demonstrators tore apart fences, grabbing iron bars and sticks for the fight. In vain, Drašković appealed to the security forces to rally behind the people against the regime.

The police beat a retreat. For a few hours in the city center the demonstrators seemed to have won. They smashed windows, leaving not a single pane of glass intact in the Serbian Presidency, the building which housed Milošević's office. But the opposition didn't know what to do next. Hijacking several fire trucks, the euphoric demonstrators massed in front of the Serbian Parliament. Upstairs, opposition leaders tried to get in touch with Milošević or anyone from the Serbian Government.

Milošević was at Dobanovci, the military compound outside Belgrade. He knew it was time to take action and rang Borisav Jović – President of the Yugoslav Presidency and Commander-in-Chief of the Army – telling him to order in the tanks. As the demonstration progressed, he grew more nervous.

The JNA Generals had also been following the events closely. They were divided. General Kadijević wanted to avoid turning the Army into another police force. A taped conversation, however, reveals General Blagoje Adžić, the hulking Chief-of-Staff, cursing the police and ordering them to beat the demonstrators.

To send in the Army, Jović needed a majority vote of the eight Presidency members. One by one, he phoned those he thought most likely to support

Milošević's demand for military intervention.[2] After the representatives from Kosovo, Vojvodina and Montenegro – all three Milošević "placemen" – he rang Vasil Tupurkovski of Macedonia to secure the fifth vote, begging: "Vasil, we need to get the Army on to the streets in a demonstration of power to stop what will happen in Belgrade. It will be very detrimental to the stability and security of the country." The Macedonian politician says the calls began in the morning, several hours before the demonstration in Belgrade got out of control. The calls became frantic: "I got calls from Jović every half-an-hour requesting a vote. At about noon Jović tells me: 'Vasil, I have five votes. Give me your vote because we want to act,'" later recalled Tupurkovski. By his own account, Jović started phoning "at eleven or twelve – at the time when they began to attack the Defense Ministry." But his memory is faulty. At midday, the crowd was nowhere near the Ministry.

Bosnia's representative to the Presidency, Bogić Bogićević, a Bosnian Serb who during the war remained loyal to the Bosnian government, also gave in. But he insisted later that Jović never mentioned the word "tank," asking only for the Presidency's approval to secure vital buildings. Despite their yes votes, both Bogićević and Tupurkovski were wary of Jović's tricks. Tupurkovski:

> *We coped with Jović for at least half a year, with all kinds of moves by him to misuse our status as Presidency members, especially pressure towards Bogićević and myself on many occasions, so we were careful about his initiatives.*

As the tanks rolled through the streets, the police raided and shut down the liberal radio station, B-92, and Studio B, the only Belgrade television station not in government hands, which were both reporting the demonstration. "The leadership of Serbia requested the dispatch of Army units since the majority of police units are engaged in Kosovo," said a statement from the Federal Presidency, explaining why the JNA was called instead of the police.

In parliament, Drašković realized he was about to be arrested.

> *One of the security men asked if I had eaten anything all day. He told me I would arrive too late for dinner and that breakfast was very bad in the Central Prison. He offered to buy me a sandwich, yogurt and cigarettes. His name was Naser Orić.* (Orić, a member of the Serbian security forces, was later to achieve renown as leader of the Muslim defenders in the eastern enclave of Srebrenica.)

Drašković was taken to jail.

Milošević's brutal tactics came as a shock to Belgrade. It was one thing to read about tanks in Kosovo, but quite another to see them on the street out-side. To make matters worse, Milošević was in no mood to compromise. He saw no reason to concede anything to the opposition, which was scrambling to make capital out of public outrage. His chilling televised speech, on Saturday evening, was a warning as blatantly obvious as the tanks that he was to remain the undisputed leader. It was also probably an attempt, cleverly devised, to prepare the public for the declaration of a state-of-emergency.

> *Today the biggest asset that our country and people have was endangered in Serbia and Belgrade. Peace was jeopardized. Peace is the basic condition without which we cannot successfully solve any single problem that we have, and we have many.*
> *Therefore, Serbia must oppose the forces of chaos and madness using all constitutional means. I am thus asking and demanding that all citizens of Serbia contribute to peace and the establishment of order, by above all extending aid to state organs.*

In other words he was calling on the people to side with the state. It was the last straw. On Sunday night 1,000 students from Studentski Grad, the biggest campus in Belgrade, broke through police cordons and headed for the city center. The police, in helmets, gas-masks and shields, seemed better suited for all-out war than controlling unarmed students. Under clouds of tear-gas, they used their batons to stop the students. But, around midnight, from dormitories all over the city, hundreds of students reached the center, Terazije, in front of the Hotel Moskva.

The students took Milošević by surprise. That first cold night, the police were poised to pounce on a handful of stalwarts encamped at Terazije's nine-teenth-century fountain. But for some reason they refrained, preferring to stand by, silent and menacing. The students issued their demands: they wanted the release of Drašković, and the dismissal of Dušan Mitević, the head of Belgrade Television, and Radmilo Bogdanović, the Interior Minister, whom students blamed for the violence of the previous day.

Over the next week, tens of thousands of Belgrade's liberal élite made their last stand. Singing "Give Peace a Chance," they re-created, fleetingly, the atmosphere of tolerance that had once been a hallmark of Belgrade, but which had disappeared from public life under Milošević. The city seemed transformed. People would stop by to bring food or blankets to the students, braving freezing temperatures on Terazije. Each night professors, writers, and actors would address the crowd from a platform on the fountain, which the demonstrators had turned into a makeshift podium, and the focal point of their city-center vigil.

Milošević was infuriated by the Terazije forum. Prominent nationalist intellectuals, such as Matija Bećković, Head of the Writer's Union, deserted him. Speakers read telegrams of support from other cities in Serbia, where local protests were being staged. A message from Zagreb was greeted with loud enthusiasm.

The crowd jeered at Patriarch Pavle of the Serbian Orthodox Church when he begged the students to abandon their protest. Milošević had persuaded the frail seventy-seven-year-old priest that violence was inevitable. Pavle believed a rival gathering, organized by Milošević, would march on Terazije.[3] But at the park on the confluence of the Sava and Danube rivers, the Ušće, the people bussed in for the rally, were too few, too old and too tired to fight. Pavle returned to the students to ask forgiveness, saying he had been deceived. "*Parents at the Ušće, Children on Terazije,*" read a headline in *Borba*, the independent Belgrade daily.

In the conviction that Yugoslavia must be pulled back from the brink of catastrophe, tens of thousands of people turned out on Terazije. But few were aware of the speed with which their country was hurtling towards violent collapse. On March 11, in a speech to an emergency session of the Serbian Parliament, which he peppered with accusations of plans to stage a Romanian-style revolution, Milošević showed that he was shaken:

> *They are trying to force Serbia to forego Yugoslavia and accept a diktat from the northwest about the disassociation of Yugoslavia into as many states as there are republics. Serbia would then have to abandon the political ideal with which it entered into the creation of Yugoslavia.*

The deputies of Milošević's Socialist Party (formerly the Communists), occupying 194 of the 250 seats, wildly applauded his speech.

Unnerved by the demonstrations, Milošević took steps to limit the damage. The regime was afraid that the student movement would inflame all of Serbia. The Serbian President decided to meet representatives of the opposition and students. Žarko Jokanović, a twenty-six-year-old student and politician, who was part of a group which met Milošević on March 11, was ushered into a huge room, empty but for a big table in the middle. "It was luxurious and fit for a tsar."

Separated by the vast expanse of the table, Milošević at first virtually ignored the group, then warned the students that they were playing into the hands of the Ustaše and Albanian separatists. "People should not destabilize things at a time when we are trying to stop the resurgent fascist Ustaše forces, Albanian secessionists, as well as all other forces of the anti-Serbian coalition which are endangering people's freedom and rights."

The students put forward their demands. But Milošević kept repeating that he did not have the authority to do anything about it – a line that was to

123

become his trademark. Looking at him intently, Jokanović asked: "Are you currently responsible for anything in this country? You are behaving like the Queen of England when you have the power of a Russian tsar."

The Serbian President sat impassive. Spiky-haired Jokanović asked if he had watched the news the previous night, "It could have provoked a civil war." The atmosphere was tense. Milošević hid his vulnerability. Tihomir Arsić, a young actor popular for his rendition of Tito, asked permission to open the window for some fresh air. The room was suddenly filled with the demonstrators' chants of "Slobo, Saddam" comparing him to the Iraqi dictator who had waged war against the entire world and brought isolation to his country. Milošević pretended not to hear. Jokanović showed him the picture of Milinović, the youth killed during the demonstration. "Is there anything human left in you?" The Serbian President turned deep red, but said nothing.

A few streets away, the Belgrade power-brokers were pressing for martial law. Jović called an emergency session of the Federal Presidency for March 12, to discuss not the demonstrations but the failure to carry out the January 25 Presidency order to disarm paramilitaries in Croatia and Slovenia. He made a late-night television announcement, publicly summoning the Presidency members. It was a deliberate attempt to heighten public fears, ominously implying that he was now acting in his capacity as commander of the armed forces. The political temperature rose.

Rumors that a *coup d'état* was under way gripped Terazije. They were well-founded. Jović was planning to repeat his attempts (which had failed in January) to get the federal Presidency to approve a military takeover. "With everything that had taken place over the weekend," said Jović, "this was our last chance."

Fearing arrest, Janez Drnovšek, Slovenia's representative on the rotating Presidency, boycotted the session. When Stipe Mesić, Croatia's representative, arrived at the Federal Presidency, the usual venue for Presidency sessions, he was alarmed to find a group of JNA officers waiting for him there. They ordered him into a military bus, which was waiting in the forecourt. Mesić took this as a sign that he was being arrested. He climbed aboard and took a seat at the back of the bus along with other members of the country's highest ruling body. He spent the journey, wrapped in his overcoat, head down, gripped by fear. The entire group of politicians was taken to Topčider, the Presidency's emergency meeting place in the event of war. When they arrived, Mesić, from the very back of the bus, asked the waiting General Kadijević, "Are we under arrest?"

The general was irritated, replying the Army would never act in an unconstitutional manner. Mesić, though still nervous, was now able to joke. "Don't be angry now, Veljko, I was just checking."

There followed a bizarre scene – filmed and later televised in a JNA pro-

124

duction entitled *Who Betrayed Yugoslavia?* – in which the country's leaders sat round a bare table in an Army command bunker in sub-zero temperatures, some dressed in military-issue furs, others shivering with cold, and discussed whether or not to impose a state-of-emergency throughout Yugoslavia. Macedonia's representative, Vasil Tupurkovski, was in no doubt about why the meeting was being convened in this extraordinary and inappropriate location. The Presidency was brought to Topčider, he said, to be intimidated, to "tremble before the military."

"It was very cold. It was scary," later recalled Mesić. "It all showed they wanted us to capitulate."

In JNA barracks, on the outskirts of Belgrade, tanks were revving up their engines – waiting for the order to move.

With Drnovšek absent, Jović hoped it would be possible to push through a state-of-emergency, which would give the JNA the authority it had long sought to impose a state-of-emergency: to save Milošević's political neck and disarm the Croatian police. He knew that he could count on his allies, Nenad Bućin of Montenegro and Jugoslav Kostić of Vojvodina. He only needed two more votes – Riza Sapunxhiu, from Kosovo, who had just been released from hospital, and Bogićević, a fellow Serb, might cave in. But he knew that it would take a lot to make them crack.

Kadijević did his bit by conjuring up nightmarish images from the Second World War. "In Yugoslavia all possible enemies of socialism and united Yugoslavia have emerged on the scene, Ustaše, Chetnik, Albanian, Beloguardist and other factors. We are fighting against the same enemy as in 1941."[4]

The first two votes came as no surprise. Mesić and Vasil Tupurkovski immediately said there were no grounds for declaring a state-of-emergency. Jović was irked by Mesić's suggestion that the Serb leaders wanted to strengthen their own positions following the turmoil on Belgrade's streets – rather than disarm paramilitary formations in Croatia. Tupurkovski saw through Jović's attempt to push through what amounted to a legal *coup d'état*:

> It was a proposal for a legal takeover. Legal because it would be by a vote of the Presidency, and it had the prerogatives to do that, but a takeover because the army would have been the main actor, the main factor of that situation.

Tupurkovski was an immensely popular political figure, both in Macedonia and throughout Yugoslavia. He was known as *Džemperovski* (sweater-man) because of his preference for casual clothes. Big and affable, he had a common touch. His habit, despite his political status, was to ride public transport, rather than take advantage of the black Audis or Mercedes favored by most of Yugoslavia's political leaders. He voted against Jović's proposal, and then asked for the floor to request warm clothing for those who had come unprepared for a meeting in such conditions.

Sapunxhiu, the delegate from Kosovo, was next to declare his hand. Frightened and ill, he voted yes. Jović now had four votes. He needed just one more to secure his state-of-emergency. The entire decision rested with Bogić Bogićević. Bogićević remained silent. Like a deer on a dark night, frozen in the headlights of an on-coming car, he seemed paralyzed. He was shaken by screams from the short-tempered Jović for him to hurry up and vote.

Like his counterpart from Serbia, Bogićević invoked the constitution, insisting on finding a legal basis for action. He balked at endorsing a procedure which bypassed the legally-elected governments of the six republics. Jović insisted that the Presidency had the authority to declare a state-of-emergency without the governments of the republics. He said any rule which said otherwise was only of an internal nature that could be changed by the Presidency itself. Bogićević, however, stood his ground. He refused to cast a vote. After a long silence, he said: "I can't vote."

Outraged, Kadijević warned that the JNA would seize the weapons no matter what the politicians decided. "The JNA has decided to take over, regardless of any decision made here, to stop the civil war. We are going to do our job."

"Kadijević, your personal army will lead to civil war," said Mesić.

"I am not going to dance along with you lot any more," said Kadijević storming out of the room.

The debate went round in circles. After half-an-hour, Kadijević came back to warn of impending war. Regardless, he said, the Serbs would form their own army within fifteen days.

Jović warned the dissenting members of the Presidency that he would resign – on the grounds that he refused to "implement the decisions causing the disintegration of the country."

It was clear that they could not agree on anything – let alone the future of Yugoslavia. But, no matter what, Serb leaders were determined to have their way.

As Commander-in-Chief, Jović sent Kadijević to Moscow that night to meet hardline Soviet Defense Minister Dimitri Yazov. The other members of the Presidency were kept in the dark about the mission.

Three months earlier, Admiral Mamula had gone to London, General Blagoje Adžić to Paris, and Admiral Stane Brovet to Moscow, to try to assess how the international community would respond to a military coup in Yugoslavia. "On balance, the Army decided the UK and France would not be opposed," said Mamula. Russia welcomed the plan, although made it clear that it would not support the move publicly.

"We were interested in their assessment as to whether the West would intervene if we tried to disarm the paramilitary units by force. There was no question – the West would not intervene," said Mamula. Word would later leak out about Kadijević's mysterious trip to Moscow. Kadijević came back believing that President Mikhail Gorbachev would not last long and that, if they could hold out just a bit longer, Communism would be shored up in the Soviet Union which, in turn, would save them.

The next day, March 13, the students believed briefly that they had won. Drašković was released. Looking out at the huge crowd on Terazije, he demanded: "Freedom for Serbia." But Drašković soon realized that he had been stronger inside prison than out. In a bid to get the students off the streets, the Serbian President agreed to fire Mitević and four other editors at Belgrade Television. The Interior Minister Bogdanović who two days before denied he was even considering offering his resignation, also agreed to step down. Milošević agreed to organize a parliamentary investigation of police actions on March 9, which could have punished the violence.

Over the next three years of war, Milošević would never again be shaken by a mass protest. The brutal police reaction signalled that although Milošević had reluctantly allowed multiparty elections in Serbia, the last of all six republics, he refused to tolerate any political opposition. [5]

On March 14, Mesić, the Croatian representative, this time backed by his Slovenian counterpart, Drnovšek, remained locked in conflict with Jović. They insisted that any JNA action would plunge the country into war.

The Presidency again refused to endorse Jović's plan for a state-of-emergency. Jović and his allies were livid. He and Kadijević warned they would take steps to allow the Army to act. The Presidency was blocking them; Jović was unable to deliver on his promise. But, to cope with this eventuality, he had crafted a fall-back plan: if the Presidency refused to support him, he would break it. An hour later, Jović was on television, putting the plan into action. Blaming "prevailing forces in the Yugoslav Presidency which do not care about the sovereignty, independence and territorial integrity of the country," Jović resigned as Head of State, declaring that he was "not prepared to be a party to such decisions which contribute to the destruction of the country." As ordered, Bućin and Kostić followed suit that same night, stepping down from the Presidency along with Jović, although with considerably less pomp.

The dismembering of the Presidency created a power-vacuum which Serbia's leadership hoped – and expected – the JNA would fill. Jović had resigned precisely so that the only body with the constitutional authority to prevent an Army crack-down would be unable to function. On the night of March 15, a statement from the Supreme Command said: "The Army would consider what measures to take after its recommendations aimed at preventing inter-ethnic armed conflict and civil war were voted down by the Presidency with a majority of votes."

The next day, Milošević declared "Yugoslavia is finished," and announced that Serbia no longer considered itself bound by federal bodies. In effect he was declaring Serbia's secession from Yugoslavia. In an address to the nation he said [I have]:

> ...*ordered the mobilization of special reservists and the urgent formation of additional Serbian militia units. Yugoslavia has entered into its final phase of agony... The Republic of Serbia will no longer recognize a single decision reached by the Presidency under existing circumstances because it would be illegal.*

Milošević threw down the gauntlet to the Federal Army, announcing that he would form his own special forces and carry out decisions bypassing the legal federal institutions. In short, he was prepared to do precisely what he had accused his rivals from the Western republics of doing. He put the finishing touches on a plan to throw the country into disarray.

That day rebel Serb leaders in Knin, the center of Krajina, declared independence from Croatia on the grounds that Jović's resignation was proof that Zagreb and Ljubljana were destroying Yugoslavia. Milošević hoped that Tudjman would send in his special police units to put down the insurrection, prompting Army intervention and a state-of-emergency, but he was disappointed.

Serbia's obedient assembly, where Milošević's Socialists had a comfortable two-thirds majority, voted to remove the recalcitrant Sapunxhiu from his seat as Kosovo's representative on the federal presidency. But the Presidency – now comprised of Mesić, Drnovšek, Tupurkovski and Bogićević – refused to accept Sapunxhiu's dismissal, saying the Parliament had no powers to remove him from the Presidency. In time, Milošević would get his way. [6]

While the public was reeling from shock, Serbia's municipal leaders were attending an important meeting. Before dawn broke that morning, the republic's local police had carried out an unusual task. They phoned all 200 of Serbia's mayors and informed them to expect an urgent message. Soon after, each municipal leader was handed a telegram summoning him to the Serbian parliament at 6 p.m. The Mayor of Valjevo, Slobodan Djukić, the only opposition mayor in office, described how 200 black sedans made quite a scene in front of the parliament. But it paled in comparison to the confusion within.

Everyone believed the secret meeting had been called in connection with the vacuum caused by Jović's resignation, and, of course, to coordinate steps to fill it. All day Djukić had speculated about various possible schemes at hand. When he said goodbye to his family that morning, he had even suspected that he might be placed under arrest while in Belgrade. But Bora Petrović, deputy speaker of the parliament, immediately tried to dispel speculation of any plan to declare a state-of-emergency.

"It seemed that those politicians who had called the meeting did not have a clear agenda, or any agenda at all," Djukić said of the meeting. Djukić later recalled that the speakers started mumbling nonsense about the economy. The mayors jeered in protest. "You, Comrades," said Jovan Cvetković of Svetozarevo, "dragged us hundreds of kilometers to this meeting to tell us the same thing we can read in our own newspapers." They were furious that Milošević was not there to meet them.

The outraged city leaders started to walk out. Cvetković led the revolt.

I asked the chairman what it was all about – Yugoslavia was disintegrating and we were supposed to receive some important information, but nobody in charge was here.
    'Where is Mr. Milošević, where is the Prime Minister?'

Finally, the Speaker of Parliament, Slobodan Unković, said he would urge Milošević to meet them. The meeting was adjourned for an hour. It was at this covert session that Milošević made clear that he was ready to drive out the Croats and Slovenes. "I understood after the meeting that he was ready to form a Yugoslavia without the Catholics," said Djukić. That evening, and over the next week, Milošević laid out his vision for the end of Yugoslavia:

The break-up of Yugoslavia is in question here. It is true that the Slovenes want to secede. It is true that the Croats want to secede. But I think that the Muslims do not have any reason to secede from Yugoslavia. Some of them have been indoctrinated, but most of the Muslims want good, tolerant, cultured and I would say civic and friendly relations with the Serbs and other nations in Yugoslavia. After all, they all live in several republics. They have no reason to destroy Yugoslavia.

Milošević outlined the possible steps the Army could take. Asked by an irate Cvetković what Serbia's strategy was, Milošević answered that the strategy would not be broadcast on the radio. His next sentences never the less leaked out to the public, and echoed throughout Yugoslavia:

If we have to, we'll fight. I hope they won't be so crazy as to fight against us. Because if we don't know how to work and do business, at least we know how to fight.
    The army has the constitutional authorization and obligation to defend

Yugoslavia's constitution. I don't doubt the Army will carry out its constitutional authorization because the Presidency stopped functioning. This is not a coup – because the army will be acting constitutionally if it disarms the HDZ tomorrow.[7]

Milošević had finally taken off his gloves. His opponents in the Presidency fought back. Mesić stood in for Jović as Commander-in-Chief. He appealed for "reasonable individuals in the Army" to refrain from using force which, he said, would precipitate a civil war. "But my influence on the Yugoslav Army (even as its Commander-in-Chief) was the same as my influence on the Finnish Army," laughed Mesić later.

On March 18, the representatives of the four Yugoslav republics, the remnants of the Presidency, found themselves alone at the immense Palace of the Federation. It was deserted – virtually the entire bureaucracy had disappeared. The clerical staff was nowhere to be found, so the Presidency members wrote their own press releases. Diplomats and reporters milled round the building. Tupurkovski hoped that they would somehow break the impasse with the JNA, which, like Milošević's proxies, was boycotting the presidency. "The Army has always obeyed the constitution and, I suppose, they will continue to do so," he said doubtfully. On Monday Kadijević boycotted a meeting of the Federal Government of Ante Marković, who threw his support behind the remaining Presidency members aware that his fate was inextricably linked with that of the other federal institutions Milošević was trying to commandeer.[8] Jović and Milošević's ploy to get the army to move had failed yet again. Kadijević, who for days had been threatening to launch a *coup*, hesitated and missed the opportunity created by Jović and Milošević. It remained unclear why he did not act.

The Serbian President apparently had no choice but to beat a retreat. The fires of protest had died down, but Milošević was still reeling. He had never before been jeered or screamed at. While he showed no feelings for anybody – he counted on the adoring masses. The students, whose predecessors during the mass demonstration in 1968 had made peace with Tito, had turned against Milošević. They hated him. The intellectuals, who had helped transform him from a floppy-eared Communist *apparatchik* to a Serbian national icon, abandoned him, at least for the time being. Nationalists joined liberal intellectuals to take a stand against Communism at the Terazije demonstrations. The nationalists realized Milošević was using them for his own personal power not because he shared their beliefs.

It seemed like a cement wall was being built up around him. He felt weak. Milošević tried to lower the temperature by consenting to an unprecedented session with 200 students and professors at Belgrade University. He squirmed in discomfort, as students, who had become his staunchest opponents, controlled the agenda. They demanded to know what he planned to do with Yugoslavia.

He repeated virtually verbatim his message to the Mayors' Meeting. The audience finally understood. It was obvious Yugoslavia, as they knew it, was finished. But he pledged that all "Serbs would live in one State."

> *It has not occurred to us to dispute the right of the Croatian nation to secede from Yugoslavia, if that nation decides of its own free will in a referendum... but I want to make it completely clear that it should not occur to anyone that a part of the Serbian nation will be allowed to go with them. Because the history of the Serbian nation in the Independent State of Croatia is too tragic to risk such a fate again.[9]*

While discarding hopes for settling the dispute with the Croats in order to save Yugoslavia, he baldly dismissed "all nationalism as discrimination; and any division along those lines as medieval."[10] He appeared to forget how he had come to power.

In vain, the students appealed for him to understand that the future of Serbia rested on transforming it into a democracy. Nebojša Milikić, a student, boldly told Milošević that his resignation would pave the way for the fall of his nationalist counterpart in Croatia and the building of democracy:

> *You have to understand that there is only one national interest, that Serbia and Yugoslavia become democratic states ...The people and the leaders will not try to escape from that kind of state. If you resign tomorrow, Franjo Tudjman would lose all support within 15 days. He built his myth on you.[11]*

Shaken, Milošević realized his attempt to impose a state-of-emergency had failed. He decided to scrap the boycott of the Presidency, ordering his Parliament to block Jović's resignation.

Milošević recovered his political balance after secret talks with Franjo Tudjman in Karadjordjevo, Tito's favorite villa for negotiations and hunting.[12] Word soon leaked out that the two Presidents had made a pact while strolling through the serene grounds of Karadjordjevo. Milošević has never divulged the details of their discussions – while Tudjman bragged how he had doubled the size of Croatia. Convened to avert war, the two men agreed on a plan which meant war.

They discussed Serbia's demand to oust Prime Minister Ante Marković. The Croatian President wanted in return the sole authority to resolve the status of the Serbian minority, which a week earlier had declared independence from Zagreb.

The two leaders also discussed the partition of Bosnia-Herzegovina. Tudjman said he proposed either the confederation or partition of Bosnia. "This partition had been started with the Croat-Serbian agreement of 1939 when the representatives of the Croatian and Serbian people agreed to create the Banovina Hrvatska," he said in reference to the *Sporazum* (Agreement) between Vlatko Maček of Croatia and his Serbian counterpart, Dragiša Cvetković. It created a Croatian *banovina* which included much of Bosnia – about thirty percent of the territory and population of Yugoslavia. Milošević was interested in whatever deal would maximize his grip on power. Tudjman was lulled into believing that his dream of an independent-and-enlarged Croatia was within reach and that war could be avoided. He could not contain himself and afterwards boasted to a handful of trusted associates that Croatia would be "even bigger than it had been under the Maček-Cvetković Agreement."

In fact, according to Mesić, Tudjman even believed that Croatia would get a chunk of Bosnia, and part of Vojvodina in northern Serbia as well. His exuberance rings true.

> *Tudjman came back in a good mood, very satisfied, red in the face saying everything was fine – the JNA wouldn't attack and that Croatia was going to be bigger than it has ever been. Milošević had agreed.*
> *It was a gentlemen's agreement.*

By contrast, Milošević denied that any such agreement was ever reached. Pragmatic as ever, he kept his cards close to his chest, never divulging what he and Tudjman had decided on that day in the first of a series of secret encounters designed to carve out their own ethnic states.

> *Tudjman told me he wanted an independent Croatia. But we simply could not agree – he wanted to destroy the federal institutions and I could not agree to that. I suggested as I had before that we should change the constitution to allow self-determination. There has been speculation that we decided how to split Yugoslavia: I can tell you now if we had decided that there we could have done it immediately.*
> *I believed that the best solution was for all to live in one country.*

The agreement between the two leaders however did not last long. Just one day later, Serb rebels moved to take control of a police station in Plitvice national park and took the first combat-casualties of the war. Within four months, backed by the Yugoslav People's Army, Serbs would be fighting a real war to build a country of their own.

1 Belgrade Television frequently broadcast films of Ustaše leader Pavelić, in 1941, woven with scenes of Tudjman and the newly-elected Croatian Democratic Union (HDZ).

2 This is one of a myriad of examples when Jović, in league with Milošević, adopted a legalistic approach to justify the abuse of power.

3 Even Radovan Karadžić, then President of the Serbian Democratic Party of Bosnia, addressed the students, who booed at his seemingly irrelevant remarks that the time of Partisans and Chetniks was over. In fact, it was just being re-born.

4 Kadijević as quoted by Mesić in his book *Kako smo srušili Jugoslaviju*, Zagreb 1992, Globus.

5 Milošević's victory was bolstered by the ethnic Albanians who, since 1990, had boycotted all official Serbian institutions and ignored the elections.

6 In place of Sapunxhiu, a former officer of the World Bank, he appointed the loyal Sejdo Bajramović, head of the Kosovo veterans' association, who ran a bingo hall in his spare time. The normally obedient Kosovo representative had not, as Milošević had expected, resigned from the Presidency. Bajramović was also a tragic figure. He died in 1993 after the Croats failed to hand over the corpse of his only son, a JNA officer, killed in Mostar.

7 *Vreme*, April 15, 1991.

8 Marković criticized the Army deployment in a rather short-sighted statement, saying JNA units should be used in disputes between nations and republics, *Borba*, March 10, 1991

9 *Borba*, document: March 19, 1991.

10 Ibid.

11 Ibid.

12 Karadjordjevo is 125 kilometers from Belgrade – 330 from Zagreb. It was surrounded by hundreds of forests, wheatfields, cane, and a lake. Tito last visited in 1980 to celebrate what turned out to be his last new year.

Despite his fondness for Tito, Karadjordjevo was an odd choice for Tudjman, since this was the location where Tito had begun his crackdown on Maspok.

10

THE DESCENT INTO WAR
Croatia and the Serbs
February–June 1991

By the spring of 1991 the Krajina Serbs' rebellion had spread. Milan Babić and Milan Martić were, respectively, the political and military leaders of the uprising, and, in February, they targeted the town of Pakrac in western Slavonia. Rebel Serbs, loyal to their self-proclaimed Serbian Autonomous Region, seized control of the local police station and the municipality building next door. They jailed those officers who refused to submit to their authority, among them many Serbs. Then they announced that they would, from now on, take instructions only from the Interior Ministry of the Serbian Autonomous Region of Krajina. Another piece of Croatian territory had fallen into rebel hands.

Serbs formed the largest community in Pakrac,[1] but the town – like its western Slavonian hinterland – was a kaleidoscope of intermingling national groups. The town's boast was that it had twenty national minorities: Czechs, Poles, Ruthenes, Italians, Slovaks, Hungarians and others. For weeks a hidden campaign of terror had stalked Pakrac: harassment of Croatian officials, machine-gun bursts in the night, threats, and intimidation.

When news of the takeover of the Pakrac police station reached Zagreb, Tudjman did not hesitate. He could not afford yet another Knin. He ordered that the renegade police station be retaken by force.

Perica Jurić, the Deputy Police Minister, assembled a force of 200 men, trained in anti-terrorist operations, in the neighboring town of Kutina. Some would go on foot, through the woods; others, crammed into the backs of civilian trucks, lying flat, and covered, on top and at each side, with flak-jackets, and then rubble. The trucks travelled separately, rather than in convoy: several Serbian villages lay along the route; Jurić did not want to alert the rebels that an intervention force was on its way.

They coordinated their arrival time. At 4:30 a.m., they entered the center of the town. The rebels were caught unawares; they had erected no barricades. The first commando unit of twenty men stormed the municipality building and arrested the Serbs inside. Some of them, according to Jurić's account later, were found sleeping off the effects of a heavy-drinking session. Jurić set up a command post for storming the police station next door. There was shooting – machine-gun and rifle fire from the police station and neighboring houses. But the intervention squad was quickly reinforced by armored police vehicles. The rebels put up little resistance and Jurić's men suffered no casualties. A hundred and eighty men were arrested, and the rest took to the wooded hills around the town. The town had suffered physical damage; broken windows and pock-marked walls and roofs. But no one was killed or injured. It was a text-book operation, perfectly executed.

The Belgrade press erupted, reporting a flood of refugees, 20,000-strong, pouring into Serbia and claimed that eleven Serbs had been killed, including an orthodox priest. The mass-circulation Belgrade daily, *Večernje Novosti*, reported in a special edition on the front page that the priest had been killed; on page two, it said the priest had been wounded, and on page three, it carried a statement from him. Jovan Rašković, still formally the SDS leader in Croatia but now waning in political influence, told a rally of Krajina Serbs that Croatia had that day "declared war on the Serb nation." In Belgrade, the President of the Federal Presidency, Borisav Jović, agreed to a request from the Defense Minister Veljko Kadijević for armed intervention. Kadijević sent in the tanks. The JNA intervened in Croatia for the first time.

Jović issued a statement. The Army had intervened, it said, in a dispute "between the two national communities." Belgrade painted the dispute throughout as an ethnic conflict which only the Army could prevent. Zagreb insisted it was a conflict between the legally-elected Croatian Government and illegal paramilitaries. It was to become a familiar pattern of events: Krajina Serbs provoking the Croatian authorities into conflict, the Army stepping in to "separate the two sides" and, in effect, protecting renegade Serb areas from the Croatian authorities' attempts to bring them back under Zagreb's jurisdiction. Under a cloak of impartiality, the Federal Army was now another step closer to becoming the army of Greater Serbia.

By four o'clock in the afternoon, the Croatian special forces had established their control of the town. The JNA tanks rolled in later that evening. There was chaos, with the Serb rebels firing into the town from the hills above, Croatian police establishing defensive positions in and around the town and the JNA, under fire for the first time, caught in the exchange.

From Belgrade, Jović sent the leading JNA Counter-Intelligence officer, Colonel Aleksander Vasiljević, to find out, in person, what was going on. From Zagreb, Tudjman sent Croatia's representative on the Federal Presidency, Stipe Mesić. The two met, by chance, in the Pakrac police station late that night. Vasiljević, according to Croatia's Police Minister Degoricija, was as "messy as a pig, covered in mud." The Croats took this as evidence that he had been tramping through the woods with the run-away rebels, and accused him of instigating, and organizing, the whole rebellion.[2] In everything the Krajina Serbs did in the early months of their rebellion, Tudjman's men saw only the hand of Slobodan Milošević.

The Croatian police regained control of the town. The Federal Presidency ordered both sides to end their stand-off by pulling back. The crisis ended, but nothing was resolved.

* * *

Martić's next target was to shake 200 Italian tourists from their beds with the rude discovery that war had come to their secluded holiday resort. The Croatian coast attracted ten million tourists a year, providing Yugoslavia with twenty percent of its hard-currency earnings.[3] There were few spots more precious to the tourism industry than the Plitvice National Park, a vast terraced lakeland, connected, lake-to-lake, by cascading turquoise waterfalls. Plitvice lies to the north of Knin, in the Serb-majority region of Lika. The main town, Titova Korenica, had, initially, resisted the SDS, electing, instead, a local authority led by the reformed Communist party, the Party of Democratic Changes (SDP). A series of popular rallies, stage-managed by Babić's people, finally chased the town's moderate leadership from office, to be replaced, eventually, by SDS hardliners loyal to Knin.

In late February, an angry crowd of Serb nationalists staged another *Meeting of Truth* rally, this time at Plitvice, to protest against the setting up of a Croatian police station in the park.[4] They accused Zagreb of trying to "appropriate" the park, and called for the resignation of the park's managers. Within days, Milan Martić had sent a force of armed militiamen, mostly civilians in combat fatigues, to impose, by armed might, the will of the demonstrators on the park. The park's managers were removed and replaced by others, loyal to Knin. Some of the workforce was dismissed.

On March 30 the Croatian government responded. It called the Plitvice uprising "the most extreme violation of the constitution and the law of the republic of Croatia... [which] threatens the sovereignty of the republic, the constitutional order and the rights of the citizens."[5] The Plitvice rebels were warned to return the park to its former managers and staff, or face police intervention. They were reminded of the precedent set by the Croatian police intervention at Pakrac.

Croatia's Deputy Interior Minister, Slavko Degoricija,[6] contacted the Serb Mayor of Korenica, Boško Božanić. But Božanić told him that he had no control over Martić's men. They had come from Knin and had imposed their will.

Degoricija sent an intervention unit. This time, the Serbs were better prepared, and met force with force.

The Croatian police special units arrived at five o'clock on the morning of March 31, Easter weekend. But Martić's men had erected barricades, and lay in wait. Two miles inside the park, the column of vehicles was ambushed. There was a fifteen-minute firefight. A rocket-propelled grenade was fired at a coach-load of Croatian policemen, but failed to explode. The Croatian police units outnumbered and outgunned the rebels. In the battle for control of the local post office, the first casualties of Yugoslavia's wars occurred, one on each side: Josip Jović, a policeman in his early twenties, and Rajko Vukadinović, a local butcher-turned-militiaman, from Korenica, in his thirties.

136

This Croat and this Serb were the first to die in Yugoslavia's wars of secession.

While the rest of the world was still preoccupied with the aftermath of the Gulf War in which a multinational force had evicted Iraqi troops from Kuwait, this first spilling of blood sent shock-waves through Yugoslavia, further polarizing public opinion in the two dominant nations. In Belgrade, the extreme nationalist Serbian National Renewal Party accused the Croatian Government of "warmongering" and warned that "the entire Serbian nation," in Yugoslavia and abroad, was behind the Serbs in Croatia. For the first time, the Serbian Government formally recognized the existence of Babić's self-declared "Serb Autonomous Province of Krajina." The SPS, Milošević's ruling party in Serbia, sent an "urgent delegation" to Knin to assess what "forms of aid" Serbia could make available to the Serbs of Croatia. In Sarajevo, the leader of the Bosnian branch of the SDS, Radovan Karadžić, called for an armed force of the Serbian people to be set up throughout the Serb lands of Yugoslavia. He goaded the federal authorities for failing in their constitutional duty. The Plitvice events had, he said, represented the "greatest defeat for the Presidency of Yugoslavia which has not even been able to implement its own decision to disarm the militias." He said the Federal Army no longer instilled the kind of trust that it had earned when it had saved Knin from armed intervention by the Croats the previous August.[7]

The Army responded. In Belgrade, Jović convened an emergency meeting of the Federal Presidency. It called for a four-point plan to defuse the tension at Plitvice:

1. a full and unconditional cease-fire.
2. JNA to ensure cease-fire is respected.
3. withdrawal of all police units from outside the area.
4. combat-readiness to be raised among certain units of the Yugoslav Peoples' Army.

For the second time in as many months, the Army was on the streets of Croatia. By the following morning, April 1, JNA-armored units were positioned at all main bridges, public buildings and road intersections in the area.

But the JNA was still not offering the kind of assistance that the Serb rebels were expecting, and were eventually – though not yet – to receive. Korenica's mayor, Božanić, had, in the early hours of March 31, sent an urgent telex to Belgrade, pleading with the over-statement that is characteristic of SDS leaders: "We are completely surrounded. Take urgent steps or we will all be liquidated." He complained bitterly that the Army had not arrived until eight hours after the shooting had begun. As the Croat forces were establishing their control in the region, he was on the phone to Radio Belgrade's main lunchtime news program, declaring that:

The Army has arrived now, but we are totally dissatisfied with it. We consider such a delay unacceptable in such a critical situation. We have two people dead and many wounded. We feel unprotected and at extreme risk, and we are calling on the whole of the democratic Yugoslav public to raise its voice against the unprecedented terror of the Croatian constabulary.[8]

Indeed, it was the Croats who praised the Army's involvement. The only part the JNA had played in the conflict was the ferrying of the wounded to hospital by helicopter. Otherwise, the Croatian police were left to do the job they had set out to do. Twenty-nine Serb rebels were arrested, eight of them, according to the Croatian Interior Ministry, wearing the uniforms of Serb special forces, the remainder, civilians in combat fatigues.

On April 1, Tudjman rejected the Federal Presidency order of the previous day to withdraw his police force, declaring that a police station would be established in Plitvice armed "with all the force necessary to keep peace and order." There followed another round of brinkmanship between the Croatian and federal governments, translated now, for the first time, into a stand-off between armored units – of the JNA on one side and the Croatian police on the other. Kadijević asked the Presidency to authorize the Army to act if the Croatian police had not withdrawn by 1 p.m. local time. That night, the Croatian special forces pulled out; but they were replaced by ninety regular police officers from the nearby town of Gospić.

All Krajina was on a knife edge. The village of Kijevo, fifteen miles from Knin, was populated exclusively by Croats, but surrounded on all sides by Serb villages (an enclave within an enclave). On April 1, the villagers grew nervous. A bomb had exploded on the outskirts of the village in the early hours, causing no damage or injury, but rocking the inhabitants into consciousness of the precariousness of their situation. They erected barricades at the entrances to the village.

In Knin, the Serb authorities began to compile lists of men of military age who were willing to fight. They boasted that throngs of young Serbs were coming forward to volunteer for combat in the wake of the Plitvice events. Milan Martić told a protest rally that "the President of Serbia has promised to send arms."[9] He said if the JNA did not take action against the new Croatian police station in Plitvice, then Krajina "would drive them out in the way it sees fit." Thirty thousand men had volunteered to defend the Krajina Serbs, he said. Hours later, in the dead of night, a series of explosions in Knin destroyed a bakery and a café, both owned by Croats.

Plitvice sent ripples of alarm throughout Yugoslavia. It hurled the Slovenes one step further down the path to secession which they had chosen. For them, the intervention of the JNA was a dangerous foreshadowing of things to come. President Kučan believed that it proved that the JNA was trying to redraw Yugoslavia's internal borders. He announced that he would immediately ask the Slovene Assembly to adopt a declaration of sovereignty because, as he put it, in the event of a JNA coup, the Assembly might not be able to meet to declare anything.

The next day, April 2, Franjo Tudjman followed suit. He addressed a Croatian Youth rally and declared himself in favor of reconstituting Yugoslavia as a confederation of sovereign republics, each with its own armed forces. But, he said, if Slovenia unilaterally seceded, Croatia "would not stay a day longer." And it would not allow an inch of Croatian territory to be taken out of the republic.[10]

It had been a tumultuous and portentous Easter weekend. The clouds of war had closed in on Croatia and, briefly, the storm had broken. Mainland Europe suffered its first casualties of war since 1948.[11] The positions of both sides had hardened. Yugoslavia had taken another – and, on the part of some of the players, wilful – lurch toward war. And 200 bewildered and frightened Italian tourists, arguably the first western Europeans to wake up to the tragedy that was about to unfold, had spent twenty-four hours in the middle of a pitched battle, only to be driven, at eight o'clock in the morning, out of the sudden war zone, and back to the holiday resorts of the Dalmatian coast. The 1991 tourist season had begun, although the industry was having its worst year for three decades. The foreign holiday-makers were largely oblivious of what was happening in the hinterland. But an atmosphere of foreboding had settled on Croatia. There seemed a terrible inevitability. Full-scale war was less than three months away.

One of the men arrested at Plitvice, and subsequently released, was the Secretary of the Vukovar branch of the SDS, Goran Hadžić. His name meant little at the time. But it was soon to loom large. Babić's rebellion was spreading far beyond the confines of his *Kninska Krajina*. The plains of eastern Slavonia, the flat, vulnerable, fertile territory, that stretches towards the Danube valley in the east, and whose cornfields had filled the bread-baskets of central Europe for generations, were now stirring to the strains of Serb and Croat nationalism. This land had been farmed, for centuries, by national communities too numerous to count. Croats, Serbs, Czechs, Slovaks, Ruthenes, Italians, Hungarians and, until 1945, Germans, had lived together on this southern rim of the Austro-Hungarian empire. The clash of the two great empires to its north and south notwithstanding, Slavonia had enjoyed a tradition of peaceful coexistence for hundreds of years.

But the twentieth century had brought disruptions to this delicate multinational patchwork. New tensions were to manifest themselves in ethnic conflict. The real divide in Slavonia was not between Serbs and Croats. It was between the old settlers and the new. The *starosedioci* of all nationalities could date their presence on this territory to the fifteenth or sixteenth centuries. After the creation of Yugoslavia, in 1918, they were shaken by two successive waves of immigration from other parts of the new state – first, after 1918, and then after 1945. The *starosedioci* spoke disparagingly of their new neighbors, the *došljaci* (newcomers), refugees from further south settling in the homes of German or Hungarian families who had been killed or expelled after the World Wars. Slavonia had regarded itself as the southern extremity of central Europe, living under the civilizing influence of Viennese hegemony. Those who came from further south were from lands that had been, for centuries, under the yoke of the Ottoman Turks, or from Herzgovina, a land that seemed to breed nationalists; whatever their nationality, the *došljaci* were, the old settlers believed, barbarians.

The Plitvice events set Slavonia on edge. The SDS immediately demanded that the entire region be annexed to Serbia. Across the great plains, in Serb villages and towns, barricades went up, and came down, rising and falling as a barometer of the suspicion and fear that was now taking hold, stoked by the paranoid rhetoric of SDS organizers. Armed village patrols were forming, to mirror those already in existence in Croat-populated areas. It became dangerous, and, in places, impossible to travel long distances – particularly at night, and particularly off the main roads – because of the fear of being stopped by an illegal patrol of armed and often masked men.

Radical HDZ activists did what they could to provoke conflict. In the middle of April, a group of highly-placed HDZ members, led by Gojko Šušak, an extreme nationalist who was one of President Tudjman's closest advisors and whose personal fortune, from an Ottawa pizza company, had helped fund Tudjman's 1990 election campaign, called on the regional police chief Josip Reihl-Kir. Although Kir was of mixed German and Slovene descent, he considered himself Croatian. He was a moderate who had worked tirelessly, on both sides of the rapidly-forming front-lines, to remove barricades and restore mutual trust. Now, Šušak asked Kir to lead him, through the cornfields and along the country paths that criss-cross Slavonia, to the outskirts of Borovo Selo, a Serb-populated village near the town of Vukovar on the Danube.

Kir was against the excursion. He knew that it would inflame the local Serbs. But, under intimidation, he agreed.

From outside the village, Šušak and his companions fired three shoulder-launched Ambrust missiles into the village. "They're crazy," Kir later confided, in disgust and disbelief, to a colleague.[12] One rocket hit a house; another landed in a potato field and failed to explode. It was later exhibited on Belgrade television as evidence of Croat aggression. Petar Gračanin, the Federal Interior Minister, took the unexploded shell to a meeting of the Federal Presidency to wave it in the face of the Croat representative Stipe

Mesić and demand an explanation. Mesić could offer no defense. It was, indisputably, an unprovoked act of aggression, by extremists in Mesić's own party, designed to provoke ethnic conflict.[13]

The three rockets caused no casualties in Borovo Selo. But it gave the Serb villagers every excuse they needed to strengthen their defenses. Kir continued his painstaking efforts to restore confidence between the Serbs and Croats.

Two weeks of heightened tension followed. Kir turned his family home into a fortified police command station. He knew that his commitment to negotiate with the Serbs, to try to defuse tension whenever new barricades appeared, had put his life in danger from Croatian extremists. A permanent police guard was stationed at his house. He took to sleeping in his uniform and boots, night after night.

Šušak's jaunt had lit a slow fuse. Then, on the night of May 1, came the event which, arguably more than any other, set Croatia irrevocably on the path to open war. Four Croatian policemen, from Osijek, learned that a farm road into Borovo Selo had been left unguarded. There was a single barricade on the road – a few agricultural vehicles blocking the way – but it had been left unmanned.

The first of May was the traditional workers' holiday. The villagers of Borovo Selo had put out flags, Yugoslav flags, carrying the Communist five-pointed star. The four Osijek policemen drove into the village in the dead of night, past the unmanned barricade, determined to remove the Yugoslav flag in the center of Borovo Selo and replace it with the Croatian flag, carrying the symbol the Serbs hated – the red-and-white checkerboard shield, the *šahovnica*.

It backfired tragically. The Serbs of Borovo Selo had not left the village unguarded at night. The Croat policemen ran into a hail of gunfire. Two were wounded, and two escaped. The wounded men were taken prisoner.

Discipline had broken down in Tudjman's police force. The influx of so many young Croats, promoted to positions of authority which their age and experience did not warrant, had weakened chains of command and accountability. In Osijek, Croatia's third city and capital of eastern Slavonia, Kir had lost control of his own force. Hardline HDZ officials had gained the upper hand in both the police and the civil administration. Precisely who gave the fateful order for what came next, on the morning of May 2, has never been properly established. But it ended in tragedy.

The two policemen who had escaped returned to Osijek and described what had happened to their colleagues. In the morning, a bus-load of Croatian policemen assembled at Vinkovci and set off for Borovo Selo, determined to rescue the wounded men. They drove straight into a massacre. The incursion the previous night had put the entire village on alert. Serb militiamen were waiting in force. They were stationed throughout the village, guarding road intersections, and covering the main streets from roof tops. Between 10 a.m. and 11 a.m., when the Croatian police bus entered the village, the waiting Serb militiamen opened fire. Twelve Croats were killed and more than twenty wounded.[14]

Borovo Selo caused a sea-change in Croatian public opinion. The Serb "enemy within" was now demonized beyond all reason. The Croatian media launched a campaign that pandered to the worst excesses of Croatian "Serbophobia." Croatian Radio and television began, routinely, to refer to the Serbs of Slavonia as "chetniks" or, frequently, "terrorists." Zagreb television carried photographs of the bodies of the twelve men, claiming autopsy evidence that they had been tortured to death, and subsequently mutilated. The newspapers did not stint in their use of the vocabulary of horror. They said the policemen had died at the "bestial hands" of chetniks. Their eyes had been gouged out before they died and their throats had been cut. One Zagreb daily reported, absurdly, that "It's quite clear that the Croatian police were victims of Romania's notorious ex-secret police, the Securitate. Running away from their own country to escape punishment, numerous agents of the Securitate crossed the Danube and found shelter in the Serbian state secret police. Thirty of them were killed in Borovo Selo. They were professional mercenaries and their bodies were taken to the Danube and thrown into the river."[15]

The extreme Serbian nationalist, Vojislav Šešelj, appeared on Belgrade television boasting that his "chetniks" had taken part in the Borovo Selo events. Radmilo Bogdanović, a close associate of Milošević, and until March 1991 Serbian Interior Minister, later admitted that the Borovo Selo Serbs had been armed by Serbia. Goading the Serbian opposition, Bogdanović asked: "Where was the opposition [then]? If we had not equipped our Serbs, who knows how they would have fared in the attack by the Croatian National Guard on Borovo Selo?"

In Zagreb, Tudjman's ministers gathered in a state of shock, for an emergency session of the State Council. None had been prepared for loss of life on such a scale. Their mood reflected public opinion. Many began to push Tudjman for an immediate declaration of sovereignty by the Croatian Parliament. Tudjman resisted. But the idea to which Tudjman had clung for months, of reconstituting Yugoslavia as a confederation of sovereign states had lost the confidence of his ministers, who now believed that Serbia – and not just the Serbs in Croatia – was determined to block, by bloodshed if necessary, Croatia's progress to full sovereignty.

In the early hours of May 3, Tudjman made a public address, broadcast by Croatian radio. Its tone was both solemn and alarming. For the first time he was alerting the people to the likelihood of war:

> *We have experienced the most tragic day in the short history of the new democratic authorities, a year after the victory of young democracy in Croatia. We are facing, I may say, the beginning of open warfare against the Republic of Croatia.*

He identified the enemy: dogmatic Communism in the JNA had united with Greater Serbian imperialists to defeat democracy and establish "Serboslavia." He blamed the Government of Serbia for sending its officials into Croatia to arm and prepare the republic's Serb minority for military insurrection. He sounded a cautionary note, calling on the Croatian people to "be patient and not to answer the calls of those [extremist Croats] who want spontaneous resistance." But he played to the radicalizing effect that Borovo Selo had had on public opinion with a final call to arms, promising that if all other means of securing Croatia's freedom were to fail, then Croatia would mobilize to defend "every inch" of its territory:

> *If that need arises, if one will have to stand up with arms in one's hands and defend the freedom and sovereignty of the Republic of Croatia, then we shall do so. We shall embark on this only when every other avenue is closed. But we will not shy away from sacrifices if need be. Rest assured that the Croatian government, the Croatian Assembly and I personally, will take all the measures necessary for defending the freedom, democracy, integrity and sovereignty of the Republic of Croatia.*

With the precedents of both Pakrac and Plitvice already established, the Army moved into Borovo Selo. By the afternoon of May 3, it had formed an armored ring around the village, guarding, in particular, the approach road from Vukovar.

The Serbian Government responded tersely and swiftly to Tudjman's open accusation that it was fomenting insurrection and plotting war. "All responsibility for the bloodshed in Borovo Selo lies with the competent bodies of the Republic of Croatia, in particular the Croatian Ministry for Internal Affairs, which without any reason carried out an organized attack on Borovo Selo." The Croatian Government was attacking not just individuals, it added darkly, but "the entire Serb nation." Serb leaders grew increasingly critical of the federal authorities – in particular the Army – for failing to defend the Serbs outside Serbia.

The Federal Presidency met on May 4, under pressure from speaker after speaker, in the Serbian Parliament and on Serbian television. It authorized the JNA to intervene to separate the two sides in disputes between Serbs and Croats. And there were many such conflicts. Throughout May, scarcely a day passed without further intimations of the war that was to engulf Slavonia the following month: a bomb destroyed the front of a house in Lipik; a café owner from Vinkovci was shot dead by unidentified masked men at a road block; a gang of forty attacked a police administration building in Erdut, near Osijek. Both sides were at work.

Voices of moderation were drowned out by those prophesying doom and counselling military readiness. Reihl-Kir, who had worked for months to promote mutual trust between Serbs and Croats began to see that his task was hopeless. He grew convinced that his life was in danger. He asked Police Minister Boljkovac for a transfer to Zagreb. He begged Boljkovac: "Please, save me. I know the situation here very well. I am going to lose my life. We are losing control down here." Hardline HDZ activists such as Gojko Šušak, had taken over, Kir told Boljkovac. They had consistently undermined his efforts to find a rapprochement with the Serbs. Boljkovac initially told Kir not to be "childish," then, in late June, finally recognizing the threat to Kir's life, he agreed to withdraw him to the Croatian capital. But it was too late. Kir was murdered by HDZ extremists on July 1, a day before he was due to leave Slavonia. It is a striking commentary on the direction in which Croatia was moving during those crucial weeks leading to the outbreak of full-scale war, that Kir's moderation, his conciliatory approaches to the Serbs, had cost him his life, while Šušak's activities, stoking tension and provoking conflict, were to win him one of the most prominent places in Tudjman's government. As Minister of Defense, he was second only to Tudjman.

The events of spring 1991 were a watershed. After Milošević's secret March meeting with Tudjman at Karadjordjevo, both leaders decided that Yugoslavia was finished, and that three, or more, successor states would emerge. Where the Serb and Croat leaders differed was on the question of which territories would fall to which new state. Croatia's war of independence, when it came, was not about the Croats' right to secede; that had already been acknowledged by Milošević. It was about which territories Croatia would be allowed to take out of Yugoslavia. The war of 1991 was to be a land-grab between two mutually, though tacitly, recognized new states.

Both presidents played a double-game, saying one thing for public, and especially international, consumption; and doing the opposite. Tudjman repeatedly stressed the inviolability of the republican borders, demanding recognition of Croatian sovereignty within its existing frontiers; but he secretly conspired throughout to deny the same right to Bosnia-Herzegovina. Milošević, similarly, argued that his republic sought to defend the territorial integrity of Yugoslavia as a whole; but he was already pursuing a plan to let the Croats and Slovenes go, but to keep Croatia's Serb-majority areas inside Yugoslavia – and by force if necessary. By March, Milošević was no longer for Yugoslavia; he was for what amounted to a Greater Serbia. But he believed Bosnia, Macedonia and parts of Croatia would remain under his control. As his man on the Federal Presidency, Borisav Jović, was later to admit:

Milošević and I decided we would limit our military activities to those territories in Croatia where the Serbs wanted to remain with us. We would protect them from the Croatian authorities and from the Croatian paramilitary units. We knew we would have to withdraw the Army from those parts which obviously couldn't remain in Yugoslavia, and to close our eyes as far as the arming of the Serbs was concerned.

But Plitvice was a turning-point of sorts, one that the Croatian leadership still did not see, or, if it did, did not admit to. Under pressure from Milošević, the army had no choice. According to Jović:

The army started changing its opinion. It realized that the only role that it had, at that time, was to protect that part of Yugoslavia where the people saw it as their own army, where they did not have to fight with the people. Basically, that is the line of the Serb territory in Croatia. From that time onwards, we started preparing for the decision [of the Federal Presidency] that was to be adopted in May – the decision to use the army to protect the Serbs in Krajina, and to act as a buffer between the Croat and the Serb sides.

In Knin, the cradle of the rebellion, the intervention of the Army was at last a sign that the Serbs would get the support they needed from Belgrade. Milan Martić could now prepare for a war in the knowledge that the JNA, under the guise of defending Yugoslavia, or of separating the two warring national factions, would protect his rebel territories from the legally-constituted authorities of the Croatian Republic. The mutual suspicion that had existed between the Krajina rebels and the JNA began to evaporate. Martić admitted that, after Plitvice, his relationship with the JNA changed:

There were contacts with the JNA at that time, but I personally didn't participate in that. The JNA was pretty indifferent to what was happening apart from a few Serb patriots among the JNA military officers. [But] when Milošević saw that Croatia was getting aggressive towards Krajina, he raised his voice then, and in certain ways gave us support, weapons for our defense. I saw it coming... JNA personnel that were on our side, and also people in police circles, got signals to prepare for war. It meant we would be getting weapons, and other logistic and material help. It came from JNA garrisons nearby, from military officers who were either Yugoslavs or Serb patriots. The help we are talking about came from JNA barracks nearby, not from Serbia as many would like to put it. There were many warehouses nearby.

It had become a standing joke among Belgrade's foreign correspondents that there were too few ways, in the English language, to say "pulled back from the brink." It had seemed that Yugoslavia had spent more than a year approaching the precipice and pulling back. The phrase had turned up in news dispatches from Yugoslavia so frequently that, on newsdesks all over the world, editors began to suspect their correspondents in the field of crying wolf. But, by the end of May, as the country entered the full heat of high summer, there was little to joke about. And there would soon be no more pulling back.

1 Serbs were forty-six percent of the population, Croats thirty-six percent.

2 Vasiljević was furious and screamed accusations at Mesić; Mesić screamed back, enjoying, for once, the upper hand. "I am your Supreme Commander," he yelled, citing, to Vasiljević's irritation, his membership of the Federal Presidency, "and I order you to sit down." The two then sat down and enjoyed a meal of beans together, along with the Federal Interior Minister Petar Gračanin and the Croatian Interior Minister Josip Boljkovac. Before eating, Boljkovac hastily swapped plates with Gračanin, explaining to Mesić as they drove together back to Zagreb afterwards: "They might have been trying to poison me!" "What if they were trying to poison me?" Mesić asked him. Boljkovac replied: "Well, Stipe, there are casualties in every war!"

3 *Financial Times*, June 27, 1991.

4 It was the strategy of Croatia's Interior Ministry to extend and strengthen its network of police stations across the republic, particularly in Serb-populated areas. These would be staffed by the officers recruited since the elections, as part of Tudjman's campaign to "de-Serbianize" the Croatian police force. It explains why so many of the conflicts, in the months that led to the outbreak of full-scale war, centered on the control of police stations.

5 Croatian Deputy Interior Minister Ivan Brezak, on Croatian television, March 30, 1991.

6 Slavko Degoricija had replaced Jurić as one of the deputy interior ministers. Jurić was fired, blamed for the casualties at Plitvice.

7 See Chapter Seven of this book *The Remnants of a Slaughtered People*.

8 Belgrade Radio, March 31, 1991.

9 This was much to Milošević's fury, who later told Babić: "Why don't you dismiss that fool [Martić]?" Martić was, however, later to become Milošević's loyal lieutenant in an internal battle between Milošević and Babić. But Milošević, trying to assert control over Krajina, changed alliances several times.

10 Zagreb Radio, April 2, 1991.

11 Excluding Northern Ireland, which is not mainland Europe, or the Greek Colonels' coup, which was not a war, or the Soviet invasions of Hungary and Czechoslovakia.

12 Zlatko Kramarić, mayor of Osijek.

13 One of Šušak's companions on that night Branimir Glavaš later boasted that Šušak had given him a good thick flak jacket as a reward for his participation. Šušak himself, though never publicly admitting his role in the affair, especially after becoming a minister in Tudjman's Government, alluded to it obliquely in 1992 when, during an election rally, he demonstrated his nationalist credentials by boasting that he had fired the first shell against the "aggressors" in eastern Slavonia.

14 The figures were announced by President Tudjman. Both the Belgrade and Zagreb press initially reported inaccurate figures; no two newspapers agreed on a death toll.

15 *Vjesnik*, May 7, 1991. The claim is ridiculous, and not supported by any evidence. But it is typical, in tone and content, of the reporting which was to dominate the Croatian news media and inflame opinion by spreading terror.

11

CONVERSATIONS OF THE DEAF
The Last Chance Squandered
May–June 1991

Throughout that spring and summer the leaders of Yugoslavia's republics held a series of meetings to try to resolve their differences about the future of the country. A travelling circus of presidential summits took to the road. The Federal Presidency met in extended session – the republics' presidents and foreign and defense ministers in attendance as well as the eight *ex officio* members. On at least half-a-dozen occasions, all the leading decision-makers from the entire country were gathered together, face-to-face, in one room, to "discuss" the future of Yugoslavia. Each time, the main players used the opportunity to reiterate their grievances and reassert their positions. There was no negotiation to speak of; no give-and-take; no progress. Croatia's President, Franjo Tudjman, dismissed the high-powered gatherings as "conversations of the deaf." They were Yugoslavia's last and missed opportunity to avoid war.

The rock on which the discussions foundered, time and again, was the stark contradiction that quickly emerged between two central articles of the Helsinki Final Act: the commitment to the self-determination of nations; and the principle of the inviolability of borders. Unity is the holy grail of modern Serb nationalism; all Serbs in a single state. Milošević did not dispute the right of the Croats or the Slovenes to secede. But he insisted that the Serbs of Croatia had the same right to secede, in turn, from Croatia,[1] and that the break-up of Yugoslavia would necessitate a redrawing of the borders.[2] The internal borders of Yugoslavia had been drawn in 1945.

Despite the failure of the presidential roadshow to find common ground, Slovenia, closely followed by Croatia, strengthened its negotiating position by forging ahead with independence preparations. Its referendum, in December 1990, had produced an overwhelming vote for independence. On May 19, in the highly-charged emotional atmosphere of the aftermath of Borovo Selo, Croatia held its referendum. The result was a foregone conclusion – more than ninety percent for what amounted to outright secession.[3] But Croatia had problems that were not shared by Slovenia, and problems which made the Croats take the road to independence with more caution, and less haste: the Krajina Serbs boycotted Croatia's referendum; there were no polling stations in the territories they controlled.[4]

As Serb and Croat leaders spent the months of spring and early summer articulating mutually-incompatible visions of Yugoslavia's future to each

147

other, it was clear to the leaders of the country's smaller nationalities that, if Slovenia and Croatia seceded, they would be left as marginal peoples in a rump Yugoslavia in which the Serbs would enjoy an overwhelming numerical superiority. In the summer of 1991, Bosnia's President, Alija Izetbegović, and his Macedonian counterpart, Kiro Gligorov, breathed temporary new life into the flagging presidential summits. They proposed what became known as the "asymmetrical federation" as a model for the country's constitution. This formula envisaged Serbia and Montenegro as the heart of the Yugoslav federation (or confederation); Bosnia and Macedonia as semi-detached, but constituent republics; and Croatia and Slovenia exercising as much sovereignty and autonomy inside the confederation as they saw fit. In this way, Izetbegović and Gligorov believed, both the Serbs' desire for a single state, and Croat and Slovene aspirations to sovereignty could be accommodated. When the travelling presidential summit rolled into Sarajevo in early June, the proposal gained the temporary support of both Milošević and Tudjman.

But its terms were obscure. It was a constitutional plan that was all things to all republics. That was both its appeal and its downfall. The Slovenes played their part in the scuttling of the plan by declaring, in the Ljubljana Parliament on June 12, less than a week after the Izetbegović-Gligorov plan had ignited a flicker of hope that the constitutional stalemate might break, that their preparations for independence would be completed by the end of the month. Tudjman had already declared that, if Slovenia seceded, Croatia would not stay "a day longer" in Yugoslavia.

On the same day, June 12, the presidents of Serbia, Croatia and Bosnia gathered in Croatia's second city, the ancient port of Split on the Dalmatian coast, at a meeting that had been agreed in Sarajevo, and the purpose of which was to discuss the Izetbegović-Gligorov plan. But by the time the meeting took place, neither of Izetbegović's more powerful neighbors wanted to discuss his proposal. Like the Slovenes, Tudjman and Milošević were already too far down the roads they had mapped out for themselves. Despite an official *Tanjug* report of the meeting, which recorded that "the maximum degree of openness and goodwill was evident in the talks," Izetbegović later admitted that he had had to keep "forcing" the other two to address themselves to the asymmetrical confederation plan, when, all along, all Tudjman and Milošević wanted to discuss was the cantonization of Bosnia. Izetbegović went back to Sarajevo dejected, but not yet fully cognizant of what was about to take place. He said the word "canton" had not been used, at least not in his presence, but he admitted that the ethnic division of his republic had been present "between the lines." In fact, it had been discussed, by the Milošević and Tudjman delegations, not between the lines, but behind his back.

While the presidential caravan was the public face of the ill-fated attempts to agree a constitutional future for Yugoslavia, the Croats and Slovenes, in private, held a series of bi-lateral talks aimed at coordinating their joint escape from the federation. These had begun in 1990. Croatia had, in the early months, counselled caution. Tudjman's advisor, Dušan Bilandžić, who later became the Croatian deputy representative in Belgrade, remembered one such meeting, at which he tried to impress upon Kučan the need to wait. "Hang on a bit," Bilandžić told Kučan. "If you take it slowly, stage by stage, the rest of us can come along – Bosnia and Macedonia, as well as Croatia. Wait for an anti-Milošević coalition." But it was easy for the Slovenes; they had no Serb population, and Milošević had already made it plain that Serbia would not fight to keep the Slovenes in Yugoslavia. In April, Slovenia and Croatia signed a joint defense agreement, promising mutual assistance and the sharing of intelligence.[5] Tudjman was to renege on the agreement the day that the JNA rolled across his territory and into Slovenia.

The Slovenes had left the Croats far behind in almost every respect. After their December referendum, the Slovene Government had embarked on a six-month plan to prepare the legislation and the executive orders that would enable the country to implement full independence by the summer of 1991. By June, they were ready. On June 15, three days after the Tudjman-Milošević-Izetbegović summit in Split, the Slovenian and Croatian leaders met. The meeting revealed to the Slovenes just how unready the Croats were. According to Bavčar:

> *This meeting was organized to coordinate all the things for the 26th of June. At that moment we decided that we will do it together on the 25th or 26th. We got to Banski Dvori, and Tudjman was there, and his ministers. We told him what we would do with the customs, the police, airports, boundaries. They were shocked to see the level of our organization.*

The Croats, whose referendum had been held only the previous month, had not even begun their preparations for full statehood. Tudjman, embarrassed by the disparity, pompously tried to disguise his republic's unreadiness. Rupel remembered Tudjman, even at this late stage, bluffing his way through the meeting.

> *We explained to Tudjman that we had our new laws ready, and that we would like to coordinate the dates for our declarations of independence, because Tudjman said that they wanted to go out at the same time as us. This was a more or less secret agreement. The deadline was June 26. We decided to do it on June 25, and Tudjman said that we should do it on the same day at the same time. The Slovene delegation was surprised about the fact that the*

Croatian government did not have anything ready. There was almost a con-
flict between Tudjman and one of his ministers, Franjo Gregurić, because
Tudjman said 'We have everything ready too, all the laws, everything is pre-
pared.' And Gregurić said 'No Mr. President, this is not true.'

The two sides agreed to coordinate their declarations of independence. But the Slovenes left the meeting convinced that the Croats could not be trusted. Slovenia would press ahead with independence unilaterally, regardless of Croatia's readiness, and without regard to the ramifications their secession would have on the rest of Yugoslavia.

On June 21, four days before Croatia and Slovenia were to declare their independence, the US Secretary of State, James Baker – preoccupied with the need to deliver his promise to bring peace to the Middle East in the aftermath of Operation Desert Storm – passed through Belgrade. The Gulf War, in the words of the then-President George Bush, had established the United States as the "respected and undisputed leader of the free world." All sides in Yugoslavia's conflict set great store on Baker's visit; all sides wanted to see him. He held eleven separate meetings in a single day: one with each of the republics' presidents, and a series with the Federal Government, on whom the international community were still putting great faith. In common with the governments of western Europe, US policy was that the unity and integrity of Yugoslavia should be preserved.

The content of Baker's meetings remain a matter of great historical controversy. What signals did he give the respective leaders about what the United States would tolerate? According to Baker's own recollections of the day, the United States was already defeatist about its chances of preventing war:

The question was whether I should go and try and put down a marker, if you
will, of what we thought would happen if there was anything other than a
peaceful break. We weren't naive but we felt that if we didn't make the effort
we would be accused of not even being willing to try. So knowing full well
that we had very little chance of succeeding, we went and made the effort.

Baker met the Slovene President Kučan in Belgrade, and asked him whether Slovenia was ready to give up the idea of independence. He warned him that the Helsinki Final Act recognized only peaceful self-determination, and not secession by force. He said the United States would not recognize unilateral declarations of independence. Kučan told him frankly that things had gone too far, and that it was not possible to preserve Yugoslavia as it had been.

When he met the Serb leadership, he told them that the US would continue to press the Slovenes and Croats not to go ahead with independence, but that, equally, the US would not countenance the use of force to prevent declarations of independence. These were the same mixed signals that the US Ambassador to Yugoslavia, Warren Zimmermann, had been issuing for months. United States policy on secession, during the crucial months that led to war, was neither one thing nor the other: support for Yugoslav unity, yes; use of force to preserve that unity, no. And to the Slovenes and Croats: support for self-determination, yes; unilateral declarations of independence should negotiations fail, no.

Baker's meeting with the Montenegrin leader, Momir Bulatović, must have made him yearn for the familiar and relatively simple dynamics of the conflict in the Middle East. Bulatović said Baker was, at the outset of the meeting, obviously confused about who he was talking to and why.

> *When I met Mr. Baker I said 'Tell me what you want from me.' He was confused about how to start the conversation with me, until they brought him his briefing book. I looked into it to see what it said about Montenegro. I peeked into it and there were just two lines:*
> *- the smallest republic in Yugoslavia.*
> *- a possible fifth vote for Mesić.*

Milošević's placement on the Federal Presidency had blocked the automatic succession of Croatia's representative Stipe Mesić as president of the country's eight-member collective-head-of-state. Under the constitution Mesić should have become Yugoslavia's president on May 15. By the time of Baker's visit, technically the country had already been without a president for six weeks. It is a measure of how little Baker understood about the distance Yugoslavia had already travelled that he still thought that securing the succession of Mesić would somehow defuse the crisis. Bulatović continued:

> *I said I'd be happy if Mr. Mesić gets elected but I'm not going to vote for him. Baker said if we didn't vote for Mesić, there would be a great crisis and war would start. I agreed with him that war would start, but I didn't expect Mesić's election would stop it.*

Baker's meeting with Federal Prime Minister Ante Marković remains the most difficult to fathom. According to the former Defense Minister, Admiral Branko Mamula, who was Veljko Kadijević's most trusted advisor throughout the crisis that led to the war, Baker told Marković to "wrap the Slovenes gently on the knuckles." Marković has been silent about his role in the run-up to Slovenia's ten-day war; neither man has confirmed that the phrase was used.

151

Baker's visit took place five days before the outbreak of war. On that day, two of Tudjman's closest ministers discovered, through personal contacts in Belgrade, which neither ever divulged publicly, that the Federal Army had decided to respond to Slovenia's independence declaration by force. Dušan Bilandžić remained in Belgrade after the Baker meeting. An old friend, whose identity he has never revealed, warned him of the invasion plan. Bilandžić went back to Zagreb immediately, and woke Tudjman shortly after midnight on the morning of June 22. Bilandžić says he told Tudjman that the Army was planning to attack Slovenia in five days time. Tudjman, according to Bilandžić, laughed and said: "Oh, Duško, don't worry so. I have an agreement with Kadijević and Milošević. They won't break it. It's impossible. Kadijević has promised that the Army won't intervene in politics." Bilandžić then told Tudjman the name of his source in Belgrade, an officer "very high up" in the JNA. Tudjman again refused to believe him. Stipe Mesić, party to the conversation throughout, stood by in silence. Tudjman's complacency left him despondent.

Tudjman's Defense Minister, Martin Špegelj, after a lifetime in the JNA, had also retained clandestine personal contacts in Belgrade. He, too, learned of the Army's plans on the day of Baker's visit:

> *I knew the JNA was going to attack five days before independence. I had my intelligence sources in Belgrade, some of them were Serbs. I notified the Slovenes, and Kučan then phoned Tudjman and asked 'Are you going to join us in common defense?' Tudjman said 'No.' The full answer was 'It is not in the Croatian interest to interfere in a war between Slovenia and Serbia.'*

Kučan was furious that the agreement the two presidents had come to only two months earlier, and reiterated at their meeting in Tudjman's presidential palace at Banski Dvori less than a week earlier, was now being flouted by the Croatian president. "I told him this was very shortsighted," Kučan said later.

> *Sooner or later the JNA would oppose Croatia. But he replied that if Croatia intervened it would involve opening armed conflict in their own territory. He said they were not ready for war and didn't have enough arms – which is all true. But I told him that helping Slovenia is the same thing as defending Croatia.*

On the very eve of war, Tudjman was still paying no heed to the advice of his Defense Minister, Špegelj. It was the closing stages in the dispute between the two. Špegelj was soon to resign in bitter protest against a president whom he blamed for blindly leading his country into a war without first preparing an adequate defense.

1 Though, of course, Milošević never conceded the same right of national self-determination to the Albanians of Kosovo or the Muslims of Serbia's Sandžak region. Milošević had risen to power on the issue of Serb rights to rule Kosovo, even though Albanians comprised more than ninety percent of the province's population.

2 This, despite the fact that only about 200,000 of the Serbs in Croatia lived in the Serb-majority areas, nearly a third of Croatia's total Serb minority. Most of Croatia's Serbs lived in Croat-majority areas that Milošević had no intention of "defending."

3 Ninety-three percent of those voting supported turning Croatia into a "sovereign and independent" country, with guaranteed cultural autonomy for "the Serbs and members of other nationalities in Croatia." To a second question, asking whether Croatia should remain part of a federal Yugoslavia, 92 percent voted "No." The turn-out was 82 percent.

4 In August 1990, the Krajina Serbs had held a referendum of their own in which more than ninety-nine percent, according to the organizers, voted to stay in Yugoslavia.

5 According to the Croatian Defense Minister Martin Špegelj, who negotiated the agreement with his Slovene counterpart Janez Janša.

PART THREE: THE EXPLOSION OF WAR

12

"THE HOUR OF EUROPE HAS DAWNED"
Slovenia's Phoney War, June–July 1991

Slovenia declared itself independent by a near unanimous vote of its Parliament on the evening of June 25, 1991, unilaterally making the first changes to the international borders of Europe since Yalta.[1] Croatia also declared independence that day.

Unlike the Croats, the Slovenes had prepared well for secession.[2] They had backed their independence legislation with executive orders, creating and staffing the independent bodies that would, on the June 26, assume control of the borders, the air traffic, and the port authorities. At the frontiers with Italy, Austria and Hungary, they removed the Yugoslav symbols, flags and noticeboards, and replaced them with the heraldry of the new independent Republic of Slovenia. They ordered federal police and customs officials off the premises. They also began to place border posts along the 600-kilometer frontier with neighboring Croatia, an act that the Federal Government had, the previous day, declared illegal.

At the formal celebrations the next day, Colonel Milan Aksentijević[3] was, by his own account "in no mood to drink Champagne." Conspicuously, he had been one of the few members of Parliament[4] to vote against the declaration, and, though the other MPs kept handing him brimming glasses, and Slovene TV crews tried to catch him sipping discreetly, he was not celebrating. It was to be Yugoslavia's last day of formal peace. Aksentijević knew – as did the Slovene leaders – that the Army had been placed on alert.

Belgrade preempted Ljubljana. On the same day as the independence declaration, the Federal Parliament met, and agreed not to recognize Slovenia's secession.[5] Milošević was playing a double game. On one hand he was encouraging Slovenia to secede, on the other hand Belgrade was accusing it of unilateral secession. The Federal Government, headed by Prime Minister Ante Marković, also met, and issued a decree of enforcement, the purpose of which has been the subject of fierce controversy ever since. The JNA was without a Supreme Commander and the state without a president because Serbia had blocked the normal rotation of Croatia's Stipe Mesić to the head of the Presidency on the grounds that he had publicly declared himself against Yugoslavia. The decree's terms were clear enough: it empowered the Defense Minister and the Interior Minister to "deploy the frontier units of the JNA with the aim of safeguarding the state frontiers at the border-crossings."[6] What is less clear is what Marković intended by the decree. He insisted, almost immediately when fighting broke out, that the decree had never been intended to authorize the Federal Army to use force against the Slovenes. But whatever Marković's motivation – almost certainly pressure from the Army – two of his most senior ministers used it as the constitutional authority on which to send in the tanks.

The Federal Interior Minister, Petar Gračanin, sent a request to the JNA's Fifth Army District in Zagreb.[7] He told the commander there, General Konrad Kolšek (who was, incidentally, a Slovene), to provide troops and transport to accompany federal police units, first to barracks in Slovenia, and from there to the border posts to which they were assigned. Throughout that day and into the night, General Kolšek, and his deputy, General Andrija Rašeta, worked out a detailed plan to bring back into federal control thirty-five[8] land border-crossings, one airport (Ljubljana's Brnik airport), and one seaport (Koper).

From the beginning, Belgrade adopted a determinedly legalistic approach to the Slovene crisis. For six months, the Federal Defense Minister, Veljko Kadijević had wanted JNA action to hold Yugoslavia together. But he did not want the JNA accused of staging a military coup. He had exercised restraint precisely because he did not want to act outside the constitution. He acted now in a way which he considered consistent with that constraint, and consistent with constitutional rule. He sought, and he believed he had received, all the constitutional authority he needed for what he intended to be a limited military intervention in Slovenia. The orders and decrees passed by Belgrade on the June 25 carried the signature of the Prime Minister. They were published in the constitutionally-prescribed way: by being lodged in the *Official Gazette of the Socialist Federal Republic of Yugoslavia*. They were due to come into effect one day after their publication therein. The Slovenes, thus, had at least twenty-four hours notice that the JNA had been ordered to act.

In fact, they had more precise information even than that. Throughout the ten-day period that Slovene leaders were later to claim as their war of independence, they were in constant telephone contact with the JNA commanders they were fighting against. According to Igor Bavčar:

> *It may sound strange but in 10 days of war we had a daily or even hourly communication with the Army. The staff that led the operations were in constant contact with us. We usually talked to each other issuing ultimatums, talking over the phone about the operations while they were going on.*

At the beginning, the Generals did not regard it as a war. They regarded it – and resourced it – as a limited policing action. And, as such, they informed the Slovene authorities in advance of what they were planning to do – including, according to the JNA, disclosing the precise routes that the Army units were to take. A force that is preparing to "invade and occupy a neighboring country" (as the Slovenes protested) does not release its invasion plans the day before D-Day.

That at least was Plan A, the plan that was in the event put into effect. But the JNA also had a Plan B: the entire Fifth Military District was standing by, ready to move against Slovenia. The élite 63rd Airborne brigade, from Niš in southern Serbia, had been deployed at Slovenia's Cerklje airforce base along with a military police battalion; they had precise plans about which positions to take and whom to arrest. They knew that the Slovene TO was well-equipped, well-organized and large. Plan B provided for the invasion of Slovenia, the military defeat of the Slovene TOs, the arrest and imprisonment of Slovene leaders and the imposition of martial law on the republic. Plan B was never to be implemented.

As his independence celebrations were getting under way, President Kučan spoke to General Kolšek in Zagreb, and asked him not to undertake any JNA operations in Slovenia on that day. Kučan feared it would enrage the people at the height of their celebrations. Kolšek was able to reassure him that no action would be undertaken that day. In fact, the plan had been laid to re-take control of the border-crossings and the airport in the early hours of the following day.

On June 25 and 26, Plan A began. A force of 400 federal police and 270 federal customs officers were taken to Cerklje air force base in Slovenia and, from there, by helicopters, to the various barracks in Slovenia and Croatia, from which they were to be dispatched. Fewer than 2,000 JNA troops were deployed to accompany them. It was scarcely the assembling of an invasion force.[9]

Early on June 27, the JNA began the operations which the Slovenes were later to characterize as the invasion and foreign occupation of their newly independent country. The JNA officers in command of the operation believed the whole thing would be over in hours. They did not expect the Slovene territorial defense to try to oppose them by force; and they were not equipped, or sufficiently armed, to fight a war against the Slovenes.

An anti-aircraft unit from Karlovac, in northwestern Croatia, left its barracks at 1:30 a.m., tasked to reach the Slovene border by 3 a.m. Its movement was spotted by Croatian police, who informed their counterparts in Slovenia.

President Kučan was getting ready for bed when, by his account of the affair, he found out that JNA troops were on the move. He had been working late, on a speech.

> *I was having a shower when the phone rang. It was my chief of cabinet. He told me the tanks had left Vrhnika barracks [in Slovenia] and said the war had started. I immediately called General Kolšek in Zagreb, but couldn't get*

him. I asked to speak to anybody from the Zagreb command, but nobody answered. I called Ante Marković in Belgrade, woke him up, told him what it was about and told him he was responsible for the order which was released then by General Kadijević.

Marković expressed surprise and appeared not to know what was happening, even though, that day, his own Government had issued the decrees on which Kadijević and Gračanin, as Defense and Interior Ministers, were now acting. Marković contacted the Fifth Military Command in Zagreb and told them to speak to Kučan. The Deputy Commander, Andrija Rašeta, called the Slovene President. "Why are you so annoyed?" he asked Kučan. "The troops that have left the barracks are not even armed. Calm down and go back to sleep."[10] Kučan exploded. He shouted down the phone that he regarded the JNA intervention as a declaration of war against Slovenia. Rašeta tried to reassure Kučan that the Army had a limited mission – to secure the border-crossings and the airport and no more. If the JNA had intended to wage war against Slovenia, he told Kučan, it would have acted in a wholly different way – by mobilizing all the units from Croatia and Slovenia.

Kučan went to his office. He called the Slovene leadership together, and, at five in the morning, convened what must rank as one of the most decisive sessions, and certainly the least loquacious, in Yugoslav political history. He asked Janša, as Defense Minister, to give an account of what was going on. Janša's report was brief. He spoke in short dramatic sentences. The 13th (Rijeka) Corps of the JNA was on its way, he said. The Slovene TO had erected barricades – agricultural vehicles and commandeered articulated trucks, mostly – but had not yet received orders to defend them. In some areas, JNA armored vehicles had simply pushed the barricades aside and carried on. Tanks had left Vrhnika barracks near Ljubljana and could be heard heading towards the airport. Janša said he had already spoken to the second-in-command of the Vrhnika barracks, General Vidmar. "General Vidmar was quiet for a while, and then said it was not something he had control of," Janša said. "I asked him then where the tanks were heading, and, after a silence, he replied '*Brnik*' (airport)." Janša then, according to his own account, said that the [Slovene] Presidency should order armed resistance to "this aggression."[11]

To each of the main players, fully aware of the gravity of the decision they had to take, the meeting seemed to last an eternity. In fact, it lasted only a few minutes, and most of these were passed in silence. Janša concluded his brief remarks by saying that there were two alternatives: either to give in, and, in so doing, sacrifice the historic opportunity for independence, or to resist. "These are the two alternatives," he said, "now it's up to you the [Slovene] Presidency to decide because you are the Supreme Commander." And then there was silence. According to Kučan:

I believe that everybody was conscious of how important the decision was, everybody had in mind the victims claimed by war, because nobody knew at that stage what kind of war it would be and for how long it would last. Everybody was occupied with their own thoughts. It was a long silence. I interrupted it by saying 'Does anybody want to speak?' There was silence again. Then I said 'Then I'll speak. I suggest we face the fact that we are at war.'

There was silence again. "Do I take it from your silence," Kučan asked, "that we have reached a consensus on this?" And that was it. The order went out to the territorial defense units to begin resisting the JNA. Kučan made a television address in which he announced that his republic would "respond with all measures to this act of aggression." The territorial defense units had, he said, been ordered to "use weapons to defend the sovereignty of Slovenia."

Yugoslavia, after almost a year of teetering on the edge of the precipice, had, at last, plunged headlong into war.

Slovene territorial defense forces moved to surround the JNA bases in Slovenia. Electricity and water supplies were cut. Telephone lines were disconnected. Igor Bavčar telephoned General Rašeta in Zagreb and warned him not to try to resupply the barracks by helicopter. Rašeta did not take the implied threat seriously. In the afternoon of June 27, Slovene forces shot down a helicopter carrying bread over central Ljubljana.[12] The pilot and mechanic on board were killed. Aksentijević, trapped, with his troops, inside his barracks, was stunned by an escalation he had not expected:

I realized that this was not a revolt or a political demonstration, but that it was war. I think that was the moment when we cracked within. We realized that they wanted to kill us, to shoot us, that there was no Yugoslavia and that there was no more life together with them.

The shooting down of the helicopter was a turning point in Slovene public opinion, too – the moment when most Slovenes realized the enormity of what their Government had decided on their behalf, and that there was now no turning back. Slovenia declared war on the JNA, not the other way around. Slovene television "milked" the conflict for every ounce of propaganda value. Throughout that first day, it carried dramatic pictures of the 1968 Soviet invasion of Czechoslovakia, to complement Kučan's explicit call to arms. Bavčar and Rašeta exchanged an angry telephone call, Rašeta, near to tears, shouting at Bavčar his disbelief that the Slovenes had dared to open fire on a target so exposed and unthreatening as a low-flying and unarmed helicopter. To Rašeta's disgust, Bavčar appeared, as the general put it, "triumphalist."

* * *

The United States, after James Baker's half-hearted efforts in Belgrade the previous week, made it clear that it regarded Yugoslavia as Europe's problem. Europe happily rose to the challenge. The year, 1991, was a bright confident age: the twelve countries of the European Community were soon to become the European Union. The single European market was due to come into effect the following year – the world's biggest single unrestricted trading block. Integrationists were talking positively about a common foreign policy, and a common security policy; mechanisms were already being devised. The British Prime Minister Margaret Thatcher, the most celebrated opponent of further European integration, had been deposed less than a year earlier, her downfall this very issue. Yugoslavia, the first armed conflict of the post-Cold-War age, presented the historic challenge that Europe needed to prove its singleness of purpose. In a phrase that would haunt him, Jacques Poos, Luxembourg's Foreign Minister, declared, "The hour of Europe has dawned."

The European Community had stated its position the previous week. A meeting of EC Foreign Ministers had agreed, on June 23, not to recognize unilateral declarations of independence. The day after fighting erupted, the British Prime Minister, John Major, reiterated the view. "The first prize is to hold the federation together in Yugoslavia," he said. The Twelve then issued a second draft statement, calling for the restoration of constitutional order and respect for the territorial integrity of the country. The JNA, of course, had sent the tanks in precisely, as it saw it, to achieve these two objectives. The unity of the Twelve began to crack. Some of Europe's leaders began to see that, inadvertently, in their support for Yugoslavia's unity, they had given a green light to the Yugoslav Generals to use force.

Jacques Poos was one of the three members of the EC troika, the group of foreign ministers which consists of the last, the current and the next presidents of the community.[13] He and his Dutch and Italian counterparts, Hans van den Broek and Gianni de Michelis, sailed into the Yugoslav maelstrom the day after war broke out. From the beginning, international mediators – and this was a pattern which, with few exceptions, was to characterize their efforts for many months – behaved as though the war had no underlying structural causes at all. They came – in the phrase of many a subsequent mediator – to "bang heads together," as though the conflict was caused by no more than some ill-defined, but frequently alluded to, Balkan temperament, a south Slavic predisposition – either cultural or genetic – toward fratricide. They behaved as though all they had to do was to persuade the belligerents of the folly of war. They failed to recognize that, in some circumstances, the resort to war was far from irrational. It was, for President Kučan's Government on that fateful night, a profoundly rational, and indeed the only, way to achieve what they wanted.

The troika arrived in Belgrade on June 28. Their first instinct was to preserve the *status quo*: Slovenia must revoke its independence declaration; Belgrade must send the JNA back to barracks. The Serbs must also be persuaded to agree to Mesić's assumption of the Presidency of the Federal Presidency.

By the time the troika arrived in Zagreb, to meet the Croat and Slovene leaders, it was already late in the evening. President Kučan drove across the mountain tracks, the main highway being blocked, mostly by his own forces. At Tudjman's presidential palace, Banski Dvori, dinner was served at two a.m. Vasil Tupurkovski, Macedonia's representative on the Federal Presidency, who had spent most of the day in Slovenia trying to find terms for a ceasefire, arrived after midnight to find a room full of between twenty and thirty Croats, Slovenes and EC officials. There was no structured discussion, no ordered negotiation. The troika had asked Kučan and Janša to revoke the declaration of independence. The Slovenes, sensing that the "war" was going their way, refused.

The troika left next morning believing they had secured a three-point ceasefire agreement: the Slovenes and Croats would put their independence on hold for three months; the JNA would return to barracks; and Mesić would be elected to take his turn as President of the Presidency, thus giving the Army a Supreme Commander, and the country a Head of State. But the Slovenes had not really agreed to anything, and were certainly not ready to give up now, just as they sensed the tide turning favorably in their direction. The agreement, in any case, left unresolved the question at the heart of the conflict: that of who should control the border-crossings and the airport. Janša said the results of the first troika-intervention were so disappointing that they were not made public in Slovenia for fear that they would damage morale, claiming that the people there had placed great faith in the idea of Europe.

> *The troika demanded that we freeze all measures of independence for 90 days, and to revoke the proclamation of independence then. This was unacceptable for us, because we had practically won the war by then. If we had accepted we would have to give back all the weapons confiscated from the JNA, and give back the airport and everything else we took over.*

The troika learned their first cruel lesson in Balkan realities: agreements are not what they seem. The fighting did not stop.

That weekend, international public opinion did, indeed, turn. Television pictures, beamed around the world, suggested a plucky little nation – in the tradition of Czechoslovakia – westward-leaning, democratically-inclined and struggling to liberate itself from a reactionary, unreconstructed Communist monolith which, two years after the fall of the Berlin Wall, was still ready to use force to impose its will.

Marković now distanced himself from the Army's actions in Slovenia. "No one in the Government expected that force would be used," he said. "The development of events goes far beyond the decisions of the Federal Government on regulating the situation at the borders." By implication, Marković was stating that the Army, in the absence of a functioning Presidency, was acting on its own authority. On June 29, General Marko Negovanović, a member of the JNA's general staff who would fix his threatening gaze on any opponent, warned Slovenia to cease hostilities or face "decisive military action." The country, he said, was "at the beginning of a civil war." His remarks compounded the growing impression of an Army off the leash and unrestrained. The next day, even the British Foreign Secretary Douglas Hurd, one of the most cautious of European statesmen, felt compelled to condemn federal actions in Slovenia. "The time has passed," he told the House of Commons, "when you could keep a state together by shooting its citizens."

On June 30, day three of Slovenia's ten-day war, Serbia finally withdrew its support for the JNA's attempt to hold federal Yugoslavia together. At a session of the council for the defense of the constitution, Borisav Jović, on Milošević's behalf, pulled the rug from under the feet of the Yugoslav generals.

General Kadijević told the session that Plan A (a limited action to recover the border crossing) had failed. There were now two options – withdrawal and by implication recognition of Slovene secession; or Plan B: full-scale invasion and the crushing of the Slovene rebellion. Jović, to Kadijević's astonishment, in effect vetoed Plan B.

Jović recalled:

> *I remember well that day because it was a day when I first announced our new policy. It was very clear to me that Slovenia had seceded, and that it would be useless to wage war there. The only thing I thought which we should do was to defend the Serb populated territories in Croatia because they wanted to stay in Yugoslavia. Concerning Slovenia, I said that we could not use a war option in Slovenia.*
>
> *I said we should allow Slovenia to leave Yugoslavia and pull the JNA out. I proposed that the Federal Assembly should recognize Slovene secession, and agree to a division of assets with Slovenia, and a territorial delineation.*
>
> *There was no discussion about my proposal because everybody was absolutely confused and stunned. They thought it inconceivable that any Presidency member could talk about the disintegration of Yugoslavia.*

Milošević knew that to get the withdrawal from Slovenia that he wanted, the Army had to be brought back under civilian control. The Federal Presidency, out of action since May 15, would have to be reconstituted.

Milošević told Jović to stop blocking the election of Mesić as President of the Presidency. When the EC troika flew back into Belgrade later that day, Milošević, ever the master tactician, was able to present this as an important concession. He told Jović to "pose some conditions... so that it won't appear that we accepted this so easily."

Late into the evening, the troika sat with Milošević in the Federal Presidency, painstakingly trying to extract from him a "concession" he had already decided to make. Meanwhile the Federal Presidency members were assembling in the same building, a few doors down the corridor, and preparing, finally, to elect Mesić as President. Mesić himself had come to Belgrade on the understanding that his election would now go ahead. Finally, close to midnight, the Federal Presidency met formally, in the presence of the three EC foreign ministers. Jović made great show of opposing the election of Mesić. "How can you force us to vote for a man who has openly said he wants the break-up of Yugoslavia?" he demanded. He asked for a formal guarantee that Europe would respect the territorial integrity of Yugoslavia, and demanded that the troika press Mesić, as President, to work to restore the constitutional order, including the return of Slovene border-crossings to the Yugoslav federal authorities. His position could not have been more disingenuous. Only hours earlier he had announced, in the closed session of the Council for the Defense of the Constitution, that Serbia was now in favor of Slovene secession. Every Yugoslav in the room knew it. Only the hapless troika seemed oblivious to what was going on.

When midnight struck, the Presidency of the European Community changed hands. A domineering van den Broek forced an obviously reluctant Milošević to clink glasses with him. Jacques Poos handed over to Hans van den Broek. "You see," said van den Broek, "this is how democracy works. I will chair the meeting now because I have taken over. Similarly, you should elect Mesić." In return, he promised: "... and I will make a public statement saying that Europe supports the unity of Yugoslavia." With a great demonstration of reluctance, the Serb members agreed. In the small hours of July 1, Mesić was finally elected head of state of a country which, in the eyes of those who elected him, no longer existed. A comprehensively out-maneuvered, but determinedly optimistic EC troika declared that further progress had been made.

The JNA made one last attempt to regain control of Slovenia before the will of the newly-constituted Federal Presidency could be imposed upon it. On July 2, twenty-four hours after the election of Mesić, a JNA armored unit, which had been camped in the Kokovski forest near Slovenia's border with Croatia, tried to move from its position, just before dawn. It came under a barrage of rocket fire by Slovene TO units lying in wait. The JNA sent an armored column from nearby Croatia to reinforce. It ran into a hail of fire as soon as it crossed the border. The JNA ordered air-strikes against Slovene forces, who then fled. A JNA noncommissioned officer later lined up several junior ranks who had refused to fight the Slovenes and ripped the insignia from their uniforms in disgust.[14]

But hostilities had resumed. General Blagoje Adžić, JNA Chief of Staff, emerged briefly to eclipse his boss, the Defense Minister Veljko Kadijević, as leader of Yugoslavia's armed intervention in Slovenia. He appeared on Belgrade television and said the JNA would wage war until it had regained control of the country. He criticized the federal authorities for trying to restrain his forces, and said: "We will make sure that the war that has been forced upon us is as short as possible." A column of 180 tanks and other armored vehicles left Belgrade heading north, cheered on by Serb villagers as it passed. The convoy never reached Slovenia, nor was it ever intended to. Its real mission was to take up positions near the Croatian border with Serbia for the coming war against the Croats.

The JNA lost the international public relations campaign. Hans Dietrich Genscher, Germany's Foreign Minister, had chosen that day to visit the Slovene capital; Kučan and he had been in regular telephone contact throughout. He boarded a train at Graz in Austria. News of the fighting reached him as it crossed the frontier. According to Bavčar:

> *Genscher's visit was of utmost importance in the sense of moral support because any contact or communication with major politicians from other countries meant recognition, giving legitimacy to us. As regards Genscher, there was an incident when they crossed the tunnel, an alarm was sounded and the train pulled back to the Austrian side.*
>
> *Our police in order to calm down Genscher's escort, showed him the arsenal of anti-aircraft missiles on the train. It was enough for them to order the train to turn back and head for Austria again.*

Genscher accused the JNA of "running amok" in Slovenia. It had forsaken all political control, he said, in order to retain its position of power and to preserve old structures. Douglas Hurd joined the refrain. He told Parliament the JNA had hastened the disintegration of Yugoslavia. Italy said it would "act in solidarity" (whatever that meant) with Croatia and Slovenia, unless the JNA respected the ceasefire. Playing to this international gallery, and consciously casting himself in the role of the leader of a small nation brutally crushed by a militaristic Communist monolith, President Kučan appealed to the international community, saying that he expected a "brutal attack, any time now." In the United States, the Chairman of the Senate Foreign Relations Committee, Claiborne Pell, urged President Bush to support Slovene and Croatian independence if Yugoslavia's "renegade army does not cease its wanton aggression." The Republican leader, Bob Dole, as usual went further, calling on Bush to "compel" Belgrade to "halt its violent crackdown on democracy and human rights."

Within two days, the Federal Presidency had reasserted control over a humiliated JNA. On July 4, as part of a ceasefire package, the Presidency ordered Slovenia to hand over control of the border-crossings to the JNA, and to withdraw Slovene forces to barracks. It was what the EC troika had wanted – the restoration of constitutional authority throughout Yugoslavia. But federal Yugoslavia had ceased to exist. The Slovenes did neither. They took advantage of the ceasefire to strengthen their barricades. In Ljubljana, the buses and trucks that had acted as makeshift defenses were replaced by tank traps made from criss-crossed iron girders, and surrounded by barbed wire. It didn't matter. The Slovenes knew that they had international public opinion on their side. More importantly, they knew that Milošević's men on the Federal Presidency would now block further JNA intervention. Indeed, that day, Milošević's party, the SPS, formally recognized Slovenia's right to peaceful secession. Menacingly for Zagreb, the same right was not, of course, extended to Croatia.

The secession of Slovenia was, in effect, formalized at a summit meeting on the island of Brioni, Tito's idyllic retreat in the Adriatic, on July 8. By the time the delegates assembled that morning, the alliance that had been born between Serb and Slovene leaders on January 24, when Milošević and Kučan had first agreed on the rights of the nations to secede, now came to maturity. It was not difficult for van den Broek, who presided, to find a formula on which the main players could agree. At lunchtime he sent a handwritten note to the Slovenes proposing joint-control of the borders, a withdrawal of troops to barracks, and a three-month cooling-off period. The three parties to the agreement were to be the EC, Yugoslavia, and Slovenia. For Kučan, it amounted to tacit recognition. It pleased him that the historic first international document communicated to his newly-independent country was a handwritten note scrawled by the Dutch foreign minister.

Van den Broek convened a session of all the delegates at eight p.m. He presented the four-point proposal, saying: "This is what the EC backs. Take it or leave it."[15] Only Ante Marković, who saw clearly that the proposal spelt the end of Yugoslavia and the death of his own efforts to hold it together, objected. Van den Broek, exasperated, called a break. He brought Marković and Kučan together. Marković spelt out his objections to the plan. Van den Broek asked Kučan whether Marković's ideas were acceptable to the Slovenes. Kučan said they were not. "Very well," said van den Broek, "we will go back to the original proposal." When Marković again objected, van den Broek stormed out of the room muttering, in English, according to Kučan: "What a people! What a country!"

Van den Broek brokered an agreement between the Slovenes and the Federal Presidency, under which Slovene police were granted control of the border-crossings, provided all customs revenue was turned over to the Yugoslav federal reserves; the JNA were withdrawn to barracks; and the Slovene forces were "de-activated" and withdrawn to base. The agreement imposed a three-month moratorium on the *implementation* of Slovene (and Croatian) independence, but not on the declarations of independence themselves. Marković was isolated. He had little choice but to accept the agreement and place his faith in the three-month cooling-off period and the talks which, the agreement stipulated, would begin on August 1 to resolve the outstanding issues between Slovenia and the federation. Marković had been out-maneuvered by a tacit alliance between Milošević and Kučan, by which Slovenia would be allowed to secede so that the JNA could concentrate its efforts in Croatia and, later, Bosnia.

During the Brioni talks, Slovenia's representative on the Federal Presidency, Janez Drnovšek, approached Borislav Jović, his opposite number from Serbia, and proposed, informally, a total withdrawal of the JNA from Slovenia. The usually argumentative Jović was sympathetic. Neither man raised the question in the formal sessions. They knew that it would never win the agreement of the Federal Government since it amounted to complete secession, and its introduction, at this delicate stage in the negotiations, could scuttle the whole Brioni accord. Drnovšek and Jović agreed to leave the question of JNA withdrawal for later.

The Federal Presidency met ten days later on July 18, and agreed that the Army should withdraw within three months. The four members under Milošević's control were certain to vote for this. Drnovšek agreed to resume his place on the Presidency to guarantee the crucial fifth vote. It was not necessary. Neither the Bosnian nor the Macedonian representative raised objections to the withdrawal when the word "temporary" was inserted in the resolution. But they all knew that it was not a temporary withdrawal, and that the departure of the JNA meant that Slovenia had seceded from Yugoslavia, and – alarmingly for Croatia – had seceded alone. Within a day, the JNA had withdrawn the troops it had sent to Slovenia during the ten-day conflict. A full JNA demobilization followed. Slovenia, as its President had been sure it would be, was, after all, free to go.

But not Croatia. The only member of the Federal Presidency to vote against the withdrawal of the JNA from Slovenia was Stipe Mesić. He knew the implications for his own country if the Slovenes gained their independence and the Croats did not. It was in order to avoid being left behind that the Croats had rushed through their independence declaration months before they were ready to act on it. The Brioni Accord dealt the fatal blow to Croatia's alliance with Slovenia. There was no love lost. The Slovenes said it was no more than the Croats deserved for having failed to enter the war when the JNA had sent the troops into Slovenia two weeks earlier. According to Dimitrij Rupel:

> *There were two theories about the connections between the former Yugoslav republics. One was that Slovenia and Croatia were the Siamese twins, that they belonged together. I think that this was also the view of the Vatican and the Germans. We didn't object to this view because we knew that on our own, we could not have constituted the critical mass to be able to leave on our own. But with Croatia, we were almost half of the country.*
>
> *But the other theory, which I think is much more true, is that Croatia and Serbia are the Siamese twins. They had the same language, and they had the same heart, which is Bosnia-Herzegovina. They are bound together by Bosnia.*

The Brioni Agreement was hailed as a triumph of European diplomacy. It was nothing of the sort. It left every important item of contention unresolved, pending the three-month cooling-off period: it did not address the question of Slovenia's sovereignty; it did not address the future of the JNA in Slovenia; it simply put everything on hold. The diplomatic triumph belonged to Milošević and Kučan, who had, between them, agreed Slovenia's departure from the federation at a series of meetings that began, arguably, in Belgrade on January 24, and ended with the July 18 Presidency session. The crucial issues were resolved without the benefit of international mediation, by the players themselves. United, Milošević and Kučan had out-maneuvered – and, in effect, destroyed – federal Yugoslavia.

Forty-four JNA soldiers were killed during Slovenia's ten-day conflict, of whom the vast majority were conscripts, still in their teens, bewildered at the mission with which they found themselves tasked. Of the thousands of federal prisoners the Slovenes held by the end, the majority had either deserted or given themselves up without a struggle. A hundred and eighty-seven JNA members were wounded. Casualties on the Slovene side were in single figures, most of them foreign truck-drivers passing through, unaware of what was taking place and caught in the cross-fire.

Slovenia's war – to the extent that it was a war at all – was crucially different to the two that followed it, in Croatia and Bosnia. It was not a war between Serbs and Slovenes, but rather a war between Slovenes and a federal system that was already in its death throes, killed off by a nationalism that had taken hold first in Serbia and – later – in Croatia and Slovenia. Serb and Slovene leaders were, by the end of June 1991, indeed, well before it, united in their central objectives, and in their opposition to the federal structures by which they both felt constrained. Kučan and Milošević were, in an important sense, in cahoots; it was the JNA generals who were outside the loop. They thought they were defending the territorial integrity of Yugoslavia. They did not know that that integrity had already been fatally betrayed, and by the very man who, publicly, continued to cast himself in the role of its principal defender. The Slovene experience tore the heart out of the JNA. It emerged from the ten-day conflict humiliated at home and abroad, vilified by the entire democratic world. And, crucially, when the JNA went to war in Croatia in the weeks that followed, its withdrawal from Slovenia meant that it was no longer able to do so in the conviction, or even the pretense, that it was defending Yugoslavia's integrity. The JNA's metamorphosis, into the Army of the Serbs, progressed apace.

Yugoslavia was also tearing the heart out of the proud, confident, new Europe. Two weeks after declaring its support for the territorial integrity of Yugoslavia, and warning that the use of force would bring no reward, the Community had turned about-face. When Kučan's Presidency, in the small hours of June 27, opted for war, it was gambling that the old Yugoslav federation had no fight left in it. The gamble paid off. Slovenia had opted for force and had won a great prize. It had taught Europe a lesson that the peace mediators never once took on board – that war is sometimes not only a profoundly rational path to take, especially when you know you can win, but is also sometimes the only way to get what you want. Despite this, successive peace-makers continued to close their eyes to the balance of forces in former Yugoslavia and behaved as though all that was necessary for peace to prevail was to persuade the belligerents of the folly of war. The Slovenes had demonstrated that war was not always folly. Belgrade knew this, too, and was to act on it in both Croatia and Bosnia.

1 Except for the reunification of Germany. The declaration envisaged few immediate changes. There were to be no new passports, and no immediate introduction of a Slovene currency. Twenty thousand federal troops, stationed in Slovenia, were given until the end of 1993 to withdraw from the republic's territory. The legislation established a Slovene central bank, and transferred customs and air-traffic control to Slovene competence. Fixed property belonging to the JNA was to be transferred to Slovene state ownership by the end of 1993.

2 Neither Slovenia nor Croatia called their actions "secession." They used the term "disassociation," claiming that Yugoslavia had been founded as a voluntary union of nations.

3 Later promoted to General, Aksentijević was to have what must rank as one of the unhappiest wars in the entire JNA officer corps. He was no nationalist. He believed passionately in a multinational Yugoslavia. But, despite asking permission to retire after the withdrawal from Slovenia, he went on to serve in both Croatia and Bosnia. He was thus present – indeed a pivotal member of the JNA command – at the outbreak of war on three separate occasions, in three republics; surely a unique record of service to an army that was, by the time he left it, exclusively Serb, the antithesis of what he had spent a distinguished military career promoting. His wife and family are Slovene, and continue to live there – in a republic where he was, incredibly, declared a war criminal.

4 Aksentijević was the MP representing the Army, which had its own representatives in each of the republics' parliaments.

5 Item 4 of its conclusions declined to recognize the legitimacy of Slovene secession:

The Federal Government and all the Yugoslav institutions, including the security agencies and the JNA need to continually take steps and measures forced upon them by the unilateral acts, in prevention of the alteration of the Yugoslav borders, disruption of the border regime on the frontiers of the SFRJ, conversion of the Yugoslav customs into republic ones, appropriation of customs duties and property belonging to Yugoslavia, and to make recourse to all legal devices to combat unilateral decisions, options and behavior aspiring to impose ones will on other parties.

6 Narodna Armija, *The Truth about the Armed Conflict in Slovenia*, Military Publishing and Newspaper House, Belgrade, 1991, and containing the full texts of the Federal Parliament and Federal Government orders and decrees.

7 The Fifth Military District covered all of Slovenia, most of Croatia, and part of northern Bosnia.

8 There was some disagreement about how many land border-crossings there were on Slovene territory. At the time, the most frequently reported number was twenty-seven. The figure of thirty-five comes from the JNA's subsequent, official account of what it called the "highly restricted scope" of its June 27 mission in Slovenia, *The Truth about the Armed Conflict in Slovenia.*

9 The figures are those released by the JNA in *The Truth about the Armed Conflict in Slovenia.*

10 This is Kučan's account of the conversation. It is consistent with Rašeta's account, in which he insists that he did not consider the JNA intervention anything more than a policing action. "I was trying actually to calm him, addressing him as the President of Slovenia and trying to explain that there were no other plans but to control the border, because if we had other plans we would have moved all the units from Croatia to Slovenia and the action would have been completed in a totally different way." (Rašeta.)

11 The accounts of this meeting, given by Kučan, Janša, and Bavčar, while broadly consistent, differ in one telling respect. Kučan and Janša both claim the credit for first insisting on the use of armed resistance. Bavčar says it was France Bučar, a Slovene policeman, who first broke the silence and apparent nervous indecision of the gathering.

12 The JNA said, and films show, that the helicopter was carrying bread, although General Rašeta later admitted that it had also been ordered to take off to check conditions on the road between Vrhnika barracks and the airport.

13 The European Community, like Yugoslavia, had a rotating Presidency, each country holding the office for six months, from January 1 to June 30. The Presidency rotates alphabetically, each country being listed according to the name it has in its own language, which makes the rules governing the rotation more impenetrable than those governing the Yugoslav Federal Presidency.

14 Associated Press, July 2, 1991.

15 According to Kučan's account of the session.

13

"AN UNDECLARED AND DIRTY WAR"
The JNA in Croatia
July–December 1991

At the July 18 Presidency session which ordered the JNA to withdraw from Slovenia, Stipe Mesić, Croatia's representative, sensed disaster for his own republic. The vote stripped away any vestige of pretense that the JNA was engaged in the defense of Yugoslavia. It was, now, openly and incontrovertibly, fighting for territory for the Serbs outside Serbia.

Zagreb saw Slovenia's phoney war for precisely what it was: a Serbian-Slovene pact to facilitate the secession of Slovenia, humiliate the JNA, and destroy what was left of Marković's Federal Government. It had succeeded in all three respects. The JNA – no longer, in any sense of the term, a genuinely Yugoslav Army – was now free to turn its attention to the growing tension in Croatia. And, after the Slovene fiasco, it badly needed a morale booster.

The JNA intervention in Slovenia brought Croatia's President Franjo Tudjman into conflict with his increasingly dissatisfied Defense Minister Martin Špegelj, for the last time. Špegelj again pressed Tudjman to declare war on the JNA. At a meeting of the state council, the day the Slovene war erupted, Špegelj urged Tudjman to order the Croatian National Guard to surround the federal barracks in Croatia and arrest leading members of the military. This time Tudjman's ministers were with Špegelj.

> *Everything was prepared. I was just waiting for the signal. In the state council meeting, Tudjman spoke for 95 minutes and said that I had dangerous intentions. Mesić backed me up 100 percent... He knew everything because he was living in Belgrade. He saw the war coming. About ten other people spoke and they either said they were for me or that they didn't have a view because they were not experts. Only one other person supported Tudjman. At five a.m., Tudjman had had enough. He collected his things and he wanted to leave without a decision. But I insisted that he make a decision. He was afraid to reject the plan and even more afraid to accept it. He wanted to decide in secret, by himself. I wouldn't leave it at that and I offered my resignation.*

Špegelj resigned hours later. Croatian radio and television announced that he had retired "for health reasons." Špegelj, in robust health, dismissed it as a "good old bolshevist trick" to cover up political division.

Tudjman's calculation was that Croatia was not in a position to take on the JNA militarily. He placed his faith, as he had done from the beginning, not on military readiness but in winning international goodwill. He believed Croatia would win its independence not through military victory over the JNA but only through international recognition. Even when war became inevitable, he wanted the world to see, and to acknowledge, that Croatia had not chosen it. Throughout the summer of 1991, Franjo Tudjman did everything he could to avoid all-out war.

To his critics on the right of his own party this looked like weakness in the face of Serb strength and singleness of purpose. Throughout July and August, the *Martićevci*, Martić's forces steadily extended the territories they controlled. One municipality after another fell to the territorial defense forces of the Krajina Republic during that summer of undeclared war between Serbia and Croatia: Glina, Kostajnica, Okučani and Dalj. On each of these occasions, the JNA stood behind the Serb paramilitaries ready to step in and "separate the warring factions." The tourist resorts of the Dalmatian coast were filling up with legions of the dispossessed: Croats who had been forcibly removed from their homes or who had fled the Serb advance. Whole communities decamped overnight, carrying what could be carried, and leaving everything else behind to be looted, or destroyed. Martić's officers began to claim the best properties for themselves. In villages abandoned by Croat civilians, the names of Serb paramilitary commanders could be seen scrawled above the door: their handwritten claim of right to the spoils of war.

Croatia's forces were no match. The Croatian National Guard, which Tudjman had formed from the ranks of his police reservists in May, was badly organized and poorly equipped, though there was no shortage of volunteers. In contrast to the armored vehicles and heavy weaponry that was increasingly available to the Serb paramilitaries, Tudjman's forces found themselves running around the battle zones in commandeered grocery vans and customized tourist buses. The two sides were hopelessly mismatched.

On August 1, Tudjman's critics moved to try to unseat him. In the Croatian parliament, right-wing deputies from his own Party proposed a declaration of war. Tudjman again argued that Croatia's future depended not on defeating the Serbs militarily, but on winning international recognition; a declaration of war would bring universal condemnation from the democratic world; it would be suicide for his fledgling state.

He turned to opposition members for support. Fearing a coup by right-wing nationalists, they gave it. A coalition of liberals, social democrats and former Communists was hastily formed and Tudjman swore in a Government of National Unity under Prime Minister Franjo Greguric, who belonged to the liberal wing of Tudjman's HDZ. The hard-right nationalists were isolated, and – in Parliament, if not on the battlefield – brought to heel.

But the Krajina Serbs, and the JNA, were to force Tudjman into war whether he wanted it or not. The JNA began a series of troop movements through Bosnia-Herzegovina in preparation for an assault on those territories which the Serbian leadership in Belgrade considered rightfully Serb. A day later, the day of the abortive coup against the Soviet leader Mikhail Gorbachev,[1] Milan Martić issued an ultimatum to the Croatian police at Kijevo, near Knin: leave the area within forty-eight hours or face attack. The Croats refused.

Kijevo was a Croat village surrounded by Serb-held territory. Since March 1, the day of the battle at Plitvice, the villagers of Kijevo had barricaded themselves in. Martić had come to regard Kijevo as an irritating anomaly – a Croat village in the "Serbian Republic of Krajina." It was also a security risk. It made communication between Knin and the Serb villages that lay beyond Kijevo dangerous, sometimes impossible. It meant that those villages could not be properly secured for the coming war against Croatia. Kijevo would have to be wiped off the map. The unfortunate distinction it enjoys now, is that it was the first victim of a process that came to characterize the wars in Yugoslavia: *čišćenje terena*, the "cleansing" of the ground.

For the Croats, Kijevo became a symbol of resistance. Tens of thousands of Croats had already lost their homes; what distinguished Kijevo was the level at which the dispossession was planned and executed. On August 20, the day that Martić's forty-eight hours' ultimatum to the Kijevo police was due to expire, Milan Babić announced that the *Martićevci* were now an integral part of the defense forces of federal Yugoslavia. Martić himself told the Belgrade daily, *Borba*, that his men were now acting in full cooperation with the JNA. He confidently announced their intention to seize the Croatian port city of Zadar. "The interests of the Army and of the Serbs coincide," he said. "We both need a harbor."[2]

The decisive player in this new unity of purpose was a young lieutenant colonel, recently arrived in Knin. Ratko Mladić was a Serb from the village of Božinovići in southeastern Bosnia. In the early summer of 1991, he was posted from Priština to Knin, where he became Chief of Staff of the Knin Corps of the JNA. Immediately on his arrival he made contact with the Krajina Serb leaders. The instant rapport he struck with the *Martićevci* removed any remaining distrust between Martić and the Knin garrison of the JNA. Ratko Mladić understood the Krajina Serb mentality. He was a life-long Communist who now switched his allegiance from defending Yugoslavia to the task, as he saw it, of protecting the Serbs against resurgent Croatian fascism. Mladić, like so many of his generation, had been shaped by the Second World War. When he was two years old his father was killed while taking part on a Partisan raid on the village of Bradina, coincidentally the home-village of the Ustaše leader Ante Pavelić. Though,

171

for now, Mladić's name meant little outside the limited military circles in which he moved, he would later achieve international notoriety as the commander of the Serb Army in Bosnia. His strength as commander was his remarkable ability to inspire loyalty among those he commanded. So enthusiastically did he take up their cause that he quickly earned the trust, even the adoration, of the Krajina Serbs.

On August 26, one week after Martić's ultimatum to the Kijevo police, he and Mladić, acting together, struck. In a twelve-hour bombardment, the village of Kijevo was levelled. Martić was filmed by a Belgrade television crew while his troops ripped down a sign post – in Latin script, of course – at the entrance to the village and triumphantly taking command of the area. Four years later the Croats would rip down those same sign posts. Martić's subsequent account of the cleansing of Kijevo was chilling in its clinical matter-of-factness:

> *It was a joint action between the police and the army and in two days we liberated Kijevo. The army provided the heavy weapons and I provided the infantry. When Colonel Mladić came to Knin, we saw that we could trust the Army. From then on we suggested that people [who came forward to volunteer for military service] should volunteer in the army and not the police. That arrangement then existed through the whole war.*
>
> *To be honest we seemed to be superior to the Croatians. They were running away. We didn't care about the victims. We wanted to liberate our blocked villages. Of course there were a few burnt houses, that's the way it goes in these actions with artillery. We thought it wouldn't last long and we were right.*

The action had the full backing of Belgrade. With the Croatian and Slovene representatives now always absent from sessions of the Federal Presidency, Yugoslavia's collective Head of State was totally under Milošević's control. In Mesić's absence, the Vice President assumed the Presidency. The Montenegrin representative, Branko Kostić, became Yugoslavia's acting Head of State and Supreme Commander of the JNA:

> *We had in Knin, the Knin corps, one of the strongest and best equipped army units there, and it is not an exaggeration to say that in these first days of the war the JNA protected the Serbs from physical liquidation and prevented a massive exodus.*
>
> *Objectively speaking, if we had not encouraged this JNA corps in Knin, the Croatian police, with their arms and everything, could have taken it easily.*

Kijevo set the pattern for the rest of the war in Croatia: JNA artillery supporting an infantry that was part conscript and part locally-recruited Serb volunteers. It was the very alliance that Tudjman had warned against in his late-night address to the nation after Borovo Selo. As he saw it, Communist militarism had joined forces with Greater Serbian hegemonists. He still hoped to avoid war against the JNA; a war he knew he could not win. But that hardly mattered now. In its cleansing of Kijevo, the JNA had unofficially declared war on him.

Franjo Greguric convened a late-night session of the Government. The pressure to act was now too great. Tudjman's reluctance to be dragged into open war could no longer be sustained. On the day Kijevo was cleansed, the Croatian Government announced a general mobilization and declared a "war of liberation."

Though Kijevo captured the headlines, it had coincided with an assault in Eastern Slavonia. On Croatia's border with Serbia, the town of Vukovar came under sustained artillery and mortar fire for the first time.[3] Vukovar's crisis headquarters, established in the town-center hospital complex at the beginning of the month, now moved to the basement, as did most of the sick and wounded being treated there.

Croatia's counter-offensive took two weeks to prepare. On September 14, the Croatian National Guard laid siege to JNA barracks and installations across the republic. Electricity, food and water supplies were cut off, and telephone lines were disconnected. The Zagreb city authorities called on all citizens to rise in defense of the capital. Tank-traps, made of iron girders and wrapped in barbed wire, were placed at the main intersections of the roads. Bridges across the Sava River were mined. Barricades were erected blocking all but one of the lanes on the major highways. Windows were sandbagged. Menacingly, JNA fighter-jets screamed low over the city, wreaking terror. A night-time black-out was imposed. An atmosphere of intense paranoia took hold. There were reports of fifth-columnists in every building, sniper nests around every corner. Though there was not a single recorded death or injury by sniper-fire within the confines of Zagreb city, its 900,000 citizens began to walk the streets in fear for their lives. Croatia, at last, after months of low-level conflict, was on a republic-wide war footing.

Fighting erupted across a broad arc, from Gospić in the south, north to Karlovac, just south of the capital itself, and then eastward through Pakrac, Okučani and, finally, to Vukovar in eastern Slavonia. To the extent that the line of confrontation established itself at all in those early days, it ran roughly – though with important exceptions – along the line that Milošević and Jović had identified in May, when they issued their instruction, through the Federal Presidency, to the JNA to start protecting the Serbs of Croatia. The JNA was now openly fighting to establish new borders for a Yugoslavia without the Croats.

Serb forces, together with the JNA, now controlled between a quarter and a third of the republic's territory. The front-line that emerged on September 14 gave them three disparate blocks of territory, linked to each other only by territory in Bosnia-Herzegovina: the first, and most established of these, was the territory around Knin; the second was in central Croatia, around the town of Glina, from which the Croats had been driven in July and August; and the third was in eastern Slavonia, and Baranja which shares a frontier with Serbia.

The Croats retaliated. In several cities and towns there was a systematic campaign of terror against Serb civilians as Croatia began to lose the war. One night in late September Croatian militia rounded up and killed twenty Serbs – professors, judges in the southern town of Gospić – loyal Serbs who had decided to stay in Croatia. It was a warning to Serbs – they were no longer safe in Croatia. There were also incidents in Zagreb, Sisak, and Karlovac.

Behind Serb lines the JNA was free to group and regroup as the demands of battle required. Behind Croat lines it was immobilized. In almost every important town in the republic, the JNA was trapped in its barracks, its guns trained outward, surrounded by the Croatian National Guard, guns trained inward, in an explosive stand-off. In Gospić the stand-off quickly erupted into a battle that heavily damaged of the town. The JNA garrison there tried to blast its way out, while reinforcements grouped outside the town added mortar and artillery support. The result was a three-day exchange of fire that left scarcely a building in Gospić habitable, and the fall of the barracks. Two hundred JNA men, mostly recruits, were taken prisoner, and the barracks' commander was killed: local Croatian Guard officers claimed he shot himself in full view of his men in the forecourt of the town hospital; Belgrade Radio said, more convincingly, that he had been murdered.

The capture of Gospić was a strategic blow to the ambitions of the Krajina Serbs. It halted the expansion, westwards, of their territory. It prevented them pushing west, towards the coast, at Karlobag, and, therefore, dealt a mortal blow to Martić's confidently declared intention to take Zadar, the Adriatic port city that was, in the eyes of Serb nationalists, the western-most point of the Serb lands, and the main outlet to the sea. Gospić was also a great morale boost to the Croats. It sent a shiver down the spine of every besieged JNA commander in the republic, who wondered whether he, too, would suffer the fate of the unfortunate Gospić general.

But many struck local deals. In Osijek, in eastern Slavonia, the JNA did not wait for the barracks to fall. It pulled out on September 17 and withdrew to new positions to the south and east of the city, from where, for the three months that followed, it played a vital role in the bombardment of Osijek. The Commander at Vinkovci did the same a week later. At Jastrebarsko, southwest of Zagreb, where the JNA had stationed one of the largest single deployments of tanks, the local JNA Commander, Radovan Tašić, struck a deal with the local police chief, warning him that: "It would be a great pity if you were to bring upon yourself the destruction of your beautiful town." His meaning was not lost on the National Guardsmen besieging his barracks. Tašić was, after weeks of negotiation, allowed to leave, taking his 600 soldiers (again, mostly conscripts) and his heavy weapons with him.[4] Local people watched ruefully as a huge column of 160 tanks, dozens of armored vehicles, surface-to-air missiles, and anti-tank and anti-aircraft batteries, trundled out of their barracks and south towards Bosnia-Herzegovina, in the knowledge that the hardware would soon be put to good use elsewhere in Croatia.

Circumstances deeper in Croatian-held territory were more difficult. The Commander, Vlado Trifunović, at Varaždin, near the Hungarian border, appealed to Belgrade for help, but got none. The Croats were determined not to let him out with his equipment. He was too far from Serb lines to expect reinforcement. He surrendered. His 200 men were stripped of their JNA uniforms and released to make their own way home in civilian clothes. By handing over dozens of tanks and armored vehicles to the Croats, Trifunović had averted a battle that would undoubtedly have cost the lives of many of the men – most of them conscripts – under his command. His actions saved them. On his return to Belgrade, he was tried for treason, and, after an exhaustive appeals procedure, sentenced to twelve years in jail in January 1995. The Kafkaesque trial horrified liberal Belgraders. But in the summer of 1991, the Belgrade regime had needed a pretext on which to base the military intervention that it had already ordered and which was, even as Trifunović was striking his deal with the Croats, on its way. Belgrade had required of Trifunović an heroic and suicidal last-stand to justify JNA intervention. He was punished for failing to offer his men up as sacrificial lambs to the slaughter.

None the less, the siege of the barracks provided the JNA with a pretext of sorts. Belgrade ordered a sharp escalation of a war whose stated purpose, now, was the relief of the JNA garrisons, but whose over-riding war aim was to secure the territory on which to build a Serb state in Croatia. On September 19 two columns of tanks and armored vehicles left the federal capital, Belgrade, and trundled down the Brotherhood and Unity highway towards the Croatian border. Foreign journalists, roused from their beds to follow the column, reported that it stretched for more than six miles, and contained at least a hundred tanks, mostly T-55s and M-84s, as well as armored personnel carriers and trucks towing heavy artillery pieces.[5] Like the force which had taken the same route, two months earlier, towards Slovenia (only to be turned back), the column was again cheered by local Serbs who lined the route, throwing food and cigarettes to the bewildered conscripts and mostly reservists in the passing trucks.[6]

Serb paramilitaries and the JNA had already secured a triangle of land in the oil-rich fertile corner of northeastern Croatia. From Baranja it stretched west, to the outskirts of Osijek, and south, to Borovo Selo, a suburb of Vukovar. The towns of Vukovar and its neighbor Vinkovci now stood in the way of further expansion into eastern Slavonia. They, and not the besieged barracks, were the target of this latest impressive deployment. The JNA surrounded Vukovar, and dug in for the start of what was to become a two-month bombardment that would turn a pretty Danubian town into the symbol of Croatia's struggle for national liberation. Stipe Mesić said Vukovar would be "Croatia's Stalingrad."

Serbs loyal to the SDS rebels had, to some extent, begun a process of "self-cleansing" as early as the spring of that year. The Mayor of Vukovar, Slavko Dokmanović, who was a Serb, said he had stopped coming to the city long before the war had begun because he feared for his life. Barricades had been erected months earlier by the inhabitants of the Serb villages on the outskirts of the town. Mortar attacks on the suburb of Borovo Naselje had begun in early July; the city center was subjected to sporadic bombardment from early August onwards. By the end of August, only 15,000 of the town's original population of 50,000 were still there. Those who were left retained the ethnic mixture that had characterized the town before the war.[7] Serbs and Croats suffered alike in the bombardment that followed.

On September 14, the day the Croatian National Guard had laid siege to the JNA barracks, Serb paramilitaries had launched a fierce assault on the southwest of Vukovar from the direction of Negoslavci. Two thousand residents had fled their homes and sought refuge in the city center. They had reported that some eighty civilians had been killed. Bodies had piled up in the streets. The dead had been collected by the advancing Serb forces, and buried in mass graves in common meadow land at Negoslavci. Croatia had not heard atrocity tales like this. The war had entered a new phase. On each of the fifteen days that followed, between sixteen and eighty wounded were brought into the hospital. On average, three-quarters of them were civilians.[8]

October 4 brought the fiercest single attack to date. It included artillery, mortar, and air assault. Two bombs were dropped from the air on the hospital. One destroyed the Department of Surgery and the Operating Theater, though much of its equipment had already been moved to the basement. The other fell through several floors, failed to explode, and landed on the foot of the bed of a wounded man, who survived. Ninety-two wounded people were brought into the hospital on that day alone.

The Serb-JNA attack brought territorial gains. The road from Vukovar to the village of Bogdanovci fell. JNA units took up positions along it, depriving the town of its last land-route out of the city. The siege was now complete, save for a dangerously exposed footpath which was overlooked by Serb gun positions in nearby woods. The Vukovar crisis committee

176

claimed that at least thirty people, using this route to try to flee the town, were killed by snipers.

At the beginning of October, the people of Vukovar began living in common shelters, some housing up to 700 people. The crisis committee, which itself was operating from a nuclear bomb-proof bunker beneath the town-center hospital, organized the distribution of food, water and medical supplies, thus keeping to a minimum the number of civilians on the streets at any one time. Each common shelter, as far as was possible, had at least one doctor and one nurse assigned to it. The Croatian National Guard provided each shelter with armed protection.

The pattern of attack was that of Kijevo writ large: the JNA providing the heavy weapons and infantry support to the local Serb paramilitaries, together with volunteers from Serbia proper. But a striking feature emerged: the failure, despite overwhelming firepower superiority, to make commensurate territorial progress. The attack on Vukovar revealed the shambles to which the dissolution of Yugoslavia had reduced the country's once-proud fighting force. The level of desertion, particularly among non-Serb officers and conscripts, was high. So was the degree to which the conscripts, in the face of battle, disobeyed orders. JNA officers complained that they couldn't get their boys to leave their armored vehicles. Morale in the JNA slumped as weeks went by and Europe's fourth-largest Army proved incapable of overpowering a small town with a handful of beleaguered and ill-equipped Croatian defenders.

In October, with the JNA's assault on Slavonia hopelessly delayed by the surprising resilience of Vukovar, the Chief-of-Staff Blagoje Adžić appointed General Života Panić to command the Vukovar operation. Života Panić was Commander of the First Army District, and he was now charged with finishing the Vukovar operation off. Panić and Adžić went to the Vukovar front together to assess why the operation had stalled so badly. They were appalled by what they found there. There was no clear chain-of-command, and no demarcation of tasks between the various units deployed. There was, by Panić's own account, "chaos." Many soldiers appeared not to know who their commanding officer was. There was desertion from the ranks, particularly among reservists who had been mobilized and sent to the front with no clear idea of why they were there and no notion of what they were trying to achieve.

Tens of thousands of Serbs were mobilized to fight in a war that was undeclared. Throughout the republic – in particular in Belgrade – men were hiding or fleeing the country. One reservist could not decide whether to join a group of deserters or remain with his unit so he shot himself. Another took a tank from the front and drove it all the way to the Federal Parliament.

When Panić assumed command of the operation, he integrated the para-

177

military groups into the command structure of the JNA. Volunteers were recruited to replace those who had been mobilized unwillingly. A single command structure was put in place. Those unwilling to submit themselves to it were removed from the of operations.

On November 3, the headquarters of the Army's First Motorized Guard Brigade announced that the "final operation" to drive Croatian forces out of Vukovar had begun. The next day, the Federal Air Force carried out sixty-five sorties against Croatian positions in Vukovar and elsewhere.[9] Ground troops advanced to within a few hundred yards of the town center.

On the same day, fifteen artillery rounds landed on the Serbian town of Šid, in Vojvodina, on Croatia's frontier with Serbia, from where some of the artillery attacking Vukovar had been deployed. no one was injured. But the outraged Serbian Minister of Defense, General Tomislav Simović, none the less felt compelled to call upon the international community to condemn the attack. As though quite ignorant of what JNA forces were doing in Vukovar even as he spoke, he addressed the Serbian Parliament to denounce the attack on Šid:

> *This attack is part of the fascists' policy. The attitudes of the Croatian armed forces are such that whenever we have spoken about peace and truce they have acted in the worst way... There will probably be blackmail in The Hague today regarding the blockades of Vukovar and Dubrovnik by the Yugoslav People's Army. They may even make the further course of the talks conditional upon liberation or withdrawal of the forces that are surrounding these two towns.*

He then vowed not to submit to international blackmail.

With Panić now in command of a disciplined operation, the situation in Vukovar grew desperate. The town's defenders turned their bitterness against their own side. They accused Zagreb of deliberately sacrificing Vukovar in the interests of winning international sympathy. The town's military commander, Mile Dedaković, went to Zagreb to appeal to Tudjman. He told him that Croatia's willingness to agree to internationally-brokered cease-fires was losing Vukovar the war. Tudjman exploded with rage, and told Dedaković to remember who was President and Head of State: "I am running this war," he is reported to have said, "and when I order that military operations around Vukovar should stop, then you will not move even a millimeter."[10] For Tudjman, who was still chasing international respectability, diplomatic considerations continued to outweigh military priorities.

In Vukovar, two weeks of hand-to-hand fighting followed. On November 10, the JNA took the town-center district of Milovo Brdo. The Croats retreated in disarray. The fall of Vukovar, long predicted, was now imminent. On the

November 16, the JNA captured the suburb of Borovo Naselje. That deprived Vukovar of its last precarious access route along the footpath through the corn-fields. There was now no way in or out of Vukovar. In terror, 700 civilians now left their shelters and fled into the hospital complex. In being "liberated" street-by-street and house-by-house, Vukovar was also destroyed in the process. By November 17, the entire town, save for a few pockets of resis-tance, most notably that of the hospital itself, was in Serb-JNA hands. The next day, during Croatia's thirteenth internationally-brokered republic-wide ceasefire, Vukovar fell. Those Croatian National Guardsmen who had not smuggled themselves out before the fall of Borovo Naselje, were now trapped. They had one night left in which to risk a death-defying dash, under cover of darkness, through Serb lines, across the cornfields and into the neighboring town of Vinkovci. Many did so, and gathered there the next day in small exhausted huddles, embittered against both Zagreb and the international community, who had continued to try to talk Belgrade into finding a "negoti-ated settlement" as their town had been reduced to rubble. Something of their mood transmitted itself to the Croatian population generally.

The commanders of Vukovar's defense conceded defeat. The JNA repre-sentative in Zagreb agreed to surrender talks. Both sides agreed to an evacua-tion of the town's civilian population, and the 700 sick-and-wounded from the hospital. It would be supervised by the EC monitors and representatives of the International Red Cross.

In the three months of the siege and bombardment that ended on November 20, the hospital treated 1,850 wounded people, most of them civil-ians. This figure represents serious injury only, and therefore understates the true figure. Those with light wounds were encouraged not to risk the journey but to stay at home. In the same period, the Vukovar police had registered 520 dead bodies for transportation to the only available burial ground. Of these, 156 had been Croatian National Guardsmen, and twenty-four, policemen. The rest had been civilians, including eight children. These figures do not include the hundreds of bodies that remained uncollected during the last days of the siege, when the intensity of the bombardment, and the proximity of advancing Serb and JNA forces, made movement through the streets almost impossible. In the three months since the JNA had begun its attack on the town in earnest, Vukovar received one convoy of international aid. It was allowed to deliver medicine to the hospital and to evacuate 114 of the wounded.

On November 19, at eleven o'clock in the morning, as Vukovar's crisis headquarters tried, unsuccessfully, to make contact with the outside world, the JNA entered the hospital complex, the last bastion of Croat resistance. To the terror of those inside, they arrived ahead of the international monitors who were to supervise the evacuation. The ICRC truck, carrying medicine for the sick, arrived at six in the evening. By then, the JNA had begun to evacuate the civilians and the sick-and-wounded, without international supervision, and in contravention of the previous day's agreement. In the center of Vukovar a JNA officer arrogantly replied to the protesting ICRC representative that this was Yugoslavia, *his* country, and if the ICRC didn't like it, it was welcome to leave. The unsupervised evacuation proceeded. By now, bands of heavily-armed Serb men, many wearing Chetnik insignia, fresh from the battlefield, were roaming the streets of Vukovar unchecked, as weeping ashen figures with dark rings under their eyes made their way out of the shelters. Many had been under ground for three months, while the battle had gone on over their heads. On November 18, they saw a different Vukovar. Corpses of people and animals littered the streets. Grisly skeletons of buildings still burned, barely a square inch had escaped damage. Serbian volunteers, wild-eyed, roared down the streets, their pockets full of looted treasures. One group grabbed a Croatian man and banged his head against the wall accusing him of fighting with the enemy. He cried that he had not fought at all. The JNA began to separate the men from the women and children. The latter were asked to choose whether they wanted to be evacuated to Serbia or Croatia. Those who chose Serbia were allowed to leave, or were given transport out of town. Those who asked to go to Croatia were taken, by bus, into Vojvodina, where they spent the night in schools and sports halls. The next day they were handed over to the Croatian authorities.

The men were not handed over; and many of them – more than three years later, at the time of writing – are presumed dead, buried in a mass grave at Ovčara, outside Vukovar. Four years later Serb militia refused access to all but a handful of officials to the suspected site. There among the dead was Siniša Glavašević, a thirty-one-year-old reporter from Croatian Radio's Vukovar studio, whose voice, in Croatia, had become the voice of Vukovar, daily chronicling the destruction of his home-town in increasingly desperate and exhausted tones. There is little doubt that the status he achieved in Croatia, and the corresponding notoriety which his work won him among Vukovar's tormentors, cost him his life.

Those men who were not singled out for execution were taken to a detention center at Sremska Mitrovica in Vojvodina. On their arrival they were stripped naked and any property they were carrying was confiscated. Many were beaten. They were herded into overcrowded prison cells where, for the weeks that followed, they slept on the wooden floors. Many were subjected to repeated interrogations. Some were offered the inducement of reward for informing on the others. They were released in January 1992, under the agreement brokered by Cyrus Vance, the US envoy.

The director of Vukovar's hospital, Dr. Vesna Bosanac, whose courageous example had done so much to keep the place going throughout the siege, had become something of a heroine in Croatia. She came to personify what the city itself now stood for in the mentality that war fashioned in many Croats. Consequently, she was vilified by the Serbs. Belgrade television called her the "Dr. Mengele of Yugoslavia," accusing her of refusing treatment to wounded Serb civilians, and of carrying out medical experiments on them. When Vukovar fell, many Croats feared for her life. For a week, nothing was heard of her. She was not on the convoy of women and children that reached Croatia after Vukovar's fall. The International Red Cross made urgent appeals in Belgrade. The hated doctor was spared the fate that Siniša Glavašević suffered. She was released after a month in detention.

It took the EC monitors three days to organize the evacuation of the sick and wounded. Several times they were loaded into JNA ambulances only to learn that the hand-over to Croatian authorities had been postponed because of continued fighting on the road. Finally, the two convoys – one JNA, the other Croatian Government – met in northeastern Bosnia. Five hundred wounded, many of them barely conscious, were stretchered out of their JNA ambulances and transferred to the waiting Croatian vehicles. An angry crowd of local Serbs turned out to scream abuse at the "Ustaše murderers" as the wounded were carried past.

Serb passions had been inflamed by a badly judged piece of journalism by a reputable news agency. On the day Vukovar had fallen, Reuter's Belgrade bureau had reported that Croatian National Guardsmen had slaughtered forty-one Serb children in revenge as they fled the city. The news spread like wild-fire across the Serb-populated areas of Croatia and neighboring Bosnia. Western news organizations, anxious for some "balance" to include in their accounts of what otherwise seemed an impossibly one-sided sequence of events, also gave the claim undue prominence. The story turned out to be nonsense. The claim had been made by an unnamed JNA Colonel to a Belgrade photographer. Reuters issued an unqualified retraction twenty-four hours later. But the damage had been done. Hundreds now screamed for the blood of the injured of Vukovar, as the grisly hand-over of the wounded took place. A single line of JNA officers held them back. Even now, the JNA could present itself to the world's television cameras as an impartial force intervening to separate the "warring factions."

The bodies of Vukovar's dead were barely cold before the JNA organized, for the Belgrade press corps, what it must have believed was a public relations triumph. On November 21 two busloads of reporters were taken, as guests of the JNA, on a tour of the liberated town. "We'll give them lunch right here," said Colonel Milan Gvero, JNA spokesman and future Deputy Commander of the Bosnian Serb forces, as he paraded through the bombed-out remains of the Hotel Dunav, setting the Army a challenge to which it rose magnificently. Marc Champion of the *Independent* captured the absurdity of the event in his dispatch:

*'Massacred civilians this way,' said the army officer, waving his arm in the
direction of a court yard opposite Vukovar's ravaged hospital. Dozens of
journalists were already huddled in the gateway for a look at Exhibit 2 of a
tour organized by the federal army in an attempt, ranging from the grotesque
to the obscene, to give its version of the siege of Vukovar.*

*'I don't see why nothing is being said about the necklaces being made of chil-
dren's fingers, or the forty children killed near here' [said Gvero]*

*Inside the courtyard... were 33 corpses. Next door were more than 50, lined
up in rows and open to the pouring rain. 'They are Serbs who were massacred in the streets,' said Colonel Miodrag Starčević, authoritatively. Many
had medical tags tied to their toes identifying them as patients who had died
in hospital – Asked how he knew they were Serbs, he shrugged.[11]*

The journalists were given JNA ballpoint pens as a souvenir of their visit.

On October 1, the JNA attacked Dubrovnik from Montenegro for the first
time. No one had expected it. Neither of the pretexts that the JNA was using
elsewhere in Croatia – the protection of Serb populations, and the relief of
besieged JNA barracks – applied in Dubrovnik. There were few Serbs living
there[12] and the town had no JNA garrison. But Dubrovnik was a sitting target,
ripe for the taking. It sits on the far tip of a thin strip of coastal land at the
southern extremity of Croatia. Its hinterland, just a few miles inland, lies
inside Bosnia Herzegovina and Montenegro.

The Army imposed a land-blockade from Montenegro to the port of
Neum, that tiny strip of coast which is Bosnia-Herzegovina's only outlet to
the sea. Early next morning, Belgrade Radio announced that "the surrender
of enemy forces is the aim of today's battles around this town." On October 2
and 3, Croatian forces, such as they were, defending that precarious strip of
Croatian territory that tapers off into Montenegro, suffered a rout in the face
of an overwhelming JNA assault. The handful of Croatian National
Guardsmen protecting Dubrovnik's hinterland turned on their heels and
fled. There was no other course of action available to them. As the Federal
Army marched through the prosperous region of Konavle it destroyed almost
everything in sight. In village after village, every house was first looted and
then put to the torch.

On 15 October, the Federal Army entered the resort town of Cavtat, south
of Dubrovnik. They met no resistance. The people of Cavtat resigned them-
selves to what amounted to occupation of their town. Though this meant that
Cavtat lost all contact with the rest of Croatia, the JNA did not allow its
Montenegrin reservists to run riot in the way that they had done in Konavle.
Cavtat was neither looted nor burned.

The Army spent the next two weeks preparing its assault on the city of

Dubrovnik itself. Because Croatia had not expected the Army to attack, the city was left practically undefended. A handful of Croatian National Guardsmen, equipped with a few field guns and mortar-launchers, now found themselves charged with the defense of the ancient city. Dubrovnik is a city built to withstand a siege. Its ancient fortified walls were again called into service. They were almost all that its citizens had by way of defense.

On October 27, after a six-day bombardment, the JNA had brought their gun positions to the very edge of the city. As though to goad the trapped citizens below, a Yugoslav federal flag was hoisted on Žarković hill, a few hundred yards from the Hotel Argentina, where the EC monitors and foreign journalists gathered each night in the basement restaurant and bar. The Hotel Argentina quickly established itself as one of those extraordinary warzone hotels whose management and staff take pride in maintaining normal service despite the collapse of all normality around them. From the seaward terrace of the Hotel Argentina, shielded from federal positions by the hotel itself, and exposed only to the occasional federal gunboat gliding silently past, the journalists, and the white-uniformed EC monitors could follow the progress of individual artillery rounds fired from Žarković as they screamed down over the hotel, and then, in a low arc, over the red roofs of the old town, before slamming into targets into the harbor area, particularly at night, when the shells would glow a fierce orange, the color of fire in the night sky. The EC monitors, pinned down in their hotel, would pass the time teaching journalists to recognize the subtle differences in the sound of ordnance – marine artillery (outgoing) here; 80-millimeter mortar round (incoming) there.[13]

On the day of the Yugoslav federal flag's menacing appearance on Žarković hill, Federal Commander, General Pavle Strugar, issued an ultimatum to the Croat defenders: he demanded that the Croats hand over their weapons, and that all military personnel should leave the city. He guaranteed a safe passage out, adding that he expected a response by eight p.m. that day.

The JNA had Dubrovnik in the palm of its hand. Zagreb panicked. It seemed certain that Dubrovnik would fall, even though both sides recognized that a land-assault down the rocky inclines that surrounded the city on all sides would be costly. Stipe Mesić called on the owners of small boats, up and down the Dalmatian coast, to join him in a convoy to break the JNA's naval blockade. As stunts go, it was bold and imaginative. But it was a stunt none the less. For two days the world watched as Mesić, in the commandeered car-ferry, *Slavija I*, inched his way south from Split, followed by dozens of smaller boats. The flotilla was halted by JNA gun-boats in the Mljet channel and ordered to turn around. Mesić, on the bridge of Slavija I, opened radio contact with the JNA. The guns of the naval patrol were trained in his direction. *Slavija I* was full of Croatian dignitaries, including the Prime Minister, the wife of the Foreign Minister and a popular middle-of-the-road singer Tereza Kesovija – a kind of Croatian Nana Mouskouri, whose home in Konavle had been destroyed in the JNA advance and who could therefore claim symbolic solidarity with the dispossessed. Mesić told the JNA Naval Commander that he intended to proceed to Dubrovnik. The Commander replied that he had orders to let no vessels pass and that, if the flotilla moved on, he would regard this as a hostile act and respond. In other words, *Slavija I* would be blown out of the water. Mesić upped the ante. He was still, after all, President of the Federal Presidency of Yugoslavia and therefore Commander–in–Chief of the armed forces, although he had admitted, more than once, that his control over the Yugoslav Army was about the same as his control over the Finnish Army. "I am your Supreme Commander," he radioed back to the JNA gun-boat, "and I defy you to sink my ship." The celebrities on board – many of them feeling bold after hours in the ship's bar – clapped and cheered. The ship's captain, responsible for the safe passage of his crew and passengers, and unsure who was now commanding the ship, rolled his eyes. Asked who was in charge, he replied, wearily, "Only God knows. Only God knows."

Mesić finally established radio contact with Admiral Stane Brovet, the Deputy Defense Minister. Brovet ordered that the JNA conduct a search of each vessel and, once it had been established that no arms were being smuggled to Dubrovnik, it should be allowed to pass unhindered. On October 30, after thirty hours at sea, *Slavija I* broke the naval blockade and docked in Dubrovnik, bringing goodwill, and precious little else. Mesić left twelve hours later, the plight of Dubrovnik unchanged.

Mesić's antics at sea served a purpose. Drawing attention to the plight of Dubrovnik worked wonders for the international reputation of the JNA. Whatever had motivated the JNA Command in ordering the attack on Dubrovnik in the first place, there seemed little doubt that straightforward malice played an important part in motivating the troops. Day after day, the men on the hills fired artillery and tank-rounds into the prosperous tourist hotels that lined Dubrovnik's modern seafront. They dropped mortar rounds into hotel forecourts and watched, with impunity, as the fire, ignited by the explosions, jumped from car to car destroying everything in its path, leaving a charred landscape of twisted metal and broken glass. The refugees who had poured into Dubrovnik, fleeing the advance, meanwhile cowered in the basements, first bombed out of their homes, now bombed from their places of refuge. There seemed little or no military rationale to much of the bombardment inflicted on Dubrovnik. It was the revenge of the poor boys from the mountains on one of the richest, most westward-leaning parts of former Yugoslavia. It culminated, in November, in the systematic destruction, by wire-guided missile, of every last yacht in the harbor of the old town.[14] The city, which Byron had characterized as the pearl of the Adriatic, was the perfect setting for such an orgy of vengeance. The normally-restrained *Daily Telegraph* – surely the most cautious of Britain's quality newspapers – splashed a front-page headline that read: *Like the Barbarian Hordes Advancing on Rome, the Federal Forces Have Abandoned All Restraint.*[15] Colonel Milan Gvero, the JNA spokesman and the man who masterminded the grotesque media tour of "liberated" Vukovar, dismissed reports of Dubrovnik's destruction throughout. The Croats were setting fire to piles of burning car tires, he claimed. And, absurdly, given the abundant evidence to the contrary, "Not a single speck of Serbian dust has fallen on Dubrovnik."[16]

The Federal Army did not succeed in forcing the surrender of Dubrovnik's defenders. After November's riot of destruction, the siege-lines acquired a semi-permanence, and the battle settled into a seemingly endless low-level stand-off. Events in the Hague and in Belgrade overtook the ambitions of the Montenegrins, and, in May 1992, with the truce in Croatia now five months old, the Croats reached agreement with the JNA.

The JNA withdrawal from Dubrovnik's hinterland was, at the time, overshadowed by the eruption of war in Bosnia-Herzegovina. The Army's reasons for so doing have never been firmly established. But by now, Serb-Croat enmity had cooled. The agreement to withdraw from the last of Croatia's coastline was brokered by Tudjman and Dobrica Ćosić, President of the remnants of Yugoslavia, on September 30, 1992. In the war in Bosnia, the interests of the former foes coincided. Serb and Croat leaders were now meeting in secret to plan the partition, between them, of Bosnia-Herzegovina. When the Federal Army withdrew from its siege-lines around Dubrovnik, many observers believed that it was part of a Serb-Croat deal in which the Croatian *quid pro quo* was a commitment to withdraw from Bosanski Brod in northern Bosnia, thus facilitating that town's capitulation to the Serbs. Certainly Brod was of much greater strategic significance to the Serbs than Dubrovnik's hinterland, guarding, as it did, the vital east-west land-corridor that linked Serb-held territories in western Bosnia to Serbia proper. Concomitantly, Croatia was much more interested in de-blocking Dubrovnik and liberating Croatian territories around it than in holding Brod. This remains the most plausible explanation of Dubrovnik's final liberation, after six months of blockade and intermittent bombardment. It was also an early pointer to the nature of the war in Bosnia: a war in which the Serbs and Croats cooperated to great effect against the common foe of Bosnia-Herzegovina as a single multi-ethnic state.

The fall of Vukovar rendered all of eastern Slavonia vulnerable. Within a week the Army had moved on. The villages of Ernestinovo and Laslovo fell to the juggernaut that had swept Vukovar aside. Federal and Serb forces surrounded and began an intense bombardment of the village of Tenjski

185

Antunovac. The city of Osijek took a battering from JNA artillery and mortar-fire, day after day.

The rationale pointed to a single conclusion. Laslovo protected the road from Osijek to the Croatian town of Djakovo, a vital supply route to Osijek's beleaguered population. Osijek was Croatia's third largest city and the capital of eastern Slavonia. It seemed certain to suffer the same fate as Vukovar. Tens of thousands of Osijek's citizens now poured out of the city in panic, their cars packed with belongings and jamming the main road west, escaping their home town before – as they believed inevitable – it had been completely surrounded.

At the same time, President Tudjman, under international pressure, agreed to the de-blocking of the JNA's Marshal Tito barracks in Zagreb. Tudjman's critics were furious. They accused him of playing into the hands of the enemy in his bid to win international respectability. As the Federal Army was making its next push deeper into eastern Slavonia, Tudjman was handing over hundreds of tanks, armored vehicles and artillery pieces that, in Croat hands, could have been mobilized in the defense of Croatian territory. Tudjman again faced a threat from the right. Croatia buzzed with rumors of a coup.

Tudjman had two of his most prominent critics arrested and detained without trial – Mile Dedaković, Commander of Vukovar's defense, and Dobrosav Paraga, leader of the extreme nationalist Croatian Party of Right. Paraga had claimed, implausibly, to have 10,000 armed men in his HOS militia. He boasted that his men had borne the brunt of Croatia's defense. Neither claim was true. When his Party called, a few days later, for a mass demonstration in Zagreb to protest against Paraga's detention, the rally that they claimed would topple Tudjman attracted only a couple of hundred activists. Paraga never enjoyed the popular support in Croatia that his opposite number in Serbia, Vojislav Šešelj, was to win.

Federal troops and Serb paramilitaries penetrated the outskirts of Osijek. Arkan, the feared leader of the Tigers and police agent, even entered the provincial capital and afterwards threatened to take the town. Panić, still in command of the operation, had orders from his Commander, General Blagoje Adžić – the Army Chief of Staff – to continue. Panić recalled the day:

> *The moment Vukovar fell, Croatia lost the war. Because we could have marched to Zagreb without any problems. Osijek was abandoned. We entered Osijek. We had orders to take Osijek and Županja the moment Vukovar fell, and to march towards Zagreb with two columns, along the Drava and the Sava rivers. And we could have accomplished that in two days. But then I was ordered to go back. I talked to Jović, and Kostić. And I also talked to President Milošević. It was his decision,*

Milošević's decision and it was approved by the rump presidency. He simply said, 'We have no job there in Croat populated areas. We have to protect the Serb areas,' and that was the line. And I told him if the task was to protect Yugoslavia we should go further. Because it would have been easy. The Croats had fled Vinkovci, Županja, and Osijek. When Vukovar fell, Croatia fell too. And we could have marched easily on. But President Milošević said, among other things, that we must stop. And that was the order from the defense minister and I just obeyed. We protected the Serb areas, and that's where the line is here today.

Adžić, the Yugoslav General who had pressed for the use of overwhelming force to keep Slovenia in the federation, was still trying to keep something resembling the old Yugoslavia together. He was thwarted again by Milošević, now firmly in control of the rump Yugoslav Presidency. By now, the collective Head of State consisted of only half its members – three from Serbia, the fourth from Montenegro.[17]

On November 24, one week after the fall of Vukovar, Tudjman addressed a panic-stricken Croatian nation on television. He said Croatia had succeeded in "internationalizing" the conflict and that the war was not, despite the claims of those who were plotting a coup to overthrow the Croatian Government, a lost war. Croatia, he said, had begun the war against the largest Communist army in Europe with virtually nothing, and had succeeded in building strong defenses, while, at the same time, pursuing successful diplomatic negotiations.

In fact, two things had happened during the long siege of Vukovar. First, Croatia, having begun the war largely undefended, built an army. In August, Tudjman had appointed General Antun Tus to take charge of Croatia's armed forces. As a Croat, Tus had been dismissed as Commander of the Federal Air Force in May. In three months, he had turned a rag-bag chaotic assembly of volunteers and reserve policemen into a disciplined fighting force. When he had taken command, the Croatian armed forces consisted of a National Guard of four brigades, together with a large reserve police force. By October, Tus had assembled all available forces into a system of thirty-five brigades, each with a specific military function. By December, he claimed to have 250,000 fighting men under arms, organized, across the republic, in sixty brigades.

At the same time, the tactic, inherited from Tudjman's former Defense Minister Martin Špegelj, of blockading barracks, had yielded rewards. In September, the surrender of the Varaždin garrison had provided Tus with the hardware to form his first tank brigade. Soon, JNA garrisons were falling to Croatian forces like dominoes. At the end of September, Tudjman had claimed that seventy JNA installations – ranging from full garrisons to arms and ammunition stores – had fallen to his forces. The evidence, despite Panić's confident assertion that he could have been in Zagreb in forty-eight hours, is that Milošević called a halt to the war when the Serbs, backed by the JNA, had won all they were capable of winning without an endlessly bloody and costly conflict.

At the same time, there were important JNA victories that gave territorial cohesion to the new Serb entity in Croatia. In September, the JNA took Petrinja, a town that had had a population that was half-Serb and half-Croat before the war. The fall of Petrinja redrew the frontier of the Serbian Krajina along the natural barrier of the Kupa River, and just thirty-five miles from Zagreb. (Serb forces then turned their guns, unsuccessfully, on the neighboring and larger town of Sisak, which the Croats managed to hold throughout the war.) And, overshadowed by the fall of Vukovar, the JNA pushed the Croats out of Slunj, thus forging what proved to be a vital land-bridge between the two largest Serb enclaves in Croatia – that of Knin Krajina and the territory around Glina in central Croatia.

Secondly, Tudjman's claim to have internationalized the war was justified. In late November, Milošević agreed to the deployment of international peace-keeping troops in Croatia. He did this largely because the troops were to be deployed on his terms, in a way that was consistent with his central war aim, which was the partition of Croatia into Serb-and-Croat entities, the redrawing of borders between Croatia and Yugoslavia, and the eventual secession, by the Serb-populated territories in Croatia, to the rump Yugoslav federation. By the end of the year, Tudjman had won his country's independence. But it was a victory that was far from complete. The war had left a third of his country under occupation. And it had almost cut Croatia in half.

1 The two events might, indeed, be connected. There is strong evidence that Kadijević's secret trip to Moscow in March had led him to believe that it would only be safe for the JNA to launch a state-of-emergency throughout Yugoslavia, once Gorbachev had been deposed and replaced by hard-liners in the Kremlin who would block any western attempt to oppose the JNA.

2 Associated Press, August 20, 1991.

3 Although Vukovar had been subjected to sporadic shelling since July.

4 Although weeks of protracted local negotiations had taken place, and relations had been relatively warm, Tašić finally left under the auspices of an EC-brokered ceasefire deal that applied to the republic as a whole. See Chapter Fourteen of this book: Yugoslavia à la carte.

5 Associated Press, September 19, 1991.

6 Many had no idea where they were going. Associated Press quoted one conscript who, when asked where the tanks were going, replied "I don't know – probably to beat the Croats."

7 According to the 1991 census, Vukovar was 43.7 percent Croat, and 37.4 percent Serb.

8 The records were kept by the hospital director Vesna Bosanac. They are credible

because of their dispassionate precise nature, and because, if anything, they are modest claims given the intensity and duration of the bombardment. They also conflict sharply with the dramatic and exaggerated accounts reported by Croatian television.

9 *Tanjug*, November 5, 1991.

10 The account of Tudjman's encounter with Dedaković is recalled by Mesić, to whom Dedaković also spoke.

11 *The Independent*, November 22, 1991.

12 Dubrovnik was 82.5 percent Croat, and 6.7 percent Serb.

13 For a graphic account of life under siege in Dubrovnik, see Alec Russell, *Prejudice and Plum Brandy*, Michael Joseph, London, 1993.

14 The destruction of the harbor area provided some of the most graphic television coverage of the war in Croatia. It was captured by ITN correspondent, Paul Davis, and his cameraman, Nigel Thomson. It did much to shift the climate of international public opinion against the Yugoslav Army and the Serb leadership.

15 *Daily Telegraph*, November 13, 1991

16 Gvero said this to Michael Montgomery, a reporter then with the *Daily Telebraph*.

17 The Macedonian representative, Vasil Tupurkovski, stopped attending Federal Presidency sessions during the Croatian war, as did Bogić Bogićević, the member for Bosnia Herzegovina.

14

YUGOSLAVIA À LA CARTE
Lord Carrington's Plan
September 1991–January 1992

When Lord Carrington took on the task of bringing peace to Yugoslavia, the President of the EC Council of Foreign Ministers, Hans van den Broek, told him to work towards a comprehensive peace settlement "within two months." Carrington accepted the job on those terms, and was later to remark that van den Broek's belief that the problems of Yugoslavia's disintegration could be resolved so quickly was, in retrospect, "absolutely ridiculous" – a sign that "we were all pretty ignorant of how difficult it was going to be."

Carrington is an urbane and likeable English aristocrat with a distinguished diplomatic career behind him, a man to whom, in class-conscious Britain, the word "statesman" naturally attaches itself. He had been Mrs. Thatcher's first Foreign Secretary and had taken most of the credit for steering the former British colony of Rhodesia out of civil war and into independence as Zimbabwe in 1980. Two years later, he took personal responsibility for failing to prevent the Argentinian invasion of the Falkland Islands and resigned from the Cabinet, relinquishing, on a point of principle, the job, which, for most of his life, he had most coveted. The political obituaries of the day declared him a man of unimpeachable integrity. He went on to serve a term as Secretary General of NATO and was now enjoying semi-retirement as Chairman of Christie's, the auction house. From the beginning, Carrington's involvement in the Yugoslav conflict had about it the feel of the part-time amateur; he did not give up his day-job. In keeping with van den Broek's naive conviction that a constitutional future for Yugoslavia could be agreed within the time-frame of his own six-month Presidency of the community, Lord Carrington divided his time between the Dutch capital and the gilded opulence of Christie's auction rooms in London's West End.

Carrington convened his first session at the Hague on September 7. It was an acrimonious gathering. He recognized, after his first meeting with Tudjman and Milošević, that, in the absence of an internationally-brokered constitutional agreement, the two largest nations would try to impose a solution on the rest of Yugoslavia by force:

> When I first talked to Presidents Tudjman and Milošević, it was quite clear to me that both of them had a solution which was mutually satisfactory, which was that they were going to carve it up between them. They were going to carve Bosnia up. The Serb [areas] would go to Serbia, the Croat [areas]

to Croatia. And they weren't worried too much, either of them, about what was going to happen to the Muslims. And they didn't really mind about Slovenia.

Slovenia already had *de facto* independence; neither the Serbs nor the Croats were concerned about the consequences of that. Carrington knew what that meant: to try to put Yugoslavia back together again would be, by now, to shut the stable door after the horse had bolted. So, he began from the assumption that Yugoslavia had already broken apart. But, very early, he also saw the implications of immediate recognition of Slovenian and Croatian independence. He insisted that independence should not be recognized until a Yugoslav-wide constitutional settlement had been found that was acceptable to all the republics. In this single respect alone, Carrington, for all that he appeared semi-detached and only partially committed to the project, came closer to producing a constitutional framework which might have facilitated the peaceful dissolution of Yugoslavia – or at least a less bloody dissolution – than any of those who came after him.

Carrington picked up where the failed Izetbegović-Gligorov Plan had left off: he recognized the six republics as the constituent units of the former federal state, and produced a Plan that would give each of them as much sovereignty as it wanted. It was, as Lord Carrington put it, an attempt to draw up a "menu" of inter-republican institutions – for foreign policy, economic affairs, a common currency, defense, and so on. Each republic would choose which institutions it would participate in.

> *It seemed to me that the right way to do it was to allow those who wanted to be independent to be independent, and to associate themselves with a central organization as far as they wanted to. Those who didn't want to be independent, well, they could stay within what had been Yugoslavia. In other words you could do it, so to speak, à la carte.*

But what became known as the Carrington Plan failed for the same reason that the Izetbegović-Gligorov Plan failed: Milošević was against it.

On October 4, Carrington achieved what he thought was a breakthrough. He brought Tudjman and Milošević together, along with the Federal Defense Minister Veljko Kadijević. They agreed to divide the peace conference into two working groups: the first, and more important of these, would work on the constitutional future of the country; and the second would concentrate on bringing about an end to the fighting in Croatia which, since the September 7 gathering, had escalated dramatically. At that meeting, all present agreed three points of principle, from which the peace conference would proceed. According to the session minutes, these were:

A. a loose association or alliance of sovereign or independent republics.

B. adequate arrangements to be made for the protection of communities, including human rights guarantees and possibly special status for certain areas.

C. no unilateral changes in borders.

It seemed that Milošević had at last, under international pressure, agreed that the republics, and not the nations, were the legitimate constituent units of federal Yugoslavia.

Four days later, the working groups went into session. The task of the working group on institutional relations was to find areas of common interest, around which pan-Yugoslav institutions could be built. The discussion immediately reverted to the sterile exchanges that had dominated the Presidential summits of the spring and summer of that year. The minute of that session recorded: "The basic position of Slovenia was to accept only very limited common institutional arrangements." Croatia was prepared to cooperate in many areas, but only on an inter-governmental basis – in other words, provided such cooperation did not compromise its independence. Both these positions were uncompromising. But they were not, in themselves, inconsistent with Lord Carrington's *à la carte* design for Yugoslavia. Serbia's position was. The minutes recorded the following:

> *Serbia could not accept the working groups continuing to proceed on the basis of the lowest common denominator of identified interests and institutional arrangements. The conference should try to identify genuine common interests which could be defended* in a common state. It was essential for all Serbs to live in one state, not in a number of independent republics bound by little more than interstate relations. *If this was not accepted by the other republics, the right course would be to recognize those republics wishing it [independence],* after having settled the question of the succession of Yugoslavia and after having agreed on border changes. *(Emphasis, in roman type, added by authors.)*

In other words, Serbia not only wanted to annex those parts of Croatia (and, by implication, Bosnia-Herzegovina) where Serbs predominated; it also wanted to be considered the sole legitimate successor state to the old federal republic. Agreeing to a voluntary dissolution would thwart both ambitions.

Carrington none the less persevered. By the middle of October, the war in Croatia was now unrestrained (see previous chapter). Carrington was under growing criticism for his eagerness to find common ground with those who had ordered what was plainly going to be the destruction of Vukovar and the siege and bombardment of Dubrovnik. On October 16, Carrington distributed to the republics' leaders a detailed seven-page proposal entitled *Arrangements for a General Settlement.*

Srdjan Ilić

Serbian police crush ethnic Albanian demonstrations in Pristina, Kosovo, on March 28, 1989, the day the new Serbian constitution was adopted. During two days of protests twenty-two Albanians and two policemen were killed.

Tomislav Peternek

Slobodan Milošević addressing a crowd of about one million Serbs at Gazimestan in Kosovo on June 28, 1989, to mark the six-hundredth anniversary of Serbia's defeat by the Turks. "Six centuries later again we are in battles and quarrels. They are not armed battles, though such things should not be excluded yet."

Srdjan Ilić

The leaders of the six Yugoslav republics in 1991 (left to right): Momir Bulatović of Montenegro; Milan Kučan of Slovenia; Franjo Tudjman of Croatia; Kiro Gligorov of Macedonia; Alija Izetbegović of Bosnia-Herzegovina; and Slobodan Milošević of Serbia.

Vreme

Slobodan Milošević greeting Franjo Tudjman in Belgrade, January 1991.

Alija Izetbegović, the President of Bosnia-Herzegovina.

Srdjan Ilić

Serbian soldiers escorting captured Croatian refugees after the fall of Vukovar, November 1991.

Srdjan Ilić

AP / Wide World Photos

(left) Yugoslav defense minister General Veljko Kadijević.

(below) Ethnic cleansing in Bijeljina, April 1992. Arkan's Serb paramilitary fighters assault a Muslim man, having thrown him out of a first-floor window.

Patrick Robert / Sygma

3,500 Muslim prisoners held by Serbs in cowsheds in Manjaca, Bosnia-Herzegovina. August 9, 1992

Rick Maiman / Sygma

Lord Owen and Cyrus Vance hold a press conference at the United Nations. February 1993.

Paul Lowe / Magnum Photos

(above) In the center of Sarajevo, UN troops stop to pick up a Bosnian civilian killed in the street during an artillery attack. 1994.

Paul Lowe / Magnum Photos

(above) The funeral for six members of the Dragnic family, all of whom were killed in a single attack, Sarajevo. 1994.

Srdjan Ilić

(left) Muslims being evacuated from Srebrenica by UN trucks in April 1993. A child has fallen off in the crush but is later picked up.

Srdjan Ilić

Bosnian Serb leader Radovan Karadžić and Ratko Mladić, the commander of the Bosnian Serb forces, reviewing their advances in Operation Goražde, April 1994.

AP / Wide World Photos

President of Bosnia Alija Izetbegović shakes hands with Serbian President Slobodan Milošević as Franjo Tudjman, President of Croatia, looks on as the Proximity Peace Talks begin at Wright-Patterson Air Force Base in Dayton, Ohio. November 1, 1995.

The Carrington Plan was overshadowed by the unfolding of war in Bosnia and the intervention of the United Nations. But it deserves greater recognition for what it tried to achieve, not least because it stands as testimony to the extent to which the international community and the other republics were prepared to go to meet Serb anxieties and aspirations. The Plan guaranteed a wide gamut of individual, cultural and political rights to the Serbs outside Serbia. In areas of Croatia and Bosnia where they formed a majority, the Serbs were, under the Hague proposal, entitled to use the national emblems and flags of their choice, the right to a second nationality, jointly held with that of the republic to which they belonged, and an education system which "respects the values and needs" of the Serbs. Finally, they were granted the right to their own parliament, their own administrative structure, including a regional police force, and their own judiciary.[1]

It did not satisfy Milošević. When the Presidents of the republics reconvened in the Hague on October 18, Carrington began by asking each of the republics' Presidents in turn whether they accepted paragraph one of *Arrangements for a General Settlement*. Milošević said he did not. Lord Carrington asked whether this meant that Serbia had changed its position since the meeting two weeks earlier when Milošević had agreed to the three points of principle. Milošević repeated that Serbia was rejecting the first and most fundamental paragraph of the Carrington Plan.

What happened between October 4 and October 18 to make Milošević change his mind? One clue to his thinking came from the Slovene Foreign Minister Dimitrij Rupel, who observed that the single greatest obsession of the delegates from Serbia was not the Serbs of Croatia at all, but the national minorities within their own borders, and, in particular, the status of the Albanians in Kosovo. The Carrington Plan applied equally throughout Yugoslavia. The far-reaching autonomy granted to the Serbs of Croatia was also, in theory, granted to the Albanians. During one of the working group sessions, attended by the republics' Foreign Ministers, Rupel had, largely for the sake of mischief since it didn't concern Slovenia one way or the other, raised the Kosovo question:

> *The only thing that really bothered the Serbs in The Hague was the question of Kosovo. In one of the commissions they started to talk about how to regulate the problem of minorities, the Serbian minority in Croatia – at that time it was only Croatia under discussion – and how painful it was for them, the Serbs, to live under Croatian rule. Then, I said, we should design in this new arrangement equal rights for all minorities, including the Albanians, ha. Jovanović [the Serbian Foreign Minister] really got mad, that was really something I shouldn't have said. It was the end of our friendship.*

Milošević had risen to power by exploiting the plight of the Kosovo Serbs; he had cemented his power by centralizing the state, and abolishing the autonomy that the 1974 constitution gave to Kosovo. By extending to the Albanians the same rights that Milošević was demanding for the Serbs of Croatia, the Carrington Plan struck at the very foundations of Milošević's power base. He could not accept it, and, knowing that the price of doing so was growing international isolation for his republic, Milošević stood alone against the Carrington Plan.

He had not expected to be alone. He had counted on the slavish loyalty of Serbia's ally Montenegro. The surprise of the October 18 session was the position adopted by Montenegrin President Momir Bulatović. The session had been delayed by more than an hour because of his late arrival: he had been attending an all-night session of the Montenegrin Parliament, convened to discuss the merits of the Carrington Plan. The Parliament had decided not to take a position on the Carrington Plan, but rather to leave the decision in the hands of Bulatović personally.[2] When his turn to speak came, everyone, including Carrington and Milošević, expected Bulatović simply to follow the Milošević line: Montenegro had been reduced to little more than a satellite of Serbia since Milošević's "anti-bureaucratic revolution" had installed Bulatović's pro-Belgrade regime in power there. Bulatović dropped a bombshell. He said simply: "I accept the first part of the Hague proposal."

Milošević's claim that the Serbs formed the legitimate successor state to federal Yugoslavia rested on the assumption that a rump federation would survive the secession of those republics which chose to leave. He had taken for granted the loyalty of Montenegro, where public opinion was known to be strongly pro-Milošević. Without Montenegro, Serbia's claim to be the sole legitimate successor state could not be sustained; there could, by definition, be no rump federal Yugoslavia unless there was at least a second republic with which to federate. Bulatović's rebellion left Milošević and Serbia isolated. Bulatović's support for the Carrington Plan shocked and angered him; equally, it shocked and delighted the other Presidents around the table. Bulatović said the Carrington Plan represented the best chance of ending the war and of redeeming his republic's damaged international reputation:

We thought the plan was quite enough. It made it possible for us to realize our own interests and to have the interests of the others also taken into account. It was an excellent means to put an end to the war, a war which affected us also in Montenegro, because 10 percent of our population was mobilized for that war. I had been under enormous pressure. During a visit to the United States, they had treated me there as a savage – who is this person whose citizens are attacking and destroying Dubrovnik? We never needed Dubrovnik and, really, we could no longer allow ourselves to have our people die in vain, to have Montenegro acquire an unfavorable international reputation.

Bulatović had, in fact, been tempted away from the Belgrade line by the lure of EC money. The Italian Foreign Minister, Gianni de Michelis had once asked Stipe Mesić, Croatia's representative on the Federal Presidency, how Montenegro could be coaxed away from its loyalty to Belgrade? "Buy them! Buy them!" Mesić had urged. "They won't cost much – they have nothing down there." De Michelis had then discussed with Bulatović an EC development package amounting to millions of US dollars. De Michelis sat between Milošević and Bulatović at lunch on October 18; Milošević speaks good English. But Bulatović speaks Italian. According to De Michelis:

> *Before the start of the conference I asked to meet Bulatović briefly, we talked quickly, I insisted that Montenegro adopt a position of its own and Bulatović told me that he was interested, that he would do that. And so he did. He told me that Montenegro was interested in peace... and on the other hand he was very interested in economic-development relations with the European Community. He considered Italy Montenegro's natural channel to Europe.*
>
> *At that time there were negotiations for the program of cooperation between Italy and Montenegro. An important program, about 30 or 40 billion lire in various projects, for Montenegro, a country of 600,000 inhabitants.*

Carrington was warned by many not to set much store on Bulatović's rebellion against Milošević. "Bulatović will have his throat cut for this," someone in the hall commented. Henri Wejnaendts, the Dutch ambassador to France, who was Carrington's aide, later claimed to have had a conversation with Milošević in a men's room where Milošević had contemptuously dismissed Bulatović's rebellion. "Bulatović," he told Wejnaendts, "will not stay President of Montenegro for long."[3]

The next day, Bulatović came under a volley of political fire. The Belgrade press accused him of treachery. Serbian newspapers were full of critical headlines – a warning that Milošević would not spare even Montenegrin brethren. Opinion in Montenegro, as far as it could be gauged, appeared to turn sharply against him. There were demonstrations in Podgorica. Milošević's travelling "Anti-Bureaucratic revolution" took to the road again. Bulatović was summoned to Belgrade for a series of meetings designed to break his will to resist.

A wave of enormous attacks came on my head after I accepted the Carrington plan.

There was a series of unpleasant meetings in Belgrade. The entire press in Belgrade labelled me a traitor. And some [of Milošević's men] would direct- ly ask me whether I was a spy, whether I had received money from a foreign country. The next days were very explosive. The media would say I stabbed Milošević in the back.

Bulatović was finally forced to agree to a referendum on the issue. He knew he was bound to lose. Montenegro, brow-beaten into submission by a Serb bandwagon that would certainly have cost Bulatović his job, had he con- tinued to resist, joined Serbia in backing an amendment to the Carrington Plan that recognized the existence of a legitimate successor state, consisting of those territories which did not choose secession.

On October 30, Serbia and Montenegro sent their amendment to the Hague, insisting that a clause be inserted in Paragraph One, declaring that the federal republic of Yugoslavia continue to exist for those who did not wish to secede. The Serb-Montenegrin amendment amounted to an out- right rejection. It was strengthened by the result of Montenegro's referen- dum, at the end of October. In response to a question asking whether Montenegro should stay in Yugoslavia there was, predictably, an over- whelming vote in favor.

Carrington declared that the amendment was "totally unacceptable." He saw in it Milošević's ambition to carve out a new territorial entity, comprised of Serb-populated areas in Croatia and Bosnia. He said:

I think it all came down as usual to the fact that he [Milošević] had come to the conclusion that Greater Serbia was the thing that was important, and that if he agreed to chapter one as it then was, which was Croatia getting their independence, and Bosnia if they wanted it, then this would not be pos- sible for him. Otherwise I don't think there was any conceivable reason because none of his arguments about the retention of Yugoslavia made sense.

The peace process never got beyond that fundamental stumbling block. Gradually, international public opinion turned against Serbia. Though Milošević was not yet widely seen as the instigator of, and guiding hand in, the war, he was now identified as the main obstacle to peace. On November 8, an EC summit in Rome recommended trade sanctions against Yugoslavia, including an oil embargo. As usual the Foreign Ministers were determinedly even-handed: EC sanctions would apply to the whole country and all sides but they were soon to be lifted for all republics except for Serbia and Montenegro. By November, international dissatisfaction with Lord Carrington's progress had produced a multi-track peace process that Milošević could turn to his advantage: Cyrus Vance entered the fray as the

UN-sponsored peace-maker, appointed by outgoing Secretary General Javier Perez de Cuellar. Vance, a former US Secretary of State, promised to work alongside, rather than against, Lord Carrington. But Vance had something to offer that Carrington did not – a UN peace-keeping force.

Croatia had appealed for international troops to be deployed almost from the beginning. It wanted "blue helmets" deployed along Croatia's borders with Serbia and Bosnia. Serbia, as always, played a double game. In public, Milošević's men rejected out of hand the very idea of foreign intervention in what they insisted was an internal Yugoslav matter. In private, they saw that foreign deployment could be turned to their advantage. It was a question of choosing the right moment. They welcomed Cyrus Vance to Belgrade and the center of gravity in the international peace process shifted from the EC to the UN.

Milošević had decided the previous month to admit UN troops. The right moment came at the end of November. Milošević's calculation was two-fold: that the JNA had achieved most of its military objective in Croatia; and that international recognition of Croatia's independence was now a matter of weeks away. According to Borisav Jović:

> At that point the war in Croatia was under control in the sense that all the Serb territories were under our control, all, that is, except central Slavonia. Slobodan and I after many conversations decided now was the time to get the UN troops into Croatia to protect the Serbs there. We saw the danger – when Croatia would be recognized, which we realized would happen, the JNA would be regarded as a foreign army invading another country. So we had better get the UN troops in early to protect the Serbs.

International mediation was now moving in three distinct directions: Lord Carrington's Hague conference, to which all parties were still formally committed, and which stressed the importance of a comprehensive settlement for all parts of the country; Cyrus Vance's plan to deploy troops in Croatia which envisaged a UN-mediated solution for Croatia alone and which did not address the other republics; and a third, coming from a new and increasingly confident player on the international stage – Chancellor Helmut Kohl of recently-reunified Germany. This was, to borrow Lord Carrington's own metaphor, international mediation à la carte. Each of the parties to the conflict was presented with a menu of peace processes from which to choose. Bosnia and Macedonia continued to place their faith in Lord Carrington; Serbia favored the United Nations and its envoy, Cyrus Vance; Croatia was under the wing of Germany.

In early December the pace of events shifted up a gear. Tudjman visited Bonn and met both Kohl and Germany's Foreign Minister Hans Dietrich

Genscher. Public opinion in Germany had been strongly anti-Serbian from the beginning. The German news media had given prominence to the Yugoslav conflict throughout. Germany considered itself the European country most intimately connected with Yugoslavia. It had a large Yugoslav *gastarbeiter* community and a powerful Croatian lobby. Tudjman returned to Zagreb clearly convinced that Germany was his country's saviour. He told Croatian television that Germany "has no hesitation about its decision to recognize Croatian independence."[4]

Two days later, Vance's work in Belgrade bore fruit. The parties, he announced, had agreed the basis on which a UN troop-deployment could be prepared. Croatia, buoyed by Germany's assurances of imminent recognition, had dropped its demand for UN troops to be deployed along its borders; Serbia had dropped its opposition to foreign intervention. Both sides had agreed to what Vance called an "ink-spot" deployment – UN troops taking control of a number of disputed territories to be agreed by both sides. Milošević calculated – with good reason – that a UN-protected ceasefire would freeze the existing lines of confrontation, which would, in time, transform themselves naturally into new, *de facto*, international borders. But he first had to persuade Croatia's Serbs to accept it.

Germany had been pushing for recognition of Croatian and Slovenian independence for months. This fuelled Serb paranoia about German ambitions in the region. Veljko Kadijević, Branko Kostić and Borisav Jović all talked menacingly about the rise of a Fourth Reich, and a new German *drag nach osten*. There is no evidence that the dispassionate, more calculating Milošević shared their anxieties. But he played on them whenever it suited his purposes.

By the end of November, the destruction of Vukovar, the displacement of half-a-million Croats and 230,000 Serbs from their homes, the occupation of almost a third of Croatian territory by Serb irregulars and the JNA, and the apparently pointless vindictive siege and bombardment of Dubrovnik, pushed German public opinion over the edge. To Bonn, Lord Carrington's peace efforts – stalemated for more than a month because of Milošević's intransigence – began to look like a smoke-screen for inaction. The arms embargo imposed by the UN Security Council on September 26 against all former Yugoslavia had helped them to preserve their huge military superiority. (Bosnia was to suffer from the effects of this resolution even more than Croatia which actually imposed its own embargo on the Muslims.) Later this embargo would pose a dilemma for international policy. The Bosnian government would argue that if the West was not ready to defend Bosnia, then they should at least allow them to get arms. The US argued in favor of lifting the embargo, while EU countries and Russia, with troops on the ground, were against. When other states – most notably Britain and the United States – argued that premature recognition would derail the peace process, political opinion in Germany, across all three main parties, was contemptuous. Bonn argued that the peace process had been derailed already – by Belgrade. Genscher was convinced that recognition would halt Belgrade's military advance through Croatia, and that Milošević was continuing to take part in a peace process he had no intention of honoring in order to buy time to complete his military task. Three years later Genscher was unrepentant:

> *This was obvious right from the start. It was obvious that they wanted to use the negotiations only to enhance their situation by military forces. I came to this opinion very quickly the Serb leadership wanted to gain time, in order to continue their military actions, and to achieve their military goals... It became more and more clear that a further delay of recognition would constitute an encouragement to continue the war.*

Germany resolved to force the issue at the forthcoming EC Foreign Ministers meeting in Brussels on December 15 and 16. Genscher made it clear that if the EC did not move towards recognition, then Germany would break ranks and recognize unilaterally. It was a bitter blow to the spirit of Maastricht. Britain vehemently opposed recognition. Hans van den Broek of the Netherlands had also become intimately acquainted with the complexities of the Yugoslav conflict during his time as President of the Council of Ministers. He, too, believed premature recognition would be disastrous. But neither Britain nor the Netherlands was prepared to put the Yugoslav peace process before EC unity. To oppose Germany would be to destroy the fragile hopes that the EC still nurtured to build a common security, defense and foreign policy structure. Britain – to Lord Carrington's astonishment and irritation – did not even send its senior Foreign Minister Douglas Hurd to the summit. His deputy, Douglas Hogg, went in his place. It was a signal that Britain had decided not to put up more than a token fight.

Lord Carrington also attended the summit. He warned the Foreign Ministers that recognition now would – as he put it – "torpedo" the peace process. Paragraph One of his draft *General Settlement* offered the prospect of independence, and recognition, to any republic that wanted it, but only after a comprehensive settlement had been reached; only after the seceding republics had agreed on their relationship with those from whom they were seceding. Carrington told the Foreign Ministers that it would be impossible to continue the peace process if recognition were granted:

> *I said very strongly that I felt that the timing of this was wrong. I pointed out that early recognition would torpedo the conference. There was no way in*

which the conference would continue after that. It would make no sense at all. And that if they recognized Croatia and Slovenia then they would have to ask all the others whether they wanted their independence. And that if they asked the Bosnians whether they wanted their independence, they inevitably would have to say yes, and that this would mean a civil war [in Bosnia]. And I put this as strongly as I possibly could.

The meeting lasted most of the night, with Germany bulldozing the other eleven members towards recognition. In the end, a compromise was reached that swept away what was left of Lord Carrington's peace conference and the carefully laid legalistic plans that the EC had been drawing up to consider applications for independence. On the morning of December 17, the eleven succumbed to what amounted to an ultimatum from Germany and agreed to invite all Yugoslav republics who wanted to apply for recognition to do so within a week: applications had to be submitted by December 24. These would then be considered by a five-member Arbitration Commission, under the chairmanship of Judge Robert Badinter of France. The Badinter Commission, as it became known, had been appointed in November to draw up a set of conditions which each republic would have to satisfy before being granted EC recognition. The Commission was to report its findings on January 15.

Even this compromise did not satisfy Genscher. Croatia was by no means certain to qualify for recognition under the Badinter criteria, which would almost certainly demand that republics seeking independence should have adequate protection for national minorities, and should demonstrate control of its own frontiers. So Genscher made it clear that Germany would not regard the findings of the Badinter Commission as binding, and that Germany intended to proceed, unilaterally, with recognition, whatever the outcome. Genscher seemed determined to make Croatian independence a *fait accompli* by Christmas. To do so, he had driven a coach-and-horses through the Carrington peace process, and rendered the deliberations of the Badinter Commission of little more than academic value. He got what he wanted. Croats began to sing a new song: *Danke Deutschland*. In the Adriatic port city of Split, a popular quayside café on the old city waterfront changed its name to Café Genscher. Chancellor Kohl declared it a "great triumph for German foreign policy." Lord Carrington was furious:

> *It seemed to me that there was no point in continuing with the conference after that. When two countries had got their independence, they had no further interest in the proceedings, and I don't suppose the Serbs had much interest in it either. The only incentive we had to get anybody to agree to anything was the ultimate recognition of their independence. Otherwise there was no carrot. You just threw it away, just like that.*

Two days later a defeated Lord Carrington took to the road again, visiting each of the main capitals in the country. Bosnia, which had consistently cautioned against early recognition of Croatia and Slovenia, was now caught in the dilemma it had most feared: its choice was now to join Slovenia and Croatia in seeking independence and, by so doing, risk provoking civil war against its own Serbs, or to stay inside a rump Yugoslavia dominated by Serbia and, by so doing, suffer the same fate, ultimately, as Kosovo, Vojvodina and Montenegro which had been brought under the complete control of Belgrade.

Four republics applied – Slovenia, Croatia, Macedonia and Bosnia-Herzegovina. When the Badinter Commission submitted its report in the new year, it did indeed impose conditions that Croatia could not meet. It recommended that only Slovenia and Macedonia be granted recognition. The EC ignored it. Croatia got its independence. Macedonia did not. Its recognition was vetoed by Greece, who objected to the name of the country on the grounds that it implied territorial ambition towards Greece's own northern province of the same name. Thus the EC's first confident experiment in common foreign policy-making ended in shambles, the Community's own carefully formulated legal and diplomatic mechanisms shot down by old-fashioned political expediency.

The United States did not join the EC in recognizing Slovenia and Croatia. President Bush's leading foreign policy-makers, Brent Scowcroft and Lawrence Eagleburger, later expressed regret that they had not done more to restrain German influence. But after his abortive mission to Belgrade, six months earlier, Secretary of State James Baker had determined that this was not an American problem and that it should be left to the Europeans who had, in any case, risen to the challenge with enthusiasm and naive optimism. According to Scowcroft:

> *Eagleburger and I were the most concerned here about Yugoslavia. The President and Baker were furthest on the other side. Baker would say 'We don't have a dog in this fight.' The President would say to me once a week 'Tell me again what this is all about.'.. We tried very hard to prevent the recognition of Slovenia and Croatia. The British and French agreed, but the Germans for the first time really asserted themselves in the Community. The French were very sympathetic to us but in the end the cohesiveness of the Community was more important.*

Milošević agreed to the deployment of UN troops in Croatia because he saw, in it, a way of achieving what he wanted – the consolidation of his military gains in Croatia. He now encountered an unexpected obstacle – a rebellion from within the leadership of the Krajina Serbs, a leadership which he had nurtured and sustained and which now, for the first time that mattered, refused to do his bidding.

The Vance Plan, which had been unveiled during the last few weeks of 1991, called for the setting up of three areas to be known as United Nations Protected Areas – or UNPAs. These would coincide roughly with the three chunks of territory held by Serb and/or JNA forces. Upwards of 10,000 UN troops would be deployed in the UNPAs, for the protection of the people there. In return, the JNA would withdraw entirely from Croatia, and the Serb paramilitaries would be disbanded and disarmed, surrendering their weapons either to the JNA before withdrawal, or, if they preferred, to the UN force, who would store them, intact, at locations inside the UNPAs. Both sides would agree to a ceasefire that would, in effect, freeze the existing front-lines. The United Nations Protection Force (or UNPROFOR, as it was to be known) would therefore form a thin blue line separating the Serb-held areas from the rest of the republic. The Plan also contained a provision for the return of all refugees to their homes.

The leader of the Krajina Serbs, Milan Babić, set his face against the Vance Plan from the beginning. He now found himself in open conflict with Milošević. For Babić, the war had been waged to secure the right of the Serbs in Krajina to stay in Yugoslavia. The JNA was the single most visible symbol, and most potent guarantor, of Yugoslav sovereignty in Krajina. Withdrawal of the JNA looked to him like a betrayal of his most fundamental war aim. In the Serb nationalist mindset, it had been the historic misfortune of the warrior Serb people always to "win the war and lose the peace." Babić argued that Milošević was trying to force the Krajina Serbs to repeat the pattern.

At the end of January, Milošević resolved to break Babić. Babić was summoned to Belgrade for a meeting with the Yugoslav Federal Presidency (all, now, loyal Milošević placemen), the High Command of the JNA, and the leaders of the Bosnian Serbs. Milošević's men began by trying to reassure. Jović – Serbia's representative on the rump Federal Presidency – gave Babić a guarantee that in the event of a Croatian attack on Krajina, the JNA would redeploy to defend the Serbs there. The Federal Presidency passed a resolution to this effect.

Babić did not budge. He argued, in turn, that if Bosnia seceded from Yugoslavia, as the Bosnian Government had recently announced it intended to do, this would leave the Krajina Serbs with no direct land link to Serbia proper. In those circumstances, guarantees of JNA protection were worthless unless the JNA stayed on Krajina territory. It was the first time the question of the northern corridor – which came to dominate so much of the fighting and strategic planning in Bosnia's war later that year – was raised as a vital issue.

It appeared to Jović that the Krajina Serbs were afraid of an independent

Bosnia and that they would be cut off from Yugoslavia – and vulnerable to a Croat attack. So Jović made clear that the Bosnian Serbs were committed to doing the same thing as the Croatian Serbs, so would never be cut off. In other words, the corridor would always exist.

The leaders of the Bosnian Serbs – Radovan Karadžić and Biljana Plavšić – were called in to reassure Babić that they had no intention of allowing what they considered the Serb territories of Bosnia to leave Yugoslavia. Should Bosnia go ahead with its independence declaration, they would follow the precedent set by Babić himself and wage a war to redraw Bosnia's borders. In the northwestern Bosnian city of Banja Luka, Serbs were the dominant national group. They depended on the northern corridor as much as the Krajina Serbs. The role of the Bosnian Serb leaders in the breaking of Babić provides a small but revealing insight: Bosnia was already locked into Belgrade's strategic thinking about the redrawn borders of what would become a greater Serbian state.

The meeting dragged on for seventy hours, Babić being required to attend most of it, almost without a break. His supporters accused Milošević's men of applying old-fashioned sleep-deprivation techniques to break Babić's resolve. After one short interval, Babić kept the Belgrade leadership waiting for two hours. When he finally arrived, the JNA Chief of Staff, General Blagoje Adžić, erupted with fury. Tempers frayed. Branko Kostić, acting President of rump Yugoslavia, who was chairing the session, takes up the story:

> *Babić's minister for religious affairs – I can't remember his name but he had a long long beard – told Adžić (who for some reason loathed him) 'Shut up. Mr. Babić is a President, and can choose when he turns up.' Adžić who is six feet tall and 220 pounds got up and faced this little minister for religion who was simply a beard and said: 'Shut up or I will strangle you.' The Minister for Religion said 'OK come and strangle me.' Adžić started moving towards him and had to be stopped. At this point I thought it wise to call a break.*

Jović then tried intimidation. He told Babić: "If you don't accept this, we will be forced to get rid of you." Babić knew that the Yugoslav secret service was not beyond the occasional tactical assassination. The thought struck him – with good reason – that his defiance of Milošević might cost him his life. Babić – according to Jović – went pale and said: "What do you mean?" "Oh, don't worry," Jović replied. "We'll do it legally – through the Parliament."

Where persuasion and intimidation failed, a combination of political guile and brute-force succeeded. Milošević's men played on a split in the Krajina Serb leadership. Babić had brought only his most loyal ministers to Belgrade. Milan Martić – the Police Chief and Commander of the Krajina Armed

Forces – was known to be closer to the JNA position. Mile Paspalj, the Speaker of the Krajina Parliament, was also loyal to Belgrade. Behind Babić's back he told Jović that he endorsed the plan. Acting on instruction, he called a meeting of the Krajina Parliament in the middle of February. Crucially, it was to take place not in Babić's stronghold of Knin, but in Glina. JNA troops mounted roadblocks around the town. Babić refused to recognize the legitimacy of the session, and did not attend. The Parliament voted to dismiss Babić from office and replace him with Goran Hadžić, the secretary of the Vukovar branch of the SDS. It also voted to endorse the Vance Plan.

Babić declared the session invalid. But it was too late. He had been successfully marginalized, and had now lost the support of his Belgrade patron. Milošević publicly denounced Babić in the state-run media. It was a scathing attack on his former ally and the first of many occasions on which Milošević would use public condemnation to destroy those who dared to challenge him.

On February 12, all obstacles now removed, Cyrus Vance formally recommended to the UN Secretary General the deployment of 12,000 UN peace-keepers. Two days later, UN Security Council Resolution 743 endorsed a proposal to send the second-largest international peace-keeping force ever deployed, for an initial period of one year. Its task was to supervise the cease-fire and begin disarming the Serb militia, and oversee the withdrawal of the JNA. On March 8, forces from more than thirty nations began to deploy under the command of General Satish Nambiar of India in four sectors of the republic. For reasons that, even at the time, seemed ludicrous, he set up his Command Headquarters in the very eye of the coming storm – at Sarajevo. In less then a month, the new storm broke, over Bosnia.

1 *Arrangements for a General Settlement*, paragraph 2.5.
2 The Serbian parliament, in a closed session, rejected the Carrington Plan.
3 Henri Wejnaendts says in his book *L'Engrenage Chroniques Yougoslaves: Juillet 1991–Août 1992* (Editions Denoël, Paris, 1993) that the brief conversation took place in a men's room. Milošević denied it, as did other members of the Serb delegation.
4 Associated Press, December 6, 1991.

PART FOUR: BOSNIA

15

BEFORE THE DELUGE
July 1990–March 1992

The march to war in Bosnia-Herzegovina was a terrible doomed procession. It gathered speed when war erupted in neighboring Croatia, but might have been prevented if the European Community had not recognized Croatia as an independent state in January 1992. Bosnia's President Alija Izetbegović then faced a stark choice – either to seek recognition or remain in Serb-dominated Yugoslavia. The EC forged ahead and the US reluctantly followed, persuading themselves that recognition would mean peace. For the Bosnian Serbs it meant war. Their leader, Radovan Karadžić, had threatened that if Bosnia were recognized as an independent state, it would be stillborn and not survive a single day. The Serbs moved and war erupted. The darkest predictions were fulfilled.

Their eyes burned out of holes in black ski masks. Stockings stretched over flattened faces. The Serb gunmen looked ragged and haphazard, but their barricades went up with military precision. A half-day later, the Muslims blocked off Sarajevo from the inside. "We put them in a sandwich – the Chetnik barricades – because we were more numerous," said Sefer Halilović, an ex-JNA officer and the first Chief of the Bosnian Army, who also complained that his political leadership was slow in approving the counter barricades.

Roads were blocked, neighborhoods cut off from each other. By dawn on March 2, 1992, Sarajevo had been transformed into a menacing labyrinth. Serb leaders claimed the barricades were spontaneous, erected in retaliation for a gangland-style attack on a Serb wedding party, in which the groom's father-in-law was shot dead and an Orthodox priest wounded. "This shot," said Momčilo Krajišnik, a Serb, who was Speaker of the Bosnian Parliament, "was a great injustice aimed at the Serb people." Muslims accused the wedding guests of provocatively brandishing Serb flags in the city's old Turkish bazaar, Baščaršija.

Serb leaders used the wedding attack as justification for the barricades. In fact, they were an early precursor of the calamity that would follow. They came at the end of a weekend referendum on independence, which was overwhelmingly backed by Muslims and Croats. As expected, the Serbs, who four months earlier had staged their own plebiscite, boycotted the poll *en masse*. This formally confirmed what was already apparent: the existence of a huge gulf between Bosnia's main communities. An independence referendum was one of the conditions stipulated by the Badinter Commission for Bosnia to receive diplomatic recognition. It was not designed to bring the sides closer to a settlement, but to legitimize subsequent recognition.

General Kukanjac, in his city-center barracks at Bistrik, had disappointed the Bosnian Serb leaders by refusing to use the JNA forces under his command to partition Sarajevo. He called Izetbegović and Karadžić together in a final attempt to avert disaster. Karadžić refused to go to the Presidency. Izetbegović refused to go to the Holiday Inn. They eventually agreed to meet at the television station, each man accompanied by a bodyguard of some twenty armed militia. It was a waste of time. Kukanjac recalled a heated exchange, but no agreement.

> *I said to them very roughly: that they were playing with people's lives, that they should sit down and talk and that we had had enough of that nationalistic behavior. Sit down, talk, come to an agreement. If not in your interest then in the interest of the people.*
>
> *They were shaking their fists in each other's faces. 'You did this! You did that!' until I had to intervene. Izetbegović blamed Karadžić for the barricades of March 1, and said the Serbs were trying to take control of Sarajevo. He was also alleging that there were troop movements from Pale to Sarajevo. Karadžić, for his part, blamed Izetbegović for the plot that was to be implemented that night in Sarajevo, and they exchanged accusations as to who deceived whom, when and how. There were other people in that room, there was thick smoke and the argument was really heated.*

Their bodyguards mingled in the corridor outside. A month later they were at war with each other.

They agreed to set up joint patrols, comprised of Bosnian police and the JNA, who persuaded Serbs and Muslims to take down their barricades. The crisis was averted, but the events of that weekend had been a dress rehearsal. 'It seems,' said Izetbegović, speaking of the Serb leaders, 'that they were not quite ready for war.'

In Bosnia, Muslims, Serbs and Croats, the three main communities, had each formed separate political parties in the run-up to the republic's first free elections on November 9, 1990. The victory of nationalist parties in the elections in Croatia and Slovenia, the previous spring, had sounded alarm bells among Bosnia's Communists. It warned that playing with Yugoslavia's borders would lead to civil war, and criticized Serbian and Croatian leaders for engendering fear among Bosnia's inhabitants.[1] This was more than a scare tactic aimed at preserving power. For the next year, the balance of fear helped to postpone a war which all the national leaders warned would leave the republic soaked in rivers of blood.

The Muslims were first, establishing the Party of Democratic Action (SDA) in Sarajevo on May 26, 1990, as a "political alliance of Yugoslav citizens belonging to Muslim cultural and historical traditions."[2] A prominent Muslim intellectual and lawyer by training, Alija Izetbegović, with clear blue eyes and broad cheek bones, became the party's first leader. Of the six Presidents who came to power after Yugoslavia's first multiparty elections in the republics, Izetbegović was the only one who had never been a Communist. Indeed, the Communists had done their utmost to make him a martyr. After the Second World War, Tito's Partisans had cracked down on religious and national groups. Izetbegović was arrested for being part of an élite nationalist group, called *Mladi Muslimani* (Young Muslims). He served three years in prison, a light sentence compared with the executions that took place a year later when the Sarajevo group tried to join forces with fellow activists in Mostar. Mladi Muslimani was broken and Izetbegović was under constant police surveillance for the next forty years.

In 1983, along with a dozen Muslim intellectuals, Izetbegović was jailed again, this time for plotting to overthrow the state. Eleven security men came to arrest him at his family flat, seizing scores of books, letters and photographs which, it was claimed, proved his role in the conspiracy.[3] During the trial, Izetbegović was a compelling presence, his keen mind instilling respect, and silence falling over the courtroom whenever he spoke. But he was convicted of counter-revolution and conspiring to create a Muslim state, and was sentenced to fourteen years in jail. The renowned Yugoslav defense lawyer, Rajko Danilović, who represented two of the accused Muslims, called the court case the culmination of political show-trials in Bosnia-Herzegovina. The authorities had concocted false information, he said, and exacted confessions through physical and psychological torture.

Bosnia had long since acquired a reputation for laboring under the most repressive of all the Communist regimes in Yugoslavia. The authorities clamped down on each of Bosnia's three communities in turn. A Muslim political trial would often be followed by a case involving a Serb or a Croat. More than anywhere else in Yugoslavia the doctrine of Brotherhood and Unity was rigidly enforced in Bosnia-Herzegovina. All institutions and functions in Bosnia were filled strictly according to the *ključ* (key) – the rotation of nationalities. After Tito's death and the ensuing political crisis, the number of political trials increased as the wounded Bosnian regime tried to sustain itself through repression.

Izetbegović only served five years of his fourteen-year sentence. In November 1988, he was released and, two years later, he was the President of the SDA. His clarity of vision made him an impressive political figure. But, when war came, his stature diminished visibly. Within a year, he appeared tired and bumbling, ill-equipped to deal with the conflict which raged around him. His rapid decline seemed to mirror the destruction of the Bosnian ideal.

Serb and Croat nationalists point to the *Islamic Declaration*, an esoteric document penned by Izetbegović, in 1973, as proof that Izetbegović planned to create a Muslim state. In fact, it was a work of scholarship, not politics, intended to promote philosophical discourse among Muslims. In it, he excluded the "use of violence in the creation of a Muslim state, because it defiles the beauty of the name of Islam."[4] A more significant indicator of Izetbegović's orientation was *Islam between East and West*, first published in the United States in 1984, and then in Yugoslavia after his release from prison four years later. This book mapped out his vision of an Islamic state in the modern world.[5] In it he charts a course between Islamic values and material progress, arguing that the benefits of secular western civilization are without meaning unless they are accompanied by the spiritual values found predominantly in Islamic societies.

Serb and Croat nationalists were able to play on the widely-held conviction that Muslims had never been a separate ethnic community, but were simply Serbs or Croats who, in the course of five centuries of Ottoman domination, had succumbed to pressure or temptation and converted to Islam. They saw them, in effect, as Serbs or Croats who had traded away their true identity and adopted the trappings of an entirely alien culture. This contempt was easily translated into yet another rationale for Serbian and Croatian territorial expansionism.

Tito's 1974 constitution granted the Muslims, the third biggest national group in Yugoslavia, the status of a separate nation. Their misfortune was to be the only nation in Yugoslavia without an undisputed claim to a separate republic.[6] Izetbegović saw Bosnia as a homeland for Muslims, but one which also included Serbs and Croats. The Muslims, he said two years before the outbreak of war, did yet not comprise a big enough majority to make Bosnia a Muslim state.

> We are not on the road to a national state, our only way out is towards a free civic union. This is the future.
>
> Some people may want that (to make Bosnia a Muslim state) but this is not a realistic wish. Even though the Muslims are the most numerous nation in the republic, there are not enough of them ...they would have to comprise about seventy percent of the population.[7]

National dreams – the emergence of ethnic parties and leaders – did not reflect ancient hatreds as was claimed later by some sectors of the frustrated international community while it struggled to comprehend the war. But the popularity of exclusively ethnic parties did serve to highlight the weakness of republican institutions when confronted by different national identities. They also illustrated a tradition of separate communities growing up side-by-side, while preserving – at least in part – their distinct identities. A fundamental difference among the three national groups was the collective perception of their historical experience. The Serbs, for example, regarded the Ottoman period as an age of occupation. For the Muslims it was an era which saw the creation and subsequent prosperity of their own particular élite. For decades, these contradictory perceptions had coexisted, but, by 1990, the rise of Serbian nationalism had turned history into the purveyor of hatred.

Nearly two months after the creation of the Muslim SDA, the Serbs established the Serbian Democratic Party (SDS), a branch of the Knin party of the charismatic Jovan Rašković. A fellow psychiatrist, Radovan Karadžić, heavy-boned with a huge mop of hair, was elected SDS president. Karadžić was a poet and long-time favorite of Dobrica Ćosić, the father of contemporary Serbian nationalism, but Sarajevo society never accepted him as a member of the urban élite. But he was bright and witty. He was an outsider, born and raised in Montenegro, before moving to Sarajevo as a teenager. Nor did he see himself as a leader until Ćosić encouraged him to turn to politics. At the SDS's inauguration, at which both Rašković and Izetbegović were guests-of-honor, Karadžić told the audience that Serbs in Bosnia must have equal rights – cultural, religious and economic. He said wrongs committed against the Serbs must be redressed and he pledged to respect freedom of political organization, elections and power-sharing.[8] Two years later his Party's troops would expel hundreds of thousands of people and destroy mosques and other relics in an effort to erase all vestiges of a Muslim presence in Bosnia.

Soon after the SDS was launched, the Croats followed suit, forming a Bosnian branch of the HDZ. Like the Serbs, the Croats were infuriated when Izetbegović announced in September that the SDA opposed the principle of national parity, and that the next government would be formed on the basis of one-man one-vote. Izetbegović was attempting to play the same game in Bosnia that Milošević had in mind for Yugoslavia. Unless civil and individual rights were secured through institutions, majority vote would guarantee Serb domination throughout the country. In Bosnia, the same principle would give the Muslims – the republic's largest ethnic group with forty-four percent of the 4.35 million population – the greatest authority. A key difference was that Milošević was striving for changes which subverted the very principles on which Yugoslavia was founded, whereas Izetbegović's proposals applied only to Bosnia. The republic's constitution, however, made each of its three groups constituent nations, which meant that no major decision could be carried out without consensus.

Despite the growing tensions, the three national parties, meeting behind closed doors in Sarajevo, agreed to form a united front against their main opponent – the Communists. For its part, the reformed Communist Party was trying – with no success – to cool nationalist fevers. It warned that tensions in Croatia were spilling over into the border regions of Bosnia and condemned the formation of village guards by the Bosnian Serbs.[9]

There was still hope that an election in Bosnia might reflect the centuries of coexistence among the main communities. An attempt by Federal Prime Minister Marković to launch his own civic party, and silence the nationalists, seemed a rational choice. The indefatigable Marković remained phenomenally popular despite the constant obstacles posed by Serbia, Croatia and Slovenia. Opinion polls said most Yugoslavs would vote for his Federal Government, which had already curbed hyper-inflation and made the dinar convertible. But his successful economic program and contagious optimism never translated into political vision. His attempts to compete in elections in Bosnia and Serbia merely infuriated Serb nationalists, who argued that he had not stood in elections in Croatia and Slovenia, allowing nationalists to win there. At the same time, the obstreperous republics blocked his efforts to call elections at the federal level. On July 30, at a rally in the Kozara mountains in northwestern Bosnia where thousands of Serbs had been murdered by the Ustaše during the Second World War, Marković announced the creation of "an alliance of reformist forces to build a new and prosperous Yugoslavia." Tens of thousands of people turned out to cheer for Ante Marković. On the same spot, two years later, Serbs would carry out unspeakable crimes against their Muslim countrymen. Three of the most notorious detention camps were built in the Kozara region. Muslims were rounded up and their homes razed to the ground.

The elections were a test, not only for Marković but also for Bosnia-Herzegovina's future stability. They failed on both counts. Despite vocal support from some of Bosnia's most popular musicians, actors and writers, Marković lost. Of the 240 seats in the bicameral parliament, Marković's League of Reform Forces won just thirteen. His only allies, the (reformed) Communists of Nijaz Duraković, won a further eighteen. Ominously, most of Bosnia's electorate voted along ethnic lines: Muslims rallied behind the SDA; Serbs, with thirty-one percent of the population, solidly supported the SDS; Croats, at seventeen percent, voted for the Bosnian branch of the HDZ. In two rounds of elections, the SDA won eighty-seven seats, the SDS seventy-one, and the HDZ forty-four. The nationalists had stolen the show, taking nearly ninety percent of the seats. They were strongest in the countryside, with reformists and ex-Communists faring better in the cities. Despite public rivalry, the nationalist leaders pledged to band together against the Communists in the event of a run-off.[10] In effect, the elections constituted another Bosnian census. The victory of these nationalist options laid the ground for the war that followed.

The three parties had secretly agreed before the elections to form a coalition government – but even they were surprised by the magnitude of their victory.

Fashioned after Yugoslavia's inefficient rotating presidency, the Bosnian model had two places each for Muslims, Serbs and Croats and one for a Yugoslav. The SDA candidates captured the most votes. Fikret Abdić, a local hero in the far northwestern corner of Bosnia, received 1,010,618 votes, compared to 847,386 for Izetbegović. When he joined the SDA, shortly before the elections, the party received a great boost. Small and rotund, with tousled grey hair, Abdić was adored by Muslims in the densely-populated region of Cazinska Krajina, which he had enriched with revenues from Agrokomerc, the huge state agro-industrial combine. But his fortunes had plummeted in 1987, when he was jailed for issuing 300 million dollars in unbacked promissory notes. His supporters claimed he was a political scapegoat framed by jealous rivals in the ruling Communist party. Critics dismissed him as Yugoslavia's most brazen white-collar criminal, but Abdić's stint in jail did wonders for his popularity, which, by 1990, had crossed ethnic lines and spread across the republic. In contrast, Izetbegović held little allure for Serbs and Croats.

In an unexplained deal, Abdić, who did not have enough support within the SDA, traded his rightful position as head of the presidency in exchange for naming his man, Alija Delimustafić, as Interior Minister. Later, Abdić would become Izetbegović's biggest opponent – declaring Cazinska Krajina independent of the rest of war-torn Bosnia.

Despite being a Muslim nationalist, Ejup Ganić was nevertheless elected on the Yugoslav ticket. The SDS's Biljana Plavšić and Nikola Koljević were elected the Serb representatives. Stjepan Kljuić and Franjo Boras won the Croat seats. Both HDZ candidates, Kljuić was dedicated to preserving Bosnia-Herzegovina while Boras dreamed of a Greater Croatia.[11]

Izetbegović became President, the Serb Krajišnik was appointed Speaker of Parliament, and Jure Pelivan, a Croat, was named Prime Minister.

The uneasy coalition would last just over a year.

In Croatia and Serbia nationalism reigned. The fires were being stoked and would soon spread to Bosnia. No one made any effort to compromise. Serbs clung to their right to remain in Yugoslavia, Croats to leave what was left of the federation, and Muslims to sovereignty. On February 27, 1991, Izetbegović told Parliament he was prepared to fight to secure Bosnia's sovereignty. "I would sacrifice peace for a sovereign Bosnia-Herzegovina, but for that peace in Bosnia-Herzegovina I would not sacrifice sovereignty." To the

Serbs, this was a war cry. At that same session, Serb deputies refused to discuss a declaration of Bosnia's sovereignty, which had been proposed by the SDA and HDZ.

As Yugoslavia descended into war in the Spring of 1991, Alija Izetbegović and his Macedonian counterpart, the wily Kiro Gligorov – whose survival through four decades of Communism had earned him the nickname "the fox" – scrambled to put forward a proposal for the future shape of the Yugoslav federation which would satisfy everyone. The chances of success, already slim, grew remote after Milošević's and Tudjman's March 1991 meeting in Karadjordjevo. Izetbegović soon received word of what the scheme had "cooked up" at Tito's old hunting lodge: not only did the Serbian and Croatian leaders plan to get rid of Ante Marković, but they had agreed to carve up Bosnia as well. Izetbegović implored the Croatian leadership to tell him exactly what was in store for his republic. Stipe Mesić, Croatia's representative on the Federal Presidency, laughed and sang an old folk song by the name of "There is no more Alija."

After repeated armed incidents in Croatia, the SDA and the HDZ declared their full support for Zagreb in its battle against the Serb rebels. At the same time, the SDS condemned Croatia's assault on the breakaway Serbs. Throughout Bosnia, villagers began to stand guard at night, often armed with hunting rifles or old guns, checking identity papers.

In western Herzegovina, adjacent to Croatia and overwhelmingly Croat, the HDZ announced that its members would come to the aid of their kith-and-kin in Croatia. The red-and-white Croatian checkerboard banner was already flying throughout the region. Bosnian flags were set on fire. Allegiances had never been in question here. Even before the rise of nationalism, Croats from western Herzegovina were the most extreme. After the Second World War, Serbs would say that "nothing grows in western Herzegovina except rocks, snakes and Ustaše."

Each community raised the stakes, pushing the other towards the abyss of war. "Throughout 1991, even in the beginning of 1992, each side thought the other wouldn't dare. And there was that terrible tense political game. Until finally we found ourselves at the point of no return," said Koljević, a grey-haired professor of English whose penchant for quoting Shakespeare in an Oxford accent was in sharp contrast to the crude and violent politics of the regime he represented. Indeed, the presence of a psychiatrist and two professors in the Bosnian Serb leadership did not prevent it from espousing some of the most destructive notions to stalk the political stage of late twentieth-century Europe.

The SDS began to undermine government institutions, first by staging a boycott of parliament. The Party repeatedly declared that Izetbegović was not entitled to preside over the Serbian people, because under his leadership

212

Bosnia-Herzegovina supported Slovenia and Croatia in their wars against Yugoslavia. This policy, they argued, would leave the Serbs scattered across several separate states. The nation would be vulnerable to extermination, said a Party statement of July 11.[12] The SDS deputies said their boycott precluded them from respecting any decision taken by the Parliament, which was now comprised of only two nations – the Muslims and Croats.

Another huge bone of contention was Izetbegović's blossoming contacts with the Islamic world. Of the Yugoslav republics, Bosnia-Herzegovina was already the most active in the Non-Aligned movement, in which Tito had been a major figure. On a visit to Turkey in July 1991 – when the war was nearly over in Slovenia and was about to begin in earnest in Croatia following their declarations of independence – Izetbegović asked to join the Organization of Islamic Countries. It was a foolish gesture which he surely knew would merely serve to antagonize his Serb and Croat opponents. The response was immediate and predictable. In Belgrade, Radovan Karadžić took the request as proof that "even our gloomiest forecasts, which say that Izetbegović wants Bosnia-Herzegovina to become an Islamic republic, are being fulfilled." Despite the secessionist aspirations of the Muslims, he warned, Bosnian Serbs would not relinquish their right to remain in Yugoslavia.[13]

Serb obstruction seemed to strengthen the coalition between Muslims and Croats. Yet their alliance was tactical – they were pursuing different goals. Sarajevo was constantly unnerved by suspicions that Belgrade and Zagreb were scheming behind its back. A scandal was caused when Tudjman, unable to keep quiet, admitted that he and Milošević agreed that a two-way partition of Bosnia was the best way to resolve the Yugoslav crisis. The Bosnian Presidency warned that this would cause civil war and urged the JNA to protect the central Yugoslav republic. Otherwise, it said, Bosnia would have to undertake measures to defend itself, by building-up the republic's police.

The alliances seemed set but behind each other's backs the partners were scheming, trying to see whether they could get a better deal. While Serbs and Croats discussed dividing Bosnia between them, and their ethnic kinsmen fought each other in Croatia, Belgrade at the same time tried to strike a deal with the Muslims. In the summer of 1991, Serbia launched a surprising move to get Bosnia to remain in a new Yugoslavia – one without the Croats and Slovenes. They argued that the Belgrade Initiative, as it was called, was the only way to prevent war in Bosnia, because if the Muslims were to secede from Yugoslavia, the republic would have to be divided. Serbs and Muslims lived cheek by jowl – any division would mean war. Izetbegović, at first, indicated to Serb leaders that the idea was worth considering. But he soon complained that the proposal was Milošević's attempt to divide Bosnia's Muslim leadership and thereby assert his own control over Bosnia. Further, Izetbegović accused the Serbs of trying to dictate who ruled the Muslims.

Indeed, there were prominent Muslims who believed the price of extricating themselves from Belgrade would be far too great. Milošević's next move was to try to side-line Izetbegović and the SDA leadership by making a deal with a wealthy Muslim businessman, Adil Zulfikarpašić, whom he saw as an alternative leader. Zulfikarpašić had made his fortune in Switzerland after the Second World War, but returned to Bosnia for multiparty elections, funding the SDA until he fell out with Izetbegović and formed his own tiny splinter party, the Muslim Bošnjak Party (MBO). Serbia gave the Belgrade Initiative a high profile. Bosnian Serb and Muslim leaders appeared for an hour on Serbian state television. Banner headlines trumpeted a deal with Zulfikarpašić as a great victory. Bosnia would remain in Yugoslavia, they declared. A crisis had been averted. But the businessman was no substitute for Izetbegović. He was an outsider, completely lacking in mass support, and the fanfare in Belgrade could not mask the failure of Milošević's scheme. Had it worked, the Belgrade Initiative might have postponed the war for a while, although probably not avoided it altogether. Moreover the Muslims would have been consigned to an uncertain fate as second-class citizens under a Serbian nationalist regime.

That was Belgrade's last overt attempt to seize the political initiative. Afterwards, with each passing day, the preparations for war became more determined. Serbs in Bosnia began declaring so-called Serbian autonomous regions (SAO). At first, these SAOs seemed laughable. The idea, for example, of proclaiming an SA, or microscopic statelet, out of Romanjia, the exquisitely beautiful mountainous region east of Sarajevo, seemed ridiculous. There were jokes about the SAOs, but checkpoints manned by Serb gunmen drove home just how serious the Serbs were.

The war in Croatia had made the pattern familiar. The Serb leadership insisted on the division of Bosnia-Herzegovina into ethnic regions as the best way to avoid an all-out civil and religious war. The absurdity of this proposal was obvious – any partition of Bosnia was a certain recipe for war.

In September, the SDA accused the SDS of violating the coalition agreement by declaring the autonomous Serb lands. "The creation of Serbian autonomous areas in Bosnia-Herzegovina, prevented the functioning of the republican government and, at the same time, was an attack on joint rule in Bosnia-Herzegovina," an SDA statement said. The SDA insisted that the Serb leaders either denounce the "spontaneous" barricades and autonomous regions or admit they represented official party policy. Izetbegović's party hinted that the Muslims could retaliate.

The war of words escalated. On October 14, 1991, the Serbs shattered the fragile consensus which had somehow kept the fractious parliament function-

214

ing. During a stormy overnight session, SDS deputies railed against proposals put forward by the SDA and the HDZ on the republic's sovereignty and Bosnia's position within Yugoslavia. A rumor spread that a bomb had been planted in the Assembly building.

"I have forgotten many events, but I'll never forget that night," said Izetbegović. "The night between October 14 and 15 of 1991, when Karadžić issued a death sentence to the Muslim people." The Serb leader admonished the Muslims to take seriously the will of the Serbian people to remain in Yugoslavia:

> *You want to take Bosnia-Herzegovina down the same highway of hell and suffering that Slovenia and Croatia are travelling. Do not think that you will not lead Bosnia-Herzegovina into hell, and do not think that you will not perhaps make the Muslim people disappear, because the Muslims cannot defend themselves if there is war – How will you prevent everyone from being killed in Bosnia-Herzegovina?*

Izetbegović was shocked by Karadžić's words. "At that moment I had the feeling that the gates to hell had opened and we were all burned by the flames of the inferno." Izetbegović addressed the Assembly:

> *His words and manners illustrate why others refuse to stay in this Yugoslavia. Nobody else wants the kind of Yugoslavia that Mr. Karadžić wants any more. Nobody except perhaps the Serbs. This Yugoslavia and the manners of Karadžić are simply hated by the peoples of Yugoslavia, by Slovenes, Croats, Macedonians, Albanians, Hungarians, Muslims, by Europe and the world.*
>
> *I want to tell the citizens of Bosnia-Herzegovina not to be afraid, because there will be no war... Therefore, sleep peacefully.*
>
> *... As President (of the Presidency) of Bosnia-Herzegovina, I am sorry that in this situation I must talk for the Muslim people. I solemnly state that the Muslims will not attack anyone. However, just as solemnly I state that the Muslims will defend themselves with great determination and survive. They will not disappear as Karadžić said. They cannot disappear.*

In his scathing denunciation of the Serbs, Izetbegović also made a tactical maneuver. He praised the "stabilizing effect" of JNA regular units in Bosnia. The Army was rapidly turning into an all-Serb force as Muslim and Croat youths ignored their call-up orders. But he singled out JNA reservists for wreaking havoc in the republic. There were frequent incidents involving reservists from Montenegro laying siege to nearby Dubrovnik. Ten days after the clash in Parliament, a mosque was damaged by a bomb in the southwestern town of Trebinje, in the hinterland overlooking Dubrovnik. The pattern of military force had been drawn, interwoven with episodes of political violence.

At two o'clock in the morning of the fifteenth, Krajišnik decided to adjourn the session. The Serbs walked out leaving SDA and HDZ deputies to continue their deliberations. Those who remained voted in favor of Bosnian sovereignty and also rejected the SDS-sponsored Belgrade Initiative. Under the menacing pall of Karadžić's words, it was a false victory. The next day General Kadijević travelled to Sarajevo, and agreed with the Bosnian leadership to set up joint police and army patrols throughout the republic. As the men said goodbye, Izetbegović told Kadijević: "I leave Bosnia to your heart and soul."

Ten days later, the Serbs declared their own parliament, voting to remain part of Yugoslavia. Any illusion that the nationalist coalition was still functioning had been destroyed.

The slide to war in Bosnia gained momentum. The Serbs held their first separate plebiscite on November 9-10. Izetbegović accused the Serbs of trying to destabilize Bosnia even further by rejecting the proposed republic-wide referendum. "It was a one-party plebiscite. Of course, the result was a triumph – the response was over one hundred percent – I can't help thinking it was Bolshevik-style voting."

On November 30, an SDA congress re-elected Izetbegović as Party President. The party urged the international community to extend diplomatic recognition to all six Yugoslav republics, insisting that Bosnia would not remain in a Yugoslavia dominated by the Serbs. In order to keep Bosnia secure, the SDA called for the dispatch of peacekeepers to areas patrolled by Serb gunmen. In his closing speech, Izetbegović said he and the leadership had rediscovered the spirit of the Muslim people, characterized by tolerance towards everything and every human being.

In December, the European Community, under pressure from Germany – which was championing Croatian independence – offered each of the six republics recognition if they pledged to adopt the EC's criteria for new states. With Croatia smoldering, Izetbegović was desperate for Bosnia to secure a promise of protection. He was afraid of the Yugoslav Army, and appeared to believe that the US would help to defend Bosnia (even though Washington has denied ever giving such guarantees). With Croatia about to be recognized, transformation of the Yugoslav federation obviously was out of the question. Izetbegović had no choice but to seek independence. The Bosnian Serbs had repeatedly said they would declare their own state if they could not stay in Yugoslavia. He was apprehensive. He said he would try to persuade the German Foreign Minister Hans Dietrich Genscher not to recognize Croatia and Slovenia, but when Izetbegović met Genscher face-to-face in November he failed even to broach the subject. His silence perhaps cleared one of the last obstacles to recognition.[14]

On December 19, after meeting the two special EC representatives, Britain's Lord Carrington and the Portuguese Ambassador Jose Cutileiro (Portugal was holding the EC Presidency), who had travelled round the republic's capitals to present their plan, Izetbegović went to the local JNA sector commander Vojislav Djurdjevac to tell him that he had decided to seek independence. The grey-haired General looked at him, and asked if Alija intended to declare a civil war. For Djurdjevac, independence was a declaration of war. The JNA seemed to believe that Izetbegović might change his mind. Top generals made several trips trying to threaten – and cajole – him into keeping Bosnia in Yugoslavia. Izetbegović had not given up on the JNA. Even long after that meeting with Djurdjevac, Izetbegović nursed hopes that at least the JNA would defend Bosnia.

But the next day, the Bosnian Presidency voted to seek EC recognition. The two Serb representatives voted against the decision. On Sarajevo television, Izetbegović explained that for Bosnia there was no choice but independence. It was either that, he said, or being part of Greater Serbia. There was no more Yugoslavia, he said. He expressed little hope for a cantonized Bosnia-Herzegovina, because the demographic distribution would leave huge parts of each national group living outside its designated cantons. On the main news bulletin, in remarks addressed to the Serbs, Izetbegović said, except for the Second World War, Bosnia's ethnic communities had lived together quite peacefully for centuries. The equality of nations should still be pursued.

In Bosnia, the Serbs had a great advantage over the Muslims and Croats: the JNA. By early 1992, the Army had withdrawn from Slovenia and Croatia, mostly moving to Bosnia, where the bulk of the military industry was based. With the withdrawal, a vast amount of military hardware was concentrated in Bosnia. According to the JNA's theory of defense against foreign attack, cultivated since Tito's break with Stalin in 1948, the mountainous central republic was deemed the safest place for the JNA's backbone.

Karadžić went to Belgrade to request that all Bosnian Serbs serving in the JNA throughout Yugoslavia be transferred to Bosnia in order to transform the TO into an army. Borisav Jović, Milošević's right-hand man, said the Army would stay put until a political solution had been found. Karadžić told us:

The entire Serb population was behind the Army and they were counting on the Army to defend Yugoslavia.

The Serbian regime secretly carried out a plan which anticipated Bosnian recognition.

In January 1992, Milošević issued a secret order to start transferring all JNA officers who had been born in Bosnia back to their native republic. By the time the JNA made its formal withdrawal from Bosnia in May 1992, the vast majority of the officers who remained there were actually Bosnian Serbs. They were not citizens of Yugoslavia, which, by then, was another country. Belgrade had planned ahead for the moment when Bosnia would be recognized, said Jović.

> *Milošević and I were talking about it. We did not talk to anybody else. We instructed the General Staff to redeploy troops and to transfer all those born in Bosnia to Bosnia and withdraw those born in Serbia and Montenegro to Serbia and Montenegro.*
>
> *Ten days later they told us it had been done very efficiently although the Army was very reluctant to accept something that clashed with its internal rules. We did not wait for the international recognition of Bosnia to redeploy the troops in Bosnia. [By the time of recognition] out of 90,000 troops in Bosnia, I think, eighty-five percent of them were from Bosnia.*

Backed in this way by the military, the Bosnian Serb politicians took steps to preempt international recognition and the planned Bosnia-wide referendum. On January 9, they declared their own Serbian Republic of Bosnia-Herzegovina (later renamed Republika Srpska), proclaiming it part of the Yugoslav federation. The Serb leadership said it was the only possible defense against the Muslims. The borders of its self-styled republic encompassed the autonomous regions and even places where Serbs were a minority. As Karadžić claimed, if the Serbs wanted to, they could take control in sixty-six percent of Bosnia. He said:

> *I was constantly aware that there was going to be war because we knew very well that the Serb nation would not leave Yugoslavia. No one could force them to leave. Territories had to be defined. As nobody respected this, a conflict had to follow.*

Aware that the pendulum was swinging towards recognition, the Bosnian Serbs grew noisier, warning that Bosnia would be awash in blood. Milošević, by contrast, did not consider it such a significant event. He joked to Karadžić that the demented Roman Emperor Caligula had declared his horse a senator, but that it had never become one. He said the same applied to Izetbegović, who had international recognition but no state. Using the same rationale he would use often in the future, Milošević explained that it would mean nothing. He had correctly calculated that the international community would not defend what it had recognized as a state.

As the Lisbon talks on Bosnia's future blueprint opened, "canton" became the new catchword. Every Serb and Croat politician in Bosnia seemed to have a copy of the Swiss constitution in his office. The talks resumed a week before the referendum on independence. All the national leaders – even the Serbs who opposed it – knew that the majority would vote for Bosnian independence. This meant that international recognition would follow soon. Each side warned of the impending doom – but made no attempt to compromise – despite rhetoric to the contrary.

Under pressure from the EC mediators, the three leaders agreed to recognize the existing external borders of Bosnia. They also endorsed the formation of *national* territorial units within Bosnia. The first represented a compromise by the Serb and Croat parties because it committed them to the preservation of a Bosnian state. The second agreement was remarkable. It was a complete turnaround for Alija Izetbegović who, until then, had rejected any division along ethnic lines. Karadžić and his Croat counterpart, Mate Boban, enthusiastically welcomed Izetbegović's concession.

No sooner had he given the go-ahead, than Izetbegović changed his mind. When he returned to Sarajevo, the Bosnian President tried to go back on the agreement. He sought to broaden its base from ethnic to geographic and economic. The SDA power-brokers denounced it, because they saw it as a partition of Bosnia. Indeed despite his reluctant "yes," Izetbegović, too, was fundamentally opposed to any division of Bosnia.

Of all the international efforts to prevent the war, and later, broker a settlement, the Lisbon Agreement has been the most misrepresented. Disappointed envoys, Serb and Croat nationalists, harp on it as the moment when Izetbegović and the Muslims cast away the last chance for peace. There is scant reason to consider seriously the nationalist claims that a partition could have been executed without bloodshed. A precise territorial breakdown had not been agreed in detail. Later it would become clear that for every claim to a town by one community, there was more often than not a counter-claim by another.

Stories instantly sprang up about why the Bosnian leader had changed his mind. This behavior, possibly the result of a decade in prison, was, however, typical of him: Izetbegović was as easily swayed by one argument as he was by another. There were later allegations that Warren Zimmermann, the US ambassador to Yugoslavia, urged him to abandon the agreement. But Zimmermann, a staunch advocate of human rights, was under instructions to support any agreement reached by the three sides. He said that he had advised Izetbegović that if the Bosnian President had made a commitment he should uphold it. Zimmermann, who left Yugoslavia three months later when western embassies recalled their ambassadors, later resigned from the State Department partly in protest against US policy in Bosnia.

Just two days after the Lisbon Agreement, the Serbs and Croats pulled out their maps. On February 26, 1992, they had the first of several secret meetings in the south Austrian town of Graz. Both sides later defended the talks, denying any conspiracy against the Muslims, saying that the EC mediators had told them to hold bilateral meetings. Karadžić told Josip Manolić, one of Tudjman's most trusted advisors, who was representing the Bosnian Croats, that the Serbs must have a land-corridor across northern Bosnia. "Without the corridor any solution is out of the question." According to Karadžić, Manolić talked extensively in terms of population transfers. "He proposed that the Croats living in Serbia go to Croatia, and that the Serbs from Krajina, Zagreb and Rijeka go to Serbia. He suggested that pressure could be exerted to make them leave," Karadžić said.

The Lisbon talks were forgotten in the excitement and confusion over the referendum and the subsequent Serb barricades which paralyzed Sarajevo. "The Serbs were almost a hundred percent sure that they wanted to stay in Yugoslavia. The Croats and the Muslims were almost a hundred percent sure that they wanted to leave. It was clear then that Bosnia could not survive," said Karadžić, who knew that the time was drawing near. An outraged Serb deputy told the new Serb "parliament": "We are witnessing the birth of a Muslim bastard on the territory of the land of our grandfathers."

In the north of the republic, the first serious incident of fighting immediately erupted in the town of Bosanski Brod. During the war in Croatia, the JNA had already launched attacks from Brod, in an effort to defend the besieged barracks in Slavonski Brod, the twin city across the Sava River. After the referendum, Serb villagers set up barricades. They were seeking to block troops and weapons from being transported over the bridge from Croatia. "It was the last bridge in our hands. It connected Bosnia with the rest of the world," said Armin Pohara, a journalist who established the Brod crisis committee which took charge of the defense of the town. "The bridges at Brčko and Šamac were already destroyed, the bridge in Gradiška was in Serb hands, also at Novi. Each day the Serbs got closer. One day before the war started we made the decision that in case they moved the barricades any closer to the bridge, that we were going to fire."

Pohara went to the Croatian army in Slavonski Brod and asked for more arms to defend the city. "I said war was inevitable, we had 300 weapons and I asked for more. We got some 50 rifles more and about 200 hand-grenades, which was funny. We got a couple of thousand bullets. For us it was a lot. The war started in Bosanski Brod, and I am sure the historians will agree."

The Croatian Army had crossed the frontier river in a move against the Serbs. Unnoticed, the war in Brod had begun.

1 Associated Press, June 26 1990.

2 SDA does not include a national attribute such as Muslim because it was illegal at the time.

3 Danilović, Rajko, *Upotreba Neprijatelja: Politička sudjenja u Jugoslaviji (1945–1991)*, Agencija Valjevac, Valjevo 1993, pp. 161-71.

4 Džaja, Srećko M., *Bosnia i Bošnjaci U hrvatskom političkom diskursu*, Erasmus, p. 33 (Prosinac 1994).

5 Džaja, Srećko M., *Bosnia i Bosnjaći U hrvatskom političkom diskursu*, pp. 33-41.

6 Ethnic Albanians, the fourth biggest group in Yugoslavia, were never granted the status of nation on the grounds they had a home-state in neighboring Albania. They were classified a "nationality" which, under the Communist system, gave them fewer rights than a "nation."

7 *Start*, July 7, 1990, p. 34.

8 *Tanjug*, July 17, 1990.

9 SWB: October 4, 1990.

10 *Oslobodjenje*, November 11, 1990.

11 Ganić (680 783 votes); Plavšić (557 218) and Koljević (541 212); Kljuić, (464 174) and Boras (408 750).

12 *Tanjug*, July 11, 1991.

13 *Tanjug*, July 18, 1991.

14 Warren Zimmermann, *Foreign Affairs* (March/April 1995), p. 16.

16

THE GATES OF HELL
The Outbreak of War in Bosnia
April 1–10, 1992

The Zvornik Police Chief's face was creased with exhaustion. Night after night of holding vigil, of waiting for the unseen enemy, had taken their toll. Less than a fortnight earlier forty of his colleagues – all Serbs – had taken walkie-talkies, weapons and cars, walked out of the station, and out of Zvornik. There was no warning, he said, no explanation. One day they just left. Now, for sure, they were coming back.

In the station cell, four militiamen from Serbia proper waited to hear their fate. They had been arrested at two in the morning sneaking around town. They had been found armed with automatic weapons, knives and a metal chain used for strangulation. The Police Chief wanted to get them out of town, and safely. He phoned the JNA counter-intelligence for help. His greatest fear was that their presence here, in Zvornik, would provide a pre-text for Serb paramilitaries to attack. It was April 8, 1992, two days after Bosnia's independence had been recognized by the European Community.

A police scout came into the station. Two thousand armed Serbs were mass-ing outside the town and were on the way, he said. "The future of Zvornik is not decided here," the Police Chief said. The town had less than a day left before its majority Muslim population would be driven out.

The Serb paramilitaries and JNA units massing outside Zvornik did not need a pretext. On April 8, they began shelling from the other side of the river – from inside Serbia proper. Thousands began to flee – two thousand alone heading across the bridge to Mali Zvornik. The next day, Arkan, commander of the feared paramilitary unit, known as the Tigers, issued an ultimatum to the Muslims of Zvornik – who made up sixty percent of the town's population – to surrender. When they failed to respond to the surrender call, Arkan moved in. Zvornik fell on April 10.

José Maria Mendiluce, the UNHCR's most senior official in former Yugoslavia, was visiting Milošević in Belgrade.

> *Milošević told me, as he did throughout the conflict, that he didn't have any con-trol over the Bosnian Serbs, but he would try to use his moral authority... His official position was that if Bosnia was independent, then the Federal Army would move out. Obviously what he didn't tell me... was that a great part of the command of the Federal Army was going to stay in Bosnia as a Bosnian army. At that moment this wasn't as clear as it was later in retrospect.*

Mendiluce left Belgrade with a promise that Milošević would do everything in his power (which, of course, was limited to whatever moral influence
he could exert) to support the UNHCR's mission in Bosnia. To return to
Sarajevo, Mendiluce had to pass through Zvornik. He chose the wrong day.

*When I arrived at the bridge [over the Drina which separates Serbia from
Bosnia] I could hear explosions of artillery and mortar fire. There was great
agitation on the Serbian side. Almost a kilometer from the bridge there were
militiamen and JNA soldiers, all along the river. The whole area was mili-
tarized. I insisted on being allowed to cross the bridge. They let me pass at my
own risk. I went over to the Bosnia side. There was a big artillery bombardment coming from the Serbian side of the Drina. I even saw smoke coming
from the cannons on the Serbian side.*

The Serb and JNA forces who held that part of town were furious to find
an outsider bearing witness to their storming of the town.

*I was detained for two hours. I realized I was at serious risk. I could see
trucks full of dead bodies. I could see militiamen taking more corpses of children, women and old people from their houses and putting them on trucks. I
saw at least four or five trucks full of corpses. When I arrived the cleansing
had been done. There were no people, no one on the streets. It was all finished. They were looting, cleaning up the city after the massacre. I was convinced they were going to kill me.*

They did not kill him. They let him go. When he crossed the front line he
did so at 140 kilometers an hour into Bosnian-held territory. There he found
the victims of the cleansing. Five thousand people sheltering in a narrow valley.

*When I arrived in the car I was surrounded by 1000 people. They were all
over me, begging 'Save us! Save us!' with such despair that I stayed there for
an hour trying to calm them down. There were lots of dead people, wounded
children on the floor looking terrified – absolutely terrified – and we could
hear the sound of mortar fire approaching.*

Mendiluce's impression that both Serbian paramilitaries and JNA units
were taking part in the capture of Zvornik is corroborated by the account of
the extreme nationalist paramilitary leader Vojislav Šešelj, who went to
Zvornik shortly after what he called its "liberation": "The Zvornik operation
was planned in Belgrade," he said.

The Bosnian Serb forces took part in it. But the special units and the best combat units came from this side [Serbia]. These were police units – the so-called Red Berets – special units of the Serbian Interior Ministry of Belgrade. The army engaged itself to a small degree – it gave artillery support where it was needed. The operation had been prepared for a long time. It wasn't carried out in any kind of nervous fashion. Everything was well-organized and implemented.

Arkan's "Tigers," bloodied by their experience of eastern Slavonia the previous year, in which they had pioneered the technique of ethnic cleansing by terror, had moved into Bijeljina, in northeastern Bosnia, on April 1. Bijeljina and Zvornik were of vital strategic importance to the Serb war effort. Together, they represented a hinge of territory that linked the two main chunks of Bosnian land that the Serb nationalists considered theirs – in the northwest, Bosnian Krajina, around Banja Luka; and in the east, the west bank of the Drina, south of Zvornik and down the eastern and southern flanks of Sarajevo to join eastern Herzegovina. Eastern Bosnia was most important to Belgrade because it bordered on Serbia.

Arkan ordered a campaign of harassment against the Muslim population in Bijeljina. His "Tigers" took up sniper positions around the town, patrolled the streets and fired bursts of machine-gun rounds into the air. They hunted down Muslim leaders, and carried out summary executions. They easily crushed a token resistance. Sporadic street-battles left at least two-dozen dead. Pictures reached Sarajevo and, for the first time, President Alija Izetbegović grasped the scale and nature of the crisis that was closing in on his country:

It was unbelievable almost. The civilians being killed, pictures showed dead bodies of the women in the streets. I thought it was a photo-montage, I couldn't believe my eyes, I couldn't believe it was possible.

Izetbegović was under growing pressure to act decisively. As though completely unaware of the role that the JNA had played for almost a year in Croatia – and was about to start playing in his own republic – Izetbegović turned to the generals for help. It was, as he later admitted, like putting the fox in charge of the chicken coop. With Izetbegović's naive blessing, the JNA rolled in on April 3, and, by three o'clock in the afternoon, occupied the town. The campaign of terror continued, with JNA complicity. It would result in the flight of almost all Bijeljina's non-Serb population. Yet again, under the guise of separating the "warring ethnic parties," the JNA had succeeded in occupying a chunk of territory which, under its protection, could now be incorporated into a separate Serb state.

Izetbegović also sent a joint delegation to Bijeljina to investigate alleged atrocities there. Fikret Abdić and Biljana Plavšić were, respectively, Muslim and Serb representatives on the republic's collective Presidency. Jerko Doko was Bosnia's Defense Minister, and a Croat. Their enquiry led nowhere. According to Abdić:

> *Bijeljina was practically empty, I met with the local authorities, they told me what had happened, but there wasn't a single Muslim there, so we couldn't discuss the problem as a whole. Muslims didn't answer our appeal. They were too scared to come out, and specially scared to talk about it all.*

Plavšić didn't hide her own interpretation of events. She greeted Arkan with a kiss. A few weeks later, a senior State Department official, Ralph Johnson, drew a blank when he questioned Milošević about Arkan. Milošević looked him in the eyes and said he had never heard of him. After a six-hour war of nerves, Milošević admitted that he had heard the name before. He said he thought that man Arkan was Biljana Plavšić's bodyguard.

On April 4, Izetbegović bowed to pressure from the Croat representatives on the Presidency, and from Ejup Ganić, the man who was establishing himself as Izetbegović's *de facto* deputy. Increasingly alarmed at the flight of Muslims from northeastern Bosnia, the President issued a general mobilization of the Bosnian territorial defense. "It was clear then that something should be done," Ganić said later. "The JNA was all over the place, and had already been transformed into a Chetnik army. The exodus from eastern Bosnia had started, atrocities were committed, and we said we have to defend ourselves with the resources we had."

The decision infuriated the Bosnian-Serb leaders, who insisted that only Muslims and Croats would heed the mobilization call. They interpreted it as a declaration of war. Karadžić made a direct appeal:

> *When we heard that Izetbegović had issued a general mobilization call, it was a great shock for us and we knew that this would lead to a war. I phoned Izetbegović and said, 'Please, withdraw the call. You know the Serbs will not join your troops.' He said he could not do it because the call had already been made public, to which I replied that he should find some kind of formula to recall it because it was never too late. But he would not do it.*

Krajišnik also contacted Izetbegović, with whom he enjoyed a warmer personal relationship.

> *I asked him whether he knew what this meant. The Serbs were still serving in the Army, but the Muslims and Croats no longer did. Now he wanted to*

organize a territorial defense. Who did he think would serve in this territori-
al defense? Against whom? Against the Serbs? I begged him to rescind this
decision. I told him this may lead to war. Izetbegović told me he was sorry
but there was nothing he could do. I felt he was under a great pressure.

Koljević and Plavšić immediately resigned from the Presidency and
declared the rump Presidency illegitimate. That night, from his headquarters
in the city-center Holiday Inn, Karadžić, looked out across a city that he
knew he was at war with. He began to feel trapped:

The atmosphere in Sarajevo was that of terror. The streets were deserted and,
from our offices in the Holiday Inn, we could see Muslim Green Beret snipers
placed on top of high buildings. Everything was blocked and we could not
leave the hotel. So we waited till the morning to see what would happen.

The next morning, Serb paramilitaries laid siege to, and then attacked, the
Sarajevo police academy on the southern edge of the city. The compound sat
high above the city and enjoyed a commanding strategic position. It also
housed a large stockpile of arms and ammunition. The military priority of the
Serb forces was to move down from their positions on Vraca hill and enter the
city from the south, from where they would cross the river near the parliament building and cut Sarajevo in half at its narrowest point. With the police
academy in Bosnian hands, they would have a well-armed enemy at their
backs. It had to be dealt with first. It now became the first point of conflict in
Sarajevo.

Until April 5, most of Sarajevo's citizens – Muslims, Serbs, Croats,
Yugoslavs, Jews alike – had clung to the complacent conviction that war
could never happen in their city. They regarded Karadžić's dire warnings of
impending disaster as the ravings of a deranged and unrepresentative fanatic.
There was a strong element of snobbery in urbane middle-class Sarajevo's
dismissal of Karadžić. Many Sarajevans were fond of reminding each other
that Karadžić was not one of them; he was not even Bosnian. He was an
urbanized peasant from Montenegro, the first in generations of his family to
be educated. Sarajevans who had known him as a young man would recall a
gauche youth unfamiliar with city ways. They would say he had turned up in
the city "still wearing peasant's pointy shoes." On April 5, they started to
take him seriously.

The previous day's mobilization call shook Sarajevo out of its complacency. A small crowd gathered in the west of the city and started to march down
the main highway towards the city center. As they progressed, the crowd
swelled, thousands of Sarajevo citizens of all nationalities joining the throng
to protest against the madness of ethnic division and conflict in a city in

which the nationalities were so intermingled and whose proudest boast was that, for centuries, it had been a model of coexistence and mutual tolerance. Serbs, Croats and Muslims alike carried Yugoslav flags and portraits of Tito. Samir Korić, a twenty-seven-year-old accountant, was among them. Two years later, working as a journalist for Reuters news agency, he remembered the atmosphere of the day:

> *We were there because we thought there was still time to change people's minds, to save Sarajevo and Bosnia as a place where Muslims, Serbs and Croats could live together as they had for 500 years.*
>
> *Late in the morning several thousand of us decided to make our way to one of the barricades on the other side of the Vrbanja bridge, behind the parliament tower.*
>
> *The idea was to cross the bridge to Grbavica, to show that the city still belonged to the people – all the people.*

As the leaders of the procession, gathering in the Parliament forecourt, declared a "National Salvation Committee," the demonstrators swung right, over the bridge, and into Grbavica. Unwittingly, they were moving up the hill towards the besieged police academy and into the Serb guns. Shots rang out. A man at the head of the procession was struck in the foot. The crowd carried on. Those at the front could see uniformed men moving about beyond the line of the trees. They saw the Serb paramilitaries running from building to building. More shots; someone threw a hand-grenade. The crowd panicked and dispersed. Unknown to most of the demonstrators – for whom the prospect of open war still seemed preposterous – Sarajevo had suffered its first casualties of war. Suada Dilberović, a twenty-one-year-old medical student from Dubrovnik, was the first to die. She was shot in the chest as she crossed Vrbanja Bridge and was dead on arrival at Koševo hospital. Samir Korić had been with her at the start of the demonstration, but lost track of her as the crowd moved towards Grbavica. His memories of the day are worth recording in full. They are a reminder of how ill-prepared Sarajevo, where the nationalist parties had polled badly, was for what was to befall it; and they give the lie to the idea that the war was fuelled by "ancient ethnic feuds."

> *Many people will tell you now that they saw the war coming then, but I didn't and I don't think Suada did either. For Suada, a Muslim from the lovely city of Dubrovnik on Croatia's Adriatic Coast, the issue was more than abstract.*
>
> *Her parents had been trapped in Dubrovnik since October of 1991 when Serbs laid siege to the city during their war with Croatia. Refugees in their*

own town, they had been driven from their home by relentless Serb shelling and were living in an hotel.

As a medical student scheduled to graduate in May, Suada could easily have stayed away from the demonstration that day. She wasn't from Sarajevo. She wasn't even Bosnian. But my friend was outraged by the division of a city she had come to know and love over five years of schooling. And her family was already paying a price for the kind of ethnic hatred that lay behind the barricades.

It was not an angry crowd. I remember Suada standing there that morning with her blonde hair and sparkling blue eyes, laughing. The people around us, most of them young, were good-humored and eager to make their point in a peaceful way.

I was about fifty meters from the bridge when a few shots – maybe five or six – rang out. Everybody began to run.

Once we got to cover behind a building I was incredibly angry. It had never occurred to me that someone would open fire on a group of unarmed demonstrators.

Strange to say, war still didn't seem inevitable. It was only a few days later that there seemed no turning back, that we began to speak of Suada as the first person killed in the Bosnian war.

What had seemed a random act of violence, a great personal tragedy, slowly took shape in our minds as the first incident in a far greater drama: Europe's worst war in fifty years.[1]

At the parliament, the National Salvation Committee continued to address those demonstrators who had ignored the volley of sniper-fire from Vraca earlier in the day. Speaker after speaker emerged from the crowd to call for the dismantling of the barricades and to denounce the leadership of all three ethnic parties, and to call for a new round of elections. The event was broadcast late into the night on Sarajevo television. General Lewis MacKenzie, who had arrived in Sarajevo less than a month earlier as the UN Force Commander there, noted, as he drove back to his residence that night, the pools of blood that still lay in the street where the victims of Serb gunners had fallen. That night, under the combined cover of darkness and artillery bombardment, the JNA seized control of Sarajevo airport, and placed tanks and armored vehicles at the terminal building and on the approach roads.

Karadžić had warned that if Bosnia-Herzegovina won international recognition as an independent state, it would not last a single day. It would, as he put it, be still-born. On the afternoon of April 6, the European Community recognized Bosnia. (The United States followed suit the next day.) Karadžić kept his word. He proclaimed the independent "Serbian Republic of Bosnia and Herzegovina," later to be renamed Republika Srpska, and announced that it would come into existence that night at midnight, with Sarajevo as its capital (currently under enemy occupation) and himself as head of state. Bosnia, he said, had disintegrated the day it was recognized.

The People's Assembly and National Salvation Committee were still meeting in the forecourt of the Parliament. From the upper floors of the Holiday Inn, Serb gunmen opened fire, killing at least six people and injuring dozens more. Bosnian militiamen stormed the building. Frightened hotel staff and guests cowered in the lobby as shots ricocheted off the walls. Six men were arrested and dragged off to an uncertain fate. But Karadžić, his monstrous daughter Sonja, and his headquarters staff had long gone.

Did Izetbegović's mobilization call cause the war, as the Serb leaders insisted? Far from it. Karadžić and Krajišnik had never hidden their determination not to live in an independent Bosnian state. They knew they had the support of the Belgrade regime, and of a Serbianized JNA. They knew, too, that if the partition of Bosnia could not be negotiated, it could be achieved by force. They gave Izetbegović the choice Milošević had given all his enemies: you can have peace, but only on our terms. A few days later, Momčilo Krajišnik, now Speaker of the parliament of Republika Srpska, risked his life by driving into Sarajevo for a last meeting with Izetbegović. They met at Krajišnik's old office in the Parliament building where the massacre of peaceful unarmed demonstrators had taken place. It was late in the day and already dark. The air resounded with the pounding of artillery and mortar rounds echoing off the surrounding hills. The bombardment of Sarajevo had begun.

Krajišnik arrived first. He found the building locked. He rang the bell. No one answered. He waited in his car. The streets of the city were deserted. Finally Izetbegović arrived with his bodyguards, who were carrying automatic weapons fitted with silencers.

"We had been sort of friends," Izetbegović recalled, "We had served together in the parliament after the 1990 elections."

Krajišnik, conscious that he was on enemy territory, and that news of a meeting with the Muslim leader would be received badly on his own side, asked Izetbegović to keep the meeting a secret. Izetbegović agreed. Krajišnik then told him that he could avoid war by doing a deal on Sarajevo.

We always had at the back of our minds the division of Sarajevo – so the Serbs could have their part and the Muslims theirs. This is no secret. We considered that Sarajevo should be split into two cities – twins. I told Izetbegović that the war could stop if we could come to an agreement on Sarajevo.

Izetbegović refused. Krajišnik gave the President a pen, a souvenir, as a token of goodwill. Izetbegović accepted it. Krajišnik turned the key in his office door, and, without clearing his desk, left. As they said goodbye, they agreed to meet again in a day or two. Izetbegović drove through the blacked-out streets to the Presidency. Krajišnik headed west, to the Serb-held suburb of Ilidža. A burst of machine-gun fire narrowly missed his car. He resolved not to return to Sarajevo until after the war. The two men never met again until Lord Owen sat them around the same table in Geneva eight months later. By then they were sworn enemies.

1 Reuters, April 4, 1994.

17

THE PRESIDENT IS KIDNAPPED
May 2–3, 1992

A low blanket of cloud covered Bosnia that day, obscuring President Alija Izetbegović's view of his country from the window of the Cessna twin-prop light aircraft carrying him back from three days of fruitless negotiations in Lisbon. He was already nervous, anxious to be home. His plane had stopped to refuel in Rome, and for an hour-and-a-half he, his daughter Sabina, and his Deputy Prime Minister Zlatko Lagumdžija had tried to telephone the Presidency building in Sarajevo. All lines to the city were down. He did not know that there had begun, that morning, the greatest single bombardment to date, the targeting of many government buildings and the destruction, by sabotage from within, of the city's central post office and telephone exchange. Forty thousand phone lines had been knocked out, including all those serving the city center where government buildings were located. It was May 2, 1992. Unwittingly, the President was flying into the eye of the storm. He was about to be delivered, not back to the seat of his Government, but into the hands of his enemy.

A few minutes into the flight, the captain announced that permission to land at Sarajevo had been refused, because of heavy fighting throughout the city. The plane was to be redirected to Belgrade, Zagreb or Graz. The captain asked the President where he wanted to go. Belgrade was out of the question. Graz was too far. He chose Zagreb. The plane banked steeply to the left and headed northward.

Then the flight-deck received new instructions. Air-traffic control had cleared the plane to land at Sarajevo. There was still heavy fighting. But the President was free to land there at his own risk. The pilot relayed the message to the President and asked him, again, to choose his destination.

Even his friends said that his years as a political prisoner in the 1980s had formed in Izetbegović the habit of consulting no one but God. Faced with this dilemma he indulged in this habit again. For several minutes he sat in nervous silence, alone with his thoughts. He consulted neither his daughter, nor Lagumdžija, nor the flight crew. Finally he said "Sarajevo."

Sarajevo airport was under JNA control. Though conflict had come to the city four weeks earlier there were still no clear lines of confrontation. Naively, given what is now known about the long preparations the JNA had made for war against Bosnia, President Izetbegović still regarded the Yugoslav Army as a neutral force that was capable of standing between the Serb militiamen and the people they wanted to drive from their homes. The second of May destroyed that delusion.

General MacKenzie had sent an UNPROFOR armored personnel carrier to the airport to escort the President and his party back to the Presidency building. Its Swedish commander waited for an hour-and-a-half beyond the scheduled arrival time and then, inexplicably, returned to UNPROFOR headquarters in the city. By General MacKenzie's own admission, no one at UNPROFOR knew where the President was, or whether he was due to return to Sarajevo that day. When the plane landed, Izetbegović's eye scanned the broad expanse of tarmac for the distinctive white-painted vehicles of the UN force. He saw only the distinctive green vehicles of the JNA. Panic began to set in. He feared not only for his own security but also for that of his daughter, his Deputy Prime Minister, and his bodyguard, Nurudin Imamović. As the President's party stepped on to the tarmac, they were surrounded by thirty men bearing JNA insignia. Imamović instinctively drew his gun, which was immediately taken from him. The party was ordered into the terminal building.

The second of May had seen a serious escalation of the war not only in Sarajevo but elsewhere in Bosnia. It was the day that Serb forces consolidated their hold on Brčko and Doboj in the north of the republic, driving the majority Muslim population from their homes and securing the vital east-west corridor from Serbia to the Serb-held lands in Bosnia and Croatia. It was also the day that Karadžić's forces tried to implement, by military might, his plan to divide the city into separate Muslim and Serb quarters.

Karadžić always made plain his ambition to partition Sarajevo. He had a vision of a city divided into Serb, Croat and Muslim sectors that was sharply at odds with Sarajevo's centuries-long tradition of peaceful coexistence and ethnic intermingling. Without shame, he would advocate to journalists and diplomats alike the need to build a wall through the heart of the city. He wanted a Berlin Wall through a city in which every district, every neighborhood, every street, every apartment block was ethnically mixed.[1] In his mountain headquarters at Pale, Karadžić would happily spread out his maps of the city and show anyone who was interested the route that his proposed wall would take. The extreme east of the city, the narrow winding streets of the Turkish old town, together with the broad boulevards of the neighboring nineteenth-century Habsburg quarters, were for the Muslims and Croats. Everything to the west of Marijindvor – including most of the city's twentieth-century industrial and commercial infrastructure, and most of its residential capacity – was to be inhabited exclusively by Serbs. This was decided on the preposterous grounds that the farmland and villages on which the modern city had been built was originally populated mostly by rural Serb communities. Karadžić made no apologies for devising a plan which would cram the vast majority of the city's people into the smallest most crowded sector of the town. "It is the habit of the Muslims to live in this way," his deputy, Biljana Plavšić, once memorably declared. "They like to live on top of one another. It's their culture. We Serbs need space."

On May 2, as Izetbegović was returning from Lisbon, Karadžić's forces tried to cut the city in half. For weeks they had occupied the high ground, encircling the city from all sides. Now they moved into the town itself. From the south, they moved down from the Vraca and Trebević mountains into the city-center district of Grbavica. One column of armored vehicles crossed the narrow bridge at Skenderija and came within a hundred yards of the Presidency building. Its progress was covered by artillery and mortar fire from the surrounding heights. Artillery- and tank-rounds slammed into the red-brick facade of the city municipal headquarters. Further west, a second armored column moved in from Serb-occupied territory near the airport, apparently closing in on the district housing the television station and the distinctive twin-towered headquarters of Sarajevo's daily newspaper *Oslobodjenje*.

In Croatia, Serb and JNA forces had proved themselves almost incapable of capturing urban territory without first reducing it to rubble. They enjoyed overwhelming firepower superiority; but they did not have the infantry to follow up artillery attacks. The pattern now repeated itself in Sarajevo. Both armored columns were halted by a relatively small number of Patriotic League, the recently-formed armed wing of the SDA[2] and Bosnian territorial defense members equipped with nothing more than shoulder-launched anti-tank missiles. At Skenderija, they immobilized the lead vehicle in a street so narrow that it blocked the passage of the rest of the column, which was then forced to retreat. The second column also dispersed in disarray at the first sign of resistance.

It was a half-hearted effort, but it was not wholly unsuccessful. For the first time it brought the Serb front line into the heart of the city. It gave Karadžić's forces control of Grbavica and part of the neighboring district of Hrasno. Further west, they now occupied the suburbs of Nedžarići and Mojmilo, as well as a strip of residential territory near the airport. Furthermore, the suburb of Dobrinja, one of the city's most prosperous districts which had been built specifically for the 1984 Winter Olympics, and which had attracted many of Sarajevo's young professional people, was now entirely surrounded by Serb forces, cut off from the rest of the city – a siege within a siege. The inner-city front lines established by the Serbs' bungled invasion on May 2 held firm for the rest of the war, and formed the basis for a *de facto* partition of Sarajevo: thus Grbavica and Nedžarići would, from now on, find themselves part of the self-declared "Serbian Republic of Bosnia-Herzegovina," separated from Bosnian Government controlled districts by a Beirut-style green line, across which rival armies (and former neighbors) faced each other in a constant, and often deadly, stand-off. It was a line that divided naturally cohesive inner-city communities, and separated parents from their children, a wholly artificial and arbitrary military barrier which, overnight, became, in effect, a new frontier between enemy states.

But there was another reason why the attempt to cut the city in half had failed. The JNA in Bosnia was not yet acting wholly on the Serb side. Many of the old Yugo-centric officer corps remained hostile to Serb nationalism and would not take orders from Karadžić. The principal culprit, from Karadžić's point of view, was General Milutin Kukanjac, the commander of the Second Military District of the JNA and the most senior Army officer in Bosnia. In April, Karadžić had asked Kukanjac to place his forces under the command of the Bosnian Serb leaders, and to help cut the city in two.

I insisted, in late April, that Kukanjac release all the Serbs from the army, and, if not, to divide Sarajevo into two parts, to prevent fighting in the city itself. Kukanjac said he could not agree to such a military operation which, he said, did not correspond to what he saw as the army's role as a buffer between the Serbs and the Muslims.

Throughout most of the republic the JNA had been successfully converted into a Serb nationalist force. The transition had passed the hapless Kukanjac by. He did not know the script, nor the role that he was expected to play in it. He now found himself trapped, in his city-center barracks at Bistrik, with the 400 officers and men of his headquarters, behind government lines. Sefer Halilović, the commander of the Bosnian TO, now ordered his men to lay siege to Kukanjac's base, the nearby JNA officers club, and the military hospital at Marijindvor. Kukanjac had, for weeks, been negotiating a phased withdrawal of the JNA from the city. Halilović now determined that the JNA forces would only be allowed to leave if they surrendered their weapons to the Bosnian TO.

The streets of downtown Sarajevo had descended into chaos. Shells were falling frequently and apparently at random. The town hall, the post office, the Hotel Evropa and nearby apartment blocks were on fire. Serb aircraft attacked the television transmitter on the summit of Mount Hum. The attempted armored invasion had brought the Green Berets, the Patriotic League, the territorial defense, all on to the streets. The city was now under the control of a series of independent Bosnian militias not answerable to a single command structure, some well organized paramilitary units, others no more than armed gangs of pre-war criminals.

At his Command Headquarters in the extreme west of the city, General Lewis MacKenzie was not aware of what was going on downtown. In his diary for May 2, he wrote: "a relatively quiet day. Only a couple of hundred rounds of heavy machine-gun fire in and out of the old city. But the firing continued all night so I wasn't able to get to a colleague's flat to watch the Spanish Formula One Grand Prix. It was just as well – the flat was partially destroyed by artillery fire during the afternoon." MacKenzie was expecting the delivery of a package from Canada, which he had been told would arrive at the post office that day. He sent an administrative assistant into town to collect it. When the officer returned he told his commander: "I have good news and bad news." "What's the good news?" the General asked. "I found the post office." "And the bad?" "It's been blown up."

The President's plane had flown into the middle of the chaos, and Kukanjac had seized the opportunity that it presented. From his besieged barracks, he ordered the airport commander General Djurdjevac to detain the President "for his own safety."

The President's party were now in the airport director's office under armed guard. Izetbegović insisted on being allowed to return to the city. Djurdjevac refused. He told the President that he had been ordered to take him and his delegation to the JNA barracks at Lukavica, a Serb-held village on the southern edge of the city, about ten-minutes drive from the airport. Djurdjevac said General Kukanjac had insisted on a meeting with the President there. Izetbegović refused:

> *I said that we can meet, but only in the Presidency. They said no, Kukanjac insists we go to Lukavica. I said there is no way that I'll go to Lukavica and talk. They said I had to go to Lukavica. I asked them whether I was their hostage. I told them I was not going to Lukavica unless I was being forced. He said, then, you have to go.*

Izetbegović had asked to be allowed to telephone the Presidency to tell his staff where he was. Djurdjevac refused, telling him that the telephone lines were down. Then the phone on the airport director's desk rang. It was a woman calling from the city to find out whether the plane her daughter had been booked on earlier that day had left. By chance, she had called the director's direct line. Izetbegović stood up, walked across the room to the director's desk and said: "Pass me the telephone." According to Lagumdžija:

> *The President took the telephone, he said 'Good evening Madam, this is Alija Izetbegović, the President of Bosnia on the phone'.*
> *There was a brief pause. She was confused. He said 'Yes, yes. That's right, Alija Izetbegović, the President of Bosnia. Could you please be so kind, I am here at the airport, sitting in the director's office, and the Army won't let us go. We are kept here. Could you please call the Presidency and tell them that*

you talked to me, that I am here, at the airport, and if you can't reach the Presidency, please call radio and TV and inform them. They insist upon my meeting with General Kukanjac, at Lukavica. Yes, General Kukanjac, yes'. The woman couldn't believe her ears. The President said 'Thank you very much, yes, yes, thank you, yes, thank you Madam'.

The woman was as good as her word. She rang Sarajevo television and told them her improbable tale. And that's how the city found out that its President had been arrested.

Meanwhile, Kukanjac was on the phone to Belgrade. He told the Army Chief of Staff, General Blagoje Adžić, that his men at the airport had Izetbegović and asked for instructions. Adžić called the President of rump Yugoslavia, Branko Kostić. Kostić was annoyed that Adžić had admitted, on an unprotected phone line, that the Army had arrested the legal head of state.

I reacted instinctively and said, 'Blagoje, you know that they didn't arrest him, they are just looking after him for his own personal safety ...' But Adžić said 'No, no, they arrested him!' ... he was rather slow to pick up what I was trying to say... I told Adžić 'Look after him well, but use this opportunity to lift the blockade of the barracks.'

Thus authority to use the President's captivity as a bargaining chip in the negotiations to de-blockade the JNA barracks in Sarajevo came from the acting head of state, the slavishly pro-Milošević Kostić of Montenegro.

At the airport, the President and his daughter were ordered into one car, Lagumdžija and Imamović the bodyguard into a second. They were escorted by a tank in front and a tank behind, and driven to Lukavica, Izetbegović protesting that he now considered himself a hostage.

Senad Hadžifejzović, the Sarajevo television news anchorman, was about to end the evening news bulletin with the closing headlines when his producer barked into his ear-piece that the program was being extended. "President Izetbegović is on the line," he said. "Interview him."

The news had reached the television station that the President was being held by the JNA at the airport. There had begun a frantic round of telephone calls to try to trace what had happened to him. The television station is in the far west of the city, and its phone lines had not been affected by the destruction of the post office. It also had a direct line to the Presidency, which was not routed through the post office. The only functioning phone-line out of the Presidency was the one connecting the building to the television station. The only way Izetbegović's fellow Presidency members could communicate

with their President, and with the outside world in general, was on live television. There began an evening of what must rank as one of the most extraordinary pieces of current-affairs broadcasting in the history of the medium.

For the first few minutes, Hadžifejzović was not clear what was going on.
He asked the President a few open questions while he collected his thoughts
– questions about the talks in Lisbon, the events in the city that day. Then
he said: "Mr. President, where are you?"

"I am in Lukavica."

Hadžifejzović was stunned. Everyone in the city knew that Lukavica was
a Serb stronghold, one of the main bases from which the attacks on the city
were being commanded.

"And what is your status in Lukavica?"

"I think I have been kidnapped."

A panic-stricken Ejup Ganić was called to the phone in the Presidency,
and put through to the studio so that he could talk to the President.
Izetbegović immediately told him that, in his absence, Ganić would be acting
President. Hadžifejzović, by chance, knew General Djurdjevac well. He had
served his national service under him, and had been a journalist on the Army
newspaper. "He was a very fucked-up soldier, the Russian type, you know,
always shouting. But I knew him and I knew he liked me, so I saw my
chance," Hadžifejzović later wrote. He asked the President to put General
Djurdjevac on the line and the television anchorman began to negotiate the
President's release.

> *During these talks, Djurdjevac ignored Ganić. He kept saying 'I'm not talk-
> ing to you, I'm talking to Hadžifejzović'. I wanted to give him something so
> I told him that he was known as an honorable soldier. And I asked him to
> guarantee the President's security. He said he would, and that he would also
> protect the President's daughter, and Lagumdžija and the bodyguard.*

To Hadžifejzović's astonishment, an unexpected guest arrived in the studio – Fikret Abdić, a Muslim member of the Presidency from the northwestern Cazinska Krajina and a rival of Izetbegović. He had made his way, that
day, by car, from Split on the Croatian coast, through central Bosnia, to
Zenica and from there to Sarajevo. No one understood how he had made the
journey: he had had to pass through Muslim, Croat and Serb checkpoints.
Abdić was known to be close to the Bosnian Serbs, their Croat counterparts
and the JNA, and to have little interest in an independent Bosnian state. In
the Bosnian Presidency, Ganić, and the HDZ representative Stjepan Kljuić,
regarded Abdić's arrival with alarm. It was, they concluded, evidence that an
attempted coup was under way. They believed Abdić had arrived to depose
Izetbegović and install a quisling regime that would take Bosnia-Herzegovina

back into Yugoslavia. Ganić convened a meeting of the Cabinet Ministers who were already in the Presidency building. Alija Delimustafić, the Interior Minister and Abdić's man, began to argue for a change of leadership. Bosnia must not be allowed to descend into open war with the JNA for the sake of one man, he said. Rusmir Mahmutčehajić, who, for the previous eight or nine months, had been one of the leading figures in the establishment of the Patriotic League in Bosnia, exploded with rage. He accused Delimustafić of attempting to stage a *coup d'état*, and, in effect, of treason. Mahmutčehajić had long suspected Delimustafić of being an agent of JNA counter intelligence KOS. His insistence now on undermining Izetbegović's leadership and Abdić's miraculous success in passing through Serb checkpoints planted the conviction firmly in Mahmutčehajić's mind that what had taken place had been planned from the beginning by Belgrade.

It is an attractive conspiracy theory, and one that still holds currency among government circles in Sarajevo. Izetbegović was to be kidnapped and exchanged for Kukanjac; both men were to be killed in a bungled exchange operation. This would provide a pretext for the JNA and Bosnian Serb forces to invade the city and cut it in half. Abdić was dispatched to Sarajevo and given clearance to pass through all Serb checkpoints despite being a leading figure in Izetbegović's SDA. He would make his way to the television station and stand by to announce his assumption of the functions of President. Alija Delimustafić, meanwhile, would prepare the ground for a new government. According to other government ministers he had been briefing his staff to expect a change of leadership all morning.

The idea that this was an attempt to replace him, had also struck Izetbegović. It explains why he immediately appointed Ganić to deputize for him; he was pre-empting any attempt by Abdić to assume power. The Defense Minister, Jerko Doko, a Bosnian Croat, was dispatched to the television station with instructions to keep an eye on Abdić and stop him from making any public announcement that would undermine Izetbegović. Abdić later denied that he had any intention of usurping the President. But he was furious that the President had appointed Ganić, who officially was not even a member of the ruling party. Abdić spent the evening in the television station but, cowed, made no public contribution. If this was a coup attempt, it had failed for a variety of reasons: a chance and bizarre phone call to the director of the airport that was intercepted by the President; the failure of the armored columns to cut the city in half; Kukanjac's determination to save his own skin, and his refusal to offer himself up as a sacrificial lamb; and Mahmutčehajić's cabinet room challenge to Delimustafić.[3]

That night, in his room at Lukavica, the President did not sleep. In the Presidency, neither did Ganić. The next morning, highly agitated and afraid, he made his way along the street that was now known as sniper alley to the headquarters of the UN and into General MacKenzie's billet. He pleaded with the UN commander to intervene. He said Izetbegović was the only leader who carried the moral authority to control the militias in the city. They had surrounded the JNA barracks, and without strong leadership the situation threatened to get out of control.

MacKenzie drove to Lukavica with the EC representative in the city, Colm Doyle, a major in the Irish Army. He found an angry crowd besieging the gates of Lukavica demanding that Izetbegović be handed over to them. What happened next reveals how little MacKenzie understood of the conflict in which he had become embroiled. Having found an English speaker in the crowd, a Canadian Serb, he stood on the hood of his vehicle and addressed the mob through translation. He understood the crowd to be angry Muslims demanding the release of their President. They were, in fact, angry Serbs baying for his blood. He reassured them he was here to try to negotiate Izetbegović's safe release. The bemused crowd none the less gave way.

Djurdjevac kept MacKenzie waiting for two hours, refusing to answer questions about the President's whereabouts or condition. Finally, exasperated, MacKenzie stood up and made for the door. Djurdjevac relented and led the UN Commander into an adjacent room. A dishevelled exhausted President Izetbegović was on the telephone. He was talking to General Kukanjac, who, like the President, was held captive behind enemy lines. The solution seemed obvious. The President replaced the hand-set and said that he and Kukanjac had agreed a swap – one-for-one.

Almost immediately Kukanjac called back, to change the terms of the deal. Izetbegović and his party would be swapped for his entire barracks – 400 men, their vehicles, weapons and equipment. MacKenzie told the President it was impossible for the UN, with only a handful of vehicles and officers in the city, to supervise such a convoy and guarantee its security. Izetbegović said he would take responsibility, and pass the order down to his militia in the city to allow the JNA convoy safe passage out of Sarajevo.

MacKenzie agreed. They assembled the vehicles at Lukavica, and the President's party made the journey into the city towards Kukanjac's Bistrik barracks. It was on that journey that MacKenzie realized how seriously the war had escalated the previous day:

> *I'd been there a couple of days earlier, but now the city and the streets were blocked. There were tanks burning, there were engines blown out of vehicles sitting on the middle of the road. There were bodies, many of them in fact looked like they were sunning themselves. There were people who had been placed on their back with their hands crossed on their chest and piled like firewood along the side of the road. So I mean, it was devastation and surre-*

239

alistic with black clouds of oil, smoke and wires sparking on the street. A lot of fuel and oil spilt all over the place. And it was a very very nasty scene.

This was not, however, the deal as it was understood by the Presidency members in Sarajevo, far less by the Bosnian militias on the ground. What Ganić claimed had been agreed was a simple one-for-one swap – Kukanjac for Izetbegović. Ganić, having been appointed acting President by Izetbegović the evening before, said he had not agreed to the evacuation of the entire headquarters. Nor had he been informed that the President himself had given it his approval.

When MacKenzie led a convoy of JNA trucks into Kukanjac's barracks, it struck the Bosnian militiamen laying siege to Kukanjac that they had been tricked. The Bosnian territorial defense was desperately under-equipped. On front-line positions around the city, TO men were defending barricades often with no more than one AK-47 between three. It quickly became characteristic of Bosnia's war that, while the Serbs enjoyed an overwhelming superiority in military hardware but lacked the men, the Bosnian forces had men but no guns. Bosnian volunteers complained of having to wait until their comrades-in-arms fell in battle before getting their hands on a gun of their own. They were not now prepared – no matter what deal had been struck – to sit back and watch a huge consignment of weapons and ammunition drive calmly out of the city, only to find its way into the hands of the Serbian forces against whom they were fighting an uphill battle.

MacKenzie's convoy – carrying the President, his daughter and Lagumdžija (the bodyguard Imamović had agreed to stay behind as collateral) – reached Kukanjac's barracks. He found the General in an upstairs office drinking coffee with Jusuf Pušina, a Deputy Minister in Izetbegović's government who had responsibility for policing. This pleased MacKenzie, who took it as a sign that the two sides were cooperating. Kukanjac told MacKenzie he needed three hours to load his trucks. MacKenzie told him he had one hour. The plan was that the convoy – now numbering some seventy trucks – would leave the barracks and drive to the city-center front line near Skenderija. Izetbegović and Kukanjac would travel in the same UN APC. The JNA trucks carrying 400 men, their weapons, equipment and ammunition, would follow. Before crossing the front line into Serb-held territory, the convoy would divide. Izetbegović and his party would board another vehicle and be driven to the Presidency. General Kukanjac and his seventy trucks would then proceed to Lukavica, and safe Serb territory.

After an hour, MacKenzie, Kukanjac and Izetbegović walked out into the courtyard of the barracks. The ground was strewn with discarded equipment for which there was no room in the trucks. Soldiers were clambering aboard the convoy, bristling with arms and ammunition. The vehicles lined up and prepared to move. At the last minute, MacKenzie's walkie-talkie crackled into life. His office at UN headquarters told him it had just received a message from Acting President Ganić: the deal was off. Only Kukanjac was to be exchanged for the President, as originally agreed. Everything else – 400 men, their trucks, arms, ammunition and equipment – must stay, and their evacuation negotiated separately.

MacKenzie walked across the courtyard to the President. Izetbegović countermanded Ganić's order, and insisted the deal was still on. Pušina, the Police Minister, said he would guarantee the convoy's safe passage. MacKenzie resolved to go ahead. He radioed back to his headquarters, instructing them to inform Ganić that the President himself had pulled rank on him, and had given the go-ahead.

The convoy inched its way, painstakingly slowly, out through the barrack gates and into the narrow twisting side streets of Skenderija – MacKenzie's small armored car in the lead, Izetbegović and Kukanjac in the APC behind. It had got about 500 yards in five minutes when the shooting started.

MacKenzie stopped the convoy and ran back to a position from where he could see the ambush site. Bosnian militiamen had waited until the President's vehicle was out of sight, and then had cut the convoy in half. Its tail end – about a third of the vehicles – was still inside the Bistrik compound. Paramilitaries were looting the trucks at gunpoint. MacKenzie's eye scanned the scene: burning vehicles, a few dead bodies, a Volkswagen Golf straining under the load of hundreds of AK-47s piled into it. MacKenzie found a Bosnian TO officer who spoke English and said that President Izetbegović had authorized the convoy's passage. The TO officer replied: "My President cannot authorize anything. He's either dead or kidnapped."

MacKenzie ran back to the President's vehicle. A Sarajevo television cameraman was capturing, on film, the chaos there. Jovan Divjak, the deputy commander of the territorial defense, had arrived to try to determine whether the President was even in the vehicle. The President ordered him to stop the ambush, and allow the convoy to continue. But Divjak was powerless. He screamed into his radio handset at commanders further down the line. Disembodied voices answered back. Izetbegović persisted: "Tell them to let the convoy pass. There will be further talks tomorrow." "Tell the President that talks tomorrow are out of the question," the anonymous voice crackled back. "Who the hell is that?" the President demanded.

MacKenzie asked Izetbegović to show himself, to prove to his own militias that he was safe. He opened the hatch in the roof of the APC and Izetbegović emerged. "It's a bad analogy," MacKenzie said later, "but it was like some kind of second coming. It had a very calming effect." Bosnian militiamen clambered onto the APC to welcome their President home, oblivious to the fact that General Kukanjac was also inside.

In a matter of minutes, it was over. Seven JNA soldiers were dead, and several others wounded. Bosnian militiamen had made off with ransacked weapons and ammunition. More than a hundred JNA personnel were still trapped in the barracks, their evacuation to be negotiated separately. After twenty-four hours as a captive of his enemy, Izetbegović was free, home, and furious. He stormed into the Presidency building where he refused to shake the hand of Ejup Ganić, his appointed deputy. "Was it really worth nearly getting me killed for the sake of grabbing forty rifles?" he demanded.

Who gave the order to attack the convoy? The JNA blamed Ganić, whom they had characterized as a Muslim extremist. There is little evidence to support the claim. The command could also have come from Sefer Halilović, who was almost certainly one of the unidentified voices at the other end of General Divjak's walkie-talkie. To some extent the question is academic. Given the level of anxiety and tension that had seized the city during the previous twenty-four hours, the prospects of the convoy making it out safely were almost negligible. MacKenzie failed to grasp the intensity of what had taken place the previous day, or the effect it had had on the mood of the militias patrolling the streets.

The incident soured relations between the Bosnian government and MacKenzie, who recorded in his diary for May 3: "this has been the worst day of my life." An operation of which he was in charge had nearly cost the lives of a Head of State and a JNA General. Seven junior officers had died. MacKenzie blamed the Bosnian Presidency for deliberately sabotaging the convoy. He never forgave Bosnia's leaders.

This was also the day Izetbegović finally understood the nature of the enemy that was ranged against him. It represented the end of his delusion that the JNA was a neutral force. Kukanjac, who also labored under that illusion, was fired within days, and replaced by officers who knew whose side they were supposed to be on. As Branko Kostić inelegantly put it:

> It was Monday. I was in Belgrade when General Adžić [JNA Chief of Staff] called me in the afternoon, and I saw from his tone... he said that this asshole in Sarajevo [Kukanjac] blew it all. Alija escaped, the column was cut in two parts, and we had casualties there... We fired Kukanjac because we had to restore confidence in the Army so that the people in Yugoslavia would know they were sending their children to people who knew what they were doing.

Kukanjac was not the only casualty. On May 8, the last of the Yugoslav Generals – thirty-eight in all – were removed in a purge of the Army which completed the transition which had begun months earlier. Under intense international pressure, Belgrade ordered the JNA to withdraw from Bosnia later that month. But the pull-out was cosmetic because by now most of the officers and soldiers stationed in Bosnia were natives. They did not withdraw. Belgrade had transformed them into a Bosnian Serb army 80,000-strong. They inherited the arms and ammunition the JNA left on "withdrawal." The JNA previously had moved key factories (such as the SOKO aircraft factory in Mostar) to Serbia, which it feared would fall under Muslim or Croat control. Kukanjac was replaced by a General who had proved his mettle in the war in Croatia: Ratko Mladić.

1 Sarajevo, in 1992, did not have distinct Serb, Muslim, or Croat neighborhoods. There was one exception. The old Turkish quarter, Baščaršija, was almost exclusively populated by Muslims. Elsewhere, the overwhelming majority of the city's population lived cheek-by-jowl without regard to nationality.

2 When war erupted in Bosnia, there were many different militia; in addition to the JNA, there was the Bosnian TO, the Bosnian Serb TO (SDS), Bosnian Serb MUP, the Patriotic League, the Green Berets, the Bosnian interior ministry forces (MUP), Croatian MUP, Bosnian Croat units, the Croatian army, Serbian paramilitaries such as Arkan's "Tigers," Seselj's Chetniks, the White Eagles, the Yellow Wasps, etc.

3 Delimustafić soon afterwards left the city in disgrace and fear. He lived out the rest of the war in Austria and never spoke publicly about the events of May 2 and 3.

18

THE CLEANSING
The Summer of 1992

They arrived in Croatia by the thousand with tales which, at first, the world did not believe: tales of harassment and torture, of mass killings and deportations, of the burning of villages and towns, of wanton, sadistic cruelty so base that they found themselves accused of fabrication to discredit their enemy. Then, in May, a new term entered the international political vocabulary, a term that has proved the enduring lexicographical legacy of the Yugoslav war: *etničko čišćenje*, ethnic cleansing. It had been practiced the year before in Croatia; in Bosnia it became the defining characteristic of the conflict.

The columns of refugees that spilled into Croatia in April and May 1992 were not fleeing the war zones. They had been driven from their homes on the grounds of their nationality. They were not the tragic by-product of a civil war; their expulsion was the whole point of the war.

In a systematic campaign, Serb paramilitary hit-squads swept through northern and eastern Bosnia in the spring and summer months and, municipality by municipality, seized control of the region without, in most places, encountering real military opposition.

Sometimes the cleansing was orderly and achieved without resort to open conflict. The village of Orašac, near Bihać in northwestern Bosnia, was one such example. Serb paramilitaries first surrounded the village and then closed in on it. There was token resistance from a handful of armed Muslims. Five were killed in gun battles and the village fell in less than twenty-four hours. Two hundred Serb paramilitaries entered the village while others blocked the entrances and exits. House by house they ordered the people out into the main street. The men were separated from the women and children; and the women and children, after being robbed of their money and jewellery, were allowed to go free – north, towards Bihać town – while their homes were looted, blown up or burned. The men – 180 of them – were taken to the village primary school, and held there for two days. On the second day a Serb officer, whom none of the village men knew, arrived with a list of six names. One man – Dubravko Handžić – was selected at random and given the list. It contained the names of prominent local Muslims. Handžić was ordered to point them out. They were then separated from the rest. Their fate was never discovered.

A common characteristic of the cleansing operation was this systematic elimination of community leaders – prominent people, intellectuals, members of the SDA, the wealthy. The existence of such lists of names was in itself an instrument of cleansing. The terror it instilled in neighboring communities, once news of the atrocities spread, encouraged many of those who feared they might be targeted to flee even before they were attacked. It was the conscious elimination of an articulate opposition, and of political moderation. It was also the destruction of a community from the top down.

After two days, the men of Orašac were separated into smaller groups. About seventy of them were interned in a unused tractor-repair plant in the neighboring village of Ripač. They were housed in open-sided storage depots with sheet-metal roofs and slept on the bare concrete floor. They were subject to random beatings by their captors, some of whom were former neighbors. They were held there until they could be safely moved to one of the larger detention centers, the existence of which was eventually revealed by an ITN television crew in early August.

Elsewhere, the cleansing was violent and accompanied by mass killing. On July 20, the village of Bišćani was singled out for a cleansing sweep. Here the paramilitaries entered and began a killing spree that left dozens dead. More than a hundred more were rounded up and marched out of town. The paramilitaries argued amongst themselves about whether to kill, or detain, the survivors. Two men were shot dead in cold blood. The others were beaten with clubs or rifle butts before being driven to the detention camp at Trnopolje.

Humiliation, terror and mental cruelty were almost universally deployed. Captured men would be told that they were to be executed the following day. At dawn they would be taken out, convinced that they were to be killed, only to be thrown into a new detention camp. They were forced to sing Serb nationalist songs to entertain their jeering tormentors, and to avoid being beaten. They were told that their wives had been raped and then killed, that their children were dead. They were forced, on pain of death, to perform atrocities against each other – mutilation, physical and sexual, and, even, mutual killing. They were forced to dig mass graves and collect and bury the bodies of their families and neighbors. Sometimes, those on grave detail would themselves be killed and thrown on top of the bodies they had just delivered. The technique had a clear political purpose that went far beyond the sadistic gratification of the perpetrators, beyond, even, the desire to send hundreds of thousands of people fleeing. It was designed to render the territory ethnically pure, and to make certain, by instilling a hatred and fear that would endure, that Muslims and Serbs could never again live together.

Karadžić had founded his new independent state at midnight on April 6. Ethnic cleansing was the instrument which gave that state territorial definition. There were two areas where the campaign was most concentrated: northwestern Bosnia, around the city of Banja Luka, and in the Drina valley.

In northern Bosnia there were 700,000 Muslims; in most of the Drina valley the Muslims formed an absolute majority of the population. Clearly ethnic cleansing could not be achieved overnight.

The cleansing of the towns and cities of northern Bosnia presented a different challenge to that of the countryside. Here, whole communities could not be rounded up so easily, because the three nationalities tended to live side by side, as in Sarajevo. Here, the lives of the non-Serbs were rendered unliveable. They were fired from their jobs. They were harassed in the street. Their homes were attacked and their businesses blown up at night. In some areas, rigid restrictions, that were hauntingly reminiscent of the early Nazi curbs on the activities of Jews, were imposed on the freedom of movement of non-Serbs. At Čelinac, near Prijedor, Muslims were forbidden, by a decree issued by the Mayor's office, to drive or travel by car, or to make phone calls other than from the post office. They were forbidden to assemble in groups larger than three,[1] or to leave without the permission of the authorities. By August, Muslim households began to fly white flags from their balconies: it was a signal that they were prepared to go quietly and make no trouble.

In this way, wholesale robbery became an organized part of ethnic cleansing. Every major population center in northern Bosnia acquired, during these months a "Bureau for Population Exchange." It was a euphemism. They were, in fact, the agents of this form of ethnic cleansing – ethnic cleansing by eventual consent. Most Muslims and Croats were not allowed to leave without first signing documents surrendering all future rights to their property. Hundreds of thousands of people willingly gave up their homes, cars, business premises, money, luxury goods, fearing for their lives at the hands of Serb local authorities and the paramilitary terror squads. Frequently, they even paid for the privilege of being robbed. They would, as a final indignity, be charged a fee for being driven out of town, robbed, and sent into exile in Croatia or government-held areas of Bosnia.

There were two main routes through which the refugees fled or were driven. From Foča and Višegrad, tens of thousands walked through the mountains often for days on end, until they found a place of safety. Some died on the way, too weak to carry on. Others arrived in organized convoys of commandeered tourist buses. One such convoy left Sarajevo in May, only to be detained for forty-eight hours by Arkan's Tigers in the Serb-held suburb of Ilidža, and then robbed. The women and children on board arrived in the Croatian port-city of Split after a subsequent twelve-hour journey across narrow twisting mountain tracks, exhausted and traumatized, only to find themselves accommodated in sports halls or gymnasiums, or in tented villages erected by the Croatian boy scouts. The UN refugee agency, UNHCR, was caught off guard by the exodus. In May it had two field officers in Split – an

Austrian and an Ethiopian – sharing a tiny office in the old harbor district with one phone and one fax line between them.

From northern Bosnia, many were packed on to sealed trains at the railway town of Doboj and driven to the Croatian capital Zagreb, where they found the city unable to accommodate them because of Croatia's own displaced half a million people from the previous year. At the end of July, Croatia's Deputy Prime Minister, Mate Granić, announced that his country could take no more. Croatia, with a population of just 4.7 million, was now also home to almost a million refugees, and was turning into a giant refugee camp. He appealed to western nations to start taking more. The twelve countries of the EC, chaired by Britain, held a one-day conference in Geneva, aimed principally at fund-raising. Germany, with 200,000 former Yugoslavs living within its borders, many of them as refugees, argued for a quota system, each country accepting an agreed number of refugees according to its size, and ability to accommodate them. Britain's Baroness Chalker, Minister of Overseas Development, led the charge against the idea, and won the support of the other ten. The refugees, she said, should be accommodated as close as possible to their homes, so that their return could be made all the more readily once the fighting had died down. She was, she said, speaking not in the interest of the British or EC tax payer, but in the interests of the refugees themselves.

But to assume that the refugees would be able to return after the fighting had ended was to miss the whole point of the war, which was being waged deliberately to ensure that they would never return. Baroness Chalker, in Geneva, would not address that question. That, she said, was a matter for the London conference which the British Foreign Secretary Douglas Hurd had scheduled for the following month. In the meantime, the world had a humanitarian, not a political, crisis on its hands, and it called for a humanitarian, not a political response.

The international aid agencies found themselves the unwitting accomplices to ethnic cleansing. In July, having been assured by the local Bosnian Serb authorities that these Muslims were leaving voluntarily, to be reunited with families elsewhere, UNPROFOR troops and UNHCR aid-workers escorted 7,000 of the cleansed from northwestern Bosnia across the Serb-controlled UN Protected Area to the Croatian city of Karlovac. Only on arrival at Karlovac did the UN workers realize the scale of the terror from which the refugees were fleeing. The refugees, now no longer cowed into silence, spoke openly about their ordeal. They had been forced, they said, to sign documents surrendering their homes and property. UN officials expressed outrage. "We're becoming collaborators," one worker said. "It's blackmail. The choice we face is either to become agents of ethnic cleansing, or to leave tens of thousands of people to continue living their nightmare."

By August, the demands of the Bosnian-Serb authorities had grown more brazen. The Mayors of Bosanski Novi, Sanski Most, Bosanska Krupa and Bosanska Kostajnica drew up a list of more than 20,000 Muslim and Croat names, took it to Topusko in Serb-held Croatia and presented it to the UN Civil Affairs Co-ordinator with a demand that the UN lay on a fleet of buses to take those listed out of the area. The people had been encouraged to gather each day in the town squares in anticipation of UN transport. They were waiting there even now, the Serb delegation said. The Civil Affairs Coordinator shook his head in despair. "I know these men personally. I work with them every day. I've tried to tell them that what they are doing constitutes a crime against humanity, a war crime. But it doesn't get through. They are acting with complete impunity."

When Croatia slammed the door on refugees, circumstances deteriorated further still for the desperate Muslims still trapped in northern Bosnia. Their escape route now led south into government-held central Bosnia. Columns of those fleeing the cleansing would take to the mountain roads. Those with vehicles soon lost them to pillaging Serb militiamen at checkpoints along the way. They were abused and intimidated as they marched south, carrying whatever belongings they had the strength to bring with them. They were shot at and beaten. Some were killed. By the time they crossed into government territory at the front-line village of Turbe, just north of Travnik, they had often been walking for days. There they joined the legions of those who had come before them. Travnik, once a model Bosnian city, and the former seat of the Ottoman Turkish rulers of Bosnia, had been home to all three nationalities. The summer of 1992 turned this beautiful ancient town into a vast refugee encampment, its delicate ethnic and social mix torn apart by the influx of the dispossessed and the gradual exodus of local Serbs and Croats.[2]

So much for the women, children and the elderly. For the men it was worse still. Rumors that the Serbs had several mass detention camps in northern Bosnia had been in the air for weeks. But most of the news media was preoccupied with the siege and bombardment of Sarajevo. Then, on July 9, the journalist Roy Gutman, of the New York paper *Newsday*, put a call through to a Muslim leader he had met in Banja Luka the previous year. "Please try to come here," the man pleaded. "There is a lot of killing. They are shipping Muslim people through Banja Luka in cattle cars. Last night there were twenty-five train wagons for cattle crowded with women, the elderly and children. They were so frightened. You could see their hands through the openings. We were not allowed to come close. Can you imagine that? It's like Jews being sent to Auschwitz. In the name of humanity, please come."[3]

Recent military advances by the Serbs had succeeded in securing a land-corridor, running east to west[4], linking Banja Luka to Serbia. Gutman was the first journalist to take advantage of the new access. His first report was on July 3, his detailed series of interviews blazing a trail that would rouse international public opinion about the nature of Bosnia's war. On July 19, *Newsday* published Gutman's first story about the camps. He had been allowed to visit Manjača.

> *Heads bowed and hands clasped behind their backs, the Muslim prisoners lined up before their Serb captors. One by one they sat on the metal stool and then knelt to have their heads shaved.*
>
> *An order was given that could not be heard from 200 yards away, and each group of twenty then returned on the double to the sheds in which they lived in near darkness. Guards at the entry swung their rubber truncheons as if in anticipation of beatings to come.*

Gutman was refused permission to enter the sheds, but interviewed Muslim men who had been released as part of a prisoner-exchange program. They told him of the random beatings they had suffered and the occasional deaths that they had witnessed. The Bosnian-Serb Army called Manjača a prisoner-of-war camp. But Gutman said it was clear, even from the testimony of the eight hand-picked prisoners he had been allowed to interview under the constant intimidating gaze of the prison guards, that many of the men detained there were not combatants. Some said they had never carried arms; others said they had owned rifles but had registered and surrendered them when the Serb paramilitaries had entered their neighborhood and issued the surrender ultimatum.

Gutman's report unleashed a media frenzy just as Karadžić and Koljević were in London for EC-sponsored talks (Britain now held the Presidency). Although this was later changed on the advice of their media spin-doctors, it was their policy at that time to make themselves as available as possible to the international press. At a press conference, they angrily denied the existence of concentration camps. There were, they admitted, prisoner-of-war camps, as was normal practice in any conflict. In at least four live television and radio interviews, Karadžić, fluent in English, challenged his interlocutor to come personally to Bosnia and see for himself that there were no concentration camps on Serb territory. He invited any journalist who wanted access to the alleged camps to visit them. It sounded like rhetoric. But ITN news and *The Guardian* had the wit to take him at his word. In doing so they scooped the world. Roy Gutman, meanwhile, upped the ante. On August 2, *Newsday* carried a story under a front-page banner headline in two-inch letters that read THE DEATH CAMPS OF BOSNIA. For the first time, the Serbs were accused not just of mass detention, but of organized extermination:

> *The Serb conquerors of northern Bosnia have established two concentration camps in which more than a thousand civilians have been executed or starved and thousands more are being held until they die, according to two recently released prisoners interviewed by Newsday.*
>
> *The testimony of the two survivors appeared to be the first eyewitness accounts of what international human rights agencies fear may be systematic slaughter conducted on a huge scale.[5]*

Gutman then described conditions at Omarska camp. Quoting the testimony of a sixty-three-year-old man whom he called only "Meho," Gutman described how more than a thousand Muslim and Croat prisoners were held in metal cages without sanitation, exercise or adequate food. It contained the entire cultural and political élite of the town of Prijedor, east of Banja Luka. The camp was located in a former iron-mining complex. "Meho" had been held there for more than a week "in an ore loader inside a cage roughly 700 square feet with 300 other men." The cages were stacked four high and separated by grates. "There were no toilets and the prisoners had to live in their own filth, which dripped through the grates." The International Committee of the Red Cross had been trying for two weeks to visit Omarska, but had been denied access by the Bosnian-Serb authorities.

Four days later, on August 6, Penny Marshall of ITN produced what was probably the most memorable single piece of journalism of the entire conflict. She went to Omarska with some British colleagues including Ed Vulliamy of *The Guardian* who wrote:

> *The men are at various stages of human decay and affliction; the bones of their elbows and wrists protrude like pieces of jagged stone from the pencil thin stalks to which their arms have been reduced... There is nothing quite like the sight of the prisoner desperate to talk and to convey some terrible truth that is so near yet so far, but who dares not. Their stares burn, they speak only with their terrified silence, and eyes inflamed with the articulation of stark, undiluted, desolate fear-without-hope.[6]*

There were, it turned out, four large detention camps that gained international notoriety. Trnopolje and Manjača were transit camps where inmates lived in appalling conditions and were subject to random beatings and the sadistic whim of their guards. But in Omarska and Keraterm (a former ceramics factory on the outskirts of Prijedor) there was evidence that the prisoners were separated into categories based on interrogation. They were intimidated into giving evidence against each other. After this screening process, they were placed in one of three categories – A, B, or C. Into category A went those who were judged to have been leaders of the Muslim community, or volunteers for one of the Bosnian militias or the territorial defense. Most of these were killed. Category B consisted of men who were drafted into the territorial defense. And category C was all the rest. They were transferred to Trnopolje or elsewhere where they were held until they could be "exchanged" for Serbs taken prisoner by the Government forces, or for Serbs living on Government-held territory who wanted to cross to the Serb side.

There were, in addition, countless smaller, more temporary, detention centers, such as that at Ripač. The total number of these will never be known and it is doubtful whether the Bosnian-Serb leadership could have known the location of them all, far less come to any assessment of the number of people detained and killed in each.

On August 18, the US Senate Foreign Relations Committee received a staff report which suggested that detailed accounts had been available to the governments of the western world and to the United Nations long before Marshall's and Vulliamy's exclusive. Its main findings were that the ethnic-cleansing campaign had substantially achieved its goals – there now existed an almost exclusively Serb-inhabited region, in territory contiguous to Serbia, and covering seventy percent of the territory of Bosnia-Herzegovina. This had been accompanied by widespread atrocities including "random and selective killings... and organized massacres... We believe the death toll associated with forcible removal of the Muslim village population far exceeds the death toll from the bombardment of cities." In the camps, organized killings were "recreational and sadistic." Most damning of all the report concluded that:

> *The United Nations did not respond in a timely manner to early reports from the field about atrocities in the prison camps. The US state department also had early reports of killings associated with the forcible transfer of populations but did not follow up on the reports. The failure to respond reflects systematic defects in the way the international community and the United States monitor human rights crises. Had the world community focused earlier on the atrocities in Bosnia-Herzegovina, many lives might have been saved.*

When did the international community know about the scale and nature of the refugee crisis? As early as May 1992, a Bosnian government agency called "Save Humanity" was collecting eye-witness testimony from those who had fled the cleansed regions. A Sarajevo-based lawyer, Zlatko Hurtić, began to collect evidence almost immediately. By June he was distributing dossiers of eye-witness accounts to journalists, aid agencies, diplomats, almost anybody who would listen. Muhamed Sacirbey, then Bosnia's Ambassador to the UN, claimed to have told Boutros Boutros-Ghali personally about the camps as early as the middle of May.

In late April we started giving information to the UN, including Boutros Boutros-Ghali that there were concentration camps. There was a meeting with the Secretary General around May 15. We were worried about doing this at first because we thought that they would react by saying we were scaremongering. All we had were eye-witness reports. But we ourselves had no idea how bad these camps were. But Boutros Boutros-Ghali and the others didn't take us seriously at the time. In July we submitted a more precise list of camp locations.

On July 3, the UNHCR circulated a report to the ICRC, UNPROFOR and the EC-monitoring missions, concerning abuses at four camps. On July 27, it also circulated a report, specifically about Omarska. George Kenny, the US State Department official who resigned in protest at American policy in Bosnia, later accused the US of a cover-up. The State Department policy at the time, he said, amounted to "Let's pretend this is not happening".

The question is important because it reveals a recurring characteristic of the foreign policy-making of the main western powers with regard to Bosnia: that it was driven substantially by television coverage. Warnings about camps issued by Zlatko Hurtić, President Izetbegović, Muhamed Sacirbey, the UNHCR and Roy Gutman, no matter how persuasive their evidence, did not have a fraction of the impact of those devastating television pictures.

Karadžić agreed, under international pressure, to order their evacuation, under the supervision of the ICRC, on condition that the detainees were removed from the combat area. The agreement suited Karadžić's purpose: he had been seen to grant an important concession and could portray himself, on the international stage, as working hard to reign in the worst excesses of his own more extreme lieutenants; while at the same time achieving his central war aim of removing Muslims from the territory mapped out for his new Serbian state.

At the end of April 1992, there were 286,000 refugees from Bosnia. Most of them had gone to Croatia. By the beginning of June this figure had risen to three-quarters of a million; to 1.1 million by mid-July. By the end of the year, almost two million Bosnians – nearly half the population – had lost their homes.[7]

Before the war, there was a saying in Bosnia, "Goodbye Bosnia, I'm going to Sarajevo," that referred to the sense of separateness that the capital enjoyed from its rural hinterland. Sarajevo is encircled by high ground, and there is something in the character of the place that is inward-looking, self-contained and more sophisticated than its surroundings. The capital's peculiar sense of separateness from the rest of the republic now had an adverse effect: for during the summer months of 1992, while everything described in this chapter was taking place, the world's media concentrated almost exclusively on the siege and bombardment of the city, even though much more decisive battles and campaigns were being waged elsewhere. It was a problem partly of access, partly of information. But it suited the Serb leaders very well. Nikola Koljević once admitted to a group of journalists that the focusing of international attention on the capital had "allowed us to get on with what we had to do in northern Bosnia."

On April 23, Lord Carrington went to Sarajevo and met President Izetbegović. He was briefed by the UN commander there, General MacKenzie, who, by his own admission and through no fault of his own, knew virtually nothing about what was happening outside the capital. He saw only the relative microcosm of repeated failed ceasefire agreements. He had grown exasperated with both sides, and would, eventually, though not yet, come to regard the Serb side as much more flexible in its approach.[8] He now offered this advice:

> *I told Carrington that we [the UNPROFOR commanders] thought the Bosnian presidency was committed to coercing the international community into intervening militarily, and was therefore in no mood to honor a ceasefire – We recommended that Carrington advise the president that he would not receive military intervention and consequently should negotiate a solution with Dr. Karadžić and the Bosnian Serbs.*

Carrington was blunt with Izetbegović. The beleaguered President recalled what the peace envoy had said:

> *Carrington advised me to start to negotiate to find the solution while their forces were attacking us. I told him that it was impossible. Their demand, their objective was to destroy Bosnia as a country. He asked me 'What will you do?' I told him we would fight back. Carrington paused. He looked me in the eye and said, 'What makes you think you can fight back? Do you know what you are talking about, Mr. Izetbegović? Do you know what you are fighting against? Do you know what weaponry they have?' I told him we had no other choice but to fight back or to capitulate. If we capitulate, we will either be captured or killed. We have no choice, no alternative. He told me 'You, Mr. Izetbegović, are not aware who you are dealing with,'*

MacKenzie was right in his central conclusion. Izetbegović's strategy was to try to force international military intervention. He agreed that the logical consequences of Serb and Croat territorial ambition was that Bosnia should be wiped off the map, and that the republic's two-million Muslims should

253

make up their minds whether they were Serbs or Croats of Islamic faith and, inevitably, second-class citizens in a state defined by ethnic identity. By the end of the summer, Izetbegović was calling for an international policy that became known as "lift and strike" – the lifting of the arms embargo against his country, and the use of NATO airpower to compensate for the Serbs' overwhelming firepower superiority and the entrenched positions Serb forces now enjoyed as a result.

None of the major powers thought it desirable. Western leaders obfuscated with talk of ancient ethnic hatreds, Balkan savagery, and warring factions. When it came to ceasefire violations "all sides are guilty." This was true. But it was hardly the point. In this context a ceasefire around Sarajevo could only assist Karadžić's forces in their implementation of the plan that is described in this chapter, since this was more likely to remove the Bosnia story from the television screens of the Western world.

The major governments of the Western world were agreed on the need to mount a huge humanitarian response to alleviate the suffering of the dispossessed. It became clear that if Sarajevo were not relieved soon, large numbers of people would start starving to death. Although there was food in the city, its acquisition and sale were rigidly controlled by black-marketeers who had organized a cabal among themselves to keep prices high. On June 8, the UN Security Council approved a plan to take control of Sarajevo airport and begin an airlift of humanitarian aid. At his own request – and with huge enthusiasm – General MacKenzie was relieved of his post as Chief of Staff to UNPROFOR (Croatia) and made Commander of Sector Sarajevo, his task now to take control of the airport from the Bosnian Serbs.

At the time, the Bosnian-Serb leadership protested vigorously. Men had died defending the airport. It was sovereign Serb territory, they argued. To leave it undefended except by a battalion of blue helmets would be to render it vulnerable to a Muslim takeover. They could not possibly agree. In fact, in private, both Karadžić and Koljević were keen to reach agreement on the airport, and were much more cooperative in their negotiations to achieve it than the Bosnian government turned out to be. According to MacKenzie, the idea to hand the airport over originated with Karadžić himself. "I learned that Dr. Karadžić had proposed to New York that the Serbs open the airport and that the UN take over the whole city with a 'green line' running down the middle."[9] But Karadžić was as concerned as anybody about preventing the starvation of Sarajevo: it would have further increased calls by senior Western politicians – including Margaret Thatcher and Bob Dole – for military intervention. Would the world really stand by and watch a European capital starve to death? Karadžić planned happily to vacate the airport, making it look like a major concession and throwing the burden of "responsible behavior" back on to the Bosnian government.

On the evening of June 27, with his attempts to open the airport stalled because of the failure of repeated ceasefire agreements to last more than a few hours, MacKenzie received a bizarre phone call. The President of France, François Mitterrand, was on his way to Sarajevo, due to land at Sarajevo airport that evening, and had requested a UN escort into the city.

It was madness. An airport landing strip is, by its very nature, the most exposed of terrain. Nothing had landed at Sarajevo for weeks. There were no runway lights; the control tower was out of action. The strip was covered in shards of shrapnel – and, if the plane were not shot down by one side or the other in the belief that it was coming to resupply their enemy – its tires would blow out on landing. The airport road was the most dangerous road in the world. To drive along it in broad daylight was to take a mortal risk; to do so after dark was suicidal. MacKenzie advised the President's flight to land elsewhere, break for the night, and come the next day. It did.

The twenty-eighth of June is St Vitus's Day – the anniversary of the Serbs being defeated by the Turks at Kosovo in 1389. In 1914, Archduke Franz Ferdinand of Austria had come to Sarajevo on this very day as a deliberate gesture of defiance to Bosnia's Serbs, who wanted to take Bosnia out of the Habsburg monarchy and into a union with the Serbs of Serbia. The historical resonances were powerful.

Mitterrand intended to visit only the Head of State. MacKenzie was shocked. "I'd never considered that the President of France would visit Sarajevo and talk with only one side in the conflict." MacKenzie impressed on Mitterrand the importance of also seeing the Serb leaders. "I could just imagine the Serbs' reaction" if Mitterrand saw only Izetbegović, he wrote in his diary. "They would take their fury out on the only permanent international mediator present in Sarajevo – me."

Mitterrand agreed to shake hands with Karadžić at the airport before his departure. MacKenzie informed Pale. Karadžić and Koljević turned up together at the appointed hour and practically accosted the French President on the apron of the airstrip. They shook hands and exchanged a few words. As always, Mitterrand's expression didn't alter. His eyes showed no flicker of recognition or interest. He gave the impression that he scarcely knew who they were. Then, as MacKenzie had predicted, shots rang out. A tank at the eastern end of the runway began to blast round after round into the already shattered Bosnian government-held suburb of Dobrinja. Three wounded Serb soldiers suddenly appeared, displaying light wounds to the leg. MacKenzie, exasperated, dismissed the whole show as theater. Someone fetched an over-sized flack jacket and dropped it over Mitterrand's diminutive frame. He did not flinch, but, for the first time that day, he looked his age. He was anxious to be off. He had been unimpressed by his hasty encounter with Karadžić, and, while the gun battle lasted, stood stoically in the lee of the terminal building. It ended after a few minutes. He boarded his plane, and took off.

His mission was successful in that he appeared to demonstrate to the world that a military intervention was not necessary to bring sanity and progress to Bosnia's chaos. A bold and heroic gesture of the type Mitterrand had self-promotingly made appeared sufficient.

It created the momentum MacKenzie wanted. The next day, as promised, the Serbs lined their tanks and armored personnel carriers up on the runway and left the airport. MacKenzie ran up the UN flag. Within days a Canadian battalion had arrived, diverted from peacekeeping duties in Croatia, and began to secure the airport. The airlift began and was soon transporting more than 150 tons of food and medical supplies a day. The international community breathed a collective sigh of relief. The crisis at Sarajevo, international public opinion seemed to feel, was over.

The opening of Sarajevo airport marked another central characteristic of the West's response to the Bosnian war. It was, almost from the beginning, treated as a humanitarian crisis. Western governments dealt with the war as though it were a flood or an earthquake, enthusiastically addressing the symptoms of the conflict, without making any real effort to challenge its causes. Mitterrand's visit, and his comical encounter with a grateful and ingratiating Radovan Karadžić, was a defining moment.

That night, June 28, more than 200 Muslims were herded into a tiny room at Keraterm detention camp at Prijedor, northwest of Sarajevo. They were beaten for hours. The other prisoners heard their screams late into the night. Then they were machine-gunned. The next morning, the wounded lay among the dead. The other prisoners had to dispose of their bodies. They estimated that at least 150 had died. It was months before the world found out. And, by then, it was too late.

By the end of that fateful summer, Serb forces had under their control about two-thirds of the republic's territory, and most of what they wanted. The fiercest battles had been fought in the north, for the vital east-west corridor linking Banja Luka (and, therefore, Serb-held territory in western Bosnia and Croatia) with Serbia proper. The corridor passed through the region of Posavina, which was predominantly Croat. Twice, Croatian forces had penetrated south, deep into territory the Serbs needed. But the corridor was a strategic necessity. Without the corridor, there could be no contiguous, unbroken Serb territorial unit. "The corridor is the very air we breathe. It is our life as a nation," the Banja Luka Serbs said. They threw their best units at it. In fact, the Serbs only consolidated their hold on the corridor after secret talks with the Croats. But it remained vulnerable. At Brčko it was only five kilometers wide. It was the Serb state's Achilles heel.

The second main area of conflict was in the southwest, in Mostar. Karadžić's early ambition had been to draw the border of his state along the Neretva river, and down towards the coast. The most ambitious Greater Serb nationalists asserted that under this plan, even Dubrovnik would be incorporated into the future Serbian state. This plan would have partitioned Mostar along the river: east Mostar would be in Republika Srpska. But in May the JNA withdrew from the east back of Mostar, and on June 17 Croatian forces drove the Serbs off the east bank and out of Mostar altogether.

But there remained four vital areas where the initial Serb onslaught had not succeeded, due to the unexpectedly effective resistance of the local Bosnian defense forces in the early days of the battle. In eastern Bosnia, the majority Muslim population retained control of Srebrenica, Žepa and Goražde. These became islands of enemy territory deep within what the Serbs considered their country. As winter descended, freezing the front lines, it became clear that these three "enclaves," as they became known, would be the Serb military priority for the spring offensive. They had to be neutralized as a military threat, and finally cleansed as unwelcome ethnic stains on an otherwise pure Serb tableau. The fourth area was the unfinished business of Sarajevo itself. Karadžić remained resolved to partition the city, by negotiation if possible, by force if necessary. But that could wait until the end.

Izetbegović's dilemma was now acute. The only alternative to defeat by the Serbs was "liberation" by the Croats. He was already profoundly distrustful of his "ally" in Zagreb – and with sound reason.

1 The ban on public gathering was last imposed against Kosovo's ethnic Albanians in 1989.

2 For a graphic evocation of the horror and despair that accompanied these long marches into exile, see Ed Vulliamy, *Seasons in Hell*, Simon & Schuster, London, 1994.

3 Gutman, Roy, *Witness to Genocide*, Shaftesbury: Element Books Ltd, 1993.

4 Fighting for control of this corridor caused some of the heaviest battles of the war, cost thousands of lives, and frequently dominated proceedings at the Geneva peace talks.

5 *Newsday*, August 2, 1992.

6 Vulliamy, *Seasons in Hell*, 1994.

7 Figures supplied by UNHCR, Geneva.

8 See MacKenzie's memoir *Peacekeeper*, Douglas McIntyre, Vancouver, 1993, for his growing disenchantment with the Bosnian Government and, in particular, his animosity towards Ejup Ganić.

9 *Peacekeeper*, p. 211.

19

"WE ARE THE WINNERS"
The London Conference
May–December 1992

The London Conference, hosted by the British Government and the UN, was the most ambitious international summit on Bosnia. More than thirty countries and organizations joined in calling for the reversal of ethnic cleansing and the restoration of territory taken by force. Held in the wake of revelations about detention camps in Bosnia, speaker after speaker condemned Serb aggression. Under the illusion that the international community would take action to save Bosnia, the participants could afford to take the moral high ground. Western powers hailed the conference as a breakthrough. A framework had been established to deal with the Yugoslav crisis. The tide of war had been turned and confidence restored in the West's ability to provide leadership. Despite this new display of international resolve, Serb leaders believed that they, too, had scored a victory in London.

The Belgrade leadership knew in advance that it would face a barrage of criticism. The President of the new Yugoslavia, Dobrica Ćosić, the nationalist writer, who had taken office four months earlier, had been told by a British minister that Milošević would be called to account.

But Milošević was jovial on the flight to London. Turning to his Information Minister, he asked: "Do you know why we're travelling to London? Because we are the winning party." The Minister was confused. "But we've got sanctions, petrol is rationed. The economy is a mess." "Forget the queues, we are the winners," Milošević said, turning round to continue his conversation with the Montenegrin President, Momir Bulatović.

Once in London, Milošević seemed more interested in settling political scores with the newly-appointed Yugoslav Prime Minister, Milan Panić, than in the Conference itself. They argued publicly and behind the scenes, Milošević even threatened to punch him. Milošević had hand-picked both Panić, the Belgrade-born millionaire from California, and Ćosić, seen as the spiritual father of Serbs. His plan was to let the unlikely pair navigate while he waited for the storm to pass. Earlier that year, he had approached Ćosić, who exerted considerable influence behind the scenes, and asked him to head the unrecognized Yugoslav state, which comprised Serbia and Montenegro, and had been formally (and hurriedly) reconstituted on April 27, 1992. "Together we can save the nation," Milošević told him. It was an offer Ćosić couldn't resist. In June, the writer rode in a battered taxi to his own presidential inauguration. His heart set on healing the divisions among

Serbs and securing a place in Serbian history, the elderly Ćosić wanted to appear above political struggles. He would not dare to risk a direct challenge to Milošević.

Serbia and Montenegro were facing increased isolation. On May 30, outraged by Serbian atrocities in Bosnia, the UN Security Council had imposed draconian economic and political sanctions on Belgrade. After the imposition of sanctions, Milošević came under intense pressure to resign. For the first time institutions in Serbia – the Orthodox Church, the University and even factories turned against him.

Milan Panić was selected as the man who would deliver what was left of Yugoslavia from the Balkan wasteland. Through his connections with the political establishment in Washington, he would help to end Yugoslavia's quarantine. But if Milošević believed that the political novice would simply follow orders, he was wrong. Surrounded by a team of his own American advisors, Panić tried to run Yugoslavia the way he ran his California-based pharmaceutical company. At one point Milošević even agreed to consider Panić's bizarre proposal that he (Milošević) should take a job in the US and retire altogether from politics. It is remarkable that Milošević was even tempted to assume a new life in the US. But he soon changed his mind, and a simmering feud between the ebullient millionaire and the arrogant politician finally erupted in public during the London Conference.

With his signature glass of Coca-Cola, Panić was a breath of fresh air in marked contrast to the dour authoritarian politicians of Serbia. His cabinet was a strange mix. Panić picked some of Milošević's men, but not enough to satisfy the Serbian President. He also included several of Ćosić's appointees, and a couple of independent and genuinely qualified ministers, for sensitive portfolios such as justice and minority rights.

Panić took the premier's job out of an unshakeable belief that he could succeed in the monumental task of ending the war. He impressed foreign dignitaries with his message of coexistence for the Balkan communities – but, in fact, revealed only the vaguest knowledge of what was happening on the ground in Bosnia. On July 13, in his apartment in Belgrade, he was informed that the Serb assault on Goražde was continuing despite his pledges to the contrary. He ordered his aides to telephone the town, completely unaware that it had been under Serb siege for three months and was completely cut off from the outside world. Reaching the town via military walkie-talkie, Panić introduced himself. He asked a local Serb Commander whether he needed any help. "Just men," answered a voice through the static. Panić did not seem to realize that Yugoslavia was still aiding the Bosnian Serbs with men and materiél.

Opening the Conference, the British Prime Minister John Major painted a grim picture of Serbia's fate, already under UN sanctions. If the Serbs failed to halt their onslaught, they would condemn themselves to complete isolation.

> *If we do not get cooperation, the pressure will inexorably increase. Condemnation, isolation. Parties who stand in the way of agreement can expect even tougher sanctions, even more rigorously policed... No trade. No aid. No international recognition or role. Economic, cultural, political and diplomatic isolation.*

At the Conference, Panić made a strong impression – clownish, erratic, but committed to ending the war. At one point, Milošević asked to speak. Panić scribbled something on a piece of paper and held it up in front of the Serbian President. It said "shut up" in English. Panić then showed the paper to the Acting Secretary of State, Lawrence Eagleburger, former ambassador to Yugoslavia and once a friend of Slobodan Milošević. Panić went a step further. In his heavily-accented English – his Serbo-Croat was also rusty – he told the Conference that Milošević was not authorized to speak.

On the second day, the EC – urged by the Dutch – put forward a draft resolution, lambasting the Serbs. The Serbs saw the draft and threatened to abandon the Conference. The British worried that if the document were not proposed, the Bosnians and the Dutch would walk out. If it went ahead, the Serbs would leave instead. The Russian Foreign Minister Andrei Kozyrev, and his deputy, Vitaly Churkin, whose perfect English and relaxed manner endeared him to the media, tried to calm down the Serbs and keep them at the Conference. The Serbs withdrew to their separate rooms at the Queen Elizabeth II Center.

There was a huge row. Milošević insisted on leaving. Panić wanted to stay. Finally, Milošević agreed the delegation could stay, but only if Panić promised to shut up. Panić tried to tough it out: "It might be best if some of us go back to the Conference and others don't," he said. In the middle of this exchange, no one noticed that Kozyrev had come into the room to propose a compromise: Major would read the document aloud, but the Conference would end without debating it. The Serbs reluctantly agreed.

Major hailed the Conference a success for providing a comprehensive framework for the first time since the conflict erupted. "We now know what needs to be done," he said, "how it needs to be done and by whom it needs to be done." The participants had agreed to tighten sanctions against Belgrade and station monitors along Serbia's international frontiers, including the Danube River, though not on Serbia's frontier with Bosnia which was controlled by Serbs on both sides.

Lawrence Eagleburger announced they had secured an agreement from the Bosnian Serb leader, Radovan Karadžić, to allow the UN to monitor all heavy weapons around the towns of Sarajevo, Bihać, Goražde, and Jajce within a week. The Bosnian Serbs had also agreed to withdraw from "a substantial" – but as yet undefined – part of the land they controlled.

The UN Secretary General Boutros Boutros-Ghali announced plans to deploy thousands more peacekeepers to protect relief convoys for Bosnia's civilians. The first winter of the war was approaching, and more than 1.3 million people were expected to rely on outside supplies of food, clothing and shelter for survival. The leaders agreed that a peacekeeping force could be created by the UN Security Council to maintain the ceasefire and control military movements. On September 14, Security Council Resolution 776 sent peacekeepers to Bosnia. France, as the single largest troop contributor, took command of UNPROFOR II, as it was to be called, while Britain as the second largest held the post of chief-of-staff. The participants also pledged to work towards a ban on military flights. In October, the UN declared Bosnian air space a "no-fly" zone.

The warring parties agreed that a settlement must include recognition of Bosnia-Herzegovina by all the former Yugoslav republics and respect for the integrity of present frontiers unless changed by mutual agreement. The declaration also called on parties to:

> – *close the 'abhorrent' detention camps and grant immediate access to the international community.*
>
> – *reject as inhuman and illegal the expulsion of civilian communities from their homes in order to alter the ethnic character of any area. Compensation and the right of return.*
>
> – *establish a frame work for peace talks in Geneva, including the creation of working groups (on such issues as the succession of former Yugoslavia) and examine the proposal for a war crimes tribunal.*
>
> – *respect all international treaties and agreements.*
>
> – *restore trade and other links with neighboring countries.*
>
> –*despatch human rights observers to Kosovo, Serbia's overwhelmingly Albanian southern province; Vojvodina, the northern province whose ethnic patchwork includes 346,000 Hungarians; and Sandžak, a region straddling Serbia and Montenegro with a large Moslem population.*

Milošević repeatedly refused the despatch of international observers to monitor the human rights of the ethnic Albanians in Kosovo, saying it constituted interference in Serbia's internal affairs. Panić backed the despatch of monitors from the Conference on Security and Cooperation in Europe to Kosovo. A year later Milošević would expel them.

In their final declaration, the Conference participants urged the warring parties to lay down their arms, or risk lasting isolation.

If...Serbia and Montenegro do intend to fulfill these obligations in deed as well as word they will resume a respected position in the international community...

If they do not comply the Security Council will be invited to apply stringent sanctions leading to their total international isolation.

The text was harsh. World powers were threatening to completely seal off Serbia from the outside world. For the Serbian President however, the outcome was better than expected. The declaration did not mention the use of force to punish the warring parties. This was an important omission and a victory for Serbia. Stinging words alone would not penalize the Serbs.

At the London Conference, the Bosnian Serbs – and particularly their leader, Radovan Karadžić – emerged from under the coat-tails of their sponsor in Belgrade. This clearly worked in Milošević's favor. Until then, he alone had had to bear the brunt of the international community's wrath. As Karadžić willingly basked in the attention of the media, the burden of responsibility shifted, almost imperceptibly, on to his broad shoulders. Milošević's close ally Dušan Mitević recalled:

> *Looking at it cynically, the London Conference virtually endorsed all the effects of the war... Until then, Serbia and Yugoslavia were being struck off the agenda everywhere... But all of a sudden, Ćosić was at the conference table as the president of Yugoslavia... and Panić was there as prime minister. You mustn't forget that the Conference ended with John Major saying 'God help us and Mr. Panić for a peaceful solution to the problem ...' Milošević was also there – with all the cards in his pocket. And this was the first time the Bosnian Serbs with Karadžić appeared, not as official members of the conference, but there anyway.*

At the very end of the Conference, the former Labor Foreign Secretary and SDP leader, Lord Owen, was appointed to replace Lord Carrington. At first the Serbs were extremely upset. Previously, Owen had called for the use of air strikes to stop the Serb offensive. Ultimately, he would build an extraordinarily warm relationship with Milošević, winning his confidence.

But as the Conference wound up, Milošević was outraged by the foolish antics of Panić, who had had the temerity to ask for monitors to be sent to the borders between Serbia and Bosnia. Two years later – when he had finally tired of Karadžić – Milošević agreed to a watered-down version of the same thing, and was rewarded by the partial easing of sanctions. None of Milošević's coterie could believe that Panić had dared to propose mutual recognition between Croatia and Yugoslavia in a twelve-point peace plan he presented to the Conference (the plan also included the recognition of all former Yugoslav republics within their original frontiers, and the opening of talks with ethnic Albanian leaders).

Milošević stormed off to the airport, leaving for Belgrade in Karadžić's plane. The Bosnian Serb delegation was forced to hitch a ride with Panić to Serbia the following day. There were no commercial airlines flying to Belgrade. It was the only way to get home. Asked if he would allow Karadžić and his colleagues on to the plane, Panić turned to an aide and said: "Who are they?" He finally agreed, but forced the delegation to sit in the rear of the aircraft while he and his team travelled first class.

After the London Conference, Milošević's henchmen took steps to get rid of Panić. They were upset by Panić's tendency to say whatever came into his head. Just three days after returning from London, a no-confidence vote was tabled. As one of Milošević's devotees, the MP Brana Crnčević, told the Federal Parliament: "We have embarked on an escapade with an irresponsible man. If we place further confidence in him, we'll be embarking on an even greater one."

Panić had managed to stay in office thanks to support from the Montenegrin deputies to the Federal Parliament. Arriving in Belgrade as Milošević's placeman, six months later, Panić had emerged as the leader of Serbia's opposition. Even the West cautiously pinned hopes on the eccentric pharmaceuticals magnate.

Ćosić, who had also clashed with Milošević, appealed to the Serbian President not to stand for re-election. Milošević retaliated, Panić was the first political casualty. A few months later, Ćosić was ousted too.

In the run-up to elections on December 20, Television Belgrade, Milošević's most important weapon, unleashed a wave of propaganda against Panić and the opposition in general. Praise for the Serbian President, coupled with vicious attacks on Panić, bolstered Milošević and spread the notion that his rival was a CIA agent, conspiring to tighten UN sanctions and give away Kosovo. In a rare television interview, Milošević said that Panić's "helmsman" was in Washington. With considerable electoral manipulation and gross abuse of the media, the Serbian President took fifty-six percent of the vote. Panić, running on the slogan "Now or Never," took thirty-four percent.[1]

The distorted and isolated political landscape of Serbia provided fertile ground for the smear campaign, which encompassed not only Panić but the West as well. By December, there was almost no one left in Serbia who was not angry that the West had imposed sanctions and afraid of what it would do next. Instructed by Belgrade Television, Serbs believed that their kinsmen in Bosnia were fighting for the survival of their nation; it was not a land-grab. By contrast, "Muslim fundamentalists" and "Croat fascists" were waging a war of aggression. Scenes of Muslims being expelled from their homes were never shown. It was easy to build on collective memories of Serb suffering under the Ustaše in the Second World War.

Later, when bloodshed and destruction rendered the prospects of a multi-ethnic Bosnia much more remote, another of Belgrade's dark prophesies was fulfilled.

1 Of the 250-seat Parliament, Milošević's Socialists won 101 seats, and, together with their ultra-nationalist satellites, the Serbian Radicals who took 73, they had a comfortable majority. The main opposition coalition DEPOS, headed by Vuk Drašković, took 49 seats, the centrist Democratic Party took 7; the bulk of the remaining seats went to smaller parties, Hungarians and Muslims.

20

THE HOTTEST CORNER
The Fall of Srebrenica and the UN Safe Areas
April 1993

Murat Efendić climbs the three flights of stairs in a remote wing of the Bosnian Presidency building in the heart of Sarajevo and enters a cramped attic room. He teases a barely audible short-wave radio into life, and, jumping from wave-band to wave-band, he issues his call sign "Sara One, Sara One." Suddenly the familiar voice of Ibrahim Bećirević, the Srebrenica radio operator, answers his call. The two men have been speaking like this, twice a day, for more than six months, at 9 a.m., and 3 p.m., Ibrahim, from his bunker in Srebrenica, is passing coded messages about the precarious military plight of the town's defenses. It has been surrounded by Serb forces for almost a year. For months, the local Muslim defenders have been fighting a losing battle as the Bosnian Serb Army has moved in to close the noose ever tighter around the town. It is mid-March, and, through this single tenuous radio link, the military commanders in Srebrenica inform Sarajevo in code that they have run out of ammunition. They cannot hold out much longer. It is the start of a devastating series of events that will humiliate the UN Protection Force, destroy the Vance-Owen Peace Plan, fatally undermine the credibility of the UN Security Council, and threaten to split the NATO alliance.

Srebrenica,[1] a two-hour's drive from Sarajevo in better days, sits in Drina Valley, surrounded, like so many Bosnian towns, by high ground. It was built on the site of a silver mine[2] – the Romans called it Argentium. When war broke out, in April 1992, the town's Muslim leaders had tried to make an agreement with local Serbs, and, at first, had succeeded. Their negotiations had been disrupted by the arrival of Serb paramilitaries from Serbia itself – the very men who had "cleansed" Bijeljina and Zvornik now moved further up river. Naser Orić, a young policeman and former body-guard to Slobodan Milošević, raised a militia and staged an uprising at the end of April, driving the Serb forces out of Srebrenica after a three-week occupation. It was one of the few places where the Serbs suffered a defeat in the early weeks of the war. The battle cost hundreds of lives and left the Bosnian territorial defense forces in control of an island of territory in the heart of the "Republika Srpska." This, and two other enclaves, were proving a military and security nightmare for the Serbs.

On January 7, 1993 (the Orthodox Christmas), Orić's forces launched a surprise attack on Serb positions to the north, killing Serb civilians and burning their villages. The Serbs rounded on Srebrenica, sweeping through the neighboring Bosnian-held villages of Cerska and Konjević Polje in February and, in March, closing in on the town itself. Thousands of Muslim villagers, many already refugees, in the hinterland fled as their villages succumbed to the onslaught. They poured into Srebrenica town seeking refuge, but the town was so over-crowded, the most recent arrivals had to sleep in the open air.

At the same time, the Serbs imposed a ban on the already infrequent aid convoys entering the enclave.[3] By March, they were opening small windows in their front line, through which trails of people were fleeing to the government-held town of Tuzla in the north. They brought tales of intense suffering and hunger. The UNHCR called this "ethnic cleansing by starvation."

In February, a group of Srebrenica citizens arrived in Sarajevo. They had smuggled themselves out, through Serb lines, under cover of darkness, and, at great mortal risk, had trekked across the mountains on foot, and into the capital. They demanded a meeting with the Government. Their bitterness shocked Deputy Prime Minister Zlatko Lagumdžija. They told him that while the world's attention was focused on Sarajevo, the plight of the eastern enclaves, where conditions were much worse, was being ignored. They demanded that for every Muslim who died in eastern Bosnia, one Serb should be arrested in Sarajevo and executed. Lagumdžija was no nationalist. He was genuinely committed to a multi-ethnic society. He admonished them for their demand that innocent people should be punished for the crimes of others, but promised more resolute support for the nearly 200,000 Muslims under siege in the three eastern enclaves.

Lagumdžija, in an attempt to tie the fate of Sarajevo to that of the enclaves, announced that Sarajevo would receive no more donations of aid, until the eastern enclaves had received at least one delivery. The airlift was being suspended, and road convoys would be turned away. He was putting the whole city, in effect, on hunger strike to highlight the plight of eastern Bosnia.

In March, after hearing the news that the Srebrenica defenders had run out of ammunition, the Commander of the Bosnian army, Sefer Halilović, warned the UN Force Commander Phillipe Morillon that a Serb offensive was about to begin, and the Muslims in Srebrenica were in no position to defend their territory. At the same time, a British doctor working for the World Health Organization had trekked over the mountains into the enclave, and informed Morillon that thousands were living in the street with no cover, and that the weakest were beginning to die from hunger. Morillon now began a series of actions that first disturbed, and then infuriated, his bosses in New York: he resolved to go to Srebrenica himself.

On March 11, he took a convoy of three vehicles across forested mountain tracks, beyond the Serb front line at Bratunac, and later recorded in his memoir of the war:

> *We crept forward though the trees, and, after a couple of hours, I decided to get on to the armored car with the UN flag so that the Bosnians would not misunderstand who we were. When we reached a little hill defending the valley, three Bosnians appeared looking amazed that we were there. 'How did you get through?' one asked. 'I personally laid the mines down the path – we were expecting you from a different direction.'*
>
> *At that moment a large explosion signalled the truck had hit a mine and had turned over into the ditch.*

Morillon's party crept into Srebrenica in the dead of night. They found hundreds of people living in the street, and dozens still pouring into town. It was cold. There was no wood left in town. People were burning plastic bottles for a little warmth and the smell clung in the cold night air.

The next day, Morillon met Orić. He told him he would do everything possible to secure a ceasefire, and get humanitarian aid through. He then got into his vehicle to head out of town. Orić had other plans for him. Efendić, back in Sarajevo, had sent Orić a coded message: "Whatever happens, prevent Morillon from leaving Srebrenica until he provides security for the people there. Do it in a civilized way. Use women and children."

Morillon now found his path blocked by hundreds of women and children sitting in the middle of the road. He was now as trapped as they were. He tried to negotiate his passage out. Orić would not budge. Finally, Morillon, trying to win the confidence of the people, walked out on to the balcony and made the public promise that was to haunt him in the following weeks: "I will never abandon you." One member of his party, the Belgian aid worker Muriel Cornelis, then with MSF, recalled:

> *We were in the hospital, and we heard the crackle of the loudspeaker, and went to the window and there was Morillon: 'You are now under the protection of the United Nations.' We just burst out laughing – it was so absurd with him standing there and all the people watching. Branko the interpreter could not keep a straight face. Up went the UN flag. Eric, our doctor, said 'This is it. We are in big shit.'*

Anxious to create the impression that he was there of his own volition and not as a hostage, Morillon behaved as though nothing out of the ordinary had taken place. He made himself scarce. He went to sleep asking to be woken at two a.m. He then tried to sneak out. He left on foot, undetected, and waited at a pre-arranged place for his vehicles to arrive. But he had been spotted. The vehicles did not come. At 4 a.m., he walked back into town to see a crowd of refugees, hundreds-strong, gathering in the town center. The situation was becoming farcical. On March 13 he was finally allowed to leave, after promising to go to Belgrade to demand an end to the Serb assault.

Morillon succeeded in persuading the Serbs to let an aid convoy in. But the convoy leaders were not ready for the reception they were to receive. When the food and medical supplies had been off-loaded, there was pandemonium as hundreds of desperate women and children stormed aboard the trucks, piling one on top of the other in their efforts to leave the besieged town. Six people died from asphyxiation on the drive to Tuzla. The UN again found itself assisting with ethnic cleansing. The bombardment of the town did not let up.

At the beginning of April, the Serbs issued a surrender demand through the UNHCR. The Bosnian Army was given a forty-eight-hour ultimatum. The most senior UNHCR official in former Yugoslavia, José María Mendiluce, attended talks in the town of Bratunac, from where the assault on Srebrenica was commanded. "Either they surrender and you get all the Muslims out of Srebrenica," the Serb Commander, Ilić, told him, "or we take the town in two days." Mendiluce started making plans for the evacuation of an estimated 60,000 people. It was to be the biggest single act of ethnic cleansing since the conflict began, and it was to be carried out by the UN. Mendiluce made no effort to hide the moral repugnance with which he approached the task he was now expected to carry out. "We denounce ethnic cleansing worldwide," he said. "But when you have thousands of women and children at risk who want desperately to be evacuated, it is my responsibility to help them, to save their lives. I cannot enter any philosophical or theoretical debate now. We just have to save their lives." Mendiluce planned to send twenty trucks a day, most of them empty, to evacuate between 1,000 and 1,500 people on each trip.

Two days later, Morillon, becoming, in the view of his advisers, dangerously obsessed with the fate of Srebrenica, and his own promise never to abandon it, set off again. He had been horrified by reports of further shelling. He announced that he was going to Srebrenica with a convoy of five vehicles, with or without the permission of the Serbs. UN peacekeeping convention is to act only with the consent of all parties to a conflict. Morillon was breaching it. The gesture was to turn out to be the most flamboyant gesture to date by the UN force in the face of Serb intransigence.

Morillon got twenty-five miles from his base in Sarajevo, to the town of Sokolac, where the local commanders detained him for seven hours. They turned back three of his vehicles. Morillon soldiered on with two. Further up the road, at Zvornik, his progress was halted again – this time by hundreds of women and children blocking his path. They clambered aboard his two white UN vehicles and ripped off the aerials and jerry cans. They sprayed them multicolored with paint. His humiliation was complete. He limped back to Tuzla by nightfall, a blue-helmeted Don Quixote. Aid workers there said he was grief stricken. Like many of them, he had been to Srebrenica, knew the condition of the people, and felt immense personal responsibility. His closest colleagues began to worry about his state of mind.

UN officials in New York and Belgrade began to worry, too. Morillon had saddled them with a responsibility they did not want and did not know how to respond to. It was clear Srebrenica was going to be defeated. UNPRO-FOR, through Morillon's well-intentioned gesture, was revealed as a paper tiger. The UN now found itself in open disagreement – even conflict – with important sectors of international public opinion, most notably the American State Department.

UNPROFOR could do nothing to stop the Serb offensive; so its officers began a public relations campaign to take the heat out of international public outrage. As the Serb advance continued, General Mladić was invited to Belgrade for "ceasefire talks" with General Morillon and UNPROFOR's most senior civilian official, Cedric Thornberry, a distinguished and highly regarded Irish lawyer who had made his reputation as a civil rights lawyer in Belfast in the 1960s and 1970s.

The UN Security Council, responding to international outrage about Srebrenica, had mandated UNPROFOR to deploy a company of Canadian troops – about 120 men – to go to Srebrenica to secure regular deliveries of aid. General Mladić would not let them through. To Thornberry's acute embarrassment, Mladić, the Bosnian Serb commander, never hid his intentions. The Canadians would only be allowed to go to Srebrenica when his Army's military task was accomplished. The US State Department was pushing for a lifting of the UN arms embargo. Thornberry was under pressure to produce signs of "progress." His public information officer, Shannon Boyd, told reporters in Belgrade that General Mladić had expressed his "support for and cooperation with" attempts to deploy a Canadian company at Srebrenica. Minutes later Mladić talked to the same reporters. The Canadians, he said, would go to Srebrenica "over my dead body and those of my family."

On April 12, news reached Sarajevo of a short, intense artillery attack that killed fifty-six in less than an hour. Some of them were schoolchildren playing on a football pitch. Louis Gentile was the only UNHCR official in the town. He telexed his head office in Belgrade that day:

> *Fourteen dead bodies were found in the school yard. Body parts and human flesh clung to the schoolyard fence. The ground was literally soaked with blood. One child, about six years of age, had been decapitated. I saw two ox-carts cov-*

*ered with bodies. I did not look forward to closing my eyes at night for fear that
I would relive the images. I will never be able to convey the horror.*

There were sixteen international personnel in the town who had gone in
with Morillon on his first jaunt a month earlier. The original intention had
been to rotate personnel on a two-week shift basis, because of the stress of
working under constant bombardment. But General Mladić had issued an
instruction that no new international personnel were to be allowed in. Those
already there volunteered to stay, because they knew that if they left they
would not be replaced. They used their vehicles as ambulances during the
forty-minute firestorm. Gentile's telex described their behavior under
extreme danger as "inspirational."

Larry Hollingworth, the British UNHCR field officer, whose long white
hair and flowing beard had made him famous in Bosnia as the enthusiastic
pioneer of the most hazardous and difficult convoy routes, was also known for
his patient, indefatigable good humor in the face of unrelenting obstruction.
He, too, departed from the language of symmetry and blamelessness normally used by UN officials, whose usual practice is never to blame any side until
you can blame all sides equally. In a careful measured tone of voice, he chose
words that he knew would be broadcast around the world that day and printed across the front pages of every newspaper the next:

> *My first thought was for the commander who gave the order to attack. I hope
> he burns in the hottest corner of hell. My second thought was for the soldiers
> who loaded the breaches and fired the guns. I hope their sleep is forever punc-
> tuated by the screams of the children and the cries of their mothers. My third
> thought was for Dr. of Medicine, Karadžić, the Professor of literature,
> Koljević, the Biologist, Mrs. Plavšić, and the geologist, Professor Lukić. And
> I wonder, will they condemn this atrocity? Or will they betray their education
> and condone it? And I thought of the many Serbs that I know around this
> country, and I wondered: do they want the history of the Serb nation to
> include this chapter, a chapter in which their army drove innocent people
> from village to village to village until finally they are cornered in Srebrenica,
> a place from which there is no escape, and where their fate is to be transport-
> ed out like cattle, or slaughtered like sheep?*

This was the last thing UNPROFOR wanted to hear. It was grist to the
mill of those in the Clinton administration who were urging the new
President to press for military intervention in Bosnia, to which UNPROFOR
was implacably opposed.

On April 14, Srebrenica's local authorities summoned Gentile, and asked
him to smuggle out a message to UNPROFOR's headquarters in Belgrade.

The Commander told me that they had decided to surrender. He said it was not simply the shelling in the center of the town but that their defensive lines had collapsed. They looked desperate and finished.

The surrender request was too sensitive to make on the radio. It would have been intercepted by the Serbs and been a green light for a final devastating push. Gentile took the message to Belgrade.

That night, Serb forces pushed through the Bosnian lines to the south and east of the town. They stormed the village of Zeleni Jadar on the southern edge of town. The Bosnian defensive positions, such as they were, collapsed. The push brought the Serb ring-of-steel to the very edge of the town. From their hill-top positions, almost every street was visible. Ibrahim Bećirević radioed to Sarajevo – again in coded messages – that the town was hours, rather than days, from collapse. The radio room in the Sarajevo Presidency fell momentarily silent. Bećirević was the thirty-year-old father of two young children. His voice was that of a trapped animal, waiting for its predator to approach. "What has happened to the sixteen Canadian soldiers?" Efendić asked Bećirević. "I don't know. We are all under cover," the metallic crackly voice answered back. And then, as an afterthought, he said of the Canadian soldiers: "Whatever happens here, please make sure they are all right." It was a moment of extraordinary unsolicited generosity from a man who felt his own chances of survival diminishing by the hour.

UNPROFOR had been talking up the prospects of a ceasefire for days, despite all the evidence that General Mladić had not the slightest intention of halting his advance until Srebrenica was neutralized as a military threat. The surrender request was a bolt from the blue, and threw UNPROFOR's officials in both Belgrade and Sarajevo into a tail-spin. No one knew what to do.

UNPROFOR's dilemma was acute. For two reasons, the political implications of a surrender were immense. First, for the credibility of the peace process, which UNPROFOR supported: the Bosnians and the Croats had agreed to the Vance-Owen Plan which was "the only show in town" and the Serbs were rejecting it; the Vance-Owen Plan put Srebrenica and the territory around it in a Bosnian Government, or Muslim, canton. How could the UN on the ground now justify administering a surrender that in effect handed the territory over to Serb control, even if the town itself remained populated by Muslims? And, secondly: with the Americans pushing for a debate at the UN about the arms embargo, how could UNPROFOR, while the world was debating whether to arm the Bosnians, justify actively disarming them on the ground? UNPROFOR's concern was that it would inevitably fuel demands for military intervention. Officials immediately began working on a way out of the mess.

271

For now, though, they were agreed on one thing, the news must not reach the ears of the press. A British aid worker who had visited Srebrenica a month earlier and was now billeted at the UN head-quarters in Sarajevo was having dinner with a group of journalists that evening. He telephoned his base to inform them that rather than break the curfew, he would check into the press hotel, the Holiday Inn, for the night. When he returned to the dinner table, he said casually "They're all in a blind panic up there. Srebrenica has surrendered. No one knows what to do." After a moment of stunned silence, the reporters scrambled for their satellite telephones. The news was out.

There was also panic in UN headquarters in New York. UNPROFOR's spin-doctors took a day to find a formula. This latest unfortunate turn of events would be presented to the world not as a surrender but as a "disarmament agreement."

On April 16, General Mladić, having got what he wanted, finally agreed to let the Canadian company go to Srebrenica. It set off the next day and experienced no difficulty *en route* because it was going, in essence, to do Mladić's bidding. Its task was not to secure the safe passage of aid convoys, but to begin to receive the surrender of Bosnian guns, and, in the words of UNPROFOR's spokesman in Sarajevo, Barry Frewer, "to assist with evacuation, and to secure the airstrip so that medical evacuations can begin."

On the same day Cedric Thornberry and General Morillon convened talks at Sarajevo airport. General Mladić and his Bosnian counterpart Sefer Halilović met face to face. Both men referred openly to what had taken place as a surrender, as did the official radio stations of both sides. Only the UN persisted with the fiction that these talks represented some kind of "breakthrough" towards "disarmament." Mladić was an hour and a half late. When he arrived he told Morillon there was nothing to discuss except the terms of surrender of the Bosnian Army, which he was now prepared to dictate. Because the Bosnian Serb Army was a very humane fighting outfit, he said, civilians – that is to say women, children and the elderly – would all be allowed to leave Srebrenica and go to "Muslim territory." He would also agree to a helicopter evacuation of the 500-or-so wounded. Men of fighting age, on the other hand, were combatants, and would have to be considered prisoners of war. They would be the subject of separate negotiations. These were his terms, he said, there was little else to discuss.

Morillon advised Halilović to accept Mladić's terms, since the situation was "hopeless" and there was an urgent need to begin the evacuations. But the previous night, the United Nations Security Council had declared Srebrenica a "United Nations safe area" (see page 274), and, although no one in Sarajevo knew what that meant, it certainly made it impossible for its UNPROFOR to broker an agreement that meant emptying the place of its

Muslim population. The meeting lasted from mid-day until two o'clock the next morning. Finally, a ten-paragraph agreement was signed, paragraph one of which provided for the freezing of existing front lines: Serb forces were not required to pull back from their achieved lines. A ceasefire was agreed, in effect from 5 a.m., that day. The agreement disarmed the Bosnian Government forces, and provided for the deployment of 140 Canadian troops to collect the weapons. This had to be achieved within seventy-two hours of their arrival, and would be overseen by Bosnian Serb liaison officers. The Serbs had agreed to allow the helicopter evacuation of 500 wounded. But these would be selected by UNPROFOR in the presence of two doctors from each side, to prevent what General Mladić called "war criminals" – in other words, men of military age – using the med-evac as an escape route. All helicopters would be required to stop for inspection at the Serb-held town of Zvornik, regardless of the condition of the evacuees.

Thornberry and Morillon had been critical of the previous day's news coverage from the Sarajevo press corps. They had objected, in particular, to the prominent use of the term "surrender." The public information officer, Barry Frewer, an intelligent and likeable Commander from the Canadian Army, had been admonished by them for failing to get across the words "disarmament" and "ceasefire." Frewer, in turn, had, uncharacteristically, shown his irritation with the persistence of the journalists in reporting a surrender. Thornberry and Morillon now indulged in a skilful piece of news management of their own.

The airport talks broke up at 2 a.m – 8 p.m., in New York. The Sarajevo journalists – confined, by the curfew, to their hotel – were not informed of the outcome until after 5 a.m. – just too late for the *New York Times* and the *Washington Post* to squeeze the story into their last editions. The United Nations press corps, on the other hand, were furnished with full-and-detailed briefings as the evening progressed, complete with quotes from General Morillon, radioed, by him, from his armored vehicle at the airport, to the UN headquarters in Sarajevo, and relayed, from there, to the UN in New York. By the time the Sarajevo correspondents had called their newsdesks to report the agreement, the New York correspondents had already written their dispatches about this remarkable UNPROFOR-brokered breakthrough in Bosnia. The unfortunate word "surrender" did not feature prominently, not, in fact, at all.

But despite the best efforts of UNPROFOR, international public opinion was outraged, and the outrage intensified as the evacuations progressed over the next few days. Aid workers described how the evacuation helicopters were mobbed by desperate people clamoring to get on board. One UNHCR official described a vast wall of amputees, hobbling down the hillside to the sports field where the helicopters landed, and told of how he had had to make an arbitrary selection from the other side of a coil of barbed wire: some to go, others to stay. One man, he said, who had lost an eye, offered to pluck out the other eye if it meant he could get aboard the evacuation flight. These scenes continued to be broadcast around the world, and continued to dominate the international news agenda. The Americans kept up their pressure.

On April 16, the day after the surrender of Srebrenica, the UN Security Council met in an atmosphere of intense international outrage. It passed Resolution 819, which declared Srebrenica a United Nations "safe area." (After the collapse of the Vance-Owen Plan the status was later extended to five other areas.) What the term meant was left vague. The term "safe haven" was studiously avoided in the hurried framing of the Resolution, since this had a precise definition in international law and implied immunity from attack for all who sought refuge there. United Nations officials saw immediately that Resolution 819 contained hidden dangers for an organization that still, resolutely, wanted to take no side in the war. Shashi Tharoor, a senior UN official, noted that:

> The difficulty with the safe areas concept at that point in the Bosnian situation was that it looked as if the declaration of safe areas would essentially benefit only one side in the conflict, and would require means – and this is a very important point – that peacekeepers do not have. The safe area resolution therefore, to us, carried the risk that it would be unimplementable.

First Srebrenica and, later, Sarajevo, Tuzla, Bihać, Žepa and Goražde, were declared "safe." But there was never any intention, in practical terms, to render them safe, since this would have involved the United Nations abandoning its position of neutrality. The term "safe area" (like "protection force") quickly became a cruel misnomer. The safe areas were among the most profoundly unsafe places in the world.

The creation of the "safe areas" represented an important point of departure for UN involvement which, until then, had been limited solely to the provision of humanitarian aid and the provision of "good offices" for a negotiated settlement. For the first time the international community had committed itself – morally, if not in any effective practical sense – to the protection of one side in the war against the other. The safe areas declaration mixed elements of peacekeeping with elements of peace-enforcement that produced the worst of both worlds: it failed to provide the protection it appeared to offer; and at the same time it aligned the UN, symbolically, with one side in the conflict. It was also the biggest single step to date down a path which Western statesmen had vowed at the beginning of the conflict, that they would not take – the path by which they would be drawn into the conflict in a series of unplanned, unthought-out, incremental steps.

In seeking a short-term "solution" to defuse a long-term crisis, the United Nations saddled itself with a responsibility it was not prepared to honor. Boutros Boutros-Ghali called for the deployment of 34,000 additional troops to police the "safe areas," but member nations only contributed 7000. The night after the Srebrenica "disarmament" agreement was signed at Sarajevo airport, General Morillon and his commanding officer, Lars-Eric Wahlgren, gave a news conference at UN headquarters in the Bosnian capital. Asked what now stood between the people of Srebrenica and the guns of their tormentors, General Wahlgren replied that Srebrenica was now "protected by the blue flag of the United Nations." General Morillon added that any further attack by the Serbs on the people of Srebrenica would constitute "a declaration of war against the entire world."

The "disarmament" plan was never implemented. Naser Orić remained in control of an organized defense force in Srebrenica and, though armed only with small arms and lacking anything comparable with the Serb heavy armor, proved a constant thorn in the side of the besieging forces. In July 1995, the Serbs completed the task they had begun in 1993.

1 Population 37,000, of whom seventy-five percent were Muslim and twenty-five percent Serb.

2 *Srebren* is the Serbo-Croat word for silver.

3 The first aid convoy since the war began had only entered in November 1992.

21

LAST-CHANCE CAFÉ
The Rise and Fall of the Vance-Owen Plan
January–May 1993

When Lord Owen returned to Belgrade on April 23 he knew that the Srebrenica crisis had given him a new weapon in his campaign to persuade the Serbs to accept the Vance-Owen Plan. In the aftermath of the rout of Srebrenica, the Security Council had passed a resolution which tightened already existing sanctions even further against rump Yugoslavia. Belgrade's assets abroad were to be frozen and transhipments through Serbia and Montenegro banned – the most comprehensive set of mandatory sanctions yet imposed in UN history.

The plan to divide – or, as Lord Owen insisted, to reconstitute – Bosnia in ten provinces was first proposed in Geneva in January 1993. Vance and Owen had worked on the plan for four months before presenting it to the three sides. It recognized Bosnia within its existing frontiers but granted substantially devolved powers to each of the ten provinces which were defined, primarily, on ethnic grounds: three of the provinces would have a Serb majority, two a Croat majority, three a Muslim, and one mixed Croat Muslim. The tenth province – Sarajevo – would retain power-sharing between all three ethnic groups. The republic would retain a central government, but its powers would be minimal.

The Serbs rejected the Plan because of the distribution of territory. It envisaged the handing back of huge swathes of land that they had taken by force in the early months of the war, which had had Muslim majorities but which had been "cleansed." Most of the Drina valley and large parts of northwestern Bosnia were to be returned to Muslim sovereignty under the Plan. It denied the Serbs the single, unbroken land mass they had fought the war to create. They argued that under the Plan the Serbs would be forced to live in isolated pockets of territory with no secure landlink either between each pocket, or to Serbia proper. Vance and Owen argued that that was the best way to ensure that Serbs continue to live as part of a multi-ethnic state, since interdependence, under the Plan, would be unavoidable.

The Bosnian government initially also rejected the Plan on the grounds that the powers allotted to the central government appeared so weak that the ethnic provinces would, in effect, be self-governing. They saw in it the ethnic partition of their country. They said the Plan sanctioned ethnic cleansing – an accusation Lord Owen bitterly rebuked. By March, though, Izetbegović, under intense diplomatic and military pressure, changed his position and

276

accepted the Plan – partly to court international approval, and partly, by his own admission, because he felt confident that the Serbs would never accept it and that therefore it would never be implemented.

The Croats loved the Plan. Mate Boban, the Bosnian Croat leader, could scarcely conceal his glee when he saw the map. It gave the Croats exactly what they wanted: their provinces formed large blocks of territory, joined to Croatia proper and stretching into the very heart of central Bosnia. They signed up to the Plan immediately. Their enthusiasm for the Geneva peace conference gave rise to the joke that the initials of the Bosnian Croat defense force, HVO, now stood for "*Hvala* Vance Owen" – 'Thank you, Vance Owen!'

By April, only the Serbs needed convincing. Owen met Milošević, Bulatović and Ćosić in a state villa on Botićeva street, in a leafy district of Belgrade just steps away from Tito's grave. According to Bulatović, "the meeting went like this – Lord Owen presented the Plan, he knew what we wanted, what our interests were, and he was showing us that the Plan did not clash with our interests. After a few hours, Mr. Milošević said: 'Okay, I'll go along with the Plan. You have convinced us. We'll invite the Bosnian Serbs to listen to your explanation.'"

What brought about this remarkable change of heart?

Lord Owen insisted that Milošević had been moved by the international coalition that was lining up against him. He knew how damaging the new package of sanctions would be to an economy already ruined by the cost of waging war, which had, for the most part, been paid for by inflationary funding. "This was a clear economic decision," Owen said later. "He did not want financial sanctions. We should have imposed financial sanctions months, even years earlier."

Milošević had, until now, trusted the Russians to veto a financial sanctions' resolution. Russia had asked the Americans not to force the issue at the Security Council until after the referendum on Russia's new constitution, due to take place on April 27, since a perceived anti-Serb measure would fuel support for Yeltsin's nationalist opponents. Eager to shore up Yeltsin's power-base, the US State Department had promised not to pursue it, provided that Srebrenica did not fall, or look dangerously close to falling. On April 16, Owen had telephoned Milošević and told him: "Look, you simply have got to stop Srebrenica being taken." Milošević told Owen that he knew the Muslim Commander there (Orić had been Milošević's bodyguard before the war) and that he knew that the local Serbs were embittered by the battles they had lost to Orić's forces the previous year, in which hundreds of Serb lives had been lost. Milošević told Owen that if the Serbs entered Srebrenica there would be havoc. "I have no doubt that he intervened with Mladić to stop them taking Srebrenica," Owen said.

There is also no doubt that the financial sanctions' resolution had a powerful impact. The Federal President, Dobrica Ćosić, later complained that they placed rump Yugoslavia "in a kind of concentration camp whose borders are guarded by the NATO airforce and fleet and the international police."[1]

There was a second reason for Milošević's decision to back the Vance-Owen Plan. At their meeting on April 24, Milošević asked Owen for "clarification" on three key areas of the Plan. The first of these was on the status of the northern corridor, linking Bosnian Serb territories in the northwest of the republic with Serbia itself. Owen confirmed that part of this corridor would, according to the Plan, run through the province of Posavina, which would have a Croatian majority. Milošević asked what kind of protection would be provided to police this corridor. Owen reassured him that a serious UN force would be deployed. (Owen later secured from the Russians a promise to deploy Russian troops along the northern corridor. This satisfied Milošević on this key point of concern.)

The second "clarification" he demanded was constitutional. The interim constitution provided for in the Vance-Owen Plan included a collective Head of State, a multi-member Presidency, with representation for all three nations. Milošević asked whether decisions would be taken by majority vote, or by "consensus." A system of majority vote would always allow a coalition of Muslims and Croats to out-vote the Serbs. "Consensus," on the other hand, would give each nation, in effect, a veto. The Serbs would, therefore, have the power to render the body unworkable. Owen reassured Milošević that decisions of the Bosnian Presidency would be reached "by consensus." Since Cyrus Vance was not present, Milošević demanded to know whether this was the view of both co-chairmen of the peace conference. Herb Okun, Vance's right-hand man, who was with Owen, telephoned Vance who confirmed that he and Owen were at one on the issue: Presidency decisions would have to be arrived at by consensus. "It was just ensuring that they [the Serbs] couldn't have anything thrust down their throats during the interim constitution that hadn't got their agreement," Owen explained later. "So they effectively had a veto – a pretty difficult form of government, incidentally, I have to say. But that was the structure that was on offer."

The third area of concern was territory which had been conquered by the Serbs, cleansed of their Muslim and Croat populations, but which would have to be surrendered to Croat or Bosnian Government (Muslim) sovereignty under the Plan: this amounted to more than a third of the territory the Serbs controlled.[2] According to Milošević, Owen gave an assurance that Croat and Bosnian Government forces would not be allowed to police those territories; "only UN forces which will guarantee personal safety, the safety of property and the security of the citizens can be deployed in those areas," he said.[3]

Milošević was thus convinced that the Vance-Owen Plan provided him with a way of achieving his central war aim – the creation of a viable Serbian state on Bosnian territory. It even appeared to hold out the prospect that that state would, in practice if not on paper, consist of a single unbroken territorial entity – even though, in theory, the Vance-Owen map gave the Serbs three distinct chunks of territory linked only by UN-protected through-routes. Milošević's calculation was that the Serbs could sign the Plan, and then obstruct its implementation, much as they had done in Croatia the year before. In fact, he realized that the Plan would never even reach that stage.

Owen remained at the villa and waited for the call. He hoped that Milošević would be able to tell him that the Bosnian Serbs had been persuaded. That, in turn, would enable Owen to signal to New York not to go ahead with implementing the financial sanctions' resolution.

Milošević called in Karadžić, Koljević and Krajišnik. He told them that Owen had given crucial "clarifications" which meant, bluntly, that the Serbs could sign the Plan without having to implement it. The Bosnian Serbs were shocked and disappointed that Milošević was trying to pressurize them into signing the Plan. "His main argument," Karadžić admitted later, "was that the Plan would be impossible to implement. But this was too risky for us, and I could not accept it because I knew that the international community needed only 10,000 troops in Zvornik and the Posavina corridor to neutralize the Serbs." Koljević, too, distrusted Milošević's judgement that, once the Plan was signed, there would be no pressure from the international community to see that it was put into practice in its entirety:

> *Milošević counted on the fact that the Vance-Owen Plan couldn't be implemented in the way it was devised and that the Serbs got enough of a political chance, so to speak, for further autonomy, for the further development of that process. He rather looked at the Vance-Owen Plan as the first positive step, rather than the final form of it. And, of course, he wanted to get rid of these sanctions as soon as possible.[4]*

Owen was candid about the implications of the "clarifications" he had given Milošević: "I think Milošević had just come to the conclusion that effectively the Serb interests have been protected in Bosnia-Herzegovina. There would be a Republika Srpska. It would be within Bosnia, but the Serb way of life would be protected." This, of course, was not at all the Plan the Bosnian government thought it had signed. It was in the nature of the Vance-Owen Plan, however, that it leant itself to radically different – even contradictory – interpretations. It left – deliberately – many matters unresolved, to be addressed by the three sides once peace had been secured and UN troops deployed.

For most of that day, Milošević tried to cajole Karadžić and Koljević into accepting the Plan. The Bosnian Serbs resisted. By six o'clock in the evening, they appeared to be wavering, and, as the meeting ended, they insisted that the matter would have to be resolved by the Bosnian Serb Assembly, which was meeting that evening in Bijeljina, in northeastern Bosnia, about two hours drive from Belgrade.

Milošević, Ćosić and Bulatović met in the same state villa in Botićeva street, in Belgrade, and drafted a long closely-argued letter nearly 2,000 words long, to try to persuade the Bosnian Serb assembly to accept the Vance-Owen Plan. The centerpiece of its argument was that the Vance-Owen Plan was consistent with the Serbs' main war aim – which was a state of their own. By implication, those parts of the Plan which appeared to divide Serb territory would, in effect, never have to be implemented. It was written in a hurry and Ćosić later regretted its high-handed tone. It read:

> *Now is not the right time for us to compete in patriotism. It is the right time for a courageous, considered and far-reaching decision. You have no right to expose to danger and international sanctions 10,000,000 citizens of Yugoslavia merely because of the remaining open issues which are of far less importance than the results achieved so far. We simply wish to tell you that you must be measured in your demands.*
>
> *During our talks [with Lord Owen] we received very important explanations and definitions:*
>
> *– Guarantees were given that... units of the Croats Defense Council (HVO) or Muslim forces cannot enter the areas, outside the Serbian provinces, in which Serbs live. Only UN forces which will guarantee personal safety, the safety of property and the security of the citizens can be deployed in those areas... It is certain that... the danger of the Serbian people being separated and divided has been eliminated;*
>
> *In other words, we do not expect that the procedure envisaged by the [Vance-Owen] Plan would be used to pass decisions highly detrimental to Serbian interests not merely because this would be illogical and unfair but also because under the procedure envisaged by the Plan, all decisions would be passed by consensus of the Serbian side, and because without the agreement of the Serbian side Bosnia-Herzegovina would not be able to function at all... We feel entitled to the same right as you to pass decisions of significance for the Serbian nation and insist that you heed our categorical stand and accept the Plan.*
>
> *This is an issue of either war or peace and we are opting for peace... an honorable peace with guarantees of your equality and freedom. The other option is an unnecessary war which, now that the Serbian nation in Bosnia-Herzegovina has gained its equality and freedom and has the chance of retaining most of its territories, will bring nothing else but adversity, suffering and violence to you and others.*

Milošević woke his Foreign Minister Jovanović and told him to go to Bijeljina and read the letter to the Bosnian Serb Assembly.

Jovanović got a hostile reception. The Bosnian Serbs resented the implication that they were being strong-armed into accepting the Plan that they had been telling their people for months meant death for the Serbian nation in Bosnia. Biljana Plavšić took the lead. "Who is this Jovanović?" she thundered. "Who is this Milošević, this Bulatović, this Ćosić? Did this nation elect them? No it didn't. President Karadžić, you have been elected President by this parliament. You can't decide. According to our constitution, the parliament decides these issues."

The assembly rejected the plea in the early hours of the morning. Karadžić told Serbian radio: "The deputies said that they would not be able to return to their constituencies if they accepted the Vance-Owen Plan in its present shape. We hope that the entire Serb nation will mobilize all of its forces to survive."

For the first time, Lord Owen realized that Milošević had lost control of the war in Bosnia. The Vance-Owen Plan, together with the financial sanctions' package, had succeeded in splitting the Serbs.

The international temperature rose. A few days earlier, Owen had suggested to the Greek Prime Minister, Konstantin Mitsotakis, that Athens should host a summit to try to persuade the Serbs to sign the Plan. Mitsotakis now called Milošević and invited him to attend. The conference was scheduled for the weekend of May 1-2. Lord Owen and Cyrus Vance clung to the hope that the Bijeljina "parliament" had rejected the Plan outright because it had been sprung on them too quickly. The Bosnian Serbs had been fed a constant diet of propaganda that was hostile to the Plan, and had even demanded Owen's resignation. Owen took the view that if public opinion had been prepared in advance – even a few days in advance – then it would have been far easier to persuade the Bosnian Serb parliament to make the jump that Milošević had made. Owen and Vance persuaded Izetbegović and Tudjman that there was good reason to hope that the Bosnian Serbs were flexible; and all agreed to attend the Athens summit.

When the Bosnian Serb leadership arrived in Athens they expected just another round of talks. It soon dawned on them that they had been – as Nikola Koljević put it – led into a trap. Everybody there had signed the Vance-Owen Plan, except them. The real purpose of the summit became clear: they were to be pressured into signing up to the Plan against the explicit instructions of their parliament.

The Bosnian Serbs had walked into a pressure cooker. They were summoned to Dobrica Ćosić's suite in the conference hotel. There, they confronted Ćosić, Milošević and Bulatović. Owen and Vance mostly kept to their distance, but Mitsotakis came and went during the course of the evening.

From six in the evening Milošević harangued the Bosnian Serbs. He said he had received secret intelligence reports that Serb positions in both Bosnia and Serbia would be bombed by NATO unless Karadžić signed, and that this could happen within hours of the break-up of the summit. He returned to his argument that the Plan would never have to be implemented. He pointed out that the hostilities that had recently broken out between the Croats and Muslims in central Bosnia made the Vance-Owen Plan even more unworkable. According to Karadžić the pressure was so great that even the waiters who were bringing in pot after pot of coffee into the suite were trying to persuade the Bosnian Serbs to sign.

Karadžić argued that a signature on the Vance-Owen Plan would recognize the legitimacy of the Bosnian state. The Serbs had never recognized any such entity. They had declared the independence of their own republic twelve hours before the Bosnian state came into existence as an independent country. Momčilo Krajišnik was even more hard-line than Karadžić and Koljević. He was reduced to tears by the unrelenting pressure from Milošević and Ćosić, whom he had always held in great and affectionate regard. At one point in the evening, Krajišnik and Ćosić confronted each other on the balcony. Krajišnik told Ćosić: "Mr. President you know best that I respect you very much, but I have to be honest with you. I would rather jump from this fifth-floor balcony on to that stone ground than accept this Plan."

The meeting dragged on until four in the morning. Ćosić, who was in his seventies and had had two heart bypass operations, began to flag. They agreed to resume early in the morning. The plenary session – with Izetbegović, Tudjman and Mate Boban – was due to begin at 10 a.m.

They snatched a few hours sleep. The next morning, according to Okun: "Vance suddenly tells them straight out that this is the last-chance café, that the US Air Force is all prepared to turn Bosnia and Serbia into a wasteland." The three Bosnian Serbs retreated to a corner of the suite. There, they realized that they were not going to be allowed to leave Athens until they had agreed to sign. They decided that, if necessary, Karadžić should sign the Plan, on condition that Mitsotakis, Owen and Vance agreed that the signature would only be valid if it was subsequently ratified by the Bosnian Serb "parliament."

The clock was ticking. The plenary had already been delayed. Tudjman and Izetbegović announced that unless the Serb delegation appear by one o'clock, they would leave Athens and return to their respective capitals.

Finally, Bulatović and Milošević went over to the Bosnian Serb huddle and told them that their time was up. Karadžić then said he would sign. Bulatović described what happened next:

And at that moment Mitsotakis appears on the scene from nowhere, takes out his pen, and invites a photographer from another room who was standing there ready to take a photograph of Karadžić signing the document. Immediately after that we called Owen who couldn't believe what had happened.

Milošević, it turned out, was so afraid that Karadžić would change his mind on the way into the plenary session that he had had a copy of the Plan, and a photographer standing by. Owen entered the room to find "a very very shaken Karadžić" who had clearly taken "a brow beating." The plenary session was hurriedly called and Karadžić signed again, this time in the presence of his enemies.

An excited Mitsotakis broke the news to the assembled journalists shortly before one o'clock. Owen declared that it was "a bright, sunny day in the Balkans." (He was right only in the literal sense.) Karadžić's plan to build a state within a state was, he said, "dead and buried." Karadžić left Athens rumpled and exhausted, but defiant, saying his state was not dead and buried, merely postponed. Owen, in television and radio interviews that afternoon, was triumphant. When it was pointed out to him that Karadžić's signature would have to be ratified by the Bosnian Serb "parliament" he was contemptuous in his dismissal. "You might choose to dignify that body with the term 'parliament'" he said, "but I do not... I'm telling you," he went on, "and believe me I have been in politics a long time, I know that Milošević is on board and that is what counts."

Cyrus Vance bowed out that day. He had already announced his decision to retire from his post as UN peace envoy, and his successor, Thorvald Stoltenberg, a former Norwegian Foreign Minister, had already been appointed. Owen was delighted that his old friend was going out on a high. "There is no doubt we were buoyed up... "

> *I described it, rather unfortunately, as a happy day. And it was a happy day. I mean, we had spilled our guts out for this settlement. And I just felt tremendously pleased. And I looked back to wave goodbye, and there was Cy Vance sitting by the swimming pool, looking years younger, and I just thought to myself, what a wonderful way to go out. And somehow we let it slip away from us in the next few weeks.*

The next stop was the Bosnian Serb mountain stronghold of Pale. A long motorcade of sleek, black, Mercedes limousines sped from Belgrade. The mood was upbeat. President Milošević and his closest international ally, Mitsotakis of Greece, were confident that their very presence would sway the "Parliament" vote. Or, if not, that they would easily convince the Bosnian Serbs to vote "yes" and abandon their decision to hold a referendum on the Plan. President Momir Bulatović of Montenegro was part of the huge pilgrimage to Pale:

On our way to Pale we passed through most of Serbia. Many people stood on the roadside, waving to us. There had not been such scenes since Tito's time. I saw that people wanted this agreement to be signed.

The cars drove even faster after they crossed the River Drina into eastern Bosnia. It was the first time any of these politicians had seen the ravages of war. "Everything was empty and devastated," said Bulatović. "In the territory under Serb control, you knew that if a village had been destroyed then it must have been Muslim."

As the gleaming fleet snaked up Mount Jahorina, above the former ski resort of Pale, Radovan Karadžić stood on the terrace of the Heavenly Valley Hotel, flanked by the rest of the Bosnian Serb leadership. Milošević and Mitsotakis headed for the receiving line. The Serbian President extended his hand to Biljana Plavšić, who left it hanging.

There was a comic formality about this: the very first visit by a Foreign Premier to this rogue state. Even if Milošević had come to convince them to endorse the Vance-Owen Plan they so passionately hated, the Bosnian Serb leaders were keen to parley the visit into an affirmation of their mini-state. The guests, who included Yugoslav President Ćosić and a slew of Serbian officials, reviewed the guard of honor, which chanted a Serbian song of resistance against the Turks set to an American square-dancing tune. Swooping low over the mountain, a US F-16 fighter-jet seemed to herald what lay in store for the Bosnian Serbs if they opposed the West. Just a few miles away across the mountain from Pale, Serb artillery had been bombarding Sarajevo for the past year.

As soon as the debate began, any optimism the visiting dignitaries might have felt about their mission disappeared. The Pale leadership had encouraged a mood of defiance, which went hand-in-glove with genuine Serb fear about the Plan. Without question Vance-Owen would be voted down in a referendum. On the eve of the Pale session, Risto Djogo, the best-known Bosnian Serb journalist, read the TV news. He looked at a blank piece of paper, signed it, pulled out a pistol and shot himself. Wiping the stage-blood off his forehead, Djogo said the Serbian people would not commit suicide. The message was clear.[5]

Even though Karadžić – under extreme pressure – had initialled the Plan in Athens, his recommendation was half-hearted at best. He called the proposal catastrophic, but stressed the possible consequences of its rejection. The deputies dismissed threats from the West – insisting that the Plan itself was more dangerous. The assembly was a motley collection of deputies from the old Bosnian Parliament, priests in long black robes, officers in battledress and a smattering of war-profiteers in shiny cheap suits.

In the first of his speeches, a confident Milošević told the assembly that a "decision in favor of peace is in the interest of the Bosnian Serbs and of the entire Serbian nation." He proclaimed that the Plan granted the Serbs equality and liberty. His speech recalled the tones of the old days, of the Communist chiefs whose authority was unchallenged and unimpeachable. As the night wore on, Milošević took off the kid gloves. He grew angry and hinted that he could isolate the Bosnian Serbs.

His threats had little effect. The deputies boasted that NATO jets would never find their target through the fog cloaking their mountain kingdom. They even derided Milošević, the man who had come to power on a pledge to defend all Serbs, for his attempts to prevent the further imposition of economic sanctions. Milošević's concern about sanctions was contemptible, they said, pledging to fight the whole world if necessary.

The decisive speaker was General Ratko Mladić, the Bosnian Serb military commander. In a blustering speech, he used a series of maps to illustrate how much land would have to be handed over to their Muslim foes. When the stocky General took out the maps, Milošević and Bulatović were concerned. Mladić was no politician, but Bulatović could see that the General's strictly military logic carried weight. One map showed the military situation on the ground. Another depicted the demographic distribution of the Serbs. But the *pièce de résistance* was a transparency of the Vance-Owen provinces, which Mladić super-imposed on the map showing the front lines. Not only would the Bosnian Serbs have to hand over huge chunks of territory, but part of the Serb population would be left in isolated and vulnerable areas. Having exposed the dangers implicit in the Vance-Owen Plan, Mladić went further and boasted that his men were not afraid of Western intervention.

The session went on deep into the night. Suicide was constantly invoked, by those who argued for acceptance as well as those who favored rejection. A slew of different amendments were proposed. One deputy even called for another condition to be placed on acceptance – that he get three cartons of cigarettes. It was a dark farce. Milošević employed all manner of arguments to persuade his proxies. The Serbs could not afford to gamble everything they had, he argued, only to lose it all "like a drunken poker player." He was obviously referring to Karadžić, whose fondness for roulette was well-known.

Ćosić, who had called Bosnia a "monstrous creation," reassured the assembly that the Serbs had won. His vision was what he called the territorial and political "recomposition of the Balkans" – the right to total ethnic self-determination. For the Balkans that meant a Greater Serbia, Greater Croatia and Greater Albania. Alija Izetbegović would never have his Muslim state. Never mind Vance-Owen, he advised them; multi-ethnic Bosnia had been destroyed.

The entire project of provinces and Bosnia-Herzegovina is historically temporary. Brothers and sisters, Alija's state does not exist. An Islamic state no

longer exists. It is over. We have to understand it. A federation will exist,
which is not yet equitable but it will be. In the places where a Serbian house
and Serbian land exist and where the Serbian language is spoken, there will
be a Serbian state.

In effect, Ćosić was urging the Bosnian Serbs to accept the Plan which he, like Milošević, knew could never be implemented.

At one point, Milošević seemed to have gained the upper hand. "One can sacrifice for one's nation everything except the nation itself, and if you don't accept the Vance-Owen Plan you are going to sacrifice your people." The Serbian President sat next to Karadžić, urging him to do more to persuade the assembly.

Sensing that the deputies had started to have doubts, the hard-line Momčilo Krajišnik, the assembly speaker, nicknamed Mr. No, called a break.

The whole time I felt a great pain from within, because we knew this Plan
meant destruction for our people. That's why at the assembly we were very
determined to see that it was not ratified. We knew it would not solve any
problems.

The Bosnian Serb deputies went to their club room, preventing guests from entering on the grounds that only members of the Serbian Democratic Party were allowed in. It was a slap in the face. Milošević was left waiting for hours, while his erstwhile protégés persuaded the deputies not to cave in.

The leadership at least tried to keep up the appearance of recommending the Plan. Nikola Koljević, the professorial "vice president," reminded the assembly of the Serbian epic hero Miloš Obilić, the bravest fighter at the Battle of Kosovo in 1389. Obilić had said there was no chance of beating the Turks – they were far too numerous. "If all of us were turned into salt there wouldn't be enough to season a Turkish dinner," Obilić told his comrades before leading them into battle. Koljević drew a parallel. "It wouldn't be enough for Clinton's boys – we should not risk a desperate battle with the biggest super power."

Out of sixty-five votes cast, fifty-one deputies voted to hold a referendum on the Plan.

An alarmed Ćosić told the assembly he had received reports that the West would launch air-strikes that very night. Afterwards, ashen-faced and exhausted, he called the decision disastrous. "I don't know what the next night and day will bring to this country."

He turned to Plavšić, asking how they could avoid the impending tragedy. The iron-willed biology professor, who was adored by troops for her willingness to shrug off Western pressure, looked at Ćosić blankly, and said:

"What kind of a tragedy? It would be a tragedy if we accepted this."

And then he said: "They are going to bomb the bridges."

And she said: "Let them bomb the bridges. They can't destroy the Serbs with bombardment."

Milošević was visibly agitated. "He was not normal. This could be seen on his face and on his hands," said Plavšić. The Serbian President never brooked any opposition. Opponents were there to be circumvented, removed or otherwise overcome. "Later the assembly booed, very loudly. He didn't know how to behave himself in parliament because he never attended parliamentary sessions."

Silent and glowering, accompanied by an exhausted Mitsotakis, Milošević boarded his car for the long ride home.

His response was swift. Belgrade announced it was cutting off all supplies except food and medicine to Republika Srpska. Nor did Milošević forget Plavšić's snub. She was prevented from crossing the frontier into Serbia. The embargo was short-lived, but the damage was done. The Pale meeting was Milošević's first public defeat since he had become the undisputed leader of all Serbs. It was the first time he had failed to out-maneuver his political challengers.

The vote in Pale came just as the American Secretary of State Warren Christopher was trying – and failing – to sell Washington's policy of "lift and strike" to Europe. In talks with the leaders of ten NATO countries and Russia, Christopher met a very cool response to a plan which called for the supply of weapons to the out-gunned Muslims and the launching of strategic air-strikes at Bosnian Serb targets. France and the UK objected because they had troops on the ground who would be vulnerable in the face of possible retaliation. Christopher himself hardly appeared convinced of its wisdom. But he was a lawyer and his client, Clinton, wanted the policy. But the Administration did not seem to have anticipated the resistance of European allies, who were trying desperately to avoid intervention and still hoping that Bosnian Serb leaders would back the Vance-Owen Plan.

After Christopher's return, Washington tried to gloss over trans-atlantic differences. Another key moment in a shift of US policy was when President Clinton and his wife Hillary read parts of *Balkan Ghosts*, by Robert Kaplan, which describes the violent past of the region. For some reason the book had an enormous impact on Clinton, convincing him that the inhabitants of the Balkans were doomed to violence.[6] Within days the Clinton Administration had abandoned two contradictory plans. It backed off Vance-Owen and "lift and strike".

There was never a more comprehensive plan than Vance-Owen, which, despite criticism to the contrary, did preserve a multi-ethnic Bosnia within its internationally recognized borders. Once Vance-Owen was rejected by the Serbs however, the US lost no time ditching it. It was cast aside ostensibly because of the Bosnian Government's complaints, but also because of fears that it was unenforceable. The fact that it would have required at least 50,000 ground-troops, of which the US had already pledged half – was probably the overriding reason.

A justifiably embittered Lord Owen on an American television program dismissed as a "delusion" the proposal to end the war by air-strikes. "You will not solve the problem at 10,000 feet," he said pointing out that the US could help by contributing troops to the UN force in Bosnia but not by bombing.

But the collapse of the Vance-Owen Plan had taken the wind out of the US sails and Christopher had already switched tack. He wanted to cut his losses and sweep Bosnia under the carpet as quickly and effectively as possible. In congressional testimony, Christopher said the killing in Bosnia was "a problem from hell." He signalled that the US would not anger its NATO allies by taking unilateral action on "lift and strike." "We will not act alone in taking actions in the former Yugoslavia."

He went even further. On May 18, he said it was essentially up to Europe to deal with "ancient hatreds." These were not the words of a country anxious to get involved. He then launched the idea of "containment." "We will do what we can in concert with our allies and friends to respond to the violence and contain the conflict." He tried, unconvincingly, to insist that Washington was not abandoning the Muslims. He said that the US was not bowing out completely and still believed in lifting the arms embargo against the Bosnian Government and limited "compensatory air action" in order to allow the Muslims to fight the Serbs on "a level playing field."

At this crucial juncture, Christopher was unwittingly rescued by Andrei Kozyrev, his Russian counterpart who had called for a Foreign Minister's meeting of the UN Security Council to consider troops for the protection of the newly-created "safe areas." The US Secretary of State deflected attention from Washington's own policy vacuum by pouring cold water on the Russian initiative to deploy troops. He announced that the meeting had been postponed, taking an opportunity to criticize the Vance-Owen Plan because the only way to implement it was by engaging troops to fight against the Bosnian Serbs. He reiterated that the United States was prepared to commit troops once all the parties agreed on a peace plan. He put a damper on engagement on any side, pointing out: "There are atrocities on all sides."

On May 22, the "Joint Action Plan" was put forward by the US, Russia, France, the UK and Spain. Billed as a recipe for containment, it was, in fact, the closest thing yet to US acceptance of the current state of play in Bosnia. The ceremony was like the emperor's new clothes – because there was no action in the Plan. The Clinton Administration announced that it would send a contingent of troops to Macedonia and traced the same line as President Bush had drawn warning that the US would not tolerate war in Kosovo, stressing that it must not be allowed to become the fulcrum of further conflict because that could drag in Albania and, in all probability, US NATO allies, Greece and Turkey. Britain and France pushed it through, but no one had considered its implication.

It called for the sealing of Bosnia's borders to prevent incursions or military support from Serbia and Croatia, and the establishing of the six Muslim "safe areas." The agreement was hailed by an ultra-nationalist Serbian leader as the "first sober public statement by the West." The Joint-Action Plan put the final nail in the coffin of Vance-Owen, formulating the embryo for the next stage of peace talks: a three-way partition whose terms were dictated by the Serbs and Croats – and mediated by Owen and Stoltenberg.

By the weekend Clinton had done a complete turnaround. He was no longer wringing his hands about the plight of the Bosnian Muslims and salvaging their state. He announced that he was looking for a deal which would give "reasonable land for the Muslims."

Karadžić praised Clinton for coming to his senses. Izetbegović lashed out at the US for abandoning Bosnia-Herzegovina to a carve-up. "The world has not left us with many choices," he complained, warning that he would no longer give time to futile negotiations. What the beleaguered President failed to see was that the stage was being set for a new round of negotiations when the Serbs and Croats could dictate the terms.

As the US tried to distance itself completely from a commitment to a unified Bosnia-Herzegovina, the Sarajevo Government was threatened with being left with nothing. It was time to investigate the options. Clinton made it clear (at least for the time being) there was no rescue for the Bosnians. "My preference was for a multi-ethnic state in Bosnia. But if the parties themselves, including the Bosnian Government... genuinely and honestly agree to a different solution, then the United States would have to look at it very seriously."

1 Belgrade Radio, April 30, 1993.

2 The final plan envisaged a demilitarized zone around a UN-monitored route – the Serb corridor. It prohibited the transport of troops or military equipment in this and ten other "blue routes" which link ethnic provinces.

Muslims and Croat troops would not be allowed to return to provinces allocated to their ethnic groups where there are Serb communities. Instead, they will be policed by UN troops. While Belgrade heralded this last-minute concession, in fact it only applied to areas designated as Muslim where the Serbs were in full control – province five, the area along the strategic Drina River.

Peace negotiators called for the despatch of 70,000 UN troops to be drawn from NATO, including up to half from the US, and possibly Russia.

Elections would be held in each of the ten provinces within eighteen months. The UN troops will protect the minorities at least until then.

Sarajevo was set to be demilitarized under the plan.

Critics pointed to the UN's failure to demilitarize Serb paramilitary troops and enable the return of refugees. But the plan's success hinges on the extent to which Serbs were ready to give up their idea of uniting Serb-held territories within a Greater Serbia, and whether Croatia would allow the independence of adjacent Croat-designated territory.

It established a timetable for peace:

UN Security Council approves the plan.

The Council endorses the implementation of the plan and levels of monitoring troops based on a report by Secretary General Boutros Boutros-Ghali.

Within 72 hours: warring parties declare troops and weapon levels, report location of front lines and minefield and prepare for UN verification. Ceasefire put in place and remains effective.

Within five days: Heavy weapons to be withdrawn from around Sarajevo under UN supervision.

Within 15 days: All other heavy weapons also placed under UN supervision. All forces separate from front lines to establish demilitarized zones monitored by the UN.

Within 45 days: All forces return to their designated provinces in co-ordination with an agreed demobilization.

Restoration of infrastructure: electricity, gas, water, railways, roads, etc.

Establishment of "free passage routes" to and from Sarajevo to guarantee movement for civilians goods and humanitarian aid.

Establishment of a UN-guaranteed corridor linking northern Serb-controlled areas with Serbia.

Establishment of an interim central government in Sarajevo comprising three members each from the three ethnic groups, with the presidency rotating every four months among the three parties.

Establishment of interim provincial governments on the basis   of the ethnic composition in each province with provision that none of the three groups can be left unrepresented in any province.

3 From the text of a letter, signed by Milošević, Bulatović and Ćosić, to the members of the Bosnian Serb "parliament."

4 Though the Vance plan that brought 14,000 UN troops to Croatia provided for the return of all refugees, and the demilitarization of the region, in fact neither took place. Ethnic cleansing of Croats from the UN Protected Areas continued well after UNPROFOR arrived; not a single Croat refugee was able to return; and, in many areas, the "demilitarization" consisted of the Krajina Serb army exchanging their military uniforms for crisp new blue "police" uniforms. Military vehicles were not, as the plan required, withdrawn but, instead, were painted blue instead of green, and reassigned from the army to the police.

5 Risto Djogo was known for his sense of humor and aggressive loyalty to the Serbs nationalist cause. In little more than a year these qualities would cost him his life. He was murdered soon after Milošević imposed a blockade against the Bosnian Serbs while in Zvornik attending a concert of the Serbian folk star Ceca, perhaps by her future husband's, Arkan's men – at the order of the Serbian secret police. Djogo allegedly knew too much and had collected documents about what he and his leadership had done during the war in co-ordination with Milošević.

6 Elizabeth Drew, *On the Edge, The Clinton Presidency*, Simon & Schuster, New York, 1994.

22

BEWARE YOUR FRIEND A HUNDRED-FOLD
The Muslim-Croat Conflict,
1992–1994

As the Neretva River enters the once beautiful city of Mostar, its broad flat banks steepen and rise until it cuts a narrow rocky canyon through the heart of the medieval Turkish town. At the narrowest point of the river, in 1566, the Turkish Sultan had ordered the building of a bridge – a single broad span of shining white cobalt. "It is one of the most beautiful bridges in the world," the novelist Rebecca West wrote. "A slender arch between two round towers, its parapets bent in a shallow angle at the center. I know of no country – not even Italy or Spain – that shows such invariable taste and such pleasing results."

The keepers of the bridge became known as the *Mostari* – the Serbo-Croat word for bridge is *most*. From them, the town that grew up around the bridge took its name. The bridge – and Mostar itself – came to symbolize the very idea of Bosnia-Herzegovina, a place where Catholic, Orthodox and Muslim peoples lived distinctively, but together and in mutual tolerance. It was despised by many Croat nationalists for whom it represented a lasting reminder of Turkish influence in what they viewed as their Christian land. It survived the fall of the Ottoman Empire. It survived two World Wars. But on November 9, 1993 (four years to the day after the tearing down of the Berlin Wall) under a sustained artillery battering by Bosnian Croat forces, its beautiful arch collapsed into the deep-blue river pool below. In a war in which multi-ethnicity was itself the enemy, the destruction of the bridge appeared to mirror that of the multi-ethnic ideal of Bosnia – a place almost defined by bridge-building – between communities, between nationalities, between faiths. For Bosnians there was no stronger image of the country they were trying to build. The Bosnian government declared a day of mourning.

The portents for a Muslim-Croat conflict in Bosnia were clear long before the Serbs launched their attack against both of them in April 1992. In 1991, as his own republic was falling under the hammer of the JNA, Croatia's President Tudjman put out feelers, via the Croats in Izetbegović's government, to try to gauge whether Izetbegović could be persuaded to bring the Bosnian territorial defense into the war, to open a second front against the Serbs. In September 1991, a few days after the Croatian national guard had laid siege to the JNA barracks across the republic, Bosnia's Defense Minister Jerko Doko, a Croat, proposed that the Bosnian TO be mobilized.

But the Interior Minister, Alija Delimustafić, a Muslim whose pro-Belgrade orientation was already well known, had already set the Bosnian TO on the opposite course. He had agreed to allow the JNA to use northern and western Bosnia as a base from which attacks against the Croatian national guard could be commanded and resourced. According to Aleksander Vasiljević, the head of JNA counter-intelligence:

> *He [Delimustafić] agreed to establish joint Bosnian police-JNA patrols and checkpoints, on railways and roads to control traffic and prevent armed movements by paramilitaries, as well as to provide for real JNA movements. Particularly since the military needed to get through to Knin from Serbia and Montenegro to the war there. If they had not got through we would never have been able to fight. Bosnia was our corridor to Krajina.*

The Croats harbored deep suspicions about the Bosnian Muslims' role in the Croatian war, accusing many of staying in the JNA throughout 1991 and well into 1992. Croatian propaganda accused the Commander of the Bosnian TO, Sefer Halilović, of playing an active part in the destruction of Vukovar.[1]

Tudjman, in any case, had never accepted the long-term viability of Bosnia as a state. He made no secret of his view that Bosnia was an artificial creation of the Yugoslav state, with no historical legitimacy. From the beginning he promoted what he called "nation-building" among Bosnia's Croats, who made up seventeen percent of the republic's population. On the very morning that Bosnia descended into open war, April 6, 1992, Tudjman told a news conference in Zagreb:

> *We have shown consistency in this respect. We said that we were for a sovereign and independent Bosnia-Herzegovina, if it secures the status of a constitutive nation in Bosnia-Herzegovina for the Croatian people there. [Izetbegović] proceeds from the thesis that the Serbian people can be pacified... and on the other hand he proposes that the rest of Bosnia-Herzegovina, i.e. a Muslim Bosnia, remain a unitary state. The representatives of the Croatian people in Bosnia-Herzegovina cannot agree to this, because they know that they as a minority would be subject to majority rule... the representatives of the Croatian population in Bosnia-Herzegovina were requesting a guaranteed status of a constitutive nation in Bosnia-Herzegovina for the Croatian people there.[2]*

Tudjman was characteristically inconsistent. While demanding international recognition for Croatia within its existing boundaries, he conspired to undermine Bosnia's territorial integrity. And while the constitution of his own republic denied the Serbian minority the status of "constituent nation" he none the less demanded this for the Croats of Bosnia.

The Croats of Bosnia fall into two distinct camps, geographically and politically. One-third of the Bosnian Croats lived in western Herzegovina, a notorious hot-bed of extreme right-wing nationalism, where Croats formed close to a hundred percent of the population – at least in the countryside.[3] Many western Herzegovinians had fought in the Croatian war, and, in 1992, returned bloodied by their experience and ready for the war in Bosnia. But the majority of Bosnia's Croats lived in central and northern Bosnia, in towns and communities where all three nationalities lived. These central Bosnian Croats were, by tradition, much less nationalistic and much more inclined to live in a multi-ethnic Bosnian state than to seek its partition into ethnically-pure units.

Of the two Croatian representatives on the Bosnian Presidency, Franjo Boras belonged to the Herzegovina tradition; and Stjepan Kljuić to the pro-Bosnian tendency. Tudjman, from the beginning, promoted the former.

When war broke out, the Croats of Herzegovina were already organized militarily, and supplied by Croatia. The first substantial military resistance the Serb-JNA juggernaut encountered was in Herzegovina, where, for three months, Serbs and Croats faced each other across the Neretva River. The Serbs occupied the east bank, the Croats the west, thus partitioning the city of Mostar itself. It had long been part of JNA strategic planning to regard the Neretva as the natural border of a new Serb-dominated rump Yugoslavia. The more ambitious Serb nationalists had even thought of Dubrovnik as the natural capital of a future enlarged Serbian republic of Montenegro-Herzegovina.

On June 17, the Bosnian Croats, after the partial withdrawal of the JNA, pushed the Serbs out of Mostar altogether and captured a swathe of Herzegovinian territory along the east bank of the river. It was the first serious defeat the Serbs had suffered since the war began.

The Bosnian Croat forces (HVO) now consolidated its hold on the territories it controlled. Arms and other supplies were channelled, from Zagreb, through the Herzegovina HDZ. A former clothing store manager named Mate Boban emerged, through Tudjman's patronage, as *de facto* leader of the Bosnian Croats, quickly eclipsing the elected representatives, Kljuić and Boras.

Boban founded his own state in western Herzegovina – the "Croatian Community of Herceg-Bosna" – with its own armed forces. He imposed Croatia's system of local government, Croatian schooling, and "Croatian" became the "official language." The Croatian dinar had already, in 1991, replaced the Yugoslav currency (Bosnia – no more than a leopard-spot collection of isolated territories by the late summer of 1992 – still had no currency of its own). Herceg-Bosna came to mirror, in almost every sense, the Serbian Republic of Bosnia-Herzegovina, with one important difference – the Muslims and Croats were, formally, partners in a military alliance signed between Tudjman and Izetbegović.

On the east bank of the Neretva, in the heart of old Mostar, stands the Turkish House, a museum depicting a typical Ottoman Muslim home from some unspecified period of Bosnia's past. On the wall in the main living-room hung an elaborately inscribed print carrying a verse from the Koran in both Arabic and Serbo-Croat. It read:

> *Beware your enemy, but beware your friend a hundred-fold. Because if your friend becomes your enemy he can hurt you all the more, because he knows the tunnels to your heart.*

By late summer, Mostar's Muslims were beginning to be wary of their Croat "friends." The HVO had made no effort, after taking control of Mostar, to follow up the victory by helping the Bosnian Army to liberate Sarajevo, as many had expected it would. Boban had dismissed almost all Muslims from positions of responsibility in public life, and replaced them with HDZ place-men. He had turned "Herceg-Bosna" into a one-party, ethnic state. The Mostar studio of Bosnian radio – which was loyal to Sarajevo – was subject to frequent harassment by Croatian police, and was, from time to time, closed down. His police mounted road-blocks around the city; Muslims found that they were not allowed to come and go freely.

Boban was never explicit about what he considered the boundaries of his state. His deputy in central Bosnia, Dario Kordić, a cocksure young journal-ist-turned-warrior with an unshakeable conviction that Bosnia belonged, properly, to Croatia, was more explicit. He set up his headquarters in the town of Novi Travnik. The central Bosnian towns of Travnik, Vitez, Jablanica, Konjic were all, he said, part of Herceg-Bosna. Three of these areas had a Muslim majority. Muslims, Kordić asserted, did not constitute a sepa-rate nation. They were Croats of Islamic faith.

By the autumn of 1992, two parallel armies coexisted on the same territory – the HVO and the Army of Bosnia-Herzegovina. A great influx of Muslim refugees, "cleansed" by the Serbs, further exacerbated tension, providing Boban with fears to play on – fears that the Croatian areas would be "swamped" by the Muslim dispossessed.

What was to become a conflict as bitter as that with the Serbs began on October 25 in the central Bosnian town of Prozor. It began as a dispute between rival mafiosi over who should take delivery of a consignment of gasoline. This gangland squabble quickly acquired the dimension of an "eth-nic" dispute, as each of the two armies jumped to the defense of its own peo-ple. Muslim men, driven out of Prozor, took to the hills, though most returned a few days later when tensions subsided. But the dispute had all the characteristics of open warfare, including shelling from outside the town, and gun-battles in the street. After a few days the center of Prozor was a burned-

and-shattered wreck of a place. Only Croat businesses were trading. Conflict also broke out to the north, in Novi Travnik. But Sarajevo radio, loyal to the Izetbegović government, would, from now on, say that Croatian fascism first entered Bosnia through the *prozor* (window).

The ensuing stand-off resulted in an immediate military disaster. A breakdown in cooperation between the HVO and the Bosnian Army, combined with intense mutual suspicion, led both to desert their positions at the town of Jajce, to the northwest of Travnik. Jajce had been surrounded by Serb forces since the beginning of the war and had suffered some shelling. There was not the slightest indication at the end of October, however, that it was about to fall. Then, on October 29, it did, not because of a Serb offensive, but because of chaos in the Bosnian and Croat defenses. The Serbs walked into Jajce as 40,000 Muslim and Croat citizens of Jajce poured down the road towards Travnik.

Few of those who fled did so by mechanized vehicle, since fuel supplies to Jajce had been so spasmodic. Their exodus, during October 30 and November 1, resembled something from a pre-mechanized age: a great train – stretching as far as the eye could see, until the road disappeared into the forested hills to the north – of weary people trudging through the damp autumn mist, some on foot, others crammed on to the back of horse-drawn carts. It took most of them two or three days to reach Travnik, seventy kilometers to the south, and, as they fled, the Serb advance continued until the Bosnian Serb Army occupied the high ground above the road down which they were fleeing. Anything that looked like a military vehicle became a target. The refugees had to endure a barrage of shelling and machine-gun fire as they fled. It was the first painful illustration of how Muslim-Croat enmity would benefit the Serbs. General Mladić was later to comment: "I will watch them destroy each other and then I will push them both into the sea." The Serbs could not contain their glee.

As Bosnia descended into its first winter of war, the front lines hardened. There was now no area of the country where the Bosnian Serb and Bosnian Croat armies had a territorial dispute with each other. But, both, on the other hand, had unfinished business with the Bosnian army. An informal tacit alliance began to take shape. In Kiseljak, a majority Croat town on the western edge of Sarajevo, hard-line nationalists, loyal to the Herzegovina Croats, took control of the local government and the HVO. They had been trading with the Serbs besieging Sarajevo, as well as with Muslim black-marketeers in Sarajevo. For months, Kiseljak became a haven of peace, a land-locked, Bosnian Casablanca, as the Croats there took commercial advantage of their position "in between" Muslims and Serbs. The Croats would buy from the Serbs and sell to Muslim war-profiteers who were, by now, operating a cartel system that kept the price of black-market goods in Sarajevo artificially high.

The result was a net export of hard currency from Sarajevo, money that had been earned, and saved, over years, by ordinary Sarajevans. Muslim gangsters, Croat middlemen and Serb suppliers, all took their cut in an extortion racket that cut across military lines and in which the Kiseljak Croats were the crucial players.

Unfortunately for Sarajevo, Kiseljak stood at the western gates of the city, the place where the Serb ring-of-armor around Sarajevo was at its most vulnerable. Any attempt to smash through the siege from outside could only have come from that direction. By the winter of 1992–93, the Croat forces there had sound financial, as well cynical political, reasons for ensuring the continuation of the siege. The Croats, although formally still allies of the Bosnian government, became, in effect, partners with the Serbs in the perpetuation of the siege of Sarajevo.

In late April 1993, the winter stand-off between Muslims and Croats erupted into all-out war. News of the defeat at Srebrenica sent a flurry of rumor flying around central Bosnia that tens of thousands of Muslim refugees were due to arrive within days. In Kiseljak and Vitez, two Croat-populated pockets north and west of Sarajevo, Croat militiamen moved to take preventive action. They entered the Muslim village of Ahmići, which was surrounded by Croatian-populated villages, and murdered dozens of civilians, including women, children and elderly, in their homes. They then set fire to the houses.

Evidence of the atrocity was discovered by British troops of the United Nations Protection Force, and by international aid workers, on April 19 – a day after the signing of the Srebrenica surrender agreement. It had happened less than a mile from the British base. The British Commander, Colonel Bob Stewart, almost in tears with rage and frustration that he had known nothing about it when it was happening, demanded access to the village. In front of the world's television cameras he screamed at an HVO checkpoint commander, who had asked him whether he had permission to enter the village: "I don't need the permission of the bloody HVO – I'm the United Nations! I want to tell you that this is an absolute disgrace. Whole families have been massacred here. Who's responsible for this?" The HVO militiamen simply drove off.

There followed a wave of forced evictions, murders, and rapes. Muslims fled Vitez and headed for Travnik or Zenica, claiming that Croat soldiers had given them three hours to leave town or be killed. The bodies of two Muslim doctors, who had been travelling from Zenica to Vitez were found on the roadside, shot at close range in the head.

In Travnik, the HVO demanded that the Bosnian Army disarm and disband. It said the Vance-Owen Plan – which the Croat and Bosnian sides had, by now, both agreed to – placed Travnik in a Croatian province, and required the withdrawal of all non-Croat forces from the province. The Vance-Owen Plan was not the cause of the Muslim-Croat fighting in central Bosnia; the conflict pre-dated the publication of the Plan. But, in the spring of 1993, the Plan gave Bosnian Croat territorial demands a stamp of legitimacy they would otherwise have lacked.[5]

Travnik was now overwhelmingly a Muslim town, having been swamped by Muslims who had been driven from their homes in northern Bosnia by Serb ethnic cleansing. These men, many of whom had been interned in the detention camps that had so shocked the world the previous year – radical-ized and embittered by their experience – determined not to go through the same thing at the hands of the Croats. Within days they had driven all HVO units out of Travnik, although thousands of Croat civilians continued to live in Travnik and were not subjected to the virulent campaigns of ethnic cleansing that the Croats were soon to inflict on Muslim minorities living in their midst. In Zenica, a stronghold of Izetbegović's SDA, and the town where the Bosnian Army had its strongest roots, talks between the Muslim Mayor and the local HVO commander that had been aimed at restoring calm broke up when HVO units in the surrounding hills shelled the town center. As in Travnik, the HVO were driven out.

Muslim central Bosnia was now surrounded on all sides by enemy forces – a land-locked island of territory, cut off from the capital Sarajevo, and from the outside world. In addition, it had to contend with three Croat-occupied areas – Novi Travnik, Vitez and Kiseljak – in its midst. These constituted sieges within the siege. Of these, Vitez was the most problematical, since it lay on the main road between Zenica and Travnik. In effect, the territory under the control of Izetbegović's Government had now been reduced to a leopard-spot smattering of isolated enclaves – around Travnik, Zenica, Tuzla, Bihać, Sarajevo, and the three eastern enclaves of Srebrenica, Goražde and Žepa. None of these enclaves was viable without the permanent life-support of international aid. Access to and from each was cut off by the besieging Serb or Croat forces. The military and strategic reality facing Bosnia in the spring and early summer of 1993 was that the country was grad-ually being wiped off the map of Europe. It seemed increasingly likely that the only future for what the Serbs and Croats now increasingly called former Bosnia-Herzegovina was that each of these enclaves should gradually be absorbed into one or other of the Croatian and Serbian states that were taking shape around them.

The fall of Srebrenica, the rejection by the Serbs of the Vance-Owen Plan, the international community's subsequent failure to enforce the Plan, and, finally, the outbreak of the Muslim-Croat war: all occurred within a few weeks in April and May 1993. Together they forced the Bosnian government and army to confront the new reality. A political and military sea-change followed: the Muslims began to fight back.

A Sarajevo psychiatrist, called Ljiljana Oruč, kept her sense of humor throughout the siege. In the summer of 1993 she described the Bosnian capital as one vast psychiatric laboratory. Sarajevans had suffered, she said, from a collective psychotic delusion – the delusion that the world would, eventually, rescue them and their country. This delusion persisted, she continued, despite all the objective evidence to the contrary. It was, therefore, a kind of inverse paranoia: a persistent belief that everything is going to turn out all right in the end even though by all rational judgement, it clearly is not. "This collective psychosis left us in May 1993," Dr. Oruč insisted. "After that, we knew we were on our own."

The fight-back began in central Bosnia. The Third Corps of the Bosnian Army[5] formed two new brigades consisting mainly of men who been "cleansed" from northern and eastern Bosnia. Many of them had been hardened by their experience at the hands of the Serb forces; most had been through the detention camps. In Travnik they formed the Seventeenth "Krajiška" Brigade, under the command of Colonel Mehmet Alagić, himself a victim of ethnic cleansing from the Kozara region of northern Bosnia. In Zenica, the heartland of Muslim Bosnia, a new force altogether appeared – the Seventh Muslim Brigade. This was explicitly Muslim, rather than Bosnian, in its orientation. Its officers were hostile to Westerners, wore Islamic insignia, long beards, and greeted each other with the Arabic "al-sallam aliekum" (peace be with you). Their families attended Islamic education classes and their wives and daughters, increasingly, wore veils in public. For the first time, a strident, xenophobic Muslim nationalism was being articulated in Bosnia: the politics of multi-ethnic tolerance, the officers of the Seventeenth Muslim Brigade argued, had led to the destruction of the Muslim people. It was time for Muslims to take matters into their own hands, not as Bosnians, but explicitly as Muslims.

Conveniently for those, in the West, who argued against intervening on the side of the Bosnian government, this fight-back gave credence to the argument – frequently voiced in defense of a do-nothing policy – that "all sides are equally guilty." But this new refugee army cared nothing for international public opinion; courting popularity in the capitals of the Western world, its officers and men argued, had brought nothing to the Muslims except military defeat, dispossession, and hand-wringing declarations of sympathy from abroad. Muslims, they argued, had learned that patient negotiations in Geneva, The Hague and London brought catastrophe; and that, in this war, victory would fall not to the just, but to the strong.

There was nothing of the multi-ethnic ideal among these men. They no longer spoke of Serbs and Croats, but of Chetniks and Ustaše. In Zenica, from time to time, the Seventh Muslim Brigade would take to the streets, smashing shops that sold alcohol and slaughtering pigs and destroying the carcasses. They became, during the summer and autumn months, a law unto themselves, frequently in conflict with the civilian police and increasingly feared by the civilian population.

The military strategy of the Third Corps was to carve out a triangle of territory in central Bosnia stretching from Tuzla in the northeast, to Sarajevo in the southeast, and Mostar in the southwest. The immediate priority was to secure lines of communication between the leopard-spot territories. The heavily populated Vitez pocket – where about 60,000 Croats lived – was too daunting a target. So the Bosnian Army began to sweep through Croatian villages in the hills above the valley that Vitez sat in. They burned and looted as they went, using the tactic which their Serb and Croat foes had proved so rewarding. By early summer, the Army had secured a road of sorts, around the back of the Vitez pocket linking Travnik to Zenica and beyond to Tuzla.[6]

The Muslim Croat fault-line ran through the town of Gornji Vakuf. Throughout the summer and winter of 1993, this town, where British troops had based a company of men to provide a way-station and logistic base for aid convoys running from Split to Tuzla, changed hands so frequently, as the tide of military fortune ebbed and flowed, that by the end of the year there was hardly a house that was left habitable.

Over the summer grisly reports of maltreatment and torture of Muslims in Croat camps emerged. In Zagreb, Stipe Mesić later recalled that he was first told of the camps by Jozo Primorac, an HDZ activist.

> *He said: "Listen Stipe, I'm surprised, I was just in Herzegovina (he had a brother there). They have camps down there. They look like in the Nazi times, even worse they don't get food and water, and are abused.'*
>
> *I asked who the people in the camps were, and he said they were former neighbors, from the same villages and towns, and their only fault was that they were Muslims. Another big group there were Muslim HVO soldiers disarmed overnight and sent there. He was very surprised, especially by the treatment there.*
>
> *I used this information, and told Tudjman. He answered that the others had camps as well.*

In mid-August the International Committee of the Red Cross finally gained access to 6,474 detainees in 51 camps – of which 4,400 were held by the Bosnian Croats (a figure the Bosnian Government claimed was far too low), 1,400 by the Muslims and 674 by the Serbs.

Muslim former prisoners held in Dretelj, a notorious camp south of Mostar, said they were beaten and woken in the middle of the night, and forced to sing songs insulting to the Muslims and Izetbegović. They were deprived of food and water. Many told of having to drink their own urine rather than die of thirst.

A statement from the UN Security Council on September 15 recalled the "revulsion and condemnation" felt among the international community when the existence of the Serb camps was revealed the year before and urged the Croats to close theirs.

Nowhere illustrated the tragedy of the Muslim-Croat conflict more than the central Bosnian town Vareš, an unlovely mining and quarry town in a pretty valley running north-south on a road from Sarajevo to Tuzla. Vareš was on the very edge of the Muslim-Croat war zone. Before the war its population had been evenly split between Muslims and Croats, with a sizeable Serb minority. The Serbs had fled, or had been moved out, at the start of the war. The local Croats and Muslims worked hard through the summer of 1993 not to become infected by the conflict that was tearing the two communities apart to the west of them.

But Vareš could not stay immune. The conflict so polarized central Bosnia that, despite the best efforts of the local leadership, Vareš soon divided along ethnic lines. But it provides an illuminating insight into the dynamic of ethnic conflict. Vareš became a microcosm of the wider conflict.

As always, the first tensions came from outside – the arrival of thousands of angry and traumatized Croats who had been driven from, or fled in terror, from their homes in Visoko, Breza, Kakanj and Zenica – towns which themselves had received floods of similarly angry and traumatized Muslim refugees during an earlier cycle. The refugees brought with them an accumulated resentment against, and fear of, the group that had driven them out. In Vareš the arrival of so many Croat refugees not only crowded the town – it tipped the delicate ethnic balance. The local Croat leadership, however, continued to cooperate with the local Muslim leaders; and this soon brought accusations from the incoming Croat refugees that they were cooperating with the "enemy" that had driven them from their homes. A split opened up among the Croats. Then, in October an armed HVO unit arrived from Kiseljak, the hard-line Croat nationalist, and xenophobically anti-Muslim, stronghold to the south. The local Croat Mayor and Police Chief were briefly jailed, then overthrown. An outsider was installed as Mayor. Muslim men were rounded up, and Muslim homes were raided and looted. Within days, almost the entire Muslim community had fled to the village of Dabravina to the south, where they waited and planned their return.

In fact, Vareš could not be defended by the Croats. Almost as soon as they had secured control of it, they prepared to evacuate it. There were two escape routes – both led across Serb territory. Since the Kiseljak Croats were on such good terms with the Serbs, this did not present a difficulty. But the existence of the village of Stupni Do, a mile from the edge of Vareš, did. It was a Muslim village, with a population of 250. It lay on the southern escape route. On the night of October 23, after a day of unrelenting bombardment of Stupni Do, Croat militiamen wearing balaclava masks, or with their faces painted, entered the village and dynamited, or torched, every house. Those villagers unable to flee were shot, or had their throats cut. Some were burned alive in their homes; others were gunned down as they tried to flee through the woods. Some bodies were thrown on to bonfires in the gardens of the homes in which they fell. By the end of the killing spree, the village lay littered with bodies and every house was in flames. Most of the villagers fled. Scores of people were killed; some of the bodies were never recovered.

For days Croat militiamen rampaged through Vareš looting the homes that had been abandoned by the fleeing Muslims. Those Muslims still trapped in the town begged the Swedish UN force billeted there to escort them safely to Bosnian-held territory. The UN did not have the trucks to do it. Instead, the Swedes positioned their armored vehicles up and down the length of the town's main street, and, for days and nights on end, Muslim women and children camped beside them, the proximity of UN forces their only protection. Then, in the small hours of November 3, the Croat Mayor went from house to house with a bull-horn instructing all Croatian families to assemble in the street, and prepare to be evacuated before dawn. The Muslim Army, he told them, was closing in on the town from the north, west, and south.

More than 10,000 fled in a single night. For a day, the town lay empty. Then, the Seventh Muslim Brigade walked in without firing a shot. The Muslim civilians returned to their homes. Within weeks the homes that the Croats had abandoned were occupied by Muslim families from towns and villages occupied by the Serbs. The entire town of Crna Rijeka in northern Bosnia, having been uprooted by Serb ethnic cleansing, resettled itself in Croat homes in Vareš.

That is how Vareš became a casualty of the Muslim-Croat war. Radicalized outsiders sowed the seeds of ethnic conflict in a community in which Croats and Muslims had been content to live together. Serb ethnic cleansing had crammed more and more Muslims and Croats into a smaller and smaller territory, causing resentment among local people that eventually spilled over into ethnic tension. Once the chain of violence was set into motion, each of the communities was ready to fight for its own separate land.

1 Halilović denied it.
2 SWB: April 9, 1992.
3 The important exception is Mostar, which Herzegovina Croats considered their

capital, and which had a typically Bosnian mix of Serbs, Croats, Muslims and other nationalities.

4 The Croat provinces, in the Vance-Owen Plan, were drawn so large in order to ensure that, although Croats would still form the largest proportion of the population, there would none the less be large Serb and Muslim minorities. The extensiveness of the Croat provinces was thus intended, by Vance and Owen, to act as a check on the exercise of Croat power inside these provinces. The HVO, at Zagreb's prompting, interpreted it as carte blanche to impose Croatian rule in Muslim and Serb towns and regions.

5 The Army of BiH consisted at that time of five corps – in Sarajevo, Mostar, Tuzla, Bihać and Central Bosnia.

6 The Muslim-Croat war never spread as far north as Tuzla. Here, the HVO were in too small a minority, and too distant from Herzegovina, to challenge the supremacy of the Bosnian Army even if their commanders had been so inclined. Their alliance held throughout the conflict until, eventually, the HVO units were incorporated into the Bosnian Army.

23

THE HMS INVISIBLE
Talks at Sea
Summer 1993

Far from the bloodshed, the three parties – the Muslims, Serbs and Croats – met for a summer of talks in Geneva. By night, the feuding leaders slept in the swankiest hotels perched on the shores of Lake Léman; by day, they argued over the future frontiers of Bosnia-Herzegovina. In late September they flew to the Adriatic to the British aircraft carrier HMS *Invincible* to settle the Muslim demand for access to the Adriatic. It was the perfect setting for a carve-up. Summoning Bosnia's main protagonists for another round of talks, the first since the collapse of the Vance-Owen Plan. The mediators Lord Owen and Thorvald Stoltenberg said: "the destruction and suffering now taking place in Bosnia – makes us both shudder for the future of your country." The appeal was dramatic. But, from the start, the mediators were anxious to distance themselves from the Plan drawn up in a new reality.

After Washington had announced the "Joint-Action Plan," the Bosnian government was reeling. Suddenly they were advised to take the hand dealt to them or risk being left with nothing. Owen, caustic and shrewd, and his affable partner Stoltenberg, prodded Bosnia's main protagonists towards an agreement, whose terms were dictated by the Serbs and Croats. Owen maintained he was trying to broker a "painful compromise" not a partition. Despite the efforts to disguise the Plan, the main adversaries knew the proposed Union of three republics would disappear as soon as, or even before, the ink was dry. The Bosnian Croat leader, Mate Boban, called the Plan, the Invisible. It is uncertain whether he had misunderstood the name of the British aircraft carrier or was referring to the vanishing Bosnian union.

On July 30, a breakthrough was announced. All three sides, even the Bosnian government, had backed a constitutional agreement for a Union of republics in Bosnia-Herzegovina – in other words, a partition along ethnic lines. In remarkably similar statements, the Serbs and Croats hailed the agreement as a compromise which could bring an end to the war. Milošević announced that the agreement "completely affirms Republika Srpska." For a member of the Bosnian Serb delegation it was simple. "The Turks (derogatory reference to Muslims) are going to be like walnuts in a Serbo-Croat nutcracker," he said. He believed the world was recognizing that the Serbs had won the war.

The Serbs' relish was paralleled by Izetbegović's anguish. "I feel," he said, "like a thirsty man sent to find water in the desert." The Bosnian President was under considerable pressure. Washington had pulled the rug out from under him. He still clung to the idea of a unified Bosnia – a homeland for the Muslims. But this priority had slipped from most Western agendas. He reluctantly admitted that a tripartite partition of Bosnia was inevitable.

> *This division will give Muslims a Bosnian state. For the moment the idea of a multi-ethnic Bosnia is dead. Future generations can hope for such a state. But only after they have sobered up from their state of drunkenness.*

Izetbegović had been backed into a corner. In June, frustrated by his intransigence, the mediators had taken steps to weaken him – in the conviction that this would hasten the peace process. They reinvented the Bosnian Presidency, and reduced Izetbegović to his pre-war constitutional role as the first among equals. At their invitation, Fikret Abdić, the canny survivor, emerged from a long silence in the northwestern Cazinska Krajina or as it came to be known during the war, the Bihać enclave, to challenge Izetbegović for the leadership of Bosnia's Muslims. The mediators believed that Abdić would cut a deal with the Serbs and Croats on partition. They were right. He was ready to do the job and joined a multi-ethnic Bosnian Presidency delegation to Geneva to begin talks on the carve-up.

A month later, driving through the arches of the Palais des Nations, the Bosnian delegation looked defeated and divided. Izetbegović sat, ringed by his bodyguards, in a black Mercedes provided by the Swiss government. The rest of the delegation arrived in a battered Honda, followed by the rotund silver-haired Abdić in a taxi. This was in stark contrast to the impression of coordinated strength and brash confidence exuded by the Serb delegation which raced to the Palais.

As the talks progressed, the fighting on the ground intensified. The armies wanted to take what they could before the final carve-up. The Serbs moved on Mount Igman, which overlooks Sarajevo from the southwest . The West threatened air-strikes if the strangulation of Sarajevo continued, as Serb political and military leaders played cat-and-mouse with the international community over their pledge to withdraw from the strategic peak. While the entire international community waited to see whether Serb troops, as promised, had pulled out of Mount Igman, Karadžić slept – waking up at 1 p.m. in Geneva, exhausted after a night of gambling in a nearby casino.

Yet he out-smarted the West, or at least gave the world an excuse for refraining from military intervention. In fiery blustering tones, he warned against air-strikes. "If a single bomb hits a Serb position there will be no more talks. We would have an all-out war and catastrophe." He played on the fears of NATO countries which had troops in Bosnia. And even went so far as to threaten that, in the event of air-strikes, he would lose control of his Army, with the implication that Bosnian Serbs would retaliate against the UN troops from NATO countries.[1] It was a strange reversal – suddenly the international community was hoping that Karadžić would remain in command.

Against the background of Karadžić's ominous warnings, Alija Izetbegović openly advocated military intervention "in the name of peace." He said that the future of the negotiations, and the entire peace process, rested on air-strikes.

The international community took no action. There were no air-strikes. Less than a month later, an announcement was made that the three sides had agreed on the future borders of their ethnic statelets. In its final version reached on HMS *Invincible*, at sea in the Adriatic, the plan gave fifty-three percent of Bosnian (contiguous) territory to the Serbs, seventeen percent to the Croats, divided into two parts, and left the Muslims with the remaining 30 percent.

The Bosnia which emerged from this plan would be virtually land-locked even though the co-chairmen insisted that they be given access to the Sava and the Sea. Through these special routes, the Plan granted the Muslims access to the sea at Neum, Bosnia's only coastline, but which was unsuitable as a port. They were also offered the use of the Croatian seaport of Ploče and the border town of Metković which is set on the mouth of the Neretva. They would also have a tenuous outlet to the River Sava to the north. The Bosnian Government wanted its country to cover all of the republic – short of that, it wanted land stretching to every frontier. Eastern Bosnia – almost completely controlled by the Serbs – although it was mostly Muslim before the war – remained a major bone of contention. The Serbs, including Belgrade, were not prepared to hand over any part of eastern Bosnia to the Muslims – this was Milošević's bare minimum, which he wanted for the security of Serbia.

Just one glance at the map, and it was clear that this bizarrely shaped and geographically disjointed state would have only a slim chance of survival. Sarajevo would be placed under UN administration for a two-year interim period, and Mostar under provisional EC control.[2] Karadžić even offered to build a tunnel leading out of Sarajevo, so that the city's inhabitants could travel to other parts of the state.

The agreement also called for demilitarization of the Union, but there was no plan to disarm Croatia and Serbia, whose armies were involved in the conflict. Stoltenberg went off to the UN, in New York, to seek 40,000 troops in addition to the 10,000 already on the ground.

After a summer of talks and misplaced optimism that a settlement would be reached, Izetbegović, after initially giving the impression he would back it, rejected the plan drawn up on the HMS *Invincible*. These sudden turnarounds were typical of Izetbegović. He had won the concessions sought by the Muslims. His foreign minister Silajdžic called it a breakthrough. Owen and Stoltenberg were disappointed, convinced that they had never been so near an agreement before. Given a boost by international attempts to bring him into the game, Fikret Abdić declared his own state, the Autonomous Province of Western Bosnia and was expelled from the Bosnian Government Presidency. Another front-line emerged, and war erupted between Muslims in the Bihać enclave.

Whenever the Serb and Croat leaders resumed their poisonous courtship, it sounded the death-knell for the Muslims. Their conspiracy defied logic, but had its own strange dynamic. These sworn enemies killed each other on the battlefield while their leaders sipped whisky together. It began in March 1991, in Karadjordjevo, when Milošević and Tudjman discussed the partition of Bosnia. They established a secret commission, comprised of their confidants, to redraw Yugoslavia's borders. The problem of Serb and Croat nationalists was not how the two communities could live together, but how they could separate. They agreed on something else. Bosnia-Herzegovina should be carved-up, then they could have their cake and eat it, too: Greater Serbia *and* Greater Croatia.

In the tightest secrecy, the two rivals had a host of meetings. In December 1991 (the war had neither started in Bosnia nor ended in Croatia) Nikola Koljević sat in a Sarajevo café with Franjo Boras, his Croat nationalist counterpart in the Bosnian Presidency. Lamenting the state-of-war between the Serbs and the Croats, Boras announced that it did not have to be that way. After all, there were plenty of Serbs who had married into his family and they got along just fine. What's more, he said, perhaps the two men could prevent a war in Bosnia if the two communities started talks. He suggested that Koljević go to Zagreb to meet President Tudjman.

The Croatian and Serbian Presidents had already discussed the division of Bosnia. By December 1991, Milošević had a valuable bargaining chip: Krajina. Milošević was not attached to Knin; privately he even said that Knin, the capital of the self-styled Serb state, always belonged in Croatia – that it had nothing in common with Serbia. But with Knin, Milošević believed he would always get the upper hand in a deal with Croatia, secure in the knowledge that he had something that Croatia could not survive without, a third of its territory.

Tudjman believed that population transfers – getting rid of the Serbs – would solve Croatia's problems. Karadžić agreed with him. Knin's Serbs should be moved, but not to Serbia – to the fertile lands of eastern Slavonia to Serb-held parts of eastern Croatia. The leader, who claimed to be a great Serb patriot, was remarkably unconcerned about the fate of his Serb kith-

and-kin in Croatia. With a smile, he said they were used to moving. After all, they had emigrated to the region, escaping the Turks centuries ago. His deputy, Koljević, established a rapport with Tudjman. President Tudjman proposed a discussion on resettlement of the population, believing that this would bring about an ethnically homogenous state. Now, there was not full agreement because, obviously, resettling, even if it's peaceful, does not bring a final solution and then that was not the main issue because the main issue was the territories.

Koljević and Boras had already devised a plan. An observer at the Zagreb meeting, Stipe Mesić, then head of the HDZ, first heard the phrase the "humanitarian movement of population."

> *The talk was about creating ethnically clean areas. In other words, the problem of Muslims had to be solved, since it was obvious that Boras and Koljević had already agreed on borders among themselves.*
>
> *Tudjman had three goals; first he wanted recognition of Croatia, and the support of the international community; second, he wanted to divide Bosnia-Herzegovina, it was his life's obsession, and third in order to do this, he had to keep communicating with Milošević.*

The first meeting was a success. Tudjman told Mesić he was very pleased with the talks. He even met Koljević on his own. "It was clear," said Mesić, "they communicated with ease, and both sides were still at war."

But Koljević knew that the seeds of the new alliance would take time to take root.

> *It was impossible to have one meeting with the Croatian leadership and destroy the already existing coalition in Bosnia because, by that time, the Muslim leaders and Croatian leaders already had made public rallies, their flags tied into knots, showing that they were together.*

Over the next six months – even after war had erupted in Bosnia, Croat and Serb leaders met in Mostar, Banja Luka and Graz. On May 6, in a clandestine meeting at the Graz airport, Karadžić made it clear that the Serbs insisted on a corridor through northern Bosnia in Posavina, the Sava River valley.

> *If they wanted war instead of a negotiating table, let's see what would happen then. And so we liberated almost all of Posavina except Orašje. I told them repeatedly that no solution would be acceptable without a broad corridor in Posavina. We believed then and we believe now that the best boundary is the one naturally formed by the Sava river.*

Karadžić and Boban agreed on some of the maps, but they also left many questions open. The Croats asked for Brčko – which according to the 1991 census was Muslim, Serb, and Croat. "The Serbs refused because they built it and it was completely Serb," Karadžić asserted.

In this war for control of the rivers, Karadžić proposed the Neretva River which runs through Herzegovina as a boundary. But Boban suggested Mostar's main street, Marshal Tito. They pledged to take into account ethnic composition of territory and agreed to accept EC arbitration – if they could not work it out between themselves – for the western region round Kupres and to the north for seven towns in the Posavina.[3]

For Karadžić, the first meeting with Boban was very useful, because he recognized himself: a fellow nationalist in his Croat counterpart. "He was more Croat than Catholic. His idea was to concentrate the Croat population in one part of Bosnia, so that they could protect their ethnicity and not Catholicism."

There were constant contacts between Zagreb and Belgrade. In January 1994, they agreed to open diplomatic offices in each other's capitals. But what was more important were the visits of Croatian ministers to Serbia and even Pale. It was a competition between the Serb-Croat and Muslim-Croat alliance. Croatia continued to pursue two separate and contradictory policies, their secret collusion with the Serbs and their formal alliance with the Muslims. The first gave the two biggest nations the power to determine the fate of the Muslims, but it seemed that Croatia would always be the weaker partner in that alliance. But the second was backed by the United States. In early 1994, the two axes seemed mutually exclusive. By the summer – and the split between Milošević and his brethren in Bosnia – the dynamics had once again shifted.

1 UK, the Netherlands, Denmark, Sweden, Norway, Spain, Canada and France.

2 The agreement for Mostar was actually carried out. Hans Koschnick, former Mayor of Brehmen, became the first EC Mayor of the divided town in 1994.

3 According to participants from both sides. They agreed that the Croats should get the western bank of Mostar and Herzegovina towns, such as Neum, Čapljina, Ljubuški, Široki Brijeg, Posušje, Livno, Tomislavgrad, and even Kupres, which was fifty-one percent Serb before the war. The Serbs did not contest Kreševo, Kiseljak, Fojnica, Busovača, Vitez, Jajce (taken by the Serbs in October 1992), Travnik, Novi Travnik, and Gornji Vakuf. There was no word of the Muslims.

24

A QUESTION OF CONTROL
The Market Square Bomb and the NATO Ultimatum
February 1994

Sarajevo thought that it knew all there was to know about incoming ordnance. But no one thought a single mortar round could take so much life, in an instant. The bomb that dropped out of the sky at 12.37 p.m. on Saturday, February 5, turned a bustling city-center market place, in the shadow of Sarajevo's Catholic Cathedral, into a human abattoir. It killed sixtynine, and left more than 200 wounded.

Why had it sown such havoc? Some survivors said they thought it had struck an overhead plastic canopy on the way down and exploded just above head height, showering the market with thousands of red-hot shards of metal. It was all the more devastating for having been fired on an otherwise peaceful day. It was one of the great tragic ironies of Sarajevo that, frequently, more people were killed on quiet days than on days when the shelling of civilian areas was intense. This was because on quiet days people came out on to the streets. The fifth of February was a bright, sunlit, spring day. The market was packed. The bomb dropped without warning.

Reaction was immediate. President Izetbegović called a news conference within hours and said it was a "black and terrible day. We Bosnians feel condemned to death. Every government which supports the arms embargo against this country is an accomplice to acts of atrocity such as this." The office of Prime Minister Haris Silajdžić, summoned American television news anchorman Peter Jennings, of ABC, for an exclusive face-to-face interview. Izetbegović and Silajdžić – both visibly shaken by the scale of what was dubbed "the market square massacre" – were, that afternoon, using the opportunity it presented to argue that Bosnia was now being pressurized by the international community into accepting a Serb-Croat authored "peace agreement" which had been repackaged by the EU, that was tantamount to complete capitulation, the dismemberment of the Bosnian state, and the dispossession of the country's two million Muslims.

Radovan Karadžić was equally quick off the mark. He denied responsibility (as he always did when civilians were killed in large numbers) and said he had ordered his forces to block all humanitarian aid convoys until UNPROFOR publicly exonerated the Serbs of blame. Only later did he develop a series of hypotheses that the bomb had been planted by "the Muslim side" or fired from "Muslim positions" or, more bizarrely still, that the bodies that were rushed from the market square to the city morgue in the immediate aftermath of the bombing were old bodies that had been planted there for the benefit of the television cameras.

Karadžić's denials always bore fruit. General Lewis MacKenzie had first given credence to the idea that the Bosnian government, as part of a strategy to bring the international community into the war on its side, had taken to bombing its own people. He had first aired this view in May 1992, when a mortar bomb crashed into Vase Miskina street in the city center where a queue of civilians were waiting for bread. Twenty-two people had been killed by that bomb. MacKenzie, who was in Belgrade at the time, because UNPROFOR headquarters had relocated from Sarajevo to the Serbian capital, gave great credence to the view that agents of the Bosnian government had planted the bomb, though no one ever revealed evidence to support the contention. Throughout the war, there was a whispering campaign to spread the notion that the worst atrocities were committed by the Muslims against their own people. The allegation was never made publicly, because this would have required evidence. If there was any evidence, it never came to light. (There were, however, UN reports of shelling by government forces from positions around the Košovo hospital, firing which provoked a Serb response.) The campaign succeeded in sowing seeds of doubt among many who might have been more resolute in their condemnation of the bombardment of Sarajevo.

No one has ever proved who fired the market square mortar. A UNPROFOR crater analysis of the impact site was inconclusive: the trajectory of the missile had been diverted by its impact with the overhead canopy; and, in any case, it is almost impossible to tell from a single impact the direction of fire and the distance travelled. Crater analysis is only accurate when several rounds have been fired from the same position, since then margins of error can be narrowed. The UN would say only that the round came from the northeast, and that both sides had positions in that direction. The common sense observation that if you fire around 500,000 mortar, artillery and tank rounds into a small city over twenty-two months (as the Bosnian Serbs did) – many of these randomly lobbed into civilian areas – sooner or later one will land somewhere where crowds are gathered, was swept away in the ensuing row. A walk down any side street in Sarajevo provides visible evidence that nowhere was safe from the random mortar: the city's streets are pockmarked everywhere with the distinctive splatter of the mortar impact point. The local people called these imprints "Sarajevo roses" – the color of blood. By February 1994, you could barely walk more than a few meters without passing one.

What is more interesting than the sterile debate about who fired the rogue round is the uses to which the UN were able to put the controversy. So great was the anti-air-strikes culture in UNPROFOR that the new commander in

Bosnia, Lt. Gen. Sir Michael Rose, worked without a break for the fifteen days that followed to produce a settlement that would, as he saw it, make airstrikes unnecessary. If there had been the slightest piece of evidence that the Bosnians had committed the market square atrocity, the world would surely have heard all about it. There would have been no surer way to counter the arguments of those (mostly in the US) who pushed for military action in the aftermath of February 5.

One plausible explanation of the market square bombing was that whoever fired it did not deliberately try to kill scores of people by landing it smack in the middle of the most crowded place in town. Mortars are not direct-fire weapons. They are not usually accurate enough to score a direct hit first time. They have to be "walked" toward their target. In any case, the February 5 massacre was different only in scale from what Sarajevo had suffered almost every day for twenty-two months. Its significance lay in its symbolic impact. Nearly 10,000 people had died in Sarajevo as the undisputed victims of Serb bombardment, most of them civilians, and many of them children. The football field in which many of them were buried in rows that were, of necessity, serried became the most potent symbol of Sarajevo's agony and of the city's lost promise: it lay in the shadow of the show-piece Zetra sports stadium, built for the 1984 Winter Olympic Games. There was no controversy about who had killed them. The market square bomb, despite the muddying of the waters by Karadžić's implausible claim that the Muslims had done it to themselves, finally made the international community say "Enough."

It was the manner in which the international community said "Enough" that alarmed Lord Owen. There were calls in every Western capital for NATO planes patrolling the skies above Bosnia to act to deter a repeat of the market square tragedy. The Americans were pushing hard for NATO intervention. They argued that the legal authority to act already existed in the current UN Security Council resolutions. The French, too – uncharacteristically in Owen's view – were pushing for a more interventionist role for NATO. Even the cautious British Foreign Secretary Douglas Hurd – always the first to put the brakes on international intervention – was now bowing to what seemed overwhelming pressure.

Owen's concern was with the Russians. He believed Kozyrev had already shown great flexibility in allowing NATO to police the no-fly zone. The Russians had agreed to this only because the policing was being done under the authority of the UN. NATO was, in this operation, carrying out the UNs' bidding. The Atlantic alliance was not acting independently. The Russians had gone still further: they had agreed that the UN commander in Bosnia should be allowed to call in close air support in defense of his own international forces, should they be attacked. Again, the Russians had conceded this role for NATO only because NATO was able to guarantee that it would act only within the limits set by the UN. Owen knew that what the Russians would not accept was NATO acting outside the auspices of the UN. Yeltsin would not be able to sell that to his own public.

> *It says something for their pragmatism that Kozyrev, Yeltsin and Churkin had all accepted that there was a legitimate role for NATO in helping the UN. So enforcement of the no-fly zone was the first thing. They were ready to accept this, as long as there were UN controls. Then we came into the question of close air support, where the UN commander could call up a NATO plane if the UN troops were under attack. The Russians bought that. So we knew we could carry the Russians with us on NATO helping the UN. What they would never agree to was that the UN would give up control of this procedure.*

Owen believed that independent NATO action would split the international community down an east-west fault line: the Russians would be forced to come to the aid of the Serbs. Much is made of Russia's historic alliance and cultural affinity with the Serbs, but, in fact, for Moscow it was a question of strategic and political interests. Russia refused to allow Washington (and to a lesser extent Europe) to dictate the new terms of conflict resolution and determine the future lines of influence.

Owen feared the world would descend, again, into a new cold war style east-west confrontation. Viktor Andreyev, UNPROFOR's Civil Affairs officer in Sarajevo and a veteran of the Soviet diplomatic service, went further still: he became convinced of the potential for Bosnia to ignite a global conflict. "Make no mistake," he said, "the great powers are aligning over Bosnia."

A former British Foreign Secretary, Owen immediately began a damage-limitation exercise, to try to rein in what he thought was a dangerous momentum toward military intervention. The day after the bombing, as Sarajevo was beginning to bury the first of its dead, Owen flew to Rome and picked up Thorvald Stoltenberg. From there, the two flew to Belgrade. They drove across the Drina into northeastern Bosnia, to the shattered town of Zvornik, for a meeting with Radovan Karadžić. On the way, Owen heard Lt. Gen. Rose speaking on the BBC World Service, giving the impression that the possibility that the bomb had not been fired by the Serbs had not even crossed his mind. "I thought to myself 'Blimey, he better be told a few things', and I made a quick phone call to the Ministry of Defense... I hope the message got across." Karadžić used the meeting in Zvornik to deny responsibility and to stress that the Serbs would respond negatively to any attempt to use force against them. Owen left convinced that any kind of ultimatum would be, as he put it, a "red rag to a bull."

The next day he flew to Brussels to a meeting of the European Union Foreign Ministers where he advised caution. There he argued strongly that NATO should not adopt an independent stance – that it should issue no independent ultimatums, but rather continue to offer action to back up UN initiatives. Owen saw this as the only way of keeping the Russians in the peace process.

There was a flurry of diplomatic exchanges. Lt. Gen. Rose went to Belgrade, and returned to Sarajevo determined to get the Serbs and the Bosnian government to agree to a ceasefire and a weapons withdrawal plan. NATO ambassadors gathered in Brussels for a meeting of the North Atlantic Council, scheduled for Wednesday, February 9. The Americans and the French arrived both pushing for a NATO ultimatum against the Serbs. The night before the scheduled session, the British tried to have the discussion cancelled, by informing their NATO partners that Lt. Gen. Rose was working on a demilitarization agreement and was on the verge of clinching it. A NATO ultimatum, the British argued, would only derail the agreement by infuriating the Serbs, and pushing them into defiance.

The NATO Secretary General Manfred Woerner consulted the other ambassadors, and found that the British were isolated in their opposition to NATO action. As one Western diplomat recalled: "The British representative said there was no need to hold the meeting because Lt. Gen. Rose had an agreement. We checked through our independent sources and found that this was not so. It was obvious that a head of steam was building up. At the meeting itself, after the British attempt to have it cancelled, we were presented with competing paragraphs (for a draft NATO communiqué). The British came up with a version that said to the Serbs, in effect, 'Please behave yourselves', without any threat to enforce this. The British wanted to cede everything to the UN."

On February 9, two crucial meetings took place in parallel. At Sarajevo airport, the commanders of the two armies were brought together by Lt. Gen. Rose; and in Brussels, despite the efforts of Britain, the NATO council meeting went ahead as scheduled.

Lt. Gen. Rose had been working on the Sarajevo airport meeting for days. He had drawn up a Four-Point Plan which he wanted to present to them as, in effect, a non-negotiable *fait accompli*: first an immediate ceasefire; second, the withdrawal of heavy weapons to at least twenty kilometers from Sarajevo, or their surrender to UN control; third, the interpositioning of UN troops between the two front lines at key locations; and fourth the setting up of a joint committee to meet daily to agree the details of the Plan's implementation.

It was not easy. The Serbs initially opposed the Plan. In his meetings with them, in the days running up to February 9, Karadžić told Rose that the

Serbs would agree to placing their weapons under UN inspection, but not UN control. He argued that the Bosnians had superior manpower (which was true) and that the Serbs needed their superior fire power to prevent their front-line positions being over-run by Bosnian infantry. "I told him to get lost," Rose claimed later. "I told them they were now operating in completely changed strategic circumstances, and that inspection was not enough." On the night of the eighth, Rose met the Serb Chief of Staff Manojlo Milovanović, who agreed to Rose's Four Point Plan, and agreed to attend the airport meeting the following day.

Later that evening he met Jovan Divjak, the deputy commander of the Bosnian army. Divjak was a flamboyant and popular officer, but he was not as influential as his rank suggested. The Bosnian Army had two deputy commanders – Divjak, a Serb, and Stjepan Siber, a Croat. Their appointments reflected the desire of the Bosnian Government to maintain at least the appearance of multi-ethnicity in the High Command. Divjak rolled out the red carpet anxious, as he put it, "to show him that the members of the Bosnian Army were militarily, intellectually and culturally on his level because we knew he was a distinguished military figure in the UK. We offered him a military dinner that evening and had a very relaxed conversation. I think we even had a bottle of wine." Rose told Divjak that the Serbs had agreed to withdraw their heavy weapons outside a twenty kilometers' exclusion zone around the city. Divjak promised that the Bosnian Army would attend the meeting at the airport the following day.

But Divjak was getting above himself. He was acting beyond his legitimate authority. Izetbegović had already decided that his government would not attend the meeting. Izetbegović took the view that it was up to the Serbs alone to take action: why should the presence of the Bosnian government be required, when all the onus was on the Serb side? The market square bombing had created an entirely new international climate. The Bosnian government sensed that it was closer than ever to winning international military intervention. Izetbegović feared that Rose was concocting a plan that would undermine NATO's new resolve and produce a compromise that would obviate the necessity for air-strikes. He was right.

Rose waited at the airport. The Serbs arrived, the Bosnians did not. Rose was furious. He was under intense pressure to produce an agreement that would allow the anti-intervention lobby in NATO to argue that the threat of air-strikes alone was enough, and that therefore no ultimatum was necessary. NATO ambassadors were meeting that very day in Brussels, and Rose knew that this was his only real chance of heading off what he thought would be a disaster – the bombing of Serb positions by NATO warplanes while the UN forces under his control were well within range of Serb guns that would be, he believed, used in retaliation.

Rose stormed into town. He went to Divjak's office and demanded to know why the Bosnian army had not honored Divjak's promise of the previous night. Divjak told him the President had over-ridden him. Rose demanded that Divjak take him to the President immediately. President Izetbegović was in the middle of a television interview with CNN, during which he said: "I think that a combination of talks and air-strikes is the only solution – talks alone cannot bring results, no. We need here simultaneous pressure on the aggressor which means one thing – to use force. If there is enough pressure from the world, then they will hand back territory."

Rose interrupted the CNN meeting and told Izetbegović that if he did not order his army command to the airport immediately he would denounce the Bosnian government before the entire world. According to Divjak, "he [Rose] said he would inform the international public that the Bosnian government and army did not want negotiations and that we would be responsible for the continuation of the conflict, and that the Serb side had agreed to negotiate and that we had refused." Menacingly, Rose also hinted that there was no proof that the Serbs had fired the market square bomb. He said the world would not forgive the Bosnians for failing to seize this chance for peace. Izetbegović, chastened and intimidated by the British Lt. Gen., sent his delegation to the airport and issued a grovelling apology for the "misunderstanding."

Within an hour, Rose had the verbal agreement of both sides. Nothing was written down, nothing signed. Rose said he had learned that in the Balkans, signatures were, in any case, worthless. The agreement was communicated to Brussels.

The NATO ambassadors, meanwhile, were drawing up their ultimatum. Britain's reluctance was swept aside by the consensus among the other members. The United States and France led the assault. By the end of the day, NATO had issued a lengthy ultimatum to the Serbs: they were to withdraw their heavy weapons to a distance of twenty kilometers from the city center, or place them under the control of the United Nations. A ten-day deadline was set to achieve this. Any weapons still in place after the expiry of the deadline would be subject to air-strikes by NATO warplanes. The ultimatum was not referred to the United Nations.

Rose now began a race against the clock. He had ten days to implement the Plan, in order to head off air-strikes. From day one, the Serbs responded to the ultimatum defiantly. Karadžić said he would shoot down as many planes as possible – up to forty percent on the first wave, he said. For days, not a single weapon was withdrawn or placed under UN control. A handful of ancient artillery pieces were dragged into Lukavica barracks and unarmed UN military observers were allowed to go and look at them. It was a farcical piece of public relations by the Serbs, which did nothing to meet the terms either of the NATO ultimatum, or of the airport agreement. But Rose's spokesmen appeared daily to declare that progress was being made.

Two days into the ultimatum period, on February 12, the Serbs inserted a new condition: in return for their withdrawal of heavy weapons, the Bosnian Army should withdraw its infantry from their front-line positions. Again this was quite outside the terms of the ultimatum and the airport agreement. The Serbs were playing hardball with NATO. Despite Rose's implausible optimism, NATO appeared to be hurtling towards the first combat action in its history. Sarajevo filled up with international television crews expecting a repeat of the Desert Storm bombing of Baghdad in 1991.

Behind the scenes Rose's staff had entered into intense negotiations with the Serb leadership. Their priority was to persuade the Serbs to do enough to convince NATO that the terms of the ultimatum had been met. Rose's first demand was that the heavy weapons of both sides should be concentrated on the only "neutral" territory in the country – at Sarajevo airport which was controlled by UNPROFOR. The Serbs rejected this. Rose then proposed five locations, which the Serbs considered and then turned down. Finally, as the deadline grew closer, the Serbs were allowed to choose the locations in which their weapons were to be concentrated and placed in UN monitored collection points. They chose eight – five outside the city and three inside. This infuriated the Bosnian government, who said the Serbs had chosen the very strategic heights from which the city had been subjected to bombardment for twenty-two months. Ejup Ganić thumped the table with rage when he saw the map of the locations, and angrily denounced UNPROFOR for colluding with the Serb side to come up with a scheme that would block airstrikes without changing the strategic reality of the siege of Sarajevo.

The ten-day ultimatum period brought the UN into a bitter public dispute with NATO over the definition of the word "control." On February 9, there seemed little doubt about what "control" meant. It did not mean supervision, or monitoring. It meant that UN forces, and not the Serbs, would command use of the weapons. The Serb finger would not only be off the trigger; the trigger would be under UN lock and key. But, early in the ultimatum period, the UN interpretation of what constituted control began to slip. Soon Rose's staff were insisting that the UN did not have to have physical possession of the weapons in order to exercise effective control over them. "There are different methods of control," Lieutenant Colonel Simon Shadbolt said. "You can observe them, you know where they are, you can react immediately. We are quite confident that they will be under our control." This, to the Bosnian government, sounded like the deliberate watering down of the NATO ultimatum by the UN on the ground.

Half-way through the NATO ultimatum period, not a single Serb gun had been handed over to the UN. On February 15, UNPROFOR stopped issuing daily progress reports. "We are no longer in the numbers' game," their spokesman said. "What matters is the overall trend." But the overall trend was clear. The Serbs had no intention of complying. They were going to take NATO to the wire.

Four days before the ultimatum expired, John Major went to Moscow to see Russian President Boris Yeltsin. After their meeting, Yeltsin made public his fury with the US. He said that the West could take no decision in the Balkans without Russia's consent, and expressed his satisfaction that Major agreed with him.

The crucial intervention came the very next day. On February 17 Yeltsin sent a letter to the Bosnian Serb leadership. Delivered by his envoy Churkin, the letter appealed to the Serbs to pull back their heavy weapons. Yeltsin guaranteed that he would send Russian troops to areas from where Bosnian Serbs had withdrawn. After intense negotiations, Karadžić and Mladić accepted his offer and, in effect, complied with the NATO ultimatum. Within hours, the convoys of military vehicles were moving across Serb-held territory regrouping weapons either to be withdrawn altogether or placed in weapons concentration points where the UN could inspect them. Four hundred Russian troops were moved immediately from their base in eastern Slavonia where they had been deployed as part of the original UNPROFOR force in Croatia in 1992. For Karadžić, it was a victory of sorts: "It was very important that Russian troops were dispatched and that no important moves could be made without President Yeltsin." For the Russians, it was a clear diplomatic triumph. Yeltsin had earlier been asked to send Russian troops to Bosnia, but had repeatedly refused. He agreed now when the stakes were higher than they had ever been, thus gaining maximum diplomatic advantage and establishing Russia as a key player in international efforts to end the war. When the Russians arrived in Pale, they were greeted by crowds of cheering Serb civilians as though they were a liberating army.

Rose was not consulted on the deployment of Russian troops. "It's news to me," he said, "but I welcome good troops from whichever country they come." Hours before the expiry of the deadline, as his officers hurried around the Bosnian countryside anxiously checking sites where rogue tanks and artillery pieces were still deployed or "stuck in the snow," Rose declared that, as the crucial hour passed, he fully expected to be in bed, sound asleep. The following day would, he said, be "just another Monday."

The NATO ultimatum was routinely referred to throughout the ten-day period as an ultimatum "to lift the siege of Sarajevo." In fact, it was nothing of the sort. Even as the Serb guns finally fell silent it became clear that the siege would remain as tight as ever. The interpositioning of UN troops along the front line, particularly in the city center, brought the eventual partition of Sarajevo – a key Serb war aim – a step closer. An embryonic green line appeared, policed by international forces. When asked whether the UN was not, in effect, dividing Sarajevo in the way they had divided Cyprus three decades earlier, UNPROFOR spokesman Peter MacFarlane said, without a hint of irony: "But this is only an interim measure, pending an overall settlement." So, of course, was the original UN deployment in Cyprus an interim measure which had become a permanent state of affairs.

Thus did Radovan Karadžić play a bad hand very well. He had been seen, by the international community, to compromise on weapons withdrawal. His guns had fallen silent; the killing in Sarajevo stopped. The partition he so badly wanted was beginning to take real shape, and he did not even have to supply troops to defend the urban frontier of his state – the UN was doing it for him. The Bosnian government felt out-maneuvered and humiliated. Karadžić, incredible though it seemed, had emerged as the principal beneficiary of the NATO ultimatum to use force against him.

But the bombardment did stop. The atmosphere in Sarajevo lightened immensely. People took to the streets again. The trams started to run. Businesses reopened. UNPROFOR opened the new "blue-route" across the airport so that small quantities of commercial goods could come into the city. Prices began to fall. For a time it was possible to believe that the city's agony was ending. It was an illusion. *Oslobodjenje* editor Gordana Knezevic summed up the bewildered mood of the city in this period. "It is as though," she said, "our death sentence has been commuted to life imprisonment. It is hard to feel happy. But we do at least feel relieved, for now."

25

GAINING MORAL GROUND
The Washington Agreement
February 1994

US policy towards Bosnia had run hot and cold since Clinton took office. In reality, there was little Washington could do. The Serbs had seized seventy percent of Bosnia and the Muslims and the Croats were killing each other for the rest. A line had been drawn – the US was unwilling to send troops into Bosnia, and NATO countries with troops on the ground were ambivalent (at best) about the use of air-power. After Vance-Owen, any proposal for ending the war was simply a disguised version of a Serb-Croat partition. The move to restore the Muslim-Croat alliance – and create a Muslim-Croat federation – put an end to their mutual bloodshed and strengthened the Bosnian Government. It came as a surprise.

The establishment of the joint federation was an impressive feat, in particular because it was a graceful diplomatic pirouette in a morass of flat-footed dancers performed by one of the clumsiest – the United States. If this fragile creation survived – and the odds were small – the Muslims would get a new lifeline. It would secure the delivery of humanitarian assistance to isolated Muslim strongholds, and perhaps what was even more attractive to Sarajevo, and pro-interventionists within the Clinton Administration, it would enable the delivery of weapons to the Bosnian army. Croatia would no longer block or skim off half of an arms shipment, only for this "taxation" to be repeated by its kin in Bosnia. Bosnian Government forces would no longer be tied up fighting the Croats – but free to face its Serb foes. It came on the heels of the failed EU action plan – in theory it solved the major problem of access to the sea for the Muslims and gave them a more normal – less disjointed state. US diplomats were pursuing a conflicting two-track policy. Publicly, Redman was negotiating the Owen-Stoltenberg, later EU, plan, yet privately trying to broker a Muslim-Croat federation.[1]

Months before the federation was formally inaugurated at the White House on March 2, 1994, Croatian, Bosnian, but most importantly American diplomats were working behind the scenes to put a deal together. The idea was on the table as early as August 1993. One night over dinner in Zagreb, Charles Redman, Clinton's special envoy, sat flanked by Haris Silajdžić, Bosnian Prime Minister, and Mate Granić, his Croatian counterpart. Redman was struck by the fact that both sides were interested in making a deal. But he said "neither was willing to take the tough steps to make it happen."

For the next six months of efforts there was no breakthrough. The fight-

319

ing between Croats and Muslims just got worse and the two sides became more entrenched. "Both sides always had good excuses. There were plenty of provocations. There were plenty of broken promises," recalled Redman.

Washington began to exert pressure on Zagreb to stop its forces fighting against the Muslims in Bosnia. In several meetings with Tudjman, Redman and Peter Galbraith, US Ambassador to Croatia, stressed that the Americans were committed to the independence and territorial integrity of Croatia. They made it clear that support for a state's territorial integrity was a universal concept which could not be applied to one country of former Yugoslavia and not to another. If Croatia wanted to grab its chunk of Bosnia, then it could forget Washington's backing for Zagreb's quest to assert authority over the nearly one-third of the country under Serb control. By visiting Serb-held parts of Croatia, Galbraith said he "made the point that we understood the nature of the suffering of the Croatian people."

The turning point came in January. Redman had lunch with someone he called a "senior Croat" who explained how Tudjman saw himself in terms of Croatian history. If the president could be persuaded that this agreement would confirm his role in history, then he might take such a step. Redman played on Tudjman's sense of destiny. Redman asked: "where is Croatia going?" The implication was clear. Croatia was being threatened with sanctions.

The Croatian Army had about 30,000 soldiers in Bosnia. Redman laid down the line, either Zagreb behaved or it could end up isolated like its counterpart Serbia. Next came the phone calls.

"It was not, by any stretch, a flurry of telephone calls or high-level pressure," said Redman. "It was enough to know that this initiative had the backing of the President of the United States as well as the European Union. I managed to arrange a few calls or messages to be delivered from key Europeans," he added, apparently referring to Germany, which from the start in 1991 had taken on Croatia as a client.

The US stressed its concern about ongoing atrocities committed against the Muslims by the Bosnian Croats, who – they again stressed – were backed by Zagreb. Galbraith secretly sent someone to visit several camps in Herzegovina. "We got a picture of absolutely appalling conditions in which prisoners were being kept without being fed, and with inadequate shelter, in which there were beatings, and so forth." He suggested that the abuse could be war crimes, and that those responsible for the atrocities might be considered war criminals. He went public with his condemnation of the camps. The threat was clear.

US efforts to persuade the Croatian Government received a boost from within Croatia itself. In Zagreb there were fears that Šušak and his henchmen were calling the shots – that western Herzegovina had taken control over

Croatia. There was also genuine shock that, suddenly, the Croats were seen to be behaving like their foes, the Serbs. Galbraith realized that Zagreb was upset.

> *The Croatian government understood first that this sort of activity was inhumane and wrong, and second, that it was very costly to Croatia in terms of its international reputation, to its relations with Europe and the United States...*
>
> *... there's a strong feeling here that Croatia is a victim of ethnic cleansing and a victim of war crimes.*
>
> *The conduct of the people that the government was supporting in Bosnia was very dangerous for Croatia. It was losing moral ground in this overall conflict.*

An agreement on September 14, 1993, to create a Croat-Muslim federation in Bosnia and then a confederation with Croatia, failed to materialize. Croatian Foreign Minister Mate Granić – who was even described by his adversaries as constructive and patient – and the impassioned Bosnian Prime Minister Silajdžić would reach an agreement, but then it immediately fell apart. Throughout the autumn, Galbraith saw that despite their feverish efforts, the bloodshed, destruction and suffering in this new war had been immense. There was not yet any support for the agreement on the ground.

> *Throughout this period, as they were trying to reach agreement, there would be some new atrocity: a Bosnian Muslim village was slaughtered by the HVO or renegade HVO factions. This would then bring their efforts to build a federation and confederation to a screeching halt.*

But it showed the Clinton Administration that there was room for maneuver. It was enough to convince diplomats that with sufficient pressure – which the US could also exert on the Muslims – a federation was possible. The first step was for the Croatian government to get rid of Boban and his allies. "It was in December of 1993," said Galbraith, "that I was informed that Mate Boban would be taking, as it was put to me, a long vacation."

For the US diplomats, making it public that Boban and his cronies did not enjoy the support of most Bosnian Croats was an important element in garnering support in Croatia. Within Bosnia, however, Mate Boban and his crew held the power. For Ivo Komšić, a long-time Bosnian Croat politician, the balance of the Croats' future in Bosnia hung on a Muslim-Croat alliance. Nearly two-thirds of Bosnia's Croats lived beyond the frontiers of Boban's Croat mini-state and did not identify with it at all. Komšić tried to undermine Boban by constantly meeting with Tudjman – fostering his relations with

Zagreb. In early February, Komšić presented his Plan to a Sabor, an assembly of eminent Croats from the diaspora and former Yugoslavia who gathered in Sarajevo. Distressed by the disastrous state of affairs in Bosnia-Herzegovina (and the fact that if the war continued there would be no Croats left anywhere but western Herzegovina), the Sabor approved the Plan.

During the NATO ultimatum – after the market square bombing on February 5 – for the Serbs to withdraw their artillery from around Sarajevo, the United States was trying to push together Muslims and Croats who, for the time being at least, were sworn enemies. Another ultimatum, this one from the United Nations, was aimed at bringing Croatia to heel. On February 3, the Security Council set a two-week deadline for Croatia to pull its regular Army troops out of Bosnia or face the consequences. The threat was that Croatia would join Serbia under UN sanctions and world isolation.

The apparent success of the NATO ultimatum round Sarajevo had given the international community new resolve. On February 16, Redman and Galbraith urged Tudjman to abandon the idea of a Croat statelet in Bosnia. They asked him to reconsider the proposal to create a federation – and finally a confederation. In return, the US promised to help (and hasten) Croatia's economic, political and military integration into the West.

By coincidence that night, Galbraith had already been scheduled to give a speech to the general public. His message was: Croatia has a choice of joining the West economically and politically or sharing Serbia's destiny – isolation, economic collapse, and never-ending warfare. Croatia could not expect international support "for Serb withdrawal from Croatia" when its Army remained in Bosnia-Herzegovina. The world community would no longer expend "vast resources to uphold Croatia's frontiers when it seeks to violate those of another country."[2]

The Croatian Foreign Ministry lost no time in summoning Galbraith. The leadership had been considering the proposals put forward by Ambassador Redman. It was the breakthrough everyone was seeking.

The entire agreement remained in the air until the parties went to Washington. "I finally decided that the best way to do this was to get all of the parties and focus them on what was at stake. The negotiations were carried out in a different way – it was very intensive," said Redman. In Washington, there was not a single face-to-face meeting between the two delegations. Redman and Galbraith would discuss the document with the Croats, then join Victor Jackovich, Ambassador to Bosnia-Herzegovina with the Bosnian delegation in the next room. For the US, said Galbraith, once the parties were there, even if in separate rooms, it was important to keep them there until they completed the job.

"It was an unlikely victory for Washington," said Silajdžić. "Mr. Redman and his aides were shuttling between us. This was the way the things were sorted out – quite efficiently. I was really surprised by the speed in which American diplomacy understood that this was a good idea and that the project was viable."

Over the next four days, they negotiated the draft agreement based on Komšić's proposal to create cantons. With a stroke of the pen, the Muslim and Croat mini-states virtually disappeared.

In the next year Tudjman exerted pressure on his proxies. It was the height of absurdity. Those very politicians who had advocated carving up Bosnia now spoke out in favor of a common state with the Muslims. It was not convincing, but as long as it remained together it would be an important element of any settlement – strengthening the Muslims even if the federation did not function as envisaged. By the one-year anniversary – celebrated in Washington with the conspicuous absence of Izetbegović – few of the major elements of the Federation (and none of the Confederation) had yet been implemented. There was, however, no fighting between the two sides and there had even been a handful of joint military operations against the Serbs. The Muslims had used the four-month ceasefire from New Year's Day, 1995, to get a limited amount of arms. Croatia, and by virtue of this, the Bosnian Croats, let weapons through. The agreement continued to depend on the support of Washington and its ability to persist in exerting pressure on both sides, so that they could see the benefits of the alliance.

1 The Owen-Stoltenberg Plan, repackaged as the EU Action Plan, collapsed in February 1994. By then the Muslims had been given nearly 33.6 percent of Bosnia. All that was needed was an additional one percent of land in western and eastern Bosnia. In an interview, Milošević expressed regret that he had not been able to persuade his Bosnian proxies to agree to the proposal, saying it was a lost chance for peace.

2 It warrants mentioning that, strictly speaking, the stated aim of the international community was not to secure Serb withdrawal from Croatia and that the UN force had not been originally deployed to uphold Croatia's frontiers.

26

TO THE MOGADISHU LINE
The Battle for Goražde
April 1994

Spring 1994 brought unexpected new hope. In the aftermath of the NATO ultimatum that had silenced the guns around Sarajevo, the US and Russia between them took control of the peace process – the US, on the back of their success in brokering the Muslim-Croat Washington Agreement; Russia after pulling off the deal that persuaded Karadžić to place his heavy weapons in and around the capital under UN collection sites. Lord Owen and Thorvald Stoltenberg, adrift since their fruitless endeavors on board HMS *Invincible*, were now side-lined. The great powers of a world that was still, despite the ending of the Cold War, stubbornly bipolar, had aligned over Bosnia. The American envoy, Charles Redman, and his Russian counterpart, the Deputy Foreign Minister Vitaly Churkin, united in their determination not to let Bosnia create a new east-west division of Europe.

By the end of March, Redman and Churkin were convinced that a comprehensive peace settlement was within their grasp. They believed they could extend the Sarajevo model to the republic as a whole: a cessation of hostilities; the interpositioning of UN troops; withdrawal of heavy weapons. They were convinced that the positions of both sides were converging. Churkin returned to Belgrade to take advantage of the momentum for peace that the Washington agreement and the NATO ultimatum had created.

> *The big goal for me when I returned to Belgrade in early April was to try to arrange, not just a ceasefire, but a complete cessation of hostilities, something along the lines of what had been achieved in Croatia, the cessation of hostilities, and the interpositioning of UN troops. I think we really did have a chance. But the moment I got to Belgrade things started to go wrong. When I walked into our embassy in Belgrade, Ambassador Redman was on the phone. He told me that Goražde had just been bombed.*

Of the three eastern enclaves,[1] Goražde was always going to be the toughest nut for the Serbs to crack. It was by far the largest of the three, and the Bosnian defenders of the city had been better armed and supplied than elsewhere. They had been a constant source of danger for the Bosnian Serbs, launching raids from inside the pocket well into Serb territory and, from time to time, inflicting heavy losses on the Serb besiegers.

Goražde was also by far the most strategically important of the three. It straddled the main road between two large Serb-held towns in the Drina valley – Višegrad and Foča. Both had had Muslim majorities before 1992, but had been "cleansed" with efficiency and little military effort at the start of the war. In Goražde the local Muslims had held out. The enclave now separated two chunks of Serb-held territory, making communication between them difficult, dangerous, and sometimes impossible without crossing into neighboring Montenegro. Furthermore, Serbs had identified Goražde as the link through which Sarajevo would forge a land-bridge to Sandžak, a Muslim-populated region of southern Serbia and Montenegro, and, from there, to Turkey. The "green transversal" as the ideologues of greater Serbia called it, would be the landlink through which Muslims would push an Islamic arrowhead into the heart of Europe.

Nor had the enclave been completely cut off from the rest of government-held Bosnia. For the first fifteen months of the war, Bosnian troops – and thousands of civilians – had been able to move in and out of the town by walking, over the mountains, under cover of darkness, through Serb lines. It was a dangerous journey. But it was undertaken frequently. Throughout 1992 and part of 1993, a regular mule train had been driven in and out of the enclave from a base camp at Grebak, near Trnovo. Soldiers and civilians carried food, medical supplies, small arms and ammunition along this route and, though the risk was great, kept the enclave alive.[2] When the Serb assault on Goražde began in early April, UNPROFOR officials played it down, dismissing it as a diversionary tactic to pull Bosnian troops away from other more important battle areas. Lord Owen thought differently:

> *We were in private discussions with Krajišnik and Koljević in Paris when it was building up and we were under no illusion that the Serbs were serious about taking Goražde. And I never doubted that they were after Goražde. It was a strategic imperative, almost, for them.*

The battle for Goražde began over the construction of a by-pass. Bosnian Serbs had been building a new road to make communications between their disparate chunks of territory safer. The construction work had been hampered by Bosnian Army raids from inside the enclave. Ironically it may have been the speed at which the peace process was moving that encouraged General Mladić to act when he did. He had, uncharacteristically, taken his eye off the ball after the suicide, in Belgrade, of his only daughter. When he returned to Pale after her funeral, he learned that a comprehensive settlement that would have frozen existing lines of confrontation, appeared imminent. The outstanding question of Goražde would have to be settled before that happened.

During the first week in April the Serb offensive gathered pace. At first

325

it looked like a re-run of the defeat of Srebrenica twelve months earlier –
Serb forces closing the noose around the town, drawing closer by the day,
sending thousands of refugees fleeing from outlying villages to seek shelter
in the town itself. But there were two important differences. First,
Goražde, unlike Srebrenica a year earlier, was – in name at least – a United
Nations "safe area" and could claim protection under successive UN resolutions. And second, the precedent of Sarajevo had shown how effective
the threat of air-strikes could be.

Rose was against air-strikes. He thought them inconsistent with his role as
Commander of a peacekeeping force. He argued that frequent resort to air-
strikes would push UNPROFOR from peacekeeping to peace-enforcement.
Peace-enforcement involved aligning oneself with one side in the conflict.
Peacekeeping required strict neutrality. It was not the job of a peacekeeping
force to intervene to alter the course of the war in favor of one side. Frequent
use of air-strikes would turn NATO, in effect, into the Bosnian Air Force and
fatally compromise UNPROFOR's neutrality. "You cannot," he was fond of
saying, "fight a war from white-painted vehicles." He was frequently at pains
to point out that he did not oppose military intervention in principle: as a soldier he took no position on it. But he insisted that if the international community opted to enter the war on the Bosnian side, it should pull UNPRO-
FOR out and replace it with a force capable of fighting a war. His staff officers joked that NATO had a supply of green camouflage paint standing by
for the day when the mandate would change. He called the fine line between
peacekeeping and peace-enforcement, between white vehicles and green,
the "Mogadishu Line," after the disastrous consequences of United States'
efforts to impose a peace settlement in Somalia. In April, under immense
international pressure, he almost crossed it.

Rose played down the seriousness of the Serb attack on Goražde: "Our
own judgement was that the Bosnian Serbs were putting pressure at the tactical level and had no serious intention of taking the pocket," he said. His
spokesmen, in early April, gave daily press briefings designed to take the
alarm out of Bosnian government claims of dozens dead and an imminent
humanitarian disaster. Rose did not want what he considered a little local difficulty derailing a peace plan which he believed was closer than ever to
achieving a lasting solution.

But his own UN military observers in Goražde, together with their
UNHCR colleagues, revolted. On April 7, a leaked document revealed that
the accounts they had been sending to Rose's headquarters were sharply at
odds with the account Rose was presenting to the public. US Chief-of-Staff,
General John Shalikashvili had publicly ruled out a repeat of a Sarajevo-style
ultimatum, arguing that the weaponry around Goražde could not be located
with sufficient accuracy to make air-strikes practical. General Mladić

behaved as though this were the green light he had been waiting for. The Serb bombardment and advance sharply escalated. The UN monitors sent an urgent appeal to Sarajevo. "The death toll continues to rise and serious losses of territory are occurring. If this is 'not serious,' as UNPROFOR seems to say in radio reports, I hope I don't see a serious situation develop," one monitor reported. "The situation today is again very serious. We have repeated that our assessment of the situation is serious and that the continued potential for loss of civilian life is very high," the report went on.

It is very disquieting to hear radio reports from the international media that the situation is not serious. From the BBC World Service news of April 5 we heard 'An UNPROFOR assessment said that it was a minor attack into a limited area'. We again do not concur with that position. It is a grave situation. It needs to be realized that the city center of Goražde is just over 3km from the Bosnian Serb army front line. Looking at a small land mass on the southeast corner and saying it is a minor attack into a limited area is a bad assessment, incorrect and shows absolutely no understanding of what is going on here.

The UNHCR, who also had representatives in the town, reported that a ten-day Serb assault had killed sixty-seven people and wounded 325, most of them civilians.

So unconcerned was Rose about the consequences of the Goražde assault that, on April 10, he was on his way to Brussels to address a NATO meeting. "When I heard in Split that in fact an attack had been launched with tanks from three different directions into the Goražde pocket, of course, I flew straight back."

Rose warned Mladić, by phone and by fax, to stop the attacks on Goražde, or face NATO action. The attacks continued. After seeking and being granted approval from the UN Secretary General's special envoy, Yusushi Akashi, Rose stepped on to the balcony of his first-floor office in the Sarajevo Delegates' Club, and, through an open window overlooking a communications cabin one floor below, he gave the order that led to the first NATO ground assault in the forty-seven year history of the organization. At 1622 GMT, two United States Air Force F16s dropped three bombs on a Serb artillery command bunker. The attacks continued as though nothing had happened. The next day, Rose ordered a second wave of air-strikes. At 1224 GMT, on Monday April 11, two US Marine Corp F/A-18 Hornets dropped three more bombs on a group of tanks and armored personnel carriers that had been firing directly into Goražde. Three APCs and a truck were destroyed. Both sets of air-strikes were directed from the ground by eight British forward air controllers whom Rose had sent to Goražde under the guise of United Nations Military Observers. They were, in fact, all men of the British Special Air Service (SAS).

What were the air-strikes meant to achieve? Rose justified the action on the grounds that Security Council resolution 836 authorized action to deter further attack, rather than to defend a territory or protect its citizens.

> *There was enormous pressure in the international community to indulge in air-strikes rather than in the sort of deterrent activity that we were engaged in. This was of course something I was resisting strongly because that would bring us in a state of war here with the Bosnian Serb Army when we were in fact here trying to stop the fighting, stabilize the situation.*

But the air-strikes did not deter. The guns stopped momentarily. But NATO's pin-prick assaults did nothing to diminish the military muscle at Mladić's disposal. It left his army intact and strengthened his resolve to continue the assault. Mladić telephoned Rose and screamed down the line for twenty minutes, threatening that no UN official would leave Serb territory alive. Mladić then implemented the plan he had prepared the previous August when air strikes were first threatened against Serb forces seizing Mount Igman on the southwestern edge of Sarajevo: he rounded up 150 UN personnel and held them hostage, while his forces in the north of the republic launched a reprisal artillery and mortar attack against the government-held city of Tuzla. Karadžić visited Mladić on the front line at Goražde and, while their forces regrouped to continue their assault, the two men, undeterred, ostentatiously played chess. If it had been Rose's intention to discredit the very idea of air-strikes he could scarcely have carried it off more effectively. Around the world those who had cautioned against military intervention from the beginning uttered a satisfied: "We told you so."

The Russians, who had not been consulted, now set out to make sure that NATO would not act independently again. To them, air-strikes, however minimal, threatened to broaden the conflict. Vitaly Churkin made his way to Pale.

> *It was a very dangerous thing. If NATO had reacted in the way that they were urged to by the Bosnian Government, if they went into some massive bombing in the Goražde area, or of the Bosnian Serb positions, there would have been all-out war with the UN and NATO participating in it. And, of course, I was also worrying about reaction back home, which could have gone the wrong way and then we would have had an international crisis on our hands. I never thought we were about to go into World War Three literally, but into major political strains, and a political crisis with long-term adverse repercussions.*

Churkin believed that if the western alliance entered the war on the side of the Bosnian government, calls among Russian nationalists to rise to the defense of the Serbs would become unanswerable. Bosnia threatened to plunge the world into a new east-west global stand-off.

On April 15 the Serbs began their final assault. The Bosnian defenses collapsed so quickly that two British SAS men found themselves suddenly on the front line. Both were injured, one critically. Their colleagues informed Rose in Sarajevo, and requested an urgent medical evacuation. Rose called for close air support, which UN Security Council resolutions authorized in defense of UN personnel. But the request had to be authorized by Yasushi Akashi, who was in Pale, meeting Karadžić. Rose telephoned Pale and found Akashi settling into a late lunch with Karadžić. Their conversation was taped and later made public.

"We need air support now," Rose told him.

"How about Dr. Karadžić ordering an immediate ceasefire allowing immediate evacuation of our people?" Akashi replied.

"By the time the message gets to the units on the ground they will all be either dead or captured," an exasperated Rose responded. "We've got casualties, we've got to use Blue Sword [close air support] to get them out. Otherwise they'll all be killed."

Akashi asked Karadžić what was going on at the Goražde front. Karadžić contacted Mladić on another line. Mladić said that if the British soldiers had been injured they must have strayed from their stated positions. "Mr. President," Mladić said. "Do you believe them and not me? I am telling you the truth and they are lying." Karadžić, now highly agitated, turned to Akashi and said "They were on the front line! What were they doing on the front line? They are not supposed to be there." Akashi overruled Rose's request for close air support.

The wounded men had not strayed from their declared positions. They had simply been overtaken by the pace of the battle. As Rose later learned: "The line collapsed so fast that they found themselves right there. The front line went past them without them knowing it."

On April 16, the Serbs announced that they had captured the strategic heights around Goražde. As they had done with Srebrenica a year earlier, they now held Goražde in the palm of their hand. They were at the very gates of the town, and their attack continued. In the afternoon, Rose again requested close air support. This time Akashi agreed. NATO aircraft took to the skies. But the weather was poor. They had to make more than one pass before they could accurately identify their targets. A British Sea Harrier jet was struck by a surface-to-air missile. The pilot ejected safely, and the plane crashed in flames. The mission was abandoned.

In Pale, Churkin grew increasingly alarmed at the escalation this represented. Karadžić had disappeared; he had gone to Banja Luka, which was twelve hours away by road, and could not be reached on the phone. The most senior Bosnian Serb leader in town was Momčilo Krajišnik, the speaker of parliament. Churkin said Krajišnik seemed reluctant to take responsibility for anything. Churkin phoned Milošević in despair. "Do I have to take on the job of President of Republika Srpska personally?" he asked the Serbian President. Churkin's concern was that NATO would respond to the downing of the British jet with further air-strikes.

> *When the shooting down of the British aircraft happened, frantic reports started coming in... I don't know whether this was true or not but we heard that something like thirty NATO aircraft were circling around Goražde and that they were about to do a lot of bombing.*
>
> *The question I had in my mind was what can I do? I had some very vigorous conversations with Milošević, and with the most senior person among the Bosnian Serbs here, Mr. Krajišnik. I was also on the phone with Mr. Akashi in Sarajevo and there was an arrangement which was worked out by which the planes would be ordered away from Goražde, and there will be no bombing.*

Churkin persuaded Akashi to call off the air-strikes. In return, Krajišnik promised three things: to stop the shelling; to pull back Serb forces to a distance of three kilometers from the town center; and to release the 150 or so UN personnel who had been taken hostage after the first air-strikes. The agreement was reached in the early evening, and was due to take immediate effect. Talks would resume in the morning.

None of the promises was honored. The next morning, Karadžić returned from Banja Luka. Yasushi Akashi returned to Pale from Sarajevo. Vitaly Churkin now found himself mediating not between the Serbs and the Bosnian government, but, bizarrely, between the Serbs and the international community. It was a measure of the extent to which the United Nations and NATO were identified in Karadžić's mind with support for the "Muslim side."

Karadžić's behavior infuriated Churkin, who later recalled:

> *They gave me this promise of three things they would do. They had not released anybody. They had not pulled back a single inch from where they were standing. And the shelling continued.*
>
> *Karadžić was procrastinating. After about two or three hours, it became clear to me that for reasons of his own he didn't want to come to any kind of agreement. So I told him of the opportunities that were being missed, including the opportunity to have sanctions lifted and I walked out of the meeting.*

Akashi, on the other hand, was more accommodating. He was anxious to grasp at any straw that he could present as a sign of "progress." Churkin continues:

> *And Mr. Akashi said 'Well why can't we at least have medical evacuation?' and Karadžić very eagerly said 'Oh yes, oh yes, let's make that announcement!' He understood that something positive needed to be announced and he walked to the waiting press people, and Dr. Karadžić invited me also to join them. But I didn't want to join them. And after their little press conference some journalists came over to me and asked me some questions and I didn't mean to say this, but I did... I said I was very disappointed because I had heard more broken promises in one weekend than I had heard in all my life. Much more should have been accomplished.*

It was vintage Akashi. He told the waiting journalists:

> *President Karadžić and I agreed that all sides should restrain themselves to the maximum from all offensive activities. In the meantime we shall review the talks and try to sign an agreement as soon as possible in order to stabilize the situation. President Karadžić agreed to an urgent evacuation of humanitarian personnel and population from Goražde. UNPROFOR is ready to do so tomorrow morning at 0800.*

That day, Bosnian Serb troops and armored vehicles entered and occupied the town on the right bank of the Drina. The shelling continued unabated.

Lt. Gen. Rose secretly ordered his SAS men to leave the town, on foot, undetected, in the middle of the night. The air-strikes had blown their cover. The Bosnian Serbs knew their true identity, not least because the Americans had released video tape of the air-strikes to the television networks on which the voice of the forward air controllers could be heard, in unmistakable south of England accents, directing the attacks. The international aid workers woke the next morning to find themselves – as they saw it – "abandoned" by Rose's men. The Mayor of Goražde, Ismet Briga, is said to have burst into tears when he learned that the SAS men had gone. The international aid workers were later evacuated by helicopter with, of course, the willing cooperation of the Bosnian Serbs. Goražde was being left to its fate.

In desperation, President Izetbegović wrote to Boutros Boutros-Ghali holding him personally responsible for the fate of the enclave:

> *The so-called safe area has become the most unsafe place in the world. The organization which you are heading proclaimed the free territory of Goražde a UN protected area almost a year ago. Security Council Resolutions 824 and 836 refer to this protected zone, but they have remained only empty*

phrases. Neither you nor your personnel have done anything to use the mandate of all those resolutions to protect the people of Goražde and the credibility of the United Nations. The result is obviously tragic. Secretary-General, my people hold you responsible for this situation. This country is bleeding, and there is not much room for diplomatic hesitation. If Goražde falls, I think that a sense of moral responsibility would command you to leave the post of UN Secretary General. This is the least you can do.

Under intense pressure from the Americans and from the NATO Secretary General Manfred Woerner, Boutros Boutros-Ghali asked NATO to use its air power to deter further attack. The NATO Council met in Brussels. It was almost paralyzed by internal division, with the Americans pushing for air-strikes and the British arguing that this was incompatible with the existing UNPROFOR mandate. US diplomats were contemptuous of the British position – which one US diplomat privately described as "really wet." The British chided the Americans for lacking the courage to put troops on the ground. The North Atlantic alliance – not to mention the so-called "Special Relationship" between Britain and the US – was under strain as never before. The Council announced that it would take "some days" before a response could be made to Boutros Boutros-Ghali's request.

On April 19 a gang of about fifty Bosnian Serbs stormed a UN-controlled weapons collection point inside the Sarajevo exclusion zone, at Lukavica barracks. It was one of the locations designated by the February 9 Sarajevo ceasefire agreement. They seized eighteen anti-aircraft guns while United Nations monitors, under whose "control" the weapons had been placed as part of the implementation of the Sarajevo ceasefire agreement, looked on helplessly. Mladić seemed to be reveling in humiliating and defying the entire Western world. By April 20, the death toll, according to international aid workers, had risen to 313 with more than a thousand wounded, in less than three weeks, though Bosnian government sources put the figure much higher. President Clinton again demanded more resolute action by NATO.

NATO reached an internal compromise, but one which, nonetheless, infuriated the British. It issued an ultimatum to the Serbs warning them that they would face further air-strikes unless they fulfilled three conditions: an immediate ceasefire; a pull-back of troops to a distance of three kilometers from the town center by the morning of Saturday April 23; and a withdrawal of heavy weaponry to a distance of twenty kilometers by the evening of Tuesday April 26. The British bowed to pressure in the interests of NATO unity; but they protested that the ultimatum set a dangerous precedent that went beyond even that concerning Sarajevo in February. It required, for the first time, action only by the Serbs; it was directed, explicitly, against one side. The Sarajevo ultimatum, issued on February 9, had required both sides to submit their heavy weapons to UNPROFOR control. To the British, who had from the beginning treated all sides equally, regardless of the role each side was playing in the war, this new ultimatum was, for the first time, singling the Serbs out as the enemy. It strained Anglo-American relations still further.

As the bombardment of Goražde continued, Yasushi Akashi went to Belgrade determined, once again, to "announce something positive" to prevent NATO carrying out its threat. The United Nations Under Secretary Shashi Tharoor later remembered:

We were of course conscious of a great amount of pressure on the part of certain NATO member states and of course of the NATO Secretary General, to see air action. Our concern was in making the judgement as to whether that was necessary, whether indeed there was a peaceful way out...

On Saturday 23, NATO southern Europe Commander, Admiral Leighton Smith, contacted Akashi to ask him to authorize air-strikes on the grounds that the Serbs had not met condition one of the NATO ultimatum – there was no ceasefire. Akashi refused on the grounds that there was evidence that the Serbs had begun to implement condition two, the pull-back of heavy weapons (even though the deadline by which this should have been completed had already passed). Akashi told Smith to give the Serbs more time. At the same time, Rose dispatched a company of 150 Ukrainians to Goražde.

Smith reported this to Woerner, who, furious that the credibility of NATO had been so compromised, intervened personally. He repeatedly called Akashi in Belgrade. Akashi, in meetings with Serb leaders, had made himself unavailable to come to the phone. The next day, he announced that the Bosnian Serbs had agreed to a ceasefire around Sarajevo, and a pull-back of troops to a distance of three kilometers. The Ukrainian troops made it into Goražde without difficulty and were due to be followed by a company from each of the French and British battalions. As they lined up on the tarmac at Sarajevo airport ready to depart, the French, who were supposed to command the operation, were suddenly ordered to turn around and go back to barracks. Over the head of the UN Force Commander they had been ordered by the French Defense Ministry, meeting in Paris, not to proceed. Rose appeared not even to be in command of his own multinational force.

The British and Ukrainians administered an agreement similar to that that had been carried out in Srebrenica the year before: demilitarization of the pocket, ceasefire monitoring and the interpositioning of UN troops between the Serb front line and the battered town.

A peace of sorts descended, though again, only after General Mladić had substantially achieved what he wanted. It is questionable whether he ever intended to take the town itself – with the single exception of a munitions factory on the East bank of the River Drina which despite Mladić's efforts remained in Muslim hands. Urban infantry had always proved costly and drawn out for any side in the Yugoslav wars. From his point of view it was sufficient to have the three enclaves encircled and, by and large, tamed. They could be traded in the future, as part of some overall settlement.

The end of the Goražde affair left unresolved the dispute that had so nearly torn the NATO alliance down the middle. The British and French announced that if the Americans continued to push for the policy known as "lift and strike," they would withdraw their ground troops. They spent the months that followed persuading the Americans that they were serious, by drawing up detailed contingency plans for an emergency withdrawal.

The whole sorry episode not only pointed up divisions within the international community. It isolated the Bosnian Serbs from their natural allies the Russians, and from their original patrons in Belgrade. Milošević, who had, before the attacks on Goražde began, sensed that with Russian help he was on the verge of clinching a deal that would have led to the lifting of sanctions, was furious with Karadžić. Milošević told Churkin that Karadžić had kept him in the dark about events in Goražde. Lord Owen said later that the Goražde crisis had driven the two rival Serb leaders further apart than ever:

> For me the main thing about Goražde was the total perfidy of the Bosnian Serbs toward Churkin and Milošević. I believe that relations between Karadžić and Milošević were never the same after Goražde. They were shown up to be bare-faced liars, all the time saying they weren't after Goražde when they were.
>
> They lost the support of the Russians for quite a while after that. Which they deserved. It was outrageous what happened over Goražde.

The Bosnian government drew a lesson too. Air strikes – the holy grail of Sarajevo's war policy – had come and gone with no effect on the course of the war. Izetbegović was, by now resigned to a long war. "We too will go for all or nothing," he told a crowd in Sarajevo at the height of the Goražde crisis. "We have learned our lesson. And the lesson is: we have to be strong because in this world only force is respected."

1 The other two, Srebrenica and Žepa, much smaller, were overrun in July 1995.
2 Trnovo fell to a Serb offensive in the summer of 1993, and the regular mule train into Goražde ceased.

27

"A DAGGER IN THE BACK"
The Serbian Split
June 1994

At first when Belgrade announced an embargo against Bosnian Serb leaders, it seemed another Machiavellian maneuver by Milošević to hood-
wink the international community.

Looking into the future Milošević realized he had little choice but to
endorse a new international Peace Plan. After two years of isolation and rising
economic deprivations, Serbia was paying a steep price for its support of the
wars in Croatia and Bosnia. By backing the Plan, Milošević hoped he could
secure the lifting of sanctions and end Serbia's isolation. It would also give
momentum to his efforts to get rid of Radovan Karadžić.

For a year, since Karadžić had rejected the Vance-Owen Plan, Milošević had
been quietly preparing the ground for a split with his brethren in Bosnia.
Under Milošević's tight control, the Serbian media began to cast Karadžić in a
different light. Less often was he depicted as a Serbian patriot, instead there
were hints that he was involved in money-laundering and war-profiteering.

Milošević was abandoning his nationalist rhetoric which had made him the
most powerful leader across former Yugoslavia. The Bosnian Serb leaders
now stood for everything Milošević no longer did – the Serbian Orthodox
Church, the Chetniks, and the other trappings of Serbian nationalism. Serbia
began to observe forgotten Communist holidays while "Republika Srpska"
celebrated traditional ones.

By trying to get rid of his rival, Milošević wanted to find a scapegoat who
could be blamed for the murder and destruction, the poverty and uncertainty.
Otherwise he realized, his rule could be cut short.

The ultimatum to the warring parties to accept the Plan put forward by
the Contact Group (comprised of the United Kingdom, Russia, France,
Germany and the United States) came a bit too early for Milošević. He ended
up having to rush the job; he would rather have slowly engineered Karadžić's
fall behind the scenes. After all, he did not want Serbs to see him as the executioner of Radovan Karadžić, who in their eyes was a hero. He wanted to
expose Karadžić as a power-hungry bloodthirsty gambler, and then make him
disappear from the political scene. In a land obsessed by its past, Milošević
did not want to be seen as a traitor in Serbian epics.

This time it would radically differ from May 1993, when Bosnian Serb
leaders spurned Milošević's efforts to promote the Vance-Owen Plan. At that
time the embargo he had threatened then was abandoned within days of

being announced. The first public warning came on June 7 from the President of the remnants of Yugoslavia, Zoran Lilić, whose remarks carried weight since he took his instructions from Milošević. It was only a hint of what lay in store for the Bosnian Serbs. He said: "ten million citizens of Yugoslavia cannot be held hostage to any leader who came from the territory of Yugoslavia, neither Republika Srpska nor Republika Srpska Krajina," in reference to the Bosnian Serb "state" and its counterpart in Croatia. In other words, Karadžić had no right to call the shots – only Milošević.

The Serbian President was convinced that it would take just a few days for the Bosnian Serbs to come to their senses. He boasted to diplomats, "Those who have confronted me have not long survived." But they did, so day by day, month by month, Belgrade turned up the heat trying to break the leadership of the Bosnian Serbs. While Milošević's influence over the Bosnian Serb leaders had evaporated, his ties with the military remained close, at the very least since Bosnian Serb officers were still on Belgrade's payrolls. Even though Karadžić's regime grew increasingly paranoid and isolated, a year later he remained in power, the first Milošević opponent to do so.

In the aftermath of the Goražde crisis, the international peace process was revived after more than a year, appearing in a different guise called the Contact Group. Owen, the EU mediator, said the new formation was necessary to involve all the interested foreign parties – in particular Russia and the US. Otherwise a settlement would never be reached, much less implemented. "You had to find a way where the Americans were involved in the nitty-gritty of negotiations and in dirtying their hands in a settlement which they then had to go out and support." He was right. The main protagonists had cleverly exploited divisions within the "international community" – the Serbs played the Russian card, or banked on the UK's reticence to lift the arms embargo, whereas the Muslim-led Bosnian government held out for a better deal in the conviction that time was on its side, in particular because of American support.

The Contact Group was reminiscent of nineteenth-century Great Power politics. The five nations gathered to dictate the future of former Yugoslavia – seeming to believe that the war-torn state was far from their borders and not bothering to conceal their wish that the problem would just go away. Its faltering start laid bare the post-Cold-War emptiness – the lack of leadership and political vision. Talks on Bosnia were more exercises in regulating relations among the Contact Group members and positioning themselves in the new political order than about the region or its inhabitants.

At a time of disunity, it was an attempt to coordinate divergent views and then present one international face to the warring parties. This proved difficult and, at times, impossible. In the months after the Plan was crafted, divisions within the Group were so deep that whatever steps were announced usually represented the minimum common denominator, packaged as a new initiative. Meeting after meeting, the Contact Group issued statements boasting that its unity was preserved.

Bosnia's main protagonists all complained about this new "second-rate" creation. The Bosnian Serbs wondered aloud why they should listen to lowly clerks, or bow to the will of this "world-wide mafia." Ejup Ganić of the Bosnian government was taken aback by their lack of knowledge about the region.

We sat with the new people from the Contact Group over the map. Some of them were trying to find Banja Luka in Romania. They had started from scratch and did not know anything. They did not know who lived where ... First we talked with the foreign ministers, then to their assistants and finally to their minions.

But the US envoy Redman and his Russian opposite number, Churkin, were old hands. They called the shots. The Group immediately started hammering out the new details of a Peace Plan, which preserved Bosnia-Herzegovina within its internationally recognized frontiers. It earmarked fifty-one percent of Bosnia for the Muslim-Croat federation and the rest for the Serbs. The Serbs would have to hand over about a third of the seventy percent of land they currently controlled. The Muslim-Croat federation made it possible to give Sarajevo a better deal. This Plan envisaged bigger chunks of contiguous territory under the Federation's control.

By late June, the maps were finished. But they were kept under tight wraps. The parties were not allowed to see them. Karadžić, jittery about what punishment Milošević had dreamed up for him, announced he "would endorse the maps if they were in the slightest bit acceptable, out of love for our brothers in Serbia and Montenegro. But on the condition that sanctions on Belgrade were lifted." This became the new Serb chorus: sanctions first, and then peace. By contrast, the mediators insisted first on peace – then the lifting of sanctions. On June 30, Russian envoy, Aleksei Nikiforov, brought the maps to Belgrade. By then Milošević had already made up his mind.

In Geneva, the Contact Group unveiled the maps and gave the warring sides fifteen days to "take-it or leave-it." After he saw the proposal, a grinning Karadžić went off to see Lord Owen. "I thought the maps would present a problem. But there is no problem. There won't be a single Serb who would accept this." The Plan called on the Serbs to surrender thirteen towns, power stations, and factories, which they had seized during the war. It whittled down their northern corridor – a route that had become so important that it was the subject of nationalist folk songs. Karadžić was "too cocky in those days," observed Owen. Karadžić dismissed as "humiliating" the maps which he said were "drawn so the Serbs would reject them and be blamed for the continuation of the war."

The maps showed two spidery states, with thousands of kilometers of proposed borders. The front-lines underscored that, despite the war, the communities remained intertwined. The three Muslim enclaves in eastern Bosnia would be part of the Muslim-Croat federation. Two of them – Žepa and Srebrenica – would be joined together, and by a tenuous link, to Goražde, which would have a road link to Sarajevo. The Bosnian capital was to be placed under provisional UN administration until its status was determined.

The Bosnian Prime Minister, Haris Silajdžić, criticized the maps for consolidating Serb military gains. "They rewarded genocide and ethnic cleansing ... the solution especially in eastern Bosnia has serious deficiencies and some genocide areas like Prijedor are going to be controlled by those who committed those crimes," he said in reference to towns, which were mostly Muslim before the war but were now under Serb control, entire communities having been expelled.

Karadžić called the maps an "American *diktat*" in remarks aimed at fracturing the united stance – painstakingly put together – of the Contact Group. For some reason Churkin, who looked out for the interests of the Serbs (in the same way that the US represented the Muslims), did not put up a fight and allowed the Serb northern corridor to be virtually cut. When Owen saw the maps he knew the Serbs would not accept them. Owen said: "He [Churkin] should have played really a slightly tougher role in the negotiations. But he was so fed up with them that he just said let them stew."

While the Bosnian Serbs rejoiced at how easy it was to turn down the maps, Milošević began to publicly side with the Contact Group, a powerful antidote to the Bosnian Serbs. In Belgrade, on July 6 the Serbian President told the Russian Foreign Minister, Andrei Kozyrev, "There is no alternative to a Serbian yes to the Plan."

A frenzied diplomatic shuttle was launched. The G-7 industrial nations,[1] joined by Russia, held a summit in Naples, and gave the go-ahead to the Contact Group Plan, dispatching British Foreign Secretary Douglas Hurd and his French counterpart, Alain Juppé, to Belgrade, Pale and Sarajevo. Despite this appearance of decisiveness, the Contact Group was torn down the middle. Europe was outraged by threats from the US that it would unilaterally abandon the UN arms embargo. Hurd and Juppé, who remained resolutely opposed to the lifting of the arms embargo, tried to convey the impression to the Bosnian Serbs that if they rejected the Plan, Europe would be forced to cave in to US demands and allow the Muslims to get weapons. Milošević took what they were saying on board. In any case, he had already made up his mind to break with the Bosnian Serbs – if they did not obey him. Lilić's earlier remarks had been only a hint of what was to come. Yet Karadžić did not appear to take seriously any of the warnings – from Belgrade or the EU. Instead, he rambled on about 600 years of history, infuriating Hurd. The British Foreign Secretary, said Nikola Koljević, tried to persuade them to back the plan. "You cannot say 'no'. And please do not say 'yes, but'. But you can say 'yes, and'. This was their neat formula of how to respond to something you don't like."

Milošević summoned his Bosnian Serb protégés, including the army and police chiefs, to Dobanovci, the military compound outside Belgrade for a meeting of the country's top leaders. They set about devising a formula that would be acceptable to the Contact Group but also convey their demands to negotiate part of the package. "The most important discussion with President Milošević in Dobanovci was to see how we could give our answer to the Contact Group so that it may sound like 'yes, and,'" said Koljević.

> *'We were talking around the clock,' President Bulatović of Montenegro later remembered. 'I spent more time with Karadžić in that period than with my wife and children. It was the decisive point.'*
>
> *We advised Karadžić to accept the Plan, to say that this is a major victory for the Serbs in Bosnia – but Karadžić went to Geneva and that's when he said that the Plan was disastrous.*
>
> *At all our meetings, from June 27 to August 4 when we decided to break off economic relations, we kept repeating that if they [the Bosnian Serbs] reject the proposal and decide to wage war against the entire world, we would not allow them to take us with them, to drag us down, too.*

The Serbian President and his Montenegrin ally repeated the warnings they had used the year before for the Vance-Owen Plan. Milošević, who had vowed that Serbia would never bend to international will, was now carrying out its bidding. He told the Bosnian Serbs that he understood their objections, but there was no choice.

Milošević told Karadžić: "I thought Krajišnik was the toughest nut to crack, but I was wrong, you are much tougher than he is." That night, trying to persuade them, Milošević made an off-hand comment, the meaning of which Koljević understood only later. "Well, if you don't want to talk this way we'll talk through the newspapers." Koljević thought this meant an end to their private all-night sessions. He was wrong.

By five o'clock in the morning, according to Bulatović, they finally agreed what to tell the Contact Group: "Republika Srpska" would accept the Contact Group Plan as the basis for negotiations about disputable issues such as the exchange of territories, international guarantees for the frontiers, and the possibility of confederal ties with Yugoslavia. In utmost secrecy, British and Russian diplomats, motivated by the desire to thwart US efforts to lift the arms embargo, helped make certain that the wording would be acceptable to the international mediators, who, at that point, were still calling it a "take-it or leave-it" Plan.

Krajišnik took out his notebook and told his Belgrade patrons: "This is our agreement and we'll write the conclusion." Bulatović said: "When we read the conclusions the next day, not a single sentence corresponded to what we had discussed and agreed during the weekend."

As the Bosnian Serb leadership left Belgrade for an assembly meeting in Pale, the parliaments of Bosnia and the Muslim-Croat federation met in Sarajevo to endorse the maps. Izetbegović called it an "unjust and unfair peace offer" and openly admitted they were accepting the Plan only because they were certain that the Serbs would reject it. "We should accept the Plan because by refusing it we would do a favor to Karadžić and Milošević." Later, Izetbegović explained:

> That's why we accepted this bad option considering all the alternatives being worse. So it's not with delight that we accepted the Plan, neither are we delighted with it now ... We realized that time is working against us, that war is destroying all the prospects of such a multinational Bosnia that peace could save it. That's why we decided to accept peace even though its terms were not fair.

Meanwhile in Pale, it was the Vance-Owen assembly revisited. Karadžić pointed to the grim consequences if the Plan was rejected. "The nation has to be prepared, for tears and hunger, if it rejects the Plan." However once again, he did not try to sell it, insisting that the Plan envisaged a life in Bosnia-Herzegovina under Muslim authority.

Shrugging off threats from Belgrade, the Bosnian Serbs switched tack. At the end of the closed session of the Pale assembly the Bosnian Serbs wrote their response to the Contact Group Plan on a piece of paper which they placed in a sealed pink envelope. A spokesman announced that the envelope would be sent to Geneva and only there would its contents be made public two days later. But it was clear from the defiant mood of the assembly members that their response had fallen well short of the unqualified yes that the Contact Group had demanded.

Nevertheless Milošević still believed that he could convince his disobedient protégés. On July 27, the heavy hitters from Russia arrived in Belgrade: the Russian Defense Minister, General Pavel Grachev and Vitaly Churkin. Milošević told the Russians that he held out hope the Bosnian Serbs would change their minds at their second assembly meeting. The Russians then met the Bosnian Serbs, and urged them to endorse the Plan.

In the eyes of the Bosnian Serbs, General Grachev commanded consider-able respect in contrast to Yeltsin and his other ministers, whom the Bosnian Serbs saw as weak and vulnerable to Western pressure. According to Karadžić, Grachev prodded him, "You must accept the Plan because if they attack you we will have to defend you, which would cause problems for us." It would mean, he said, a new political and, possibly, military confrontation in the Balkans, and a dangerous stand-off between Russia and the West. Without changing his mind Karadžić said he left the meeting confident the "Russian Army was supporting us. We knew that before, but now it was clear that the Russian Army had a sympathetic ear for the Serbs." At the assembly meeting the next day there was no change. The Bosnian Serbs, as usual, were in a defiant mood. Milošević prepared for war against his by-now former proxies.

For the first time, unequivocally, the Serbian President publicly lashed out at the Pale leadership: "Nobody has the right to reject peace in the name of the Serbian people."

Public opinion in Serbia was confused by the venom unleashed on the peo-ple who had been previously portrayed as martyrs and victims. In a letter to the Bosnian Serb assembly, the Serbian government warned: "If you reject the proposed Plan you are on the best route to carrying out a crime against your own people. You do not have the right to the lives of the citizens of Yugoslavia."

The Bosnian Serbs seemed deaf to the thunderous condemnation from Belgrade. On August 3 the assembly rejected the Contact Group Plan for the third time and called a referendum to be held three weeks later.

The reaction was immediate. That night Bulatović was enjoying a fish dinner in the Montenegrin coastal town of Herceg Novi. He got a message to ring Milošević. Their conversation was brief.

> *'Unfortunately they rejected the Plan, we must put into force that decision to close the border. Do you agree?' Milošević asked. I said yes. He answered, 'They made their decision, our decision is taking effect tomorrow.'*

The Federal Government announced Milošević's decision. On August 4 a blockade went into force. Traffic came to a halt. Except for a handful of lines, telephone connections were cut. The Serbian media exploded with claims that the Bosnian Serb leaders were criminals and war profiteers. "They are against peace, now when there is no alternative to peace" became the new slogan of the regime journalists who for years had sowed the seeds of hatred, whipping up nationalist hysteria, insisting that there was no alterna-tive to the war "foisted on the Serbs."

The blockade was complete. Biljana Plavšić was the first victim of the new rules. The year before, she had also been first to be banned from crossing the frontier to Serbia. Even the steely Plavsić was taken aback by the slap in the face from her former protectors.

> 'The only thing we hadn't expected was that we would live to see Serbia impose sanctions against us. No one said that. No one could have expected such a dagger in the back.'

The dagger plunged deep. Under Milošević smear campaigns have become an art form. His statement led a host of stinging accusations.

> They reject peace in a moment when Republika Srpska has been granted half the territory of former Bosnia-Herzegovina and when, by accepting peace they would lift sanctions from those, without whom they would not exist ...
>
> Their decision to reject peace cannot be according to any real criteria in the interest of the people but only for the benefit of war profiteers and those people who have guilty consciences. Those who fear the time when peace will come and all the crimes will be revealed ...
>
> Countless times they gave us a reason to sever every link with them. They did not keep a single one of their promises: from Sarajevo to Athens; from Athens to Goražde; from Goražde to Parliament; from Parliament to this last referendum, which they had told us would not be held ...

The pièce-de-résistance was unleashing Lilić. In a wide ranging interview he blamed the Bosnian Serbs for everything. Milošević's hand was plain to see. His former protégés had become the universal scapegoats. But it was not so easy to wash his hands of them.

Lilić painted the Bosnian Serbs as the architects of war in Sarajevo and blamed them for a senseless attack on Goražde.[2]

> How many times have they promised that they would not shell Sarajevo, and perpetuate the agony of civilians in this city? How many times have they promised to arrest the bands and paramilitary units which are terrorizing civilians and besmirching the honor of the Serbs? – They went back on their word of honor that they would halt the insane attack on Goražde, which led to many people being killed and resulted in the NATO ultimatum and the (Serbs') withdrawal to a distance of 20 kilometers.

The Bosnian Serbs behaved as if the embargo were an embarrassing family quarrel, which they did not quite seem to believe was real. Instead, they claimed, it was a secret deal between the two leaderships. Karadžić tried to use the split to his advantage; refraining from direct attacks on Milošević, and expressing pity. The poor Serbian President, laboring under the strain of economic hardship, was caving in to Western pressure. They were implying that Milošević had weakened and fallen under the thumb of the West. By contrast, the Bosnian Serbs were strong and uncompromising – the people of Serbian myth.

The Bosnian Serbs went ahead with the referendum. Despite a fierce campaign waged by the Belgrade media machine, they overwhelmingly rejected the Plan.

In Sarajevo, the Bosnian Government waited for a Western response. There was none. Silajdžić complained that even though the Serbs had rejected the Plan, the Contact Group had remained silent. "They should have said if the Bosnian Serbs do not accept the Peace Plan, then this would happen: tightening the sanctions against Serbia, expanding the safe zones and lifting the arms embargo." But the divided Contact Group could not agree what to do. They chose the path of least resistance, imposing complete isolation against the Bosnian Serb leaders, who, they said, would be excluded from the peace process until they had accepted the Plan.

Milošević, too, took steps to enforce their quarantine. He then gave the go-ahead to a real border between Yugoslavia and Bosnia-Herzegovina; but real only in the sense that he was sending a message to the politicians and, as importantly, to the West. There is strong evidence that the border remained porous. The Bosnian Serbs still received essential military supplies from the Yugoslav Army as well as their salaries from Belgrade. The central point was that Milošević wanted to see a political and not a military defeat.

While Belgrade carried out its verbal *blitzkrieg* against the Bosnian Serbs, international mediators Owen and Stoltenberg negotiated the despatch of monitors along Serbia's and Montenegro's frontiers with Bosnia. Milošević finally consented to what the ebullient Panić had called for at the London Conference two years earlier. In return, he got certain sanctions suspended – the ban on international air traffic, sports and cultural exchanges.

For the West, increasingly frustrated by the successive failures of all peace initiatives, Milošević ironically became their linchpin for achieving peace and stability in the region.

At least for the time being, perhaps just to get rid of his political rivals, Milošević took away the Serb *casus belli*, the creation of a unified Serbian state on the ruins of Yugoslavia.

Without the guiding light of a Greater Serb state, Serbs became confused. When they went to war against their neighbors, Serbs believed Milošević knew where he was taking them. They thought their sacrifices were in the name of Serb unity. It was the price for Milošević's promise "all Serbs in one state."

By breaking with his kin in Bosnia, Milošević had betrayed the slogan known to every Serb – *Samo Sloga Srbina Spašava* – only harmony saves a Serb. All that remained of this harmony, and the singleness of purpose with which the Serbs had as a united forced embarked upon the war, were the four *s*'s scrawled in red paint or charcoal on burnt-out houses and ruined villages throughout Bosnia and Croatia.

1 The G-7 – The Group of Seven Most Industrialized Nations, the seven countries with the largest economies in the world, the US, Germany, Japan, France, Italy, the UK and Canada.

2 Lilić also blamed Karadžić for being involved in the kidnapping and suspected murder of twenty men from Serbia – nineteen of whom were Muslims, in an effort to spread the war to Yugoslavia. Three years after they were dragged from a train at Strpci – despite Milošević's promises, the families of those men never found out what happened to their loved ones that night on February 27, 1993.

PART FIVE: ENDGAME

28

THE FALL OF KRAJINA
August 1995

Croatian soldiers casually loot a grocery store, two old women grab a pair of eyeglasses through a smashed shop window and stray cattle stroll aimlessly through the streets of Knin, the capital of the self-styled Republika Srpska Krajina which fell on August 5. The euphoria blanketed Croatia for days. Drinking beer and flashing victory signs, the soldiers walk among the gutted cars, children's bicycles and a dead dog. Time was not wasted. Already walls had been plastered with posters of Franjo Tudjman, his arms raised in exultation over the old Knin fortress and the caption "the man who wins."

A foreshadowing of what was in store for the Krajina Serbs had come much earlier. Croatian troops in January 1993 launched a lightning strike across UN lines to capture the straits of Maslenica, which linked central Croatia, and the capital Zagreb, with the Dalmatian coast and the country's second city, Split. In a matter of days the Croats had seized back swathes of territory they had fought over, in 1991, for more than five months without success. Luckily for Zagreb, world attention was focused on Bosnia, and, in any case, the international reaction was mild.

The limited Maslenica offensive pointed the way in two respects. It was an early indicator of growing military strength and self-confidence on the part of the Croats. It revealed how they now would brush aside the United Nations whenever they wanted. And, perhaps as importantly, it made clear the diminishing territorial ambitions of Slobodan Milošević. Despite his January 1992 promise to Milan Babić that the Yugoslav army would defend Krajina in the event of a Croatian attack, Belgrade did not lift a finger.

May 1995 brought catastrophe for the Krajina Serbs closer still. The Croatian Army seized control of western Slavonia – which was always the most vulnerable of the Serb-held lands in Croatia – and 18,000 Serbs fled, their army scarcely putting up a fight in their defense. Accusations of complicity by Belgrade attended the fall of western Slavonia. Not only did Milošević's army stay on the sidelines, but even his television was blasé, mentioning the defeat only in the twentieth minute of the nightly news.

Since the adoption of the Vance plan in January 1992, there had been no progress towards ending the stand-off with local Serbs who had declared a third of Croatia as their own state. The Croats were frustrated, fearing they would never integrate the territory into Croatia. Meeting in the Russian embassy in Zagreb, international mediators, led by the US and Russia, tried to jump-start the peace process in February 1991. They were aware that the failure to broker a lasting solution in Croatia would make it impossible to end the war in neighboring Bosnia. They tried to secure a three-point, phased agreement by which the Serbs and Croats would first agree on a ceasefire line and withdraw their forces from it to a distance of at least one kilometer. UN troops would then place themselves between the two sides. The second phase was the gradual re-establishment of transport, trade and communication links, including telephones, although, ludicrously, talks on this point ran into difficulty, too, on the question of whether the international dialling code for Krajina should reflect its status as part of Croatia (385) or as part of the same entity as the rump Yugoslavia (381).

The third phase of this attempted settlement would, if it ever got that far, be the return of Croatian sovereignty to Krajina, parts of which would enjoy autonomy within the Croatian state.

The US ambassador to Croatia, Peter Galbraith, championed the prospects of the plan for peaceful integration to succeed. There was progress. The main Zagreb-Belgrade highway, the road of Brotherhood and Unity built by Tito's youth brigades and, later, Western loans, was reopened under UN supervision after four years. Traffic was light but Croats could now drive straight from Zagreb to Slavonski Brod, in eastern Croatia, in two rather than five hours. Upset with the current round of talks, Milan Martić, former police chief of Knin who was now president of Krajina, closed the road for a day at the end of April.

By May Day weekend it was open again. It was four years to the day since the Croatian police went into Borovo Selo to hoist the Croatian flag above the Serb village – a prank which left twelve policemen and two Serbs dead in the first major casualties of the Serbo-Croat war. This time the game was different. At a gas station on the highway near the Serb town of Okučani, a Croatian man stabbed dead a Serb, whose brother later allegedly starting firing a passing cars, killing three Croats in revenge. In the chaos, Martić once again closed the country's biggest road. It was the last time the Serbs would control the highway. Tudjman finally had the pretext for intervention he had been seeking since Maslenica: the second step of a carefully laid plan, which would bring about the downfall of Krajina.

At 4:30 am, Hrvoje Šarinić, Tudjman's chief advisor, telephoned the UN. Earlier that day the government had told the UN that the troop build-up was just a military exercise. This time, Šarinić said it was a police operation, aimed at reopening the highway.

The UN was caught off guard. All efforts had been focused on renewing an all-party ceasefire in Bosnia, mediated by former US President Jimmy Carter in December, which had broken down and would expire that weekend. The Bosnian Muslims were trying to avoid signing after scoring their biggest win to date against the Serbs, seizing control of a television transmitter on Mount Vlasić in central Bosnia. "We were taken by surprise. We were all terribly preoccupied with Bosnia," later remembered UN spokesman Christopher Gunness. Yasushi Akashi, special representative to the UN Secretary General, had been in Sarajevo to try and shore up the ceasefire.

In just thirty hours, the Croats swept through the region of western Slavonia from three directions. A convoy of tractors, cars and horse-drawn wagons stretched endlessly – it was the first wave of tens of thousands of Serbs who over the next four months would flee in their tractors. Civilians were being fired on by Croatian soldiers. There was a line of wrecked vehicles. The Croatian army quickly sealed off certain areas, giving the impression that they were on a man-hunt for Serb rebels. Even Defense Minister Šušak announced in parliament that 450 people were killed in an operation where there was scarcely any fighting. The next day refrigerator trucks were seen going down the newly opened highway and the Croats began a massive clean-up campaign, using chemicals to wash down the roads.

Left by Belgrade to fight on their own, the Krajina Serbs on May 3 desperately retaliated. They fired Orkan rockets into the Zagreb city center killing one person and wounding 40. International condemnation was swift, and Martić was indicted for war crimes by the International Tribunal at The Hague, which had been established by the UN Security Council.

Operation Flash, by which the Croats took western Slavonia by storm, caused turmoil in the Krajina Serb leadership. The army chief was fired. Belgrade dispatched General Mile Mrkšić, a former commander of the army special forces, to shake up the depleted and demoralized Krajina Serbs. He set up a mobile reserve force near Slunj which he said would respond to any Croatian army attack either from the north or from the south.

But the Krajina Serb army had already been fatally weakened. For four years Krajina had by necessity been a garrison society, in which every adult male was, in effect, either a policeman or a soldier. The Krajina republic was collapsing under the weight of its own unsustainability. The region's leaders seemed more concerned with black-marketeering than making military preparations for what was certain to be a Croatian offensive. Foot soldiers complained that by August only "peasants and laborers" were left defending the territory, with, despite Mrkšić's reorganization, little or no strategic thrust. Colonel Andy Leslie, a Canadian officer who arrived in Knin at the start of 1995 as Chief of Staff of the small UN Contingent there, was struck by the lack of military readiness.

If my home was about to be over-run by my enemy, I'd be digging like a bas-tard. I'd have my troops on maneuver, I'd be rehearsing defensive opera-tions, I'd have a second defense line prepared, I'd be stockpiling. We saw none of that. Until the very end the leadership of the Krajina Serbs seemed more interested in defending their own positions within the Krajina state than in taking real measures to defend the territory. It was appalling. They were corrupt, incompetent, and complacent. And there's no excuse for them.

For four years, the Krajina Serb leadership had sustained themselves in power by selling the people a lie – the lie that their state was invincible, and that the idea of Serb self-determination in Krajina could triumph over the geo-economic reality that Krajina and the Dalmatian coast were utterly inter-dependent. In their isolation, the Krajina Serbs became more convinced than ever that they could never live in safety under Croatian rule. This fear was borne out. For international consumption, the Croatian government would make great play of appealing to the Krajina Serbs to stay in their homes and live as citizens of Croatia. But these appeals did little to mask the real ambi-tion of the Croatian government, which was to drive the Serbs out of Croatia altogether and resettle the land they had lived on for centuries with Croats from elsewhere. After the fall of Knin, Tudjman even said this publicly.

At the eleventh hour, the Krajina leadership tried to salvage a deal that would save their state. On July 29 Yasushi Akashi, who had lost any leverage he may have had in the conflict, met Milan Martić, who turned up in a cam-ouflage t-shirt with his belly hanging out. On the following day, Akashi saw President Tudjman. Both sides agreed to talks in Geneva on August 3. But by then the die was cast. Croatia went into the talks knowing that the next day they would launch an offensive. They demanded that the Serbs accept Croatian rule immediately. This was too much for the Serbs, even though they knew what was coming.

On the day those talks convened, Šarinić informed the UN force comman-der General Janvier that an attack was imminent. It was to be called Operation Storm.

By then Milošević was ready to accept almost any thing on offer. For him the overriding priority was the lifting of sanctions. He had been trying to force the Krajina Serb leadership into striking a deal with Tudjman for months. On the day of the Croatian offensive, the main Serbian newspaper, *Politika*, which was Milošević's mouthpiece, was unambiguous in its condem-nation of the Krajina and Bosnian Serb leaders for "leading their people into a virtual dead end."

Politika blamed the Krajina leadership for breaking off negotiations with Zagreb and causing the loss of western Slavonia. It was a year to the day since Milošević had imposed a blockade against the Bosnian Serb leadership for refusing to obey his orders and endorse the Contact Group plan. It was also a year since Martić, in bold defiance of Milošević, had crossed the frontier to Bosnia to vote "no" in a Serb referendum on the peace plan. He had wanted to make the point that the destinies of the Krajina and Bosnian Serbs were bound together. Belgrade now condemned both. "Without justifying the behavior of the international community, we must underscore that both Pale and the Knin leaders have caused great harm to the Serb people with their politics," wrote the Serbian newspaper.

A clear sign that Milošević would remain on the sidelines was the behavior of the tightly controlled Serbian media. In sharp contrast to the warmongering of the preceding years, where any incident was used to whip up national hysteria and ethnic hatreds, the Belgrade media now played down the storm brewing in Croatia. Indeed, Television Serbia was alone in reporting that the Geneva talks of August 3 ended on a successful note.

In Knin the UN garrison hit the air raid sirens at four a.m. on August 4. The first shells landed at 5:02. Croatian troops outnumbered the Serb defenders five to one.

It was not only numerical superiority that favored the Croats. It was a military expertise that could only have derived from their increasingly congenial relationship with the United States. In July, the Croatian Army had prepared the ground for their attack on the Krajina by a swift incursion into western Bosnia, during which they took two key towns from the Bosnian Serbs, Glamoč and Bosansko Grahovo. The seizure of these two towns isolated the Krajina capital, Knin, from the Bosnian Serbs by cutting the Knin-Drvar-Banja Luka supply route. The Croats had already taken the high ground of Mount Dinara, and from its summit Knin was within easy striking distance. Three years of military planning had prepared the Krajina Serbs for an attack from the south or the north. They were not ready from an attack from behind. Colonel Andy Leslie, of the UN garrison in Knin, recognized the strategy immediately as the Croats moved in Bosnia:

It was a textbook operation, though not a JNA textbook. Whoever wrote that plan of attack could have gone to any NATO staff college in North America or Western Europe and scored an A-plus.

The attack came from two directions in the first instance. In the north, there were two main assaults – one from Karlovac, the other from Sisak – both towards the Bihać pocket. At the same time, there was a three-pronged assault from the south, covered by heavy artillery and mortar bombardment. At least two thousand rounds struck Knin alone during the first day of Operation Storm. Gunness said:

The shelling of Knin was a key strategic move. Soldiers on the front heard that Knin was being pummeled. They simply abandoned their positions and rushed back to their families. It was a deliberate policy by the Croats to shell the women and children in their beds. This exposes the lie that this was a legitimate military action. But the Security Council was barely able to condemn it.

Western governments turned a blind eye to the shelling. The diplomatic acquiescence in the storming of western Slavonia in May had, in effect, given Croatia the green light to take Krajina by force.

The collapse of the Krajina Serb defense was swiftest in the south. By the middle of the afternoon, Radio Knin reported that Drniš and Obrovac – two front-line towns neighboring Knin – had fallen. The Krajina Serb leadership convened a meeting in the late afternoon and gave instructions that an organized evacuation should begin. The Croats had left escape routes through the villages of Srb and Lapac. Milan Martić and the leadership fled. The evacuation order was communicated to the UN garrison in the early evening, and, that night, tens of thousands of Krajina Serbs took to the road. It was the first stage in what would become, during the next few days, the biggest single forcible displacement of people in Europe since the Second World War. Colonel Leslie, who spent much of the day ferrying the wounded to hospital, estimated that five hundred people were killed on that day in the Knin area alone. Attempts to contact the leadership of the Krajina Serbs came to nothing:

Martić and Babić were nowhere to be found. We tried to contact them. They were just gone. They left one elderly colonel and an old captain to ask us for help in evacuating the civilians. There's no excuse for that. The population of Knin fell from thirty-five to forty thousand to around five or six hundred in less than twenty-four hours. It was chaos. Absolute chaos.

In the north, the Krajina Serb Army recovered quickly from the initial surprise attack and put up a more effective defense. They held out in pockets, particularly in Glina and Petrinja. But the overwhelming might of the Croatian army swept past them, isolated them, and rounded on them from behind within days.

The Croatian Army arrived at the outskirts of Knin at 11:30 on the morning of the August 5 – Day 2 of Operation Storm. They met no resistance; Knin was deserted. They entered the town at around mid-day. They parked a tank at the gates of the UN compound and refused to allow UN personnel to leave. "So there we sat, for two and a half, maybe three days, while they mopped up the city," Colonel Leslie recalled. "It was very frustrating."

It was on this day that the mass exodus of Serbs began to gather pace. By evening, the Croats were certain they were on their way to securing a rout of Serb forces. Croatian radio announced the fall of Knin, and the flight of Martić, who was reported to be in Banja Luka. The Croatian media also broadcast details of safe routes through which the Serbs could leave for Serb-held parts of Bosnia. Though Tudjman was making public statements calling on "loyal" Serbs not to flee their homes, there was no doubt in the minds of those on the receiving end of Croatian artillery that the attack had more than a military objective. Tudjman wanted all the Serbs to leave Croatia.

Eight thousand fled that evening through Dvor, on the Bosnia-Croatia border, to add to the tens of thousands who had fled the Knin region the previous day. Within hours at least twenty thousand refugees gathered at Topusko to demand United Nations protection. The civilian population was now hopelessly intermingled with troops fleeing in disarray.

On August 6, the Croatian advance continued. Petrinja, so bitterly fought over in 1991, fell in the morning. The Serbs asked for ceasefire talks so that they could arrange a safe evacuation. The Croats agreed, but demanded unconditional surrender. Sporadic resistance continued. The Croatian Army began hitting the very road that the refugees, escorted in places by UN troops, were using to flee into neighboring Bosnia. In his first public statement, Martić claimed:

The Serb army has not lost a single battle and has not sustained any serious losses in manpower...some settlements have been abandoned because there were no conditions for the people to remain here, as the Croatian Army has limitless supplies of rockets and shells, with which it kept destroying Serb villages and towns for hours.

By the next day, most of his statelet had been swept away. To the north, the Bosnian Army Fifth Corps had broken out of the Bihac pocket, pressing towards Topusko. Croatia's incursion into Bosnia earlier in July had been justified by the agreement of July 12 between Izetbegović and Tudjman to relieve the pressure on the 10,000-strong Bihać Fifth Corps who, for three years, had been fending off the Serbs – from Krajina and Bosnia. For the Bosnian government, the loss of Bihać would have meant an end to the last vestiges of control over western Bosnia. For the Serbs, Bihać was the missing link needed to join Serb-held land in Croatia and Bosnia to Serbia itself, which is what Croatia wanted to avoid at all costs.

The UN brokered a ceasefire, designed to ease the evacuation of tens of thousands of refugees in safety, but not before many had been killed. They were forced to run a gauntlet of angry Croatian townspeople who took to the streets round Sisak to stone the columns of refugees. The Croatian authorities had mapped out this route. An old woman died, her face swollen beyond recognition, of injuries suffered when hit by a rock. The Serbs were spat on. The Croats got their revenge.

A curious symmetry attaches itself to the events of August 4-8, 1995, and to the town of Knin in particular. Knin is, in a sense, where the war began, when rebel Serbs refused to submit to Croatian sovereignty during Yugoslavia's disintegration. It was where the Serb expansionist project in Yugoslavia first resorted to open warfare. It was the town, in this sense, that sent Yugoslavia so decisively down the road to catastrophe.

And it was also with the fall of the town, five years later, that international envoys believed they could put the country on the long road back to peace. August 4 was the date when the war began, for the first time, to go badly wrong for the Serbs, the day the Serb nationalist project began to unravel in the face of overwhelming military opposition. August 4 shattered the already fractured myth of Serb invincibility. It demonstrated that the Serb state in Croatia had rotted from within, so that by the time the Croats had built an army capable of turning the military tide they were, in fact, tilting at a decayed structure.

But the Croats had built it with the help of the West. Retired US generals helped them plan their operation. NATO was on their side, too. In fact, during Operation Storm, on August 4 NATO warplanes bombarded Serb communications systems, ostensibly because the Serb radar had locked on to NATO jets, but really giving a helping hand to the Croats.

Western politicians kept quiet. Carl Bildt, the European Union mediator, was a lone voice of outrage (other than Moscow's predictable response), suggesting that Tudjman could be indicted for war crimes. In response, he was declared unwelcome in Croatia, which in turn, Bildt said was "yet one more sign that they have chosen the path of war over negotiations."

While Warren Christopher, US Secretary of State, denied that Washington had even tacitly encouraged the Croatian offensive, he conceded that Croatia's successes could help the process of a wider settlement in the region. Behind the scenes, Ambassador Galbraith had returned from Washington and, according to UN officials, told Tudjman that the US would tolerate military action to take Krajina provided the battle was "short and clean."

Short it was but clean it was not. While the German Foreign Minister Klaus Kinkel had expressed a certain understanding – that Croatia must do what it has to, within five days all but a few thousand Serbs had fled the region where they had lived for centuries.

There was an officially-sanctioned campaign of burning and looting which damaged over 20,000 houses owned by Serbs. During the weeks that followed, well after the Croatian army was firmly in control of the territory, elderly Serbs were being killed. "We are still finding the bodies dumped on the roadside each morning," one UN official said more than two months later.

The Bosnian Serbs watched the collapse of their compatriots in Krajina with dismay and alarm. They, too, were sitting on more territory than they could possible hold; they, too, were stretched across hopelessly extended front lines; their state, too, was eroding from within, cut off from its former patron in Belgrade by an embargo imposed by Milošević the previous year. Radovan Karadžić knew that his fate could be similar. In an open letter, he accused Milošević of abandoning the goal shared by all Serbs to live together in one country – in Greater Serbia. "You have turned your back on the Serbs. You have relented under foreign pressure to the extent which could be compared only to treason," said Karadžić.

The collapse of Krajina was the clearest illustration to date of the peace strategy being pursued by Milošević. The Croatian offensive was planned and executed not so much on the assumption as on the certainty that Milošević would do nothing to defend the people whose armed rebellion he had, five years earlier, embraced. He sacrificed the Krajina Serbs because he knew it was the only way he could preserve what he already had. He wanted to get sanctions lifted and, after years of isolation, to be received by the international community as a peacemaker. Milošević and Tudjman wanted the biggest possible Serbia and Croatia on the territory of former Yugoslavia.

By August, Croatia was the centerpiece of US strategy. It was the counterbalance to Serbia, with a population half the size but with the might of international backing. When the Croatian army began its string of successful offensives – it came as a surprise. But in fact, the seeds of this success had been planted by Washington with the creation of the Muslim-Croat federation. In February 1994, American envoys had offered Tudjman a straight choice: abandon your war against the Muslims of Bosnia and, we, the US, will back your plans to take Krajina and even more; if not, you will face international isolation and economic sanctions. The fall of Krajina led to a complete shift in the balance of power in Bosnia, favoring the Croats and the Muslims against the Serbs. In the months to come, the Serbs would lose much more.

The Croatian President now had come into his own. At a military parade in May celebrating the fifth anniversary of Croatia's declaration of sovereignty, he donned a white martial uniform, one Tito would have worn. Among the guests of honor were foreign ambassadors, who after a brief struggle with their consciences, turned out to review the Croatian army which had managed to become a regional force by breaking their weapons embargo, and whose violation they were celebrating as well. Tudjman, who had never seen the UN as more than a fig leaf behind which he could arm himself, later boasted that diplomats and military attachés had approached him to say that not only were Croatia's weapons impressive, given the embargo, but the troops were even more so.

By November 1995, Tudjman was preparing for another offensive against eastern Slavonia. The prize was Vukovar, which his government had described as the Stalingrad of Croatia.

In Belgrade's strategic planning, the borders of Greater Serbia were redrawn, the territorial objectives scaled down radically. The Krajina Serbs, who, until the very day they fled, kept faith with the idea that they too would be part of a Serbian state, paid the price. Ironically, they ended up in a Serbian state. But it was a far cry from Greater Serbia. Instead, they brought their shattered lives to isolated and impoverished Serbia proper.

29

A PAX AMERICANA?

The three presidents of Serbia, Croatia, and Bosnia shake hands, perfunctorily, poised to take part in the most ambitious attempt to reach a settlement in former Yugoslavia since the wars began in 1991. The venue is the Bob Hope center at the Wright-Patterson Air Force Base in Dayton, Ohio. They are flanked by US Secretary of State, Warren Christopher and his assistant, Richard Holbrooke.

They began with a phase known as "proximity talks" in which the three parties to the conflict would live in separate but identical premises while international mediators moved from one to the other. It is a technique pioneered by the Middle East peace talks which had taken place in Norway and had led to the dramatic handshake on the White House lawn between Yitzhak Rabin and Yasser Arafat. Those talks had taken place under conditions of absolute secrecy. The parties had had no opportunity to wreck the negotiations by denouncing each other in public; similarly they were, under the cloak of privacy, able to consider concessions and entertain compromises without the pressure of having to adopt, for the sake of their respective hard-line constituencies, inflexible, non-negotiable preconditions. Richard Holbrooke now tried to bring the Norway Channel, as it had become known, to the Balkans.

The road to Dayton was hazardous and long. The humiliation of UN peacekeepers chained to lamp-posts and military installations to head off further NATO air strikes in June, the defeat of Srebrenica, and, finally, the gradual emergence of evidence of the mass murder of Muslims, apparently on General Mladić's instructions, brought international efforts to end the war to an all-time low. In the capitals of the western world, in the summer of 1995, the talk was all of withdrawal, particularly if the region's main protagonists wanted to wage more war.

A consensus was taking shape, particularly in Europe, that humanitarian aid had simply prolonged the war without much affecting its eventual outcome. France and Britain, the main troop-contributing countries, resented bearing the brunt of responsibility for the failure of the United Nations mission. More and more frequently, they griped that Washington should remain silent or do something. While their foreign ministers talked up the prospects of a UN withdrawal, Britain and France hugely reinforced their military presence in Bosnia by each contributing to a newly created Rapid Reaction Force. The Dutch also contributed. The Rapid Reaction Force had combat capability, and would be operating not under the auspices of the UN but rather on orders directly from London and Paris. But both capitals were ambiguous about the purpose of the new force. Was its purpose, as Clinton suggested, to "put some real steel into the UN mission"? Or were they there to protect UNPROFOR troops from retaliation in the event of a humiliating withdrawal? London and Paris would say only that nothing was being ruled out.

The prospect of a UN withdrawal rang alarm bells in Washington. Clinton knew that he would be called upon to honor his promise to send up to 25,000 US troops to help extract the allies from Bosnia. That opened up the possibility that US troops would lose their lives doing what no military leader ever seeks to do – reinforcing defeat. For Bill Clinton to put American lives in danger for so inglorious an operation, and in the year when he would be running for a second term in the White House, spelled electoral disaster. He began to look for a more robust option. On June 29, the White House committed 50 million dollars towards funding the force in Bosnia, but conceded that only 15 million had been secured, with slim prospects of finding support in Congress for the rest. Looking like a real fighting force with vehicles painted in camouflage rather than the good samaritan white of the UN, the Force, although it was initially blocked by both Bosnian government forces and the Croats, finally arrived on July 23 on Mount Igman, their base outside Sarajevo.

But by then, a sequence of events had begun that was to change fundamentally the dynamic of the conflict, and enhance the prospects for peace. That sequence began inauspiciously, with the fall of the Muslim-populated eastern Bosnian enclave of Srebrenica.

The fall of Srebrenica was the darkest moment in the international involvement in Bosnia. The United States and Europe did nothing to stop the murder of perhaps as many as eight thousand Muslim men who were rounded up while trying to escape to Bosnian government-held territory. Srebrenica was one of six UN designated "safe areas." Its defeat exposed the complete lack of international commitment to defend them. It was the terrible culmination of a series of badly-laid plans and half-hearted guarantees: from the beginning of the safe-areas policy, western governments had contributed no more than 7,000 of the estimated 34,000 troops needed to implement it; and in the end, the Serb offensive – though predictable – caught the world off-guard. International observers misread it even when it was in full swing.

Crouched in a field, surrounded by the rolling green hills of the Drina valley in summer-time, countless Muslim men await execution. The image was captured by a US spy satellite, but never released to the public. In the days following the capture, by the Bosnian Serb Army, of the Muslim enclave of

Srebrenica in eastern Bosnia, thousands of Muslim men met this chilling fate: some shot while running; others were simply lined up, executed, and dumped in mass graves.

Serb forces had begun shelling Srebrenica in earnest on July 6, after Naser Orić's Bosnian army forces staged raids into Serb-held territory from what was supposed to be a UN-protected, and demilitarized, 'safe area'. The Dutch peace-keepers stationed there did not know what to do. The following day a peace-keeper retreating with his unit after Serb forces had overrun their observation post had his head blown off – hit, not by Serbs, but by Bosnian government soldiers who had wanted to stop the retreat of the Dutch troops from government front-line positions. NATO planes swooped low over the thickly wooded hills. Within two days, the Serbs had overrun three observation posts and taken 30 Dutch soldiers hostage.

In The Hague on July 9 the Dutch Defense Minister Joris Voorhoeve starkly outlined the situation his troops found themselves in: "surrounded, outnumbered, and afraid of further actions" by the Bosnian Serbs. Incredibly, he still not did not believe that the Serbs would try to take the town. But that same day the Serbs delivered their first ultimatum – the United Nations and the Muslims must evacuate the enclave within 48 hours. In response, the UN ordered the Dutch to put up what was called a blocking position, 30 soldiers forming a thin blue line with armored personnel carriers and anti-tank missiles trying to stop thousands of Serb soldiers approaching from the town's southern perimeter.

Lieutenant Colonel Tom Karremans, the Dutch commander at Srebrenica, called for robust air strikes. The night of July 10. he tried to get some sleep, believing that by morning the situation would have changed dramatically, that NATO would bomb the Serbs. His request, however, was turned down by the UN force commander General Bernard Janvier. To the shock of his colleagues, Janvier said air strikes would be too dangerous. It was well known that Janvier was convinced that there was little point in trying to save Srebrenica; his view was that the enclave was fundamentally indefensible. Indeed, Janvier on May 24 urged the UN to pull out of the three eastern enclaves:

> *We have little time ahead of us. We must take measures which allow us to limit the risks incurred by our forces.*
>
> *Let us be pragmatic and above all honest, especially towards those whose security we hold in our hands: without lightning rods, stay out of the storm.*

By the time the alert was sounded, thousands of Serbs were already massing. Little heed had been paid to Serb threats – and the subsequent build-up of troops – following a guerrilla foray in June by Orić's troops into a Serb village. These hit-and-run trips gave the Serb commanders their casus belli to strike at Srebrenica. At the start, Western governments were convinced that the offensive was aimed at neutralizing the Muslim enclave but not at taking it.

By noon on July 10, the Serbs entered the town. By then NATO strikes were finally approved. But their target was limited – at most two tanks were taken out.

It was too little, too late. The Serbs advanced, as the Dutch withdrew to their main camp at Potočari along with thousands of panicked civilians, almost all but a handful of whom had suffered this fate before. A third and final request for air strikes was called off because Voorhoeve said the Serbs had threatened to execute the Dutch hostages.

The poorly-armed Muslim defenders of Srebrenica offered no resistance. They fled, leaving behind thousands of civilians. On July 12, General Mladić drove into the center of Srebrenica, escorted by local journalists, one of whom filmed his appearance. He is shown smiling, patting young children on the head. There was an uglier video that was not shown abroad. Mladić is ordering the Muslim men to move faster, to line up one by one.

The final slap in the face of the Dutch, and in fact of the entire international community, took place when General Mladić summoned Lt.-Col. Karremans to meet him. There was a live pig tied up in the room. Flush with victory, the General offered Karremans a glass of *sljivovica* and together they watched as a Serb soldier deftly slaughtered the pig – his knife dripped with blood. "That's how we deal with our enemies," Mladić told Karremans.

In Belgrade, Rudolf Perina, the US chargé d'affaires, went to see Milošević to convey American concern for the plight of Srebrenica's Muslims and urged him to halt the delivery of all military supplies to the Bosnian Serbs, warning that the capture of Srebrenica could derail the current peace process. "Why blame me? I have been unable to contact Mladić." Milošević's claim was unconvincing and familiar, reminiscent of previous instances in years before when he had looked his foreign collocutors in the eyes to say they had come to the wrong address.

In an interview, Milošević did not conceal his approval for the Srebrenica operation. After all, he said, shrugging his shoulders, look at what they have been doing to Serb villages alongside the enclave. He gave the impression that the Serb offensive was aimed at neutralizing the enclave as a military threat, rather than an attempt to over-run it altogether; an attempt to cripple rather than kill. Milošević clearly reserved high praise for Mladić. He was hoping that the general would be able to get rid of Karadžić.

Srebrenica was locked into Milošević's thinking about the shape of the Serbian state that would emerge from the ruins of the old Yugoslavia. Eastern Bosnia had always been strategically vital to him. Milošević may have proved

himself willing to trade away territories (regarded as sacred by Serb nationalists) further west, but the Drina valley was vital to his concept of a secure,
enlarged, Serbian state. For Serbia, Srebrenica was crucial. Just ten miles
from Serbia's frontier with Bosnia, it would have been a constant security
threat to Serbia proper, had it remained in Muslim hands. Eastern Bosnia is a
buffer zone for Serbia. For the Muslims, Srebrenica was a symbol of Bosnian
resistance. By eradicating Srebrenica the Serbs believed they made even
more remote the dream of one day re-establishing Bosnia within its internationally recognized borders.

Harrowing accounts by refugees who had made it safely to Tuzla told how
Dutch peacekeepers, 370 in all, had failed to stop the Bosnian Serb forces.
The Dutch had done what they could: they had shared their own dwindling
supplies of food and medicines with some of the most desperate of
Srebrenica's trapped Muslims. But their numbers were down to less than half
their full complement of 730 troops and they were poorly placed to do anything to halt the offensive that was taking place.

Srebrenica was one of the most arduous UN assignments in Bosnia. The
condition of the 40,000-strong population, crammed into a town where 8,000
had lived before the war, was wretched. Srebrenica was ruled by warlords and
black marketeers. Food supplies had been meager throughout the war – the
Bosnian Serbs had consistently blocked relief convoys. UN troops in the
enclave had always operated under similarly harsh conditions, with no fresh
food, no electricity and little fuel, and able to undertake only foot patrols.
They were hopelessly isolated, and when the final offensive came, they had
no reliable intelligence about its nature or scale.[1]

The Serb triumph over Srebrenica was the ultimate in international
humiliation, and not just because the world had stood by and watched the
biggest single mass murder in Europe since the Second World War. There
was a second, more revealing reason for international shame: hidden behind
international condemnation and outrage there lay a very real sense of relief; a
certain satisfaction that the messy, unresolved matter of the eastern enclaves,
which cluttered up the peacemakers' maps, had at last been settled. Neater
maps, on which a peace settlement could be based, could now be drawn.
Peacemakers saw that the game plan had been changed. Once Žepa had
been over-run a fortnight later, the map would be easier still to enforce.
When, the following month, Croatia launched its blitzkrieg against the
Krajina Serbs, it became clear that the forced movement of hundreds of thousands of people (which had been the war aim of Serb and Croat leaders from
the beginning), though deplorable, was actively helping the peace process
gain momentum. By means of ethnic cleansing and mass murder, ethnically
pure territorial units were emerging; world leaders might denounce the
method, but the end result brought peace nearer than ever before.

* * *

The plight of the hapless Dutch peacekeepers in Srebrenica provides one small illustration of the way the UN and western governments had begun to think about the eastern enclaves: the Dutch were scheduled to rotate out of Srebrenica. Like their British counterparts in Goražde, there was no replacement waiting. It was the end of the line. In the spring of 1995, there had emerged a quiet consensus among the UN and western governments that the enclaves could not be sustained.

But the fall of Srebrenica was a watershed in the international community's response to the war. After that, nothing would ever be the same. All reticence about stepping over what General Sir Michael Rose had called the Mogadishu line, that separated peace-keeping from peace-enforcement, was swept aside. The United Nations, led unambiguously now by the United States, in effect went to war with the Bosnian Serbs, all pretense of impartiality now abandoned. And the European allies, who, for three and a half years had warned against becoming embroiled in the 'Balkan quagmire,' who had warned repeatedly that 'you cannot make peace from 15,000 feet,' followed the American lead.

On July 19 the Krajina Serbs attacked the Bihać pocket, in an apparent attempt to cut it in half. Bosnia's war now formally spilled over into neighboring Croatia.

Two days later, the foreign ministers of the troop-contributing nations met in London, in the highly charged atmosphere that followed the humiliation of the fall of Srebrenica. The memory of taking hundreds of UN peacekeepers hostage, in response to NATO action, haunted the gathering. The ministers resolved not to let it happen again.

They agreed – in the parlance of the Gulf War of 1991 – to "draw a line in the sand" over Goržade. There had been no attempt to defend Srebrenica and Žepa; indeed, the Rapid Reaction Force had not been deployed in such a way as to enable it to be used in the defense of these two enclaves. Goržade, the foreign ministers decided, would be different. Should it come under attack by the Bosnian Serbs, NATO air strikes would be used – and in "disproportionate response" – to defend it. They also agreed to scrap the so-called "dual key" in which the approval of the UN civilian chief, Yasushi Akashi, had to be obtained before air strikes could proceed. NATO was now authorized to bomb on the direct request of the UN force commander on the ground.

The next day, in response to the Krajina Serb attack on Bihać, Izetbegović and Tudjman met in Split and agreed on a joint defense plan in a meeting engineered by the US. Croatia agreed to use its troops to defend Bihać. Tudjman ordered his army into Bosnia. Croatian forces quickly overpowered

Glamoč and Bosanko Grahovo, thus encircling the Krajina Serb capital, Knin. Though the US ambassador to Croatia, Peter Galbraith, hurriedly convened talks between Zagreb and the Krajina Serb leadership, by the first week in August, the order to take the Krajina had already been given. The Croatian Army attacked on August 4, and four days later the Krajina Serb state was swept away.

Srebrenica; Bihać; Glamoč and Grahovo; Krajina: the war appeared to be escalating on all fronts. But amid the apparent chaos, the US never lost sight of the main prize. Krajina was still burning when, on August 10 and 11, Clinton's National Security Adviser, Anthony Lake, toured the main capitals of Europe with the rudiments of a new plan. It was based on the assumption that a future Bosnia-Herzegovina, within its existing borders, would by necessity consist of two distinct entities: a Serbian entity, based on the current unrecognized Republika Srpska; and the Muslim-Croat federation. It also made tentative suggestions about the trading of territory, proposing, for example, that the only remaining 'enclave', Gorazde, should be swapped for parts of Sarajevo, thereby giving the Serbs security in eastern Bosnia in exchange for an undivided Sarajevo as the capital of the Muslim-Croat federation.

Richard Holbrooke began a frenzied race around the three main capitals. He had been pressing for a more robust American approach for months. He now came into his own.[2] Unparalleled in his ability to get tough with his collocutors, the inexhaustible Holbrooke believed that Milošević was ready to put the military squeeze on the Bosnian Serbs, in return for the gradual lifting of sanctions. Then, on August 28, came the pretext that many in NATO had been waiting for. In a near carbon copy of the incident which had brought about the first NATO ultimatum in February 1994, a mortar landed near Sarajevo market square, killing thirty-seven people. This time, there was none of the ambivalence that had so muddied the waters the year before: within twenty four hours, the UN had carried out a crater analysis and had declared that, beyond reasonable doubt, the shell had been fired by the Bosnian Serbs.[3] The usually reticent UN Secretary-General, Boutros Boutros-Ghali, condemned the "continued and senseless shedding of blood in Bosnia," calling on UN military commanders to "investigate the attack and take appropriate action immediately." An embittered Izetbegović warned:

We will use all means to get out of this misery. I want to stress: all means. And regarding the (Serb) criminals, I want to let them know that we will pay back in kind, and very soon. That day is not far away.

The next day more than 80 peacekeepers secretly left Goražde. The UN would not make the same mistake. There would be no hostages this time. In the night sky on August 30, wave upon wave of NATO warplanes blasted Serb targets across Bosnia. Izetbegović finally got what his government had sought since the very beginning of the war: massive NATO intervention on his side.

That night, Milošević convened a meeting of the Serb leadership in Belgrade, to be attended by the Montenegrin President Momir Bulatović, the Bosnian Serb leadership, including the hard-line nationalist Biljana Plavšić, and the patriarch of the Orthodox Church. Milošević made no secret of his attitude to the NATO intervention: the Bosnian Serb leadership had brought it on themselves by years of refusing to compromise to win peace. Even Plavšić was reported to be chastened. The Bosnian Serb leaders agreed to allow Milošević to represent them at peace negotiations in future.[4]

The NATO attacks continued for three days. The US, believing progress was being made with Milošević, then pressed for a halt to the bombing. But in Bosnia General Mladić repeatedly refused to withdraw his heavy weapons from around Sarajevo, arguing that to do so would be to leave his troops exposed, as in 1994, to the numerical superiority of the Bosnian Army infantry. The NATO bombing continued. In a two-week campaign, NATO flew 3,400 sorties, including 750 attack missions against 56 ground targets. Ammunition stores, anti-aircraft batteries, radar installations, communications facilities, warehouses, artillery units, command bunkers and bridges were destroyed. The result was to cripple Bosnian Serb communications and temporarily incapacitate their ability to respond and reinforce. Even the civilian telephone system was knocked out.

In the middle of this onslaught, talks resumed in Geneva. Nikola Koljević and Aleksa Buha, representing the Bosnian Serbs, were included as part of the Yugoslav delegation. All sides agreed to accept the Contact Group map of 1994 (which the Bosnian Serbs had, until now, repeatedly rejected) as the basis for future negotiations. It was here that the US began to bring all three sides around to accepting the plan that was still being hammered out. They agreed on a number of 'Basic Principles': Bosnia-Herzegovina would continue to exist within its recognized borders; it would comprise two distinct entities; and the territorial split between them would be 51 percent (Muslim-Croat federation) to 49 percent (Bosnian Serbs).

Talks were due to resume on September 14 but were postponed. They had been overshadowed by events on the battlefield. By now, the Croatian and Bosnian Armies were chalking up huge and rapid victories in northwestern Bosnia. On September 15, Jajce fell to the Croats and Donji Vakuf to the Bosnian Army. The Bosnian Serb army was in retreat. Huge swathes of territory that had been considered unassailable since 1992 began to fall to the juggernaut of the combined Croatian-Bosnian advance. Sarajevo began to talk excitedly about the fall of Banja Luka.

But Banja Luka did not fall. The Bosnian Serb army rallied. Washington told the Croats to halt their offensive and withdraw their troops from western Bosnia. Tudjman called a halt to the operation. By the end of September the front lines had shifted beyond recognition. The territory that the Bosnian Serbs had controlled had been reduced from almost seventy percent to about half; the Croats and Muslims, roughly speaking, controlled what was left in equal measure.

The map that emerged from September's battles – or, at least, the share of territory that it allocated – was consistent with the peace plan that was being put together by Holbrooke and Lake. It is a remarkable coincidence in a region where remarkable coincidences are scarcely what they seem. That Banja Luka never fell; that Tudjman called off the offensive before that critical phase, was widely interpreted at the time as evidence that the map that was emerging was consistent with what Milošević and Tudjman had planned from the beginning – the two-way partition of Bosnia (although by now Milošević was no longer calling the shots). As the former EU peace envoy Lord Owen noted:

> *Karadžić, when challenged that Serb forces had deliberately withdrawn, hotly denied it, but the suspicion remained that with General Mladić undergoing hospital treatment in Belgrade, it was more than a coincidence that the soldiers' map had begun to reflect a design which Tudjman had long wanted. Also, it was a map that Milošević could easily endorse, since it was no longer necessary, following the fall of Knin, for the Serbs to maintain access to the Krajina from Banja Luka.*[5]

The shuttle diplomacy continued. The map, the obstacle that had thwarted so many previous peace plans, was now a fait accompli, achieved by force of arms (NATO, Croatian and Bosnian) and the willing complicity of Belgrade. The foreign ministers of Croatia, Bosnia and the rump Yugoslavia met in New York later in the month and consolidated the 'Basic Principles' arrived at in Geneva. They further agreed that the two entities that would constitute Bosnia in the future would each honor the financial obligations of Bosnia-Herzegovina as a whole. They also agreed on a set of procedures for elections in each entity, leading to the establishment of a single parliament, presidency, cabinet and constitutional court.

The commitments were vague and did not yet add up to a blueprint for peace; far from it. But so confident was the US administration that the crucial breakthrough had been made, and so concerned was it that the momentum should be maintained, that on October 5, President Clinton, in person, announced that a ceasefire would come into effect five days later.[6] The ceasefire would last sixty days during which time "proximity talks" would take place, leading eventually to a comprehensive peace settlement to be endorsed by a treaty to be signed in Paris.

Yet western peacemakers found it convenient to ignore Milošević's role. Driven by the United States, the peace process now offered the first serious prosect for a political settlement since the outbreak of war. Milošević – despite his guiding role in the war in Bosnia – would be the cornerstone of any settlement. Shortly before the convening of all-party talks at Dayton, new evidence about the scale of the crimes committed at Srebrenica hit the headlines. Most US officials, except for US Ambassador to the United Nations Madeleine Albright, who had stridently championed the Bosnian government, bent over backwards to avoid pointing the finger at Belgrade. "There is not what you would call a smoking gun," Holbrooke said later, determined not to let the accusations derail his peace plan.

The fall of Krajina and Croatian and Muslim gains in Bosnia opened a new chapter in international involvement in former Yugoslavia. The change in the balance of power on the ground was brought about by new resolve abroad. After four years in a political stalemate, NATO had launched a bombing campaign against the Bosnian Serbs which was, as promised a few weeks before, a "disproportionate" response. These factors coalesced into an unprecedented display of unity among Western actors. That, not the military losses, was arguably the greatest problem for the Serbs. Since the start of the conflict, Serb leaders had artfully played on divisions among the international community, exploiting them and counting on diplomatic and military paralysis.

As the world's press converged on Dayton, Ohio, peace seemed closer than ever. No one in the international community spoke any more about honor, or justice. As Lord Owen concluded in his memoir, it would be, unmistakably, a "peace without honor." It would be a peace that would, in large measure, meet the principal war aim – partition – of both Croatia and Serbia. It would also be a peace that would reward the use of force; a peace, indeed, that had been achieved by the forcible creation of ethnically pure territories. And it was for this reason that Holbrooke recognized that, as the Dayton talks began, it was the Muslim-Croat federation, much more than the Serbs, who would pose the greatest threat to the future stability of any settlement. The temptation facing both Zagreb and Sarajevo was to demand maximum concessions from the Serbs and, should the talks break down, to press for further military victories now that they had established themselves as the militarily stronger parties. Holbrooke took it upon himself to see that Washington exerted pressure on both former underdogs to choose peace, even though the tide of war had turned in their favor.

Chapter 29: A Pax Americana?

1 Three months later, the Dutch government would publish an investigation which absolved its peacekeepers of any wrongdoing or even negligence in Srebrenica. They were not guilty for failing to halt the Serb onslaught, said an investigative report which determined that the lightly armed forces were helpless to stop the killing of thousands of Muslim men and the expulsion of some 25,000 women, children and elderly. "The fall of Srebrenica was caused by Bosnian Serb aggression, not by the way in which Dutch had operated," Voorhoeve said putting the blame with those government which refused to commit sufficient troops to protect the enclaves.

"What must be learned for the future is that enough military power must be provided from the start, so that you can escalate when the enemy adopts terror tactics," Voorhoeve said. "You also need a clarity of command that never existed with the UN operation."

2 Holbrooke was treading ground that had been prepared by his deputy, Robert Frasure, who had conducted hours of patient negotiations with the main players of the region, but in particular Milošević. Frasure, along with two members of the delegation, was killed when the armored personnel carrier they were travelling in slipped off the treacherous Mount Igman road. They had refused to ask the Bosnian Serbs for permission to travel a less treacherous route. It was a great loss for the US initiative, but Holbrooke only redoubled efforts to secure an agreement.

3 In the case of the earlier market square bombing which left 68 people dead in February 1994, it was never really established beyond a reasonable doubt who had fired the mortar – making it on ongoing subject of controversy. UN officials privately believed that it was fired by the Muslims, but were never able to identify the perpetrator with certainty.

4 Radovan Karadžić was, by now, along with General Ratko Mladić, indicted on suspicion of war crimes. He would not be able to attend future peace talks without risking arrest.

5 David Owen, *Balkan Odyssey* (London: Gollancz, 1995), p.336.

6 The ceasefire was conditional on the restoration of utilities to Sarajevo, and was consequently delayed by several days.

30

CONCLUSION

At the time of writing, the future of former Yugoslavia hung in a precarious balance between war and peace, the scales tipping between the two in the unlikely setting of the Wright-Patterson Air Force Base at Dayton Ohio. The United States, in the shape of Assistant Secretary of State Richard Holbrooke, was driving the peace process. After four years of watching its European allies repeatedly fail to produce a settlement, and eighteen months of preparation behind the scenes, the US had seized control of the process in the summer of 1995. Washington had, until now, been reluctant to give full backing to any of the preceding peace plans, which had always made it possible for any one of the parties to exploit divisions within the international community.

By now, five new states had emerged from the ruins of Communist Yugoslavia. Of these, Slovenia had fared best. Its leaders, fed up with Milošević's attempts to commandeer Yugoslavia, steered the northwestern republic to independence with little difficulty and with the connivance of the Serbian regime. They waged a brief war that had more to do with television screens than with front lines. By the end of 1995, its two million people, enjoying a standard of living much higher than that of their former country-men, had developed a genuinely multiparty culture. Slovenia now stood at the doors of the European Union, ready, almost, to be drawn fully into the economic and political mainstream of the western world, its back turned away from its southern neighbors.

The southern-most republic, Macedonia, escaped the war that many Cassandras had forecast for it, a war which threatened – and still threatens – to carry the conflict outside the frontiers of former Yugoslavia by pulling in Albania, Bulgaria, Greece and even Turkey, thus pitting current NATO allies against each other. The fragile peace survived an attempt to assassinate Macedonia's president Kiro Gligorov in October 1995; he was so seriously injured by a car bomb in Skopje, that his long political career came to an abrupt and tragic end. Gligorov's skilful stewardship helped save his republic from the ravages that had afflicted his neighbors to the north. Macedonia's tragedy was that it was the only one of the six republics not to have fought a war, and the only one to have lost its president. In the other five republics, the presidents who had led Yugoslavia into open conflict in 1991 were all still in power.

Macedonia remains surrounded by predatory neighbors, and is haunted by the specters of unresolved conflicts. For now, peace has been bolstered by the presence of UN peacekeepers – the first case of preventive deployment in UN history. Cyrus Vance, the US mediator, brokered a landmark agreement in September 1995 which called for Athens to lift an economic embargo against its northern neighbor in exchange for Skopje adopting a new flag. Greece had imposed the embargo in protest against the use of the name Macedonia and its 16-pointed golden star of Vergina on the grounds that they were exclusively Hellenic property.

Four years after declaring independence, and promptly losing a third of its territory to its rebel Serbs and the JNA, Croatia emerged, in 1995, with the backing of the United States, as the great power in the region. In an offensive tacitly encouraged by Washington and quietly ignored by the rest of the world, it swept away the self-styled Republika Srpska Krajina in a matter of days, gaining control of almost all the territory of the Croatian republic. Of the 600,000 Serbs who lived in Croatia in 1991, little more than 100,000 remained. The Serbs of Croatia had been part of the Croatian national identity, a legacy Tudjman wanted to destroy.

Despite the arms embargo against former Yugoslavia, Zagreb had built a powerful army that, with NATO's help, had little difficulty in crushing the Krajina Serb statelet and driving its inhabitants out of Croatia. The Krajina state had, by now, been weakened by the combined effect of four years of economic isolation and Belgrade's decision to withhold military support. The fall of Krajina reflected Slobodan Milošević's strategic thinking about the future shape of the region, every bit as much as it reflected Franjo Tudjman's. But Milošević had no choice: he knew he had to jettison the Krajina Serbs. It was the newly confident Tudjman who had seized the initiative.

In Zagreb, the resort to military means was applauded. Tudjman called snap elections in the euphoric aftermath of the capture of Krajina, a year before they were scheduled to take place. His party, the HDZ, cashed in on the atmosphere, winning 45 percent of the popular vote and a comfortable majority of the seats in the Sabor. The last piece of Tudjman's puzzle fell into place just after the October elections, when the tireless and dedicated UN envoy Thorvald Stoltenberg and US Ambassador Peter Galbraith brokered an eleventh-hour agreement, aimed at averting another Croatian offensive against the last piece of Serb-held territory in Croatia, eastern Slavonia and Baranja. Under the deal, an international force, as yet to be defined, would administer the region for a maximum two-year period before it would be fully integrated into Croatia. The only parts of the former Krajina state that bordered Serbia directly, it was strategically less vital to Croatia than the Knin region, but was rich in oil and agricultural produce. It contained, on the banks of the Danube River, the town of Vukovar, regarded by Croats as their Stalingrad. A bellicose Tudjman had boasted that he would be drinking coffee in Vukovar by Christmas; if the Serbs did not hand over the land, he said, he would use force to get it. By then, Tudjman held all the trump cards. With the agreement, however, there was no more reason to fight against the Serbs. Both Zagreb and Belgrade announced they could now proceed with the normalization of relations between the two republics, a crucial step towards an overall settlement in former Yugoslavia.

The rise of a powerful Croatia illustrated two aspects of the war and the peace that the US hoped to achieve to end it: it demonstrated that might, rather than reason, brought rewards; and it showed that the carving out of ethnically pure territorial units produced neater maps on which to build a peace settlement. The war had been fought in pursuit of ethnic separation; the war would end only when that was achieved. To that extent, the Dayton talks represented the pursuit of peace through ethnic cleansing. The ramifications for those areas of former Yugoslavia (most of them now in Serbia) that were still ethnically mixed were ominous – casting a shadow over prospects for long-term stability.

Tudjman remained obsessed by the symbols of statehood, and driven by an almost Messianic sense of destiny that it had fallen to him to deliver the freedom his people had – in his eyes – dreamed of for a thousand years. But he proved himself much less enamored by the essential tenets of democracy which he claimed to have brought to Croatia. He stifled a once diverse and impressive independent media, silencing public dissent. There was no outcry about the blitzkrieg against Krajina. On the contrary, the Croatian opposition backed the operation – reminiscent of the way the Serbian opposition had failed to condemn the wars in Croatia and Bosnia. Tudjman never tried to win over the Serb minority in Croatia with credible guarantees of human rights and was determined to reduce their numbers to a tiny and powerless few. And he continued to harbor expansionist ambitions in Bosnia. In the general election which followed his victory in Krajina, ethnic Croats in Bosnia-Herzegovina were allowed to vote and to stand for office in Croatia. This infuriated Bosnian President Alija Izetbegović, with whom Tudjman was formally bound in a military and political alliance. Most of the areas of Bosnia that were controlled by the HVO (the Bosnian Croat armed forces) continued to operate as though they were part of Croatia proper. The Croatian flag flies above western Herzegovina and the currency is the Croatian Kuna. The Muslims had little leverage over the Croats. When Izetbegović complained, Tudjman was imperious: "We liberated eighty percent of that territory for you," he told the Bosnian leader. "Without us, you would not be capable of liberating anything."

The Federal Republic of Yugoslavia remains unrecognized and isolated, comprising Serbia and Montenegro in a sham federation. The junior partner enjoys as much autonomy as Milošević allows. The first flashpoint in Yugoslavia's road to disaster – Kosovo – continued to simmer. The Kosovo

Albanians were the first to be brought under Milošević's heel. By 1995, the visual symbols of repression had gone : there were no longer tanks on the streets. But the province remained a police state. Kosovo's Serbs were still disgruntled and nervous. Although they controlled all positions of power in the province, they claimed that Milošević did not fulfill his pledge to defend them and to make Kosovo Serbian. Minorities continued to make up a third of the population of rump Yugoslavia. A peace settlement based on the principle that statehood derives from ethnicity sent powerful signals to Serbia's minorities – particularly to Albanians – that could lead to further conflict in the future.

The fate of Bosnia-Herzegovina was the most tragic. The mountains and valleys of this beautiful republic were scarred with the charred and battered towns and villages from which at least half the population had either fled, been expelled, or killed. Under the pressure of NATO bombs, the Serbs had relaxed their siege of Sarajevo and the eastern enclave of Goražde. While the guns no longer perched on the surrounding hills, there was still no freedom of movement in or out of Sarajevo for the city's people. During the war the Bosnian government had also tightly controlled the movement of its citizens, afraid the capital would empty out.

After the NATO campaign and the subsequent military gains, the territory under effective Bosnian government control had yet to rise above twenty-five percent of the war-torn country. From the Vance-Owen plan to the Dayton summit, despite the intervention of Washington, each successive peace plan gave the Muslims less territory than that which preceded it. None of the plans had allotted the Croats more than 17 percent; but they now controlled a quarter of Bosnia. In the shock of successive defeats in the summer of 1995, the Serbs had been pushed back from seventy percent to about half the land. In the Serb-held areas, visible evidence of previous settlement by Muslims and Croats was erased: Mosques and Catholic churches were razed to the ground. The tolerant spirit of the capital Sarajevo and other multicultural towns and cities was all but obliterated by Serb guns.

The Bosnian government had entered the war disastrously ill-prepared. They placed their faith in an international community which, they believed, would not stand by and watch a European country so recently admitted as a sovereign member of the United Nations be wiped off the map. As the realization dawned that the Western world would not come to Bosnia's rescue, the republic's leaders dug in for a long war to redeem lost territory. Though starved of weapons by the UN arms embargo, which the Croats enforced against their sometime allies, the Bosnian army had no shortage of foot soldiers. It drew its infantry from the legions of the dispossessed, many of them embittered and humiliated with nothing left to lose, and everything to fight for. In 1993, when bitter fighting erupted between Muslims and Croats, formerly allies against the Serbs, Bosnia's dispossessed seemed to be applying Auden's dark prophecy 'I and the public know what all school children learn. Those to whom evil is done do evil in return.' The Muslims had learned that peaceful negotiation, through the 'good offices' of successive mediators, had brought them only defeat and dispossession. Only self-defense, and, later, when they were stronger, offense, could save them from obliteration. They begged the world to lift the arms embargo to allow them the means with which to fight back. The Security Council upheld the arms embargo, most of the permanent members arguing that lifting it would only create a 'level killing field'.

The US-brokered Washington Agreement was the first tangibly successful international initiative. It ended the war between Muslims and Croats, and was the beginning of what would prove to be a decisive turn-around in the fortunes of both, and an equally decisive reversal in the fortunes of the Serbs. The initial effect was that the Muslims, at last, began to receive some military supplies, though these were still strictly regulated by the Croats, the only conduit through which the Bosnian Army could be armed. Sarajevo prepared to fight another day.

By the summer of 1995, the US would take matters into its own hands. The Serb states in Bosnia and Croatia were corroding from within. Abandoned by Belgrade, they were proving themselves increasingly unviable garrison societies with little or no sustainable economic life – states in which every adult male was was pressed into service either as a policeman or as a soldier, called upon to defend thousands of miles of impossibly extended front lines against an enemy that had been weak but could only grow in strength.

The event that brought about a change of heart in the US government and on the part of its European allies was to constitute the gravest war crime in Europe since the Second World War. The Serb capture of Srebrenica was followed by the mass murder of thousands of Muslim men. Their bodies were dumped into mass graves. Dutch peacekeepers stood by, powerless to halt the slaughter. International humiliation was complete. Failure to intervene now looked inescapably like complicity.

A two-week campaign of strategic bombing, together with a joint Bosnian and Croatian offensive, pushed the Serbs back from a third of the territory they had occupied for more than three years.

The war had come full circle. The Serbs, who had launched it with a singleness of purpose that had allowed them to slice through their enemies like a knife through butter, were now divided. They had broken their own pledge that 'Only Unity Saves the Serbs'. Milošević, who had led them into battle with an apparent clarity of vision that had brought all Serbs together under a single banner, had lost his way. The instigator of Yugoslavia's bloody disintegration, and the guiding hand behind the Yugoslav wars, proved himself no nationalist at all. Milošević, the man once seen as a brilliant tactician, maneuvered himself, and the Serbs, into a corner. For the Serbs, Milošević's rule will be seen as one of the most disastrous periods in their modern history. He had held all the cards in former Yugoslavia, and one by one, played them and lost. The Serbs, who throughout the wars had been seen as the winners, nearly overnight became the losers. Yet with tight control of the media and the police, Milošević succeeded in channeling public opinion in Serbia. After the fall of Krajina, there was no public outcry; the sense of defeat just set in deeper.

Demonized by the Western press, Milošević was liked by international mediators almost without exception. They found him intelligent and witty – though they frequently failed to appreciate that he would lie to them, play with them like a cat who has caught a mouse. It seemed he met his match in Holbrooke, the first mediator who had an arsenal far bigger than Milošević's, which he had already put to use. By the time of the Dayton summit, Milošević was the most cooperative of the Balkan players. He wanted peace more than his counterparts. In order to secure the lifting of sanctions, he would sell short the very war aims with which he had led his people into battle in the first place. He refused to lift a finger in the defense of the Krajina Serbs, the very people he had claimed to champion. He knew that each day the war continued brought the Serbs closer to total defeat.

The fall of Krajina was part of a process that fundamentally altered the balance of power. After four years of indecision and being warned by their allies that military intervention would be disastrous, the US finally demonstrated that a combined use of force and diplomacy could produce a realistic prospect – the first in years – for a peaceful settlement.

As the presidents gathered in Dayton, Ohio, they did so having agreed, for the first time, on a bipartisan division of Bosnia into two distinct entities: one based on the current territory of 'Republika Srpska', the other on land held by the Muslim-Croat federation. The land distribution on the ground reflected a territorial share which all parties had, in the past, accepted as reasonable. The US had an unprecedented hold over both sides: over the Serbs, on the one hand, who knew that without a deal now they could face further military defeat and the loss of still more territory; and the Muslim-Croat alliance on the other. Though Zagreb and Sarajevo sensed the war turning in their favor, they also knew that their military prowess depended on the tacit support of the United States.

Further, from successive military victories, there emerged in former Yugoslavia discreet territorial units, on each of which one ethnic group prevailed. The defeat of the Muslim-populated eastern enclaves of Srebrenica and Žepa, and the Croatian victory over the Krajina, though publicly denounced by all sectors of the international community, were privately welcomed by the peace mediators because they offered the prospect of neater maps on which to reach an agreement over territory.

The US, like the European Union and the United Nations before it, recognized Milošević as key to finding a solution, and turned a blind eye to his complicity in the crimes that were committed in the prosecution of Serbian war aims. Milošević will be rewarded with a gradual lifting of economic sanctions. But the big winner will be Franjo Tudjman's Croatia. His complicity in atrocities committed particularly, but not exclusively, in Bosnia and Herzegovina has also been conveniently overlooked in the interests of securing peace. If Washington brings peace to the Balkans, there will be little talk of honor or justice. Peace will come as a result of dealing with the guilty men of Yugoslavia's killing fields. A settlement will have the effect of strengthening the hand – in their respective states – of the two men on whose shoulders the lion's share of the responsibility for Yugoslavia's tragedy lies. It will come close to realizing the vision for Yugoslavia's future that they first mapped out between themselves at their secret meeting at Karadjordjevo in March 1991: a straight division of the spoils between the country's two biggest and most powerful nations.

The losers will be Bosnia's Muslims, and those dwindling few Serbs and Croats who have remained loyal citizens of Izetbegović's vanishing republic. They will have as their homeland a landlocked island of territory completely surrounded by both their former enemies. The Muslim entity that will emerge from the US peace plan will find itself utterly dependent on Tudjman's Croatia, a small and powerless satellite republic – Lebanon to Croatia's Syria.

The Washington peace initiative contained a pledge to deploy 20,000 US troops to Bosnia as part of a NATO force to make the agreement stick. Without those troops, there can be no permanent peace. But as the Dayton talks progressed, prospects for a lasting settlement seemed to depend more on the outcome of infighting among power brokers in Washington than on the Balkan players themselves.

With the fall of Krajina and the weakening of Republika Srpska in Bosnia, the Croats and Muslims have come to understand – and are applying – the great lesson of the Yugoslav wars, a lesson the Serbs demonstrated in the days of their military supremacy: that in the post-Cold-War world there is no collective security, no international will to protect the weak against the strong; the lesson that to win freedom and security for one's people requires neither a sound argument nor a good cause but a big army. Victory, in former Yugoslavia, will fall not to the just, but to the strong.

ACKNOWLEDGEMENTS

T his book accompanies a five-hour television documentary series made by Norma Percy, Paul Mitchell and Angus Macqueen of Brian Lapping Associates in London. Their eye for detail and corroboration has helped unveil, at every stage of the narrative, truths about Yugoslavia's destruction that had not, hitherto, been known. It is based on hundreds of interviews, lasting thousands of hours, conducted over eighteen months with all those who played a part – some great, some small – in Yugoslavia's tragedy. Our thanks also to Michael Simkin for his relentless search through archives in London, Washington, Belgrade, Zagreb and – in the most difficult of circumstances – in Sarajevo; to the extraordinary efforts of Bonnie Boskovic and Lisa Gartside without whose patience and persistence in keeping track of, and co-ordinating our efforts to deliver the manuscript, this book would not have appeared; and to Paul Adams, Selma Latifić, Liam McDowall, Azra Nuhefendić, Danja Šilović, Miloš Vasić, Nina Vlahović, Dina Hamzić and Bojan Zec whose assistance and advice was invaluable. Thanks also to our committed and creative publisher in New York, TV Books. Chris Wyld at the BBC and Quentin Peel at the *Financial Times* were generous in their indulgence of our obsession both in the writing of the book and in encouraging our efforts to report the war itself. Our sincere gratitude to them. Also to Sheena McDonald, whose belief in the importance of telling the tale was a constant incentive, at every stage of the writing. Finally to Dušan Knežević, in a sense the third co-author of this book, whose fine and dedicated scrutiny greatly improved the text.

It is a truism that war brings out the best as well as the worst in people. We owe an immense personal debt to the countless colleagues whose courage, dedication and determination to tell the tale as they saw it, regardless of the immense difficulties that stood in their way, were never less than inspiring. Some have become friends for life. There is no need to list them by name. They know who they are, and what they have contributed to this book.

To work in former Yugoslavia is to enter a world of parallel truths. Wherever you go, you encounter the same resolute conviction that everything that has befallen the region is always someone else's fault, except one's own side. The war wiped out any habit of self-scrutiny that Serbs, Croats, Muslims, Slovenes might once have possessed. Each nation has embraced a separate orthodoxy in which it is uniquely the victim and never the perpetrator.

Many, but by no means all, of the interviewees who contributed to the series, and the book, were speaking from an unshakeable conviction that their nation is blameless, or their actions without fault. To write any contemporary account of the Yugoslav wars is to navigate the quick waters, not so much of deliberate dishonesty, but of a contrived self-deceit. This applies not only to many of the combatants, but also, sadly, to those who came with good intentions to try to make peace. We have been navigating these waters, between us, for well over a decade. Eventually the currents grow familiar; but they are still treacherous. Any errors of judgement this book contains as a result are, of course, our own.

INDEX